8/50

QUOTABLE QUOTATIONS

"He who never quotes
is never quoted."

CHARLES H. SPURGEON

QUOTABLE QUOTATIONS

COMPILED BY

Lloyd Cory

VICTOR BOOKS®

A DIVISION OF SCRIPTURE PRESS PUBLICATIONS INC.
USA CANADA ENGLAND

Second printing, 1987

Bible quotations are from *The New Berkeley Version in Modern English* (MLB), © 1945, 1959, 1969 by Zondervan Publishing House; *The Living Bible* (TLB), © 1971 by Tyndale House Publishers, Wheaton, Illinois; *The New American Standard Bible* (NASB), © the Lockman Foundation, 1960, 1962, 1963, 1968, 1971, 1972, 1973; *The New Testament in the Language of the People* (WMS), by Charles B. Williams, © 1966 Edith S. Williams, Moody Press, Moody Bible Institute of Chicago; *Today's English Version of the New Testament* (TEV), © American Bible Society, 1966, 1971; *Norlie's Simplified New Testament* (NOR), © Zondervan Publishing House; *The Holy Bible: An American Translation* (BECK), © 1976 Mrs. William F. Beck, by Holman Bible Publishers; *The New Scofield Reference Bible* (SCO), © 1967 by Oxford University Press, Inc.; reprinted by permission; *The Bible: A New Translation* (MOF), by James Moffat, © 1954, Harper and Row Publishers, Inc., New York. All Bible quotations used by permission.

Library of Congress Catalog Number:
ISBN: 0-88207-823-2

VICTOR BOOKS
A division of SP Publications, Inc.
P.O. Box 1825, Wheaton, IL 60189

P R E F A C E

alias

the Introduction

Here's a book for communicators—teachers, preachers, emcees, writers, speakers, salespeople, parents, kids who need well-stated ideas for written homework and speech classes, and everybody who wants others to remember what he said or wrote. This may include everyone except hermits and fugitives from the law.

Besides being a handy reference volume for communicators, these thousands of quotations, on 1,007 subjects, can give you leisure-time pleasure as you browse among them.

This is not a devotional book or a study book. Instead, you'll find an intriguing combination of gravity and levity, facts and opinions, underwhelming and overwhelming ideas. There's just a partial balance between sense and nonsense, distilled wisdom and trivial tidbits. No apology is offered for humor, as "Most good jokes are funny, in part, because they express a truth" (*Psychology Today*). Humor, used aright, is great to wake up meetings, to spark discussions. So what's here can help you make more of an impact in imparting your ideas and motivating people to action. Too, humorous illustrations are like windows, which let light in through solid walls.

Quotable Quotations is not a mere rehash of the golden oldies (though some choice ones which are still apt are included) but majors on quotations that apply to human lives today.

While compiling these quotes I asked all six of my friends if they'd ever said anything quoteworthy, anything worth perpetuating in print. Only three of them did. Apparently few people have the knack of originating memorable statements, which is probably why Charles H. Spurgeon said, "He who never quotes is never quoted."

A wide variety of people are quoted, from presidents to peons, from a skid-row denizen to a billionaire. In the realm of philosophy, for example, they range from Socrates to Snoopy; public speakers vary in their viewpoints, all the way from Adolf Hitler to Howard Hendricks. So naturally neither the publisher nor the compiler vouches for the character, theology, or anything else of everybody quoted. The Bible quotes from Satan, Jezebel, and Herod, thereby teaching us valuable lessons. So though we are theologically conservative we've quoted from liberals and knaves, when they've stated truths better than we do. (May you find it in your great heart to forgive.)

Whenever I had them, names of authors or publications were included.

Often the same quotation, sometimes worded slightly differently, appeared with two or more different by-lines. So some false credits are given, and probably some authors' names are misspelled. Sorry about that.

In case you're wondering, most of the quotes were selected mainly because of their ideas, but some mainly because of the arresting way in which they were worded. When I started collecting and filing quotations about 30 years ago (for talks, lessons, and articles), I had no idea that they'd add up to a book. But they do, so here it is. I hope that you'll derive as much profit and fun reading it as I did compiling it.

LLOYD CORY
Wheaton, Illinois 60187

DEDICATION

*This quote book is duly dedicated to
(1) all the scores of people who wrote it,
(2) everybody who reads it.
May it not only amuse and inform,
but may it also stir up and bless
all who peruse its pages.*

ABILITY

Abilities are like tax deductions—we use them or we lose them.

(SAM JENNINGS)

We are all dropouts from something; from the things we could not do well.

(DON ROBINSON)

The average person puts only 25 percent of his energy and ability into his work. The world takes off its hat to those who put in more than 50 percent of their capacity, and stands on its head for those few and far between souls who devote 100 percent.

(ANDREW CARNEGIE)

Some of the best truly creative minds in the world are very poor management people, and some of the best management people somehow have little patience or sympathy with the creative function.

(ROBERT ESKRIDGE)

Ability is a good thing but stability is even better.

There is something that is much scarcer, something finer by far, something rarer than ability. It is the ability to recognize ability.

(ELBERT HUBBARD)

ABORTION

In every abortion, something living is killed. That is an indisputable biological fact, not a moral judgment.

(GEORGE F. WILSON)

ABSENCE

If your absence won't make any difference, your presence won't either.
(DECISION)

ACCOMPLISHMENT

What I can do, plus what God can do, equals enough.(FREE METHODIST)

Being able to do something well is one of life's great joys.(FRANK TYGER)

It is better to master one mountain than a thousand foothills.
(WILLIAM A. WARD)

I am only one, but still I am one. I cannot do everything, but still I can do something; and because I cannot do everything, I will not refuse to do something that I can do.   (EDWARD EVERETT HALE)

If you have accomplished all that you have planned for yourself, you have not planned enough.   (MEGGIDO MESSAGE)

ACCOUNTANTS

When her accountant husband proposed, he said, "I'd like to make a joint income tax return with you."

ACHIEVEMENT

Four steps to achievement: Plan purposefully. Prepare prayerfully. Proceed positively. Pursue persistently.   (WILLIAM A. WARD)

The most rewarding things you do in life are often the ones that look like they cannot be done.   (ARNOLD PALMER)

A somebody was once a nobody who wanted to and did.

The great composer does not set to work because he is inspired, but becomes inspired because he is working. Beethoven, Wagner, Bach, and Mozart settled down day after day to the job in hand with as much regularity as an accountant settles down each day in his figures. They didn't waste time waiting for inspiration.   (ERNEST NEWMAN)

No matter what your lot in life, build something on it.

The hard part of making good is that you have to do it every day.
(RABBI BEN ZION)

The world is not interested in the storms you encountered, but whether you brought in the ship.   (JOURNAL OF TRUE EDUCATION)

The secret of achievement is not to let what you're doing get to you before you get to it.

ACTION

To *look* is one thing. To *see* what you look at is another. To *understand* what you see is a third. To *learn* from what you understand is still something else. But to *act* on what you learn is all that really matters, isn't it? (EDUCATOR'S DISPATCH)

It is great to have your feet on the ground, but keep them moving. (P-K SIDELINER)

Whether you believe you can do a thing or not, you are right. (HENRY FORD)

Perhaps it is a good thing that you haven't seen all your dreams come true. For when you get all you wish for you will be miserable. Alexander the Great conquered the world, died of sheer boredom. To be forever reaching out, to remain unsatisfied, is the key to spiritual progress. (N.C. CHRISTIAN ADVOCATE)

People should never become so indifferent, cynical, or sophisticated that they are not shocked into action. (MARGARET CHASE SMITH)

Action may not always bring happiness; but there is no happiness without action. (DISRAELI)

Some people have such a talent for making the best of a bad situation that they go around creating bad situations so they can make the best of them. (JEAN KERR)

Doers get to the top of the oak tree by climbing it. *Dreamers* sit on an acorn.

Two hours after the chaplain at the federal penitentiary in Atlanta had given a sermon on the subject "Go Ye Forth into the World," two of the inmates escaped. (SUNDAY SCHOOL TIMES AND GOSPEL HERALD)

The world is looking for the man who can do something, not for the man who can explain why he did not do it. (CARL BOWEN)

To a student: You remind me of an irritated individual trying desperately to balance himself on a bicycle standing still. If he would only pedal ... and start forward his vexation would disappear. If he gave it momentum and a direction, he might run into something. He might have an accident. But he would certainly no longer be bored and he might possibly get somewhere. (CHRISTIAN GAUSS)

No statue was ever erected to the memory of a man or woman who thought it was best to let well enough alone. (WATCHMAN-EXAMINER)

When all is said and done, we usually wish we had done more and said less. (RICHARD ARMOUR)

[When it comes to a big job] too many people avoid plunging in. They wait till they know more about it before they start. They meditate about the task until they finally lose interest in it. Sure we need to approach a situation thoughtfully. We need to inform ourselves about the need. But sooner or later we must plunge in and begin by "peeling one potato at a time." (WALTER MACPEEK)

One thing you can learn by watching the clock is that it passes the time by keeping its hands busy. (YORK TRADE COMPOSITER)

A man should share the action and passion of his times at the peril of being judged not to have lived. (OLIVER W. HOLMES)

All mankind is divided into three classes: those that are immovable, those that are movable, and those that move. (BEN FRANKLIN)

The easiest way to have your way is to go out and make it. (THOUGHTS FOR TODAY)

Parking meters should remind us that we lose money standing still. (BERT KRUSE)

The secret of getting action: What the mind attends to, it considers. What it does not attend to, it dismisses. What the mind attends to continually, it believes. And what the mind believes, it eventually does. (EARL NIGHTINGALE)

A man has to choose the battles he will fight, and he has to weigh the consequences of his actions against the importance of the issue. (ALLAN GLATTHORN)

It's easy to be passively willing, not doing much for God. We have to be venturesome to get ahead in the Christian life. (ART GLASSER)

Let's not only read and hear, but also believe and do. (MALCOLM CRONK)

ACTIVITY

It is more important to know where you are going than to get there quickly. Do not mistake activity for achievement.   (MABEL NEWCOMER)

If a man is to live a full life, an appropriate amount of physical activity must be mixed with mental activity and spiritual activity. Without the existence of spiritual activity, man's life would be void. Without mental activity, man would be numb. Without physical activity, man would be vegetable.   (LINUS DOWELL)

ACUPUNCTURE

There must be something to acupuncture—you never see any sick porcupines.   (BOB GODDARD)

Acupuncture doctor on phone: Take a safety pin and call me in the morning.

ADAM AND EVE

Adam: Do you love me, Eve?
Eve: Who else?

ADJUSTING TO OTHERS

It is not necessarily the well-adjusted man who makes the world a better place. . . . Certainly Jesus was poorly adjusted to the society in which He lived and moved, but He gave the world such mature insights into human nature that we have not yet grasped their full significance. The founding fathers of America were poorly adjusted to the society of their day; for this very reason they gave birth to new concepts of government.
   (WILBUR McFEELY)

ADOLESCENTS (see TEENS)

Adolescence is of necessity a time of conflict between one's own capabilities and what one is expected and permitted to do. It is a time of ambiguity. The adolescent is forever being told by the adult world to "act his age," that is, to behave according to his chronological maturity. But he is also being told to stay out of adult concerns, that is, to behave according to his cultural age. Whatever he does, he is wrong. He does violence either to his chronological or to his cultural age. He is, therefore, inevitably a problem to himself as well as to society.
   (PETER DRUCKER)

ADOPTION, EXPLAINING IT

You adults really "adopt" each other in the wedding ceremony, yet feel closer to your mate than to the blood brothers and sisters with whom you grew up as a child. Use this analogy of your adoption of your marital partner when it comes to explaining the adoption of your son or daughter. (GEORGE CRANE)

ADULTS

Every human being, but especially the adult, prefers to keep on believing what he already believes, and to accept ideas only when they reinforce the ideas he already has. He tends, in other words, to become less and less intellectually curious, to have a more and more closed mind as he grows older. (CHARLES ADRIAN)

Adults are used to talking, to giving orders; but when it comes to living with teens, adults need to listen with both ears and with their hearts. (WARREN WIERSBE)

ADVANCEMENT

Personal advancement is worth very little if in achieving it one loses one's own sense of peace.

ADVENTURE

The greatest contribution we can make to our youngsters in order to prepare them for the inevitable is to imbue in them a genuine sense of adventure. Without that sense, one may easily despair. And we need rather desperately the patience and courage of men and women who refuse to despair. (EDWARD EDDY)

Gullibility is the key to all adventures. (G.K. CHESTERTON)

ADVERSARIES (see ENEMIES)

Next to a happy family and a few good friends, the best human gift that God can give to any man is a worthy adversary. (THE CRESSET)

ADVERSITY (see TROUBLES)

Botanists say that trees need the powerful March winds to flex their trunks and main branches, so that the sap is drawn up to nourish the budding leaves. Perhaps we need the gales of life in the same way, though we dislike enduring them. A blustery period in our fortunes is often the prelude to a new spring of life and health, success and happiness, when we keep steadfast in faith and look to the good in spite of appearances. (JANE TRUAX)

Adversity has the effect of eliciting talents which in prosperous circum stances would have lain dormant. (HORACE

Adversity causes some men to break; others to break records.
(WILLIAM A. WARD)

Some men work hard and save money so their sons won't have the problems that made men of their fathers.

No man is more miserable than he that hath no adversity. . . . Softness is for slaves and beasts, for minstrels and useless persons.
(JEREMY TAYLOR)

Adversity is not necessarily an evil. Because of it understanding, patience, endurance, sympathy can be learned. . . . Beethoven composed his deepest music after becoming totally deaf. Pascal set down his most searching observations about God and man and life and death in brief intervals of release from a prostrating illness. Robertson Nicoll wrote an essay on the thesis: "That the best letters are written by the mortally wounded." (ROBERT McCRACKEN)

The real test in golf and in life is not in keeping out of the rough, but in getting out after we're in. (JOHN MOORE)

The stars are constantly shining, but often we do not see them until dark hours. (EARL RINEY)

Adversity is the only diet that will reduce a fat head.

ADVERTISING

Good advertising is the product of two types of minds, widely different: the orderly, systematic, business mind, and the freewheeling, creative, inventive mind. The two sets of qualities are seldom found in one head, and if then, unequally. (ERNEST CALKINS)

Modern advertising has created an expectation gap. Young people have been taught to expect instant solutions . . . expecting the world to be transformed and changed instantly. They do not realize how slowly history moves and how long it takes to change a social condition.
(BILLY GRAHAM)

When business is good, it pays to advertise; when business is bad, you've got to advertise.

Before releasing advertising to the newspapers, let me suggest that we submit our ads to the final judgment of the charwoman. If she doesn't know what we are talking about, change the ad. (WILLIAM BURSTON)

ADVICE

Nothing is more confusing than the fellow who gives good advice but sets a bad example.

An executive: About 95 percent of the advice I get is no good, but I have to listen to all of it to get the 5 percent that's worth having.
(FRANK KLEILER)

Asking for advice is how some people trap you into expressing an opinion they can disagree with. (FRANKLIN P. JONES)

The two quick ways to disaster are to take nobody's advice and to take everybody's advice. (DUBLIN OPINION)

Being told things for our good seldom does us any.(ARNOLD H. GLASOW)

It takes a great man to give sound advice tactfully, but a greater to accept it graciously. (J.C. MACAULAY)

You save a lot of unnecessary conversation if you remember that people are not going to take your advice unless you charge them for it.
(GOPHER CHATTER)

There is nothing we receive with so much reluctance as advice. There is nothing so difficult as the art of making advice agreeable.
(JOSEPH ADDISON)

Advice is seldom welcome. Those who need it most like it least.
(MEGGIDO MESSAGE)

If you can tell the difference between good advice and bad advice, you don't need advice. (ROTARY CLUB BULLETIN)

The man who seeks your advice too often is probably looking for praise rather than information.

A good scare is more effective than good advice. (BANKING)

Fear less, hope more; eat less, chew more; whine less, breathe more; talk less, say more; hate less, love more; and all good things are yours.
(SWEDISH PROVERB)

Most of us would get along well if we used the advice we give others.

The most unrewarding task in the world is trying to tell people the truth about themselves before they are ready to hear it; and even Aesop, who cast such truths in fable form, was eventually thrown off a cliff because his morals struck too close to home. (SYDNEY HARRIS)

We give advice by the bucket, but take it by the grain. (W.R. ALGER)

The trouble with giving advice is people want to repay you.
(FRANKLIN P. JONES)

A schoolteacher asked the children to define the word *advice.*
    "Advice," said a little girl, "is when other people want you to do the way they do."

AFFLICTION (see TROUBLES)

Affliction can be a treasure. Absolutely functional, it triggers life's greatest insights and accomplishments. It is the year of the locust (Joel 2:25). (FRED GREVE)

AFFLUENCE (see MONEY)

Affluence is a problem in every society all during history. It becomes a problem because people lose their intellectual values, and there is nothing more to struggle for. (ROBERT MOSKIN)

AGING (see LONGEVITY, MIDDLE AGE, SENIORITY)

Some lives, like evening primroses, blossom most beautifully in the evening of life. (CHARLES E. COWMAN)

I remember Dr. Pepper when he was an intern. (ED COOPER)

An old-timer is one who remembers when we counted our blessings instead of our calories. (KATE M. OWNEY)

You're getting old when you reach the Metallic Age. Your teeth are gold, your hair silver, and you have lead in your pants.

Preparation for old age should begin not later than one's teens. A life which is empty of purpose until 65 will not suddenly become filled on retirement. (ARTHUR MORGAN)

After you lose your membership in it, the younger generation seems pretty bad. (ARKANSAS BAPTIST)

Obsolescence too quickly follows adolescence. (JACK KRAUS)

Sign of age: The women I see on the street now consider it perfectly safe to return my smiles. (BURTON HILLIS)

You're getting over the hill when most of your dreams are reruns. (SUNSHINE)

We are happier in many ways when we are old than when we are young The young sow wild oats. The old grow sage. (WINSTON CHURCHILL)

Many people think old age is a disease, something to be thwarted if possible. But someone has said that if any period is a disease, it is youth. Age is recovering from it. (T.C. MYERS)

As soon as you feel too old to do a thing, go out and do it. As soon as you feel critical, say something kind in a kindly way. As soon as you feel neglected, send a cheery note to a friend. (OLIVER WILSON)

When a man's friends begin to compliment him about looking young, he may be sure that they think he is growing old. (WASHINGTON IRVING)

People often ask, "What's new?" I've come to that stage in life when if anything's new it's apt to be a symptom. (LLOYD CORY)

To keep young, associate with young people. To get old in a hurry, try keeping up with them. (GOOD READING)

I don't feel old. I feel like a young guy that something happened to. (MICKEY SPILLANE)

People who are the least active mentally and physically age earlier, and are the most prone to disease. (JOHN GIBSON)

Life begins at 40—but so do fallen arches, lumbago, faulty eyesight, and the tendency to tell a story to the same person three or four times. (BILL FEATHER)

Age is a high price to pay for maturity. (TOM STOPPARD)

Now that I'm a senior citizen and in my second childhood, they once again allow me to ride on the bus for half fare. (EUGENE JAEGER)

You are as young as you feel after trying to prove it. (LOU ERICKSON)

The older a man gets, the better he was as an athlete in his youth.

The elderly are the only outcast group that everyone eventually expects to join. (TIME)

Old age: When actions creak louder than words.   (DANA ROBBINS)

The good thing about old age is that you only go through it once.
(HERB TRUE)

For the ignorant, old age is as winter; for the learned, it is a harvest.
(JEWISH PROVERB)

There's no use trying to get younger. A fellow'd better just try to keep on getting older.   (FRANK CLARK)

Forty is the old age of youth; 50 is the youth of old age.(VICTOR HUGO)

Old age is when you get out of the shower and you're glad the mirror is all fogged up.

The seven ages of man: spills, drills, thrills, bills, ills, pills, wills.
(RICHARD J. NEEDHAM)

The older we get the less we are sure that the man who disagrees with us is a bigot, a moron, or a scoundrel. We even suspect that he may be as close to being right as we are.   (LADYSMITH [WISC.] NEWS)

None are so old as those who have outlived enthusiasm.(HENRY THOREAU)

If you are over the hill, why not enjoy the view?
(MACK McGINNIS)

By the time a man gets to greener pastures he can't climb the fence.
(FRANK DICKSON)

I'm not getting old. My mirror is just getting wrinkled.

There's the shaving lotion for husbands over 65—Old Spouse.
(SHELBY FRIEDMAN)

It does not pay to get sour as you get old. I pity a man who lives in the past. He lives on stale manna. He gets stunted.   (D.L. MOODY)

In the central place of every heart there is a recording chamber; so long as it receives messages of beauty, hope, cheer, and courage, so long are you young. When the wires are all down and your heart is covered with the snows of pessimism and the ice of cynicism, then, and then only, are you grown old.   (DOUGLAS MACARTHUR, ON 75TH BIRTHDAY)

If you live long enough, the venerability factor creeps in; you get accused of things you never did and praised for virtues you never had.(I.F. STONE)

We ought to treat our elderly as if we expect to become one of them.
(FRANK CLARK)

The ideal way to age would be to grow slowly invisible, gradually disappearing, without causing worry or discomfort to the young.
(SHARON CURTIN)

I'm glad I'm growing old in England. Americans are dedicated to the new and super efficient. It must be depressing to be old in the U.S.
(ARNOLD TOYNBEE, ON 80TH BIRTHDAY)

Many individuals are more comfortable in the presence of blind or deaf people, amputees, and stroke victims, than they are in the presence of old people. People want to remain young.   (RIA SUPERVISORY ALERT)

Anonymous prayer: Lord, Thou knowest better than I know myself that I am growing older. Keep me from getting too talkative, and thinking I must say something on every subject and on every occasion. Release me from craving to straighten out everybody's affairs. Teach me the glorious lesson that occasionally it is possible that I may be mistaken. Make me thoughtful, but not moody, helpful but not bossy; for Thou knowest, Lord, that I want a few friends at the end.

The neglect of older people is becoming an increasing sin in America.
(BILLY GRAHAM)

I'm at that age where if you flattened out all the wrinkles, I'd be seven feet tall.   (ROBERT ORBEN)

You know you're getting old when your back starts going out more than you do.   (PHYLLIS DILLER)

You are as young as your faith, as old as your doubt; as young as your self-confidence, as old as your fear; as young as your hope, as old as your despair.

There is an active prejudice in this country against old people that causes a great deal of cruelty and unnecessary loss to the community.
(HUGH DOWNS)

Never lose sight of the fact that old age needs so little but needs that little so much.   (MARGARET WILLOUR)

AGREEMENT

If you find a man who always agrees with you, you have to watch him, because he is apt to lie about other things too.   (ROBERT A. COOK)

There are times when you have to change your tune to keep harmony.

We may not always see eye to eye, but we can try to see heart to heart.   (SAM LEVENSON)

At every moment of our lives we should be trying to find out, not in what we differ with other people, but in what we agree with them.
(JOHN RUSKIN)

My idea of an agreeable person is a person who agrees with me.
(BENJAMIN DISRAELI)

AIMS (see GOALS, OBJECTIVES)

Many people have the right aims in life. They just never get around to pulling the trigger.   (SUNSHINE MAGAZINE)

I am appalled at the aimlessness of most people's lives. Fifty percent don't pay any attention to where they are going; 40 percent are undecided and will go in any direction. Only 10 percent know what they want, and even all of them don't go toward it.   (KATHERINE A. PORTER)

Others aim to do right but are just poor shots.   (OHIO GRANGE)

The aim of your instruction should be love, a love that issues from a pure heart, a good conscience, and a sincere faith. (1 TIMOTHY 1:5, NORLIE)

Peace . . . and the building up of each other, these are what we should aim at.   (ROMANS 14:9, MOF)

AIRPORTS

An airport is where you go to waste time waiting that you're going to save flying.

ALCOHOL

An inebriate is a man who thinks the whole world revolves around him.   (O.A. BATTISTA)

Many guys and girls drink to prop up their sagging courage—to help them do what they really want to do, and what they know is the wrong thing to do. Alcohol could be called a false set of guts.   (BILL GLASS)

When a girl says she never drinks anything stronger than pop, maybe you'd better check and see what Pop drinks.

Alcohol is used by a majority of the adult population and creates more problems than all other drugs combined. (ROBERT ELLIOTT)

Skid-row alcoholics frequently report that they started drinking young, in imitation of adults. Children should learn that alcohol is a potentially dangerous drug. The nonalcoholic "kiddie cocktail," downed amid adult approval, does not convey this message. (TODAY'S CHILD)

ALIMONY (see DIVORCE)

Alimony is a contraction of "all his money." (FRANK DICKSON)

"Alimony" is one of the most hated words in the English language. One of the divorced pair hates it because it is not enough, and the other hates it because it is too much; which is to say, alimony is like feeding quarters into an empty slot machine. (CARL RIBLET, JR.)

ALONENESS (see SOLITUDE)

Every man must do two things alone; he must do his own believing, and his own dying. (MARTIN LUTHER)

ALTERNATIVES

Never believe that you have only two alternatives until you have made a thorough search for others. (NATION'S BUSINESS)

AMBIGUITY

Church bulletin: Tuesday afternoon there will be meetings in the north and south ends of the church. Children will be baptized at both ends.

Newspaper ad: On sale in bargain basement: shirts for men with minor flaws...shoes for women with slight imperfections.

Restaurant sign: Wanted: man to wash dishes and two waitresses.

AMBITION

If your ambition ladder is too short, you will reach the top too soon and be left without a ladder to climb. May the Lord give us ambition that will take a lifetime to reach. It is too bad when one runs out of ladder before he arrives anywhere. (J.I. COSSEY)

Keep away from people who try to belittle your ambitions. Small people always do that, but the really great make you feel that you too can become great. (MARK TWAIN)

No power in the world can keep a first-class man down or a fourth-class man up. (DEFENDER)

Undertake something that is difficult; it will do you good. Unless you try to do something beyond what you have already mastered, you will never grow. (RONALD OSBORN)

Some people get up and go. Others get up and goof.

Ambition may progress through the following stages: to be like Dad . . . to be famous . . . to be a millionaire . . . to make enough to pay the bills . . . to hang on long enough to draw a pension.

AMERICA

What is hurting America today is the high cost of low living.
(BROOKS MOORE)

Who but Americans can afford chairs that vibrate and cars that don't?

We Americans seem to have an excess of everything except parking space and Christianity.

While three-fifths of the world's population worries about hunger and survival, we anxiously wrestle with overweight and boredom. Every newspaper supplies increasing evidence that in terms of gross national product, comfort, and personal income, we are . . . superior . . . yet, in personal relationships and inner peace, we are revealing that we do not know how to live. We are artists at having and failures at being.
(CHARLES GARRIGUS)

ANCESTORS

We can't choose our ancestors, but they probably wouldn't have chosen us either. (WILLIS JOHNSON)

ANGER (see TEMPER)

Anger is an acid that can do more harm to the vessel in which it's stored than to anything on which it's poured. (BAPTIST BEACON)

Anyone who angers you conquers you. (SISTER KENNY'S MOTHER)

Nothing so reduces us to protoplasm, that seethes with turmoil, than does animosity toward someone else. (HAROLD WALKER)

Blood is thicker than water—and it boils much quicker too.(WILDROOTER)

Folks who fly into a rage always make a bad landing. (GLOBE GAZETTE)

Anger is a thief that seizes control of man's faculties and uses them blindly and destructively. Usually a man who loses his temper also temporarily loses his ability to think logically.   (Lowell Fillmore)

Anger, like fire, finally dies out—after leaving a path of destruction.

For every minute you are angry you lose 60 seconds of happiness.
(Ralph Waldo Emerson)

The worst-tempered people I've ever met were people who knew they were wrong.   (Wilson Mizner)

Anger is often more hurtful than the injury that caused it.(Old proverb)

The loss of temper is, in effect, like a sharp nail that tears and breaks the threads that make up something which should be durable as well as lovely. And though, a moment later, we may regret the tear or break, though we use every bit of our patience and skill in mending the break, we cannot make it new again. The darned place will always be conspicuous.   (Margaret Sangster)

Never get mad at somebody who knows more than you do. After all, it isn't his fault.

You can't always be hitting the ceiling without making people think there's something wrong upstairs.   (Franklin P. Jones)

Next time you feel the surge of anger, say to yourself, "Is this really worth what it's going to do to me and others emotionally? I will make a fool of myself. I may hurt someone I love, or I might lose a friend." Practice realizing that it is not worth it to get so worked up about things, and always remember Seneca, who said, "The greatest cure of anger is delay."   (Norman V. Peale)

Swallowing angry words is much easier than having to eat them.(Grit)

Anger is quieted by a gentle word, just as fire is quenched by water.
(Megiddo Message)

ANNOYANCES

Whatever gets your goat gets your attention. Whatever gets your attention gets your time. Whatever gets your time gets you. Whatever gets you becomes your master. Take care, lest a little thing horn in and get your goat.   (William A. Ward)

ANTIQUES (see JUNK)

Antiques are things one generation buys, the next generation gets rid of, and the following generation buys again.

Antique dealer, when asked if the objects in his stores were authentic:
   "Obsoletely."

An antique is something that no one would want if there were more of them. (VISTA [CAL.] PRESS)

ANXIETY (see WORRY)

Your growth depends on your willingness to experience anxiety.
(HERB TRUE)

Up to a certain point anxiety is good, for it promotes action. Beyond that point we freeze any fixed attitudes or rush about without thinking deeply from one decision to another. (JULES HENRY)

APATHY

The crime against life, the worst of all crimes, is not to feel. And there was never, perhaps, a civilization in which that crime, the crime of torpor, of lethargy, of apathy, the snake-like sin of coldness-at-the-heart, was commoner than in our technical civilization. (ARCHIBALD MACLEISH)

APPEARANCE

A dear old Quaker lady, distinguished for her youthful appearance, was asked what she used to preserve her appearance. She replied sweetly, "I use for the lips, truth; for the voice, prayer; for the eyes, pity; for the hand, charity; for the figure, uprightness; and for the heart, love."
(JERRY FLEISHMAN)

Beauty is mind-deep. You are as pretty—or as ugly—as you think you are. Visualize yourself as a pleasant, friendly, cheerful, laughing, sparkling person, and your imagination will make you into that kind of person. (ROBERT SCHULLER)

APPETITES—AND REASON

People who are driven by their appetites perish by ignoring their reason; and people who are governed by their reason too often perish by ignoring their appetites; and . . . only a few wise or lucky ones are able to sustain a *creative tension* between these opposites. (SYDNEY HARRIS)

APPLIANCES

Some household appliances seem to have built-in timers which enable them to self-destruct within two weeks after their warranties expire.

APPRECIATION

A word of approval for work well done is far more helpful than the most logical criticism which overlooks human sensibilities.   (EDWIN WITTE)

Brains are like hearts—they go where they are appreciated.
(ROBERT McNAMARA)

APTITUDES

Men are so constituted that everyone undertakes what he sees another successful in, whether he has aptitude for it or not.   (GOETHE)

ARCHEOLOGISTS

An archeologist is a man whose career lies in ruins.

I married an archeologist because the older I grow, the more he appreciates me.   (AGATHA CHRISTIE)

ARCHES

Samson died of fallen arches.

He crossed McDonald's with Dr. Scholl and got arch supports.

ARGUMENTS (see CONTROVERSY, QUARRELS)

There's nothing so annoying as arguing with a person who knows what he's talking about.   (VOICE FOR HEALTH)

The only right way to settle an argument is on the basis of what's right, not who's right.

Some arguments are sound, and nothing more.   (RICHARD ARMOUR)

The best way I know of to win an argument is to start by being in the right.   (LORD HAILSHAM)

London lawyer: Counselor Brown says that this case is half a dozen of one and six of the other. But I must emphatically say no! It is exactly the opposite.

Hurling a witty, devastating answer in an argument is like swatting a fast fly. By the time you've swung, the opportunity has flown.

The mind of the bigot is like the pupil of the eye; the more light you pour upon it, the more it will contract.   (OLIVER W. HOLMES)

Never argue with a man who talks loud. You couldn't convince him in a thousand years. (MEGIDDO MESSAGE)

The way to convince another is to state your case moderately and accurately. Then scratch your head, or shake it a little and say that is the way it seems to you, but that, of course you may be mistaken about it. This causes your listener to receive what you have to say, and, as like as not, turn about and try to convince you of it, since you are in doubt. But if you go at him in a tone of positiveness and arrogance, you only make an opponent of him. (BENJAMIN FRANKLIN)

When I'm getting ready to reason with a man, I spend one-third of my time thinking about myself and what I am going to say—and two-thirds thinking about him and what he is going to say. (ABRAHAM LINCOLN)

Don't engage in arguments, but if cornered, ask an irrelevant question and lean back with a satisfied grin while your opponent tries to figure out what's going on—then quickly change the subject. (SPARKS)

ARMY

"How is your son doing in the Army?"
"Very well. They just made him a Court Marshal."

Our outfit destroyed six bridges, blew up two ammunition depots, and leveled a key military installation. Then we were sent overseas.
(JIM CROWLEY)

"How does your uniform fit?"
"The jacket seems OK, but the pants could be taken in about an inch around the armpits."

Armed Forces radio announcer: For you Navy men, it's now 8 bells. For you men in the Army, it's now 0800. And for all you officers, the little hand is on 8, and the big hand is on 12.

ART

All art is a wedding of technique and emotion. Without emotion, all the technique in the world will not produce art. (RICHARD RODGERS)

Michelangelo was also a superb applied psychologist. At first, he was ignored and disdained by his own generation. But he had faith in his ability and decided to use some psychology on his critics. Knowing that they were fascinated by excavating in old ruins to dig up supposedly priceless works of art, he tinted one of his masterpieces and then had it buried where an excavating party would be sure to find it. The critics were enraptured. They pronounced it an antique of rare value. The Cardinal of San Giorgio was so impressed that he paid a huge sum to add it to his art collection. Then Michelangelo deftly let the cat out of the bag. The art critics . . . were so far out on a limb that they had to admit that he was an artistic genius. After that, Michelangelo was commissioned to do important work. (GEORGE CRANE)

ARTHRITIS

Twinges in the hinges. (ARNOLD GLASOW)

ATHEISM (see UNBELIEF)

An atheist does not find God for the same reason a thief does not find a policeman.

I met a watch that did not believe in the existence of watchmakers. (HEINRICH HEINE)

An atheist is someone who believes that what you see is all you get.

One trouble with being an atheist is you have nobody to talk to when you're alone.

Nobody talks so constantly about God as those who insist there is no God. (HEYWOOD BROUN)

ATTITUDES

There is no danger of developing eyestrain from looking on the bright side of things. (CHEER)

Things are for us only what we hold them to be. Which is to say that our attitude toward things is likely in the long run to be more important than the things themselves. (A.W. TOZER)

Our attitude toward the world around us depends upon what we are ourselves. If we are selfish, we will be suspicious of others. If we are of a generous nature, we will be likely to be more trustful. If we are quite honest with ourselves, we won't always be anticipating deceit in others. If we are inclined to be fair, we won't feel that we are being cheated. In a sense, looking at the people around you is like looking in a mirror. You see a reflection of yourself. (GOOD READING)

I respect those who resist me, but I cannot tolerate them. (CHARLES DE GAULLE)

You can go hopping around all over the world and never find out anything, because that ain't the way to find out anything. All you got to do is change your attitude. (WILLIAM SAROYAN)

Attitude is the first quality that marks the successful man. If he has a positive attitude and is a positive thinker, who likes challenges and difficult situations, then he has half his success achieved. On the other hand, if he is a negative thinker who is narrow-minded and refuses to accept new ideas and has a defeatist attitude, he hasn't got a chance. (LOWELL PEACOCK)

Keep your heart right, even when it is sorely wounded.(J.C. MACAULAY)

Be like a duck—keep calm and unruffled on the surface, but paddle like crazy underneath.

The man who is not hungry says that the coconut has a hard shell. (AFRICAN TRIBAL SAYING)

Let's not be narrow, nasty, and negative. (VERNON GROUNDS)

To one man, the world is barren, dull, and superficial; to another rich, interesting, and full of meaning. (ARTHUR SCHOPENHAUER)

The simple act of squeezing a lemon can seem most unpleasant and irritating to the person with a cut finger. The most casual and innocent remark can cause pain to the individual with a chip on his shoulder. (WILLIAM A. WARD)

The one attitude which gives rise to hope amidst misunderstanding and ill will is a forgiving spirit. Where forgiveness becomes the atmosphere, there hope and healing are possible. (C. NEIL STRAIT)

The quickest way to correct the other fellow's attitude is to correct your own. Try it. It works. (KING VIDOR)

If you can figure when to stand firm and when to bend, you've got it made. (JOSEPH SHORE)

Attitudes are much more important than aptitudes.

Instead of weeping when a tragedy occurs in a songbird's life, it sings away its grief. I believe we could well follow the pattern of our feathered friends. (ROBERT S. WALKER)

An easy task becomes difficult when you do it with reluctance.(TERENCE)

You can buy a man's time. You can buy a man's physical presence at a given place. You can even buy a measured number of skilled muscular actions per hour per day. But you cannot buy enthusiasm. You cannot buy initiative. You cannot buy loyalty. You cannot buy the devotion of a heart, mind, and soul. You have to earn these things.   (ED LIDEN)

Reflect upon your present blessings, of which every man has plenty; not on your past misfortunes, of which all men have some.(CHARLES DICKENS)

There is little difference in people, but that little difference makes a big difference. The little difference is attitude. The big difference is whether it is positive or negative.   (CLEMENT STONE)

A chip on the shoulder indicates that there is wood higher up.
      (JACK HERBERT)

In plain language, boredom is a most common affliction in our so-called civilized society. It is a well-known fact, medically, that the stress and strain which drive many men and women to our psychiatric clinics and mental hospitals are often the fruits of emptiness and frustration in a meaningless way of life.   (JOSEPH KRIMSKY)

What good did it do to be grouchy today?
Did your surliness drive any trouble away?
Did you cover more ground than you usually do,
because of the grouch you carried with you?
If not, what's the use of a grouch or a frown,
if it won't smooth a path, or a grim trouble drown?
If it doesn't assist you, it isn't worthwhile.
Your work may be hard, but just do it—and smile!   (ANONYMOUS)

AUCTIONEERS

Only an auctioneer can admire all schools of art.   (HARRY THOMPSON)

AUTHORITY

Never bow to authority, but always tip your hat.   (JIM FIEBIG)

AUTOMOBILES

Statistics show that motorists injure and kill a thousand times more innocent victims than all criminal elements put together.
      (LORRAINE CARBARY)

The worst kind of car trouble is when the engine won't start and the payments won't stop.   (WAGON WHEEL)

One way to solve the traffic problem would be to keep all cars that aren't paid for off the streets.   (WILL ROGERS)

If you have a cheap car, it breaks down. If you have an expensive car, it malfunctions.

The difference between estimated miles per gallon and what you actually get is about like the difference between salary and take-home pay.
(DOUG LARSON)

"I've just discovered oil on our property," said the husband as he came into the house.
    "Wonderful!" exclaimed his wife. "Now we can get a new car."
    "We'd better get the old one fixed," he replied. "That's where the oil is coming from."   (R & R MAGAZINE)

Good advice to parents whose teenagers are learning to drive: Don't stand in their way!   (BALANCE SHEET)

The last car I bought must've been owned by a little old lady who drove it only in stock car races.   (CURRENT COMEDY)

The reason they put safety belts in autos is that people are getting killed before they have their cars paid for.   (HERB SHRINER)

AVERAGE (see NORMAL)

It's strange about being average. Average is the worst of the good and the best of the bad.   (PHINEWS)

Not doing more than the average is what keeps the average down.
(WILLIAM WINANS)

BABIES

Popular belief to the contrary, babies who are more passive during their first few days of life are the ones most apt to mature into intelligent and responsive youngsters.

(SCIENTISTS AT HEW's NATIONAL INSTITUTE OF MENTAL HEALTH)

He got off the hospital elevator on the wrong floor, heard many babies crying, and asked a nurse what was wrong. "You'd cry too," she said, "if you had just arrived and found you owed the government thousands of dollars on the national debt and had wet pants."

What's the best way to drive a baby buggy? Tickle its feet.

(AMERICAN OPINION)

History prof: We'll name that baby Theophilus.
  Why such a name?
  Because he's Theophilus looking baby I've ever seen.

A physician says babies don't need that traditional slap on the rear end when they're born. But at least it gives them an immediate idea of what life is going to be like.

A baby is an inestimable blessing and bother.   (MARK TWAIN)

Out of the mouth of babes comes a lot of what they should have swallowed.   (FRANKLIN P. JONES)

BABY-SITTER

A baby-sitter is a teenager who comes in to act like an adult while the adults go out and act like teenagers. (HARRY MARSH)

A baby-sitter who's on her toes doesn't do much sitting.
(FRANKLIN P. JONES)

BACHELORS

Old classmate: I was sorry to hear that your brother died. Had he finished his education?
Other classmate: No, he died a bachelor. (JIM KELLY)

All married men profess to be puzzled about the fact that bachelors are not wealthy. (AMERICAN OPINION)

A bachelor is a guy whose romances go off without a hitch.

Bachelors, like detergents, work fast and leave no rings.

A bachelor is a man who doesn't have much help in discovering his faults. (FRANKLIN P. JONES)

An old farmer, asked why he never married, explained: "Well, I'd rather go through life wanting something I didn't have than having something I didn't want." (INDIANAPOLIS STAR)

BACKS

Had a bad back, so I took a pill. But it had a side effect. Now I have a bad side. (NONEE COAN)

BACKSLIDING

Collapse in the Christian life is seldom a blowout; it is usually a slow leak. (PAUL E. LITTLE)

However deep you fall, you are never out of God's reach.

BALDNESS (see HAIR)

He isn't bald—he has inverted hair. (ARNOLD GLASOW)

When God made heads, He covered up the ones He didn't like.

BANKERS AND POETS

A banker may write a bad poem, but a poet had better not write a bad check. (HOUGHTON LINE)

BANKS

I called the bank and asked if their interest rate sign was Fahrenheit or Celsius.   (TIGER LYONS)

One of life's big disappointments is discovering that the man who writes the advertisements for a bank is not the same guy who makes the loans.   (HERB TRUE)

BARBERS

A new barber who was shaving a customer nicked him badly, then asked solicitously, "Do you want your head wrapped in a towel?"
   "No, thanks," said the customer. "I'll carry it home under my arm."
                                              (MAYNERD BRADFORD)

BARGAINS

When you buy things for a song, watch out for the accompaniment.
                                                (BALANCE SHEET)

BARRIERS

Bulldozers can break down brick barriers, and jet power can break sound barriers, but only Jesus Christ can crack the toughest barrier of them all—the barrier between people.   (SPIRIT)

BASKETBALL

Abraham Lincoln freed the slaves because he thought it would be good for basketball.   (RED BUTTONS)

BATHROOM

Stomping-angry two-year-old: Every day I have to go to the bathroom!   (MARCIA CORY)

BEAUTY

I'm tired of all this nonsense about beauty being only skin-deep. That's deep enough. What do you want—an adorable pancreas? (JEAN KERR)

The more beautiful a girl is, the less likely she is to make a lasting deep relationship.   (JOHN OCKERT)

The great beautifier is a contented heart and a happy outlook.
                                              (GAYELORD HAUSER)

There is only one kind of beauty that can transcend time, and many women possess it. It is, of course, beauty of the spirit that lights the eyes and transforms even a plain woman into a beautiful one. Women with wit, charm, and warmth, who are interested in others and forget themselves, and who accept each stage of life gracefully, are the lasting beauties of this world—and the happiest. (DEIRDRE BUDGE)

Nothing is more beautiful than cheerfulness in an old face. (J.P. RICHTER)

Beauty is more important to a woman than brains because most men can see better than they can think.

BEHAVIOR

Be kind. Remember everyone you meet is fighting a hard battle.
(HARRY THOMPSON)

Always hold your head up, but keep your nose at a friendly level.
(AUTOMOTIVE SERVICE DIGEST)

It's easier to learn good behavior by watching it than by hearing about it. (FRANK A. CLARK)

What really matters is what happens *in* us, not *to* us. (JAMES W. KENNEDY)

There is seldom an inner urge to preach what one practices.
(HESKETH PEARSON)

When a person is shouted at, he simply cannot help but shout back. . . . You can use this scientific knowledge to keep another person from becoming angry; control the other person's tone of voice by your own voice. Psychology has proved that if you keep your voice soft, you will not become angry. Psychology has accepted as scientific the biblical injunction, "A soft answer turneth away wrath." (LES GIBLIN)

No man, for any considerable period, can wear one face to himself and another to the multitude without finally getting bewildered as to which may be the true. (NATHANIEL HAWTHORNE)

Most of us don't put our best foot forward until we get the other one in hot water. (ARNOLD GLASOW)

It does a person no good to sit up and take notice if he keeps on sitting. (BALANCE SHEET)

Some people are so intractably vain that when they admit they are wrong they want as much credit for admitting it as if they were right.
(SYDNEY HARRIS)

President Eisenhower's rules for his staff: "I want everybody smiling around here. Always take your job seriously, but never yourself. Don't forget to pray."

The more hot arguments you win, the fewer warm friends you'll have.
(BURTON HILLIS)

The underdog who condemns the behavior of the overdog rarely stops to consider whether his attitude would be any different if destiny had consigned him to the role of the overdog. (SYDNEY HARRIS)

Nobody has a right to do as he pleases, except when he pleases to do right.

Fun is a word we once reserved for children. Adults did not "have fun"; they had "pleasure." Today, in our national passion to be *happy*, we are not only substituting childish pleasures for adult behavior; we are subtly changing the very goals of that behavior. *Relax* has replaced *try*. *Spend* has replaced *save*. *Be happy* has replaced *achieve something*.
(LEO ROSTEN)

Not knowing how to spend our time, we take what satisfaction we can in spending our money. (JOHN ISE)

Some persons never say anything bad about the dead—or anything good about the living. (DAN KIDNEY)

One test of a person's strength is his knowledge of his weakness.

The world is full of cactus, but we don't have to sit on it. (WILL FOLEY)

Sixteen-year-old's explanation of much teenage behavior: "We are too old to do the things that children want to do and not old enough to do the things that grown-ups want to do, so all that's left are the things that nobody else wants to do." (ROSEMARY)

Think it's going to be a bad day for you? Then make a definite point of not letting anyone at home or at work find it out. Assign yourself the task of making someone happy, and thereby give yourself a gift, for by noon you will already have forgotten that this was going to be a bad day. (ANNABELLE)

Two qualities make the difference between leaders and men of average performance. They are curiosity and discontent. These deep human urges work together, I believe, to motivate all human discovery and achievement. I have never known an outstanding man who lacked either curiosity or discontent. And I have never known a man of small achievement who had both. The two belong together. Without discontent, curiosity is merely idle. Without curiosity, discontent is only useless handwriting. (CHARLES BROWER)

BELIEFS (see THEOLOGY)

What we believe about God is the most important thing about us.
(A.W. TOZER)

To let go is surrender. To let God is belief.

It takes no brains to be an atheist. Any stupid person can deny the existence of a supernatural power because man's physical senses cannot detect it. But there cannot be ignored the influence of conscience, the respect we feel for moral law, the mystery of first life ... or the marvelous order in which the universe moves about us on this earth. All these evidence the handiwork of the beneficent Deity. For my part that Deity is the God of the Bible and of Jesus Christ, His Son. (DWIGHT EISENHOWER)

One person with a belief is equal to a force of 99 who only have interests.

Even the greatest of men sometimes lack the courage of their convictions. Einstein himself doctored up one of his formulas to conceal an apparent "absurdity" that later turned out to be true. (SYDNEY HARRIS)

We are apt to believe what is pleasant rather than what is true.

Barnum was not only a great showman, but also a philosopher. He said that more people were humbugged into believing too little than were humbugged into believing too much. This is true of people's attitude toward prayer. Most of us believe and expect too little. Our God is a great God. He can do exceeding abundantly above all that we can ask or think [Jeremiah 33:3]. (HOUSTON TIMES)

BELITTLERS

One of the worst ways to spend your time that I know of is to let yourself become a "belittler" or a complainer. Yesterday I heard such phrases as these—"Oh, you're an idealist," or "He's an 'eager beaver,'" or "He's a 'do-gooder.'" The belittler does not detract very much from those whom he calls such names, but he does give you a pretty good idea of his own sense of values and thinking process.
(WALTER MACPEEK)

Many who belittle themselves do it because they want to be "bebigged."

BELONGING

Social workers point to an enormous psychological problem in our society: many young people have never experienced a deep emotional attachment to anyone. They do not know how to love and be loved. The need to be loved translates itself into the need to belong to someone or something. Driven by their need, these young people become the victims of cults, of peer group pressure, of fads, in short, of any mass movement at hand. They will do anything to belong. (ALBERT LaLONDE)

BENEFITS

He who receives a benefit should never forget it; he who bestows one should never remember it. (CHARRON)

BIBLE

No one ever graduates from Bible study until he meets its Author face to face. (EVERETT HARRIS)

Some seminaries offer a "Dalmatian theology," one holding that the Bible is inspired only in spots. (PAIGE PATTERSON)

It is not enough to own a Bible; we must read it. It is not enough to read it; we must let it speak to us. It is not enough to let it speak to us; we must believe it. It is not enough to believe it; we must live it. (WILLIAM A. WARD)

Men do not reject the Bible because it contradicts itself but because it contradicts them. (E. PAUL HOVEY)

If a man's Bible is coming apart, it is an indication that he himself is fairly well put together. (JAMES JENNINGS)

Preparing for a long trip, the young Christian said to his friend, "I am just about packed. I only have to put in a guidebook, a lamp, a mirror, a microscope, a telescope, a volume of fine poetry, a few biographies, a package of old letters, a book of songs, a sword, a hammer, and a set of books I have been studying."
    "But," the friend objected, "you can't get all that into your bag."
    "Oh, yes," replied the young man, "it doesn't take much room." He placed his Bible in the corner of the suitcase and closed the lid. (THE EMPLOYMENT COUNSELOR)

The Bible is not like a slot machine. If you put in five minutes' reading time, you don't necessarily get a "blessing" (or anything else) out of it. (A. MORGAN DERHAM)

Plenty of people who are under the Word are not in it.

(HOWARD HENDRICKS)

A skeptic in London, in speaking of the Bible, said it was quite impossible in these days to believe in any book whose authority was unknown.

A Christian asked him if the compiler of the multiplication table was known.

"No," he answered.

"Then, of course, you do not believe in it," persisted the other.

"Oh, yes, I believe in it because it works well."

"So does the Bible," was the rejoinder, and the skeptic had no answer.

(BAPTIST & REFLECTOR)

The family Bible is more often used to adorn coffee tables or press flowers than it is to feed souls and discipline lives. (CHARLES COLSON)

A readiness to believe every promise implicitly, to obey every command unhesitatingly, to stand perfect and complete in all the will of God, is the only true spirit of Bible study. (ANDREW MURRAY)

The Bible is a book of prayers. Out of 667 recorded prayers, there are 454 recorded answers. (DEFENDER)

The Bible is a storehouse of whose contents no one can afford to be ignorant. It repays reading and study whether it be approached merely because of its literary value, or its ethical teachings, or its practical bearing on everyday life. (DWIGHT MOODY)

There are many ways to read the Bible. Such reading may be an arduous duty or a pleasant exercise, or it may become a transforming experience.

(CHRISTIAN OBSERVER)

It is not how many Bibles are sold that counts, nor even how many people read them; what matters is how many actually believe what they read and surrender themselves in faith to live by the truth. Short of this the Bible can have no real value for any of us. (ALLIANCE WITNESS)

The Bible has given us the most marvelous record of family life of any civilization on earth. . . . The Bible never grows old. We grow old. Our houses grow old. Our businesses become outdated. Our wardrobes change quickly. But the Bible, a study of man's relationships to God, never changes. That's why the way of life of the family of Israel has survived the centuries. Faithful records of the family life of other civilizations contemporary with the Bible—the Babylonian, the Hittite, even the Greek—have perished, but the family record of Israel is alive and vital today. (EDITH DEEN)

The Bible dramatically deals with difficulties that discourage us, temptations that test us, and problems that plague us. It richly reveals the Christ who can change us, the Friend who can free us, and the Light who can lead us. (WILLIAM A. WARD)

Why is it that our kids can't read a Bible in school, but they can in prison? (MARSHALLTOWN TIMES-REPUBLICAN)

When I am thirsting for revenge, I quote the biblical injunction about "an eye for an eye"; when you are thirsting for revenge, I quote the biblical injunction about the superiority of "turning the other cheek." (SYDNEY HARRIS)

Professor A.T. Robertson used to say that one proof of the inspiration of the Bible is that it has withstood so much poor preaching. Likewise one proof that the church is God's instrument is that it has not blown apart with all of us in it. (DUKE MCCALL)

The Bible is a very dangerous book for dictators. Hitler knew it, and so did many other totalitarian rulers. If they are to remain in power, repressing liberties and keeping their subjects ignorant, they should use every means possible to keep the Bible out of the hands of their people. (CHRISTIANITY TODAY)

The Bible, God's inerrant Word, is forever true whether or not anyone reads or believes it; but it becomes of value to you when you get hold of it for yourself. Never leave a passage of Scripture until it has said something to *you*. (ROBERT A. COOK)

BIFOCALS

Show me a man with his head held high, and I'll show you a man who can't get used to his bifocals.

BILLS

Ornithologist: Many birds sing without opening their bills. We would too.

BIRDS

Scientists tell us that birds dream, but not what about. A likely subject would seem to be statues. (FRANKLIN P. JONES)

BIRTH CONTROL

Perhaps nothing makes a man think more seriously of birth control than driving the school bus. (FRANKLIN P. JONES)

I don't believe the Bible teaches that sex is just for the propagation of the human race. I believe it's also for enjoyment within marriage. I think we have a right to plan families and practice birth control, due to the population explosion. (BILLY GRAHAM)

BIRTHDAYS

Birthdays are mentioned only twice in the Bible. On the first one, Pharaoh's birthday, he had his chief baker beheaded. On King Herod's birthday, the King had John the Baptist beheaded. (BERNICE T. CORY)

You know it's going to be a bad day when your birthday cake collapses from the weight of the candles.

Some men take a day off on their birthday, and many women take a year off. (SCANDAL SHEET)

You've got what separates the men from the boys—lots of years.

BITTERNESS

Bad temper is its own scourge. Few things are more bitter than to feel bitter. A man's venom poisons himself more than his victim. (MEGIDDO MESSAGE)

BLAME

One of today's problems is that everybody is fixing the blame, and nobody is fixing the trouble. (ROBERT ORBEN)

To err is human. To blame it on the other guy is even more human. (BITS & PIECES)

Law of business blame: People in a company who quit or are fired or demoted are held responsible for everything that goes wrong. (LESTER CASE)

The man who can smile when things go wrong has probably just thought of somebody he can blame it on. (GRIT)

BLESSINGS

Life would be more pleasant if we could forget our troubles as easily as we forget our blessings. (TOM HAGGAI)

Try *claiming* God's blessings instead of merely *longing* for them. (HENRY JACOBSEN)

The things that count most cannot be counted.   (ETHICAL OUTLOOK)

The more we count the blessings we have, the less we crave the luxuries we haven't.   (WILLIAM A. WARD)

BLUNTNESS

A strange thing about blunt people is that they usually come to the point first.

BOOING

Fans don't boo nobodies.   (REGGIE JACKSON)

BOOKS

The value of a book is not determined by its cost, but its use.   (JERRY WALKER)

Books are the broadest-spectrum pharmaceuticals in the world: they can stimulate us when we are young, tranquilize us when we are old, sedate us when we are restless, sterilize us when we are infected with the virus of prejudice, fortify our intellectual anemia, and detoxify the emotional bloodstream by providing us with vicarious adventure and discovery.   (SYDNEY HARRIS)

Someday I hope to write a book where the royalties will pay for the copies I give away.   (CLARENCE DARROW)

Above a rack of books in a secondhand store in Louisville, Ky. hangs a sign that reads: "These books were owned by a little old lady who never read faster than 50 words a minute."   (CAPPER'S WEEKLY)

A pharmacist wrote a book, but it was a drug on the market.

If you believe that no one was ever corrupted by a book, you have also to believe that no one was ever improved by a book (or a play or a movie). You have to believe, in other words, that all art is morally trivial and that, consequently, all education is morally irrelevant.   (IRVING KRISTOL)

A book becomes a classic when people who haven't read it start pretending they have.   (DAVENPORT [IOWA] TIMES)

A bookstore specializing in religious reading advertises its wares as "blessed sellers."   (PRU PRATT)

There should be a law compelling all courting couples to read a few

good books together. Then they will know whether or not they are
spiritually in harmony. (LEE SHIPLEY)

Law of books: Important books which contain no errors will develop
errors in the mail.

A rare book is one that comes back after you've loaned it out.
(JOURNEYMAN BARBER)

BOREDOM

Boredom is as positive a sensation as a toothache. (LEE. S. GUNTER)

It is not the fast tempo of modern life that kills but the boredom, a lack
of strong interest, and failure to grow that destroy. It is the feeling that
nothing is worthwhile that makes men ill and unhappy.(HAROLD DODDS)

The most bored people in life are not the underprivileged but the
overprivileged. (FULTON SHEEN)

One of the leading illnesses of our time is boredom, which is just another word for denial of life and romancing with death. With the increase of
leisure, boredom threatens to become endemic in our society.
(CHARLES McCABE)

America is said to have the highest per capita boredom of any spot on
earth! We know that because we have the greatest number of artificial
amusements of any country. People have become so empty that they
can't even entertain themselves. They have to pay other people to amuse
them, to make them laugh, to try to make them feel warm and happy and
comfortable for a few minutes, to try to lose that awful, frightening,
hollow feeling—that terrible, dreaded feeling of being lost and alone.
(BILLY GRAHAM)

BORES

Everyone is a bore to someone. That is unimportant. The thing to avoid
is being a bore to oneself. (GERALD BRENAN)

To a man who asked if he was making a bore of himself by talking too
much, Franklin P. Adams replied, "Well, sir, I would put it this way—you
never seem to have an unexpressed thought." (CONSTRUCTION DIGEST)

A bore is a person who lights up the room when he leaves.

The art of evading bores was brought to a high point by the late Alexander Woollcott. Once when he thought the monologue of a certain actor

had gone on far too long, he interrupted the flow of talk. "Excuse me, my leg has gone to sleep. Do you mind if I join it?"   (PAGEANT)

BOSSES (see MANAGEMENT)

A survey revealed the 10 most common complaints of workers about their bosses: (1) arbitrariness, (2) arrogance, (3) failure to show appreciation or give credit, (4) failure to see the other person's point of view, (5) failure to size up employees correctly, (6) lack of leadership, (7) lack of frankness and sincerity, (8) failure to delegate responsibility, (9) indecision, (10) bias—letting emotions rule reason.   (BITS AND PIECES)

BOWLING

A sign on the wall of the men's room at Alfred's, a San Francisco restaurant: "The family that bowls together—splits."

In one night my wife lost 12 pounds. Her bowling ball was swiped.
                                                              (SHELBY FRIEDMAN)

BOYS

In a recent survey, 22 percent of the boys in our neighborhood raised small animals, 29 percent raised plants, and 97 percent raised their voices excitedly.

There was the mother who said, "Junior, put on a pair of clean socks every day." And by Friday he couldn't get his shoes on.

Many a small boy is the kind of kid his mother wouldn't want him to play with.   (BURLINGTON [WISC.] STANDARD)

When a small boy puts something down in black and white, it's apt to be a towel.

A young man entered an office in response to a sign: "Boy Wanted."
    "What kind of boy do you want?" he asked the manager.
    "Why, we want a clean, well-groomed, neat youngster," replied the manager, "who is quiet, quick, and obedient."
    "Phooey!" said the youth disgustedly, turning to leave. "You don't want a boy; you want a girl."

A boy is a stick of dynamite, a bundle of energy and potential power, waiting to be ignited. Guard him zealously from careless sparks that would dissipate his energies or detonate his power for the demolition of society. Guide him carefully to a place where his vigor and strength will be used to build a better world.   (OPTIMIST MAGAZINE)

The central difficulty in becoming a man nowadays is that a boy sees so little of his father or other men. A man's work is now separated from his home. There are no men around for boys to model themselves after. Boys are almost exclusively brought up by their mothers and taught by women teachers. (S.I. HAYAKAWA)

BRAGGING

Nobody's so apt to be a soloist as the fellow who blows his own horn. (FRANKLIN P. JONES)

BRAIN

The brain is not a container to be filled but rather something to be ignited. (G.K. NIELSON)

The day starts off bad when you have to get your brain jump-started. (WENDELL TROGDON)

I use not only all the brains I have, but all I can borrow. (WOODROW WILSON)

A fellow's mind, like his stomach, might be better off if it stayed a little bit hungry. (FRANK A. CLARK)

BRAINSTORMING (see THINKING)

"With the kind of boss I've got," said an enrollee in a recent executive training seminar on creative thinking, "it starts out as brainstorming and ends up as brainstomping." (NATION'S BUSINESS)

BRAVERY

Learned people know it; brave people do it.(BERTELSMANN BILD-KALENDER)

It is easy to be brave from a safe distance. (AESOP)

BREATHING

The way you breathe affects how you feel, how well you think, and how much energy you have. Complete breathing involves three motions. Each breath should begin in your abdomen, move up into the middle section of your body, or stomach, and finally fill your upper chest and collar bone region. Such breathing is not only invigorating, but also exercises muscles and helps tone your digestive system. When you are scared or anxious, your breathing normally becomes rapid and shallow. Continuing to breathe in that manner maintains or increases your feeling of fear. By slowing down your rate of breathing and breathing deeply, it is possible for you to become relaxed. (NEW WOMAN)

BREVITY

The most valuable of all talents is that of never using two words when one will do. (THOMAS JEFFERSON)

When a man takes a paragraph to say what could be said in a sentence, he is either a sloppy thinker or is trying to pull the wool over someone's eyes; brevity in expression is more than the soul of wit—it is the mark of clearheadedness and honesty. (SYDNEY HARRIS)

Unless you are brief, your complete plan of thought will seldom be grasped. Before you reach the conclusion, the reader or listener has forgotten the beginning and the middle. (HORACE)

A bank robber handed a teller a 68-word note, the message of which was "your money or your life," but by the time the teller had finished reading the note, such a crowd had collected that the robber was caught. This is the best argument for short copy that I have ever read. (CHARLES RAMOND)

A book, formerly called *How to Be Brief*, is now out in paperback with a new title, *How to Express Yourself Clearly and Briefly*. (WARREN ROBERTSON)

BROKEN THINGS

I have been reflecting on the inestimable value of "broken things." Broken pitchers gave ample light for victory (Judges 7:19-21); broken bread was more than enough for all the hungry (Matthew 14:19-21); broken box gave fragrance to all the world (Mark 14:3, 9); and broken body is salvation to all who believe and receive the Saviour (Isaiah 53:5-6, 12; 1 Corinthians 11:24). And what cannot the Broken One do with our broken plans, projects, and hearts? (V. RAYMOND EDMAN)

BROTHERHOOD OF MAN

The brotherhood of man has been turning out too few brothers and too many hoods. (TIES)

BUILDS OF BODIES

Ectomorph—tall and lean
  Mesomorph—average
  Endomorph—chubby

BURDENS

It isn't the burdens of today that drive men mad. Rather it is regret over yesterday or fear of tomorrow. (ROBERT J. HASTINGS)

BURIAL COLLECTION

To writer: "Could you give me $1 to help bury an editor?"
Hands her $5 bill: "Here—bury five of them."

BURNOUT

What causes burnout? The immediate cause is a mismatch between effort and results. Burnout victims start out full of fire and good intentions, but their efforts are not repaid in kind. The reality is that it is difficult to help people. Add to that low pay, impossible workloads, miles of red tape, inadequate training, low prestige, and ungrateful clients. There is, moreover, the fact that society does not really understand what the helping professions are all about. (PAUL CHANCE)

BUSINESS

Business is what, if you don't have any, you go out of. (EARL WILSON)

A company needs to be constantly rejuvenated by the infusion of young blood. It needs smart young men with the imagination and the guts to turn everything upside down if they can. It also needs old fogies to keep them from turning upside down those things that ought to be right side up. Above all, it needs young rebels and old conservatives who can work together, challenge each other's views, yield or hold fast with equal grace, and continue after each hard-fought battle to respect each other as men and as colleagues. (HENRY FORD II)

It takes something other than wages to hold good employees; and it takes something other than low prices to hold a good customer.
(IMPERIAL METAL & CHEMICAL CO.)

A lot of men are too busy trying to get ahead to do a good job.

Moses . . . trained Joshua to take his place, so that Moses might become dispensable. So did Jesus train His disciples versus His ascension. So should all useful persons train others to take their place. Success without a successor is failure. (FOOTNOTE TO DEUTERONOMY 34:9, BERK)

Nobody inside an organization ever looked ready to move into a bigger job. I use the rule of 50 percent. Try to find somebody inside the company with a record of success (in any area) and with an appetite for the job. If he looks like 50 percent of what you need, give him the job. In six months he'll have grown the other 50 percent and everybody will be satisfied. (ROBERT TOWNSEND)

One businessman says he has friends who really believe in recycling. They've used him time after time.

Corporate growth is something like riding on a bicycle. If you coast too long you fall off.   (GORDON WEIL)

Our grand business is not to see what lies dimly at a distance, but to do what lies clearly at hand.   (THOMAS CARLYLE)

The Christian need not be anti-business; the Christian need not be anti-possessions. The Christian cannot help but be anti-exploitation and anti-materialistic. Exploitive corporations and individuals only masquerade as "business." They in fact behave like economic war lords—as ruthless as the law and circumstance allow.   (ARTHUR JONES)

No organization can feed and grow upon self-satisfaction.
                                          (DETROIT BOARD OF COMMERCE)

After working in an office for many and many a year, I remain more firmly convinced than ever that the most useful piece of equipment in it remains the scrap basket.   (MALCOLM S. FORBES)

Business is a lot like a game of tennis—those who don't serve well end up losing.   (DOC ANKLAM)

Every business needs some promising young men—in order to attract and keep good secretaries.   (MARJORIE VICK)

A generation ago most men who finished a day's work needed rest; now they need exercise.

Everybody should be paid what he's worth. No matter how big a cut he might have to take.

Boss: This is the end. You're fired.
    Worker: Fired? I thought slaves were sold.   (PEN MAGAZINE)

They say that the late Henry Ford had no use for a private office of his own in his company's huge administration building. The reason was, he said, "I can get out of the other fellow's office a lot faster than I can get him out of mine."

The office manager frowned at the elderly clerk and said: "I'm afraid you're ignoring our efficiency system."
    "Maybe so," admitted the clerk, "but somebody has to get the work done."   (GENERAL FEATURES)

Ten Commandments of Business:
1. Handle the hardest job first each day. Easy ones are pleasures.

2. Do not be afraid of criticism—criticize yourself often.
3. Be glad and rejoice in the other fellow's success—study his methods.
4. Do not be misled by dislikes. Acid ruins the finest fabrics.
5. Be enthusiastic—it is contagious.
6. Do not have the notion that success means simply money-making.
7. Be fair, and do at least one decent act every day.
8. Honor the chief. There must be a head to everything.
9. Have confidence in yourself; believe you can do it.
10. Harmonize your work. Let sunshine radiate and penetrate your relationships. (GOOD READING)

There's a large ad agency in New York whose quick-tempered boss fires about four employees a day. Anybody who lasts a full year is secretly given a prize by astounded colleagues. One of the vice-presidents of the agency was recalling the first day he started work.

"I didn't mind too much," he sighed, "that my name was printed on the door with chalk—but I did think that the wet sponge hanging on the doorknob was highly unethical." (WINSTED [COLO.] EVENING CITIZEN)

I believe my father's overall business philosophy may be accurately summed up in the following tenets he frequently quoted to me when I was young, and which were the principles by which he lived and worked:

Moral responsibility can never be avoided.

The last thing you should ever do is borrow. The first thing you must always do is repay your debts.

If you can trust a man, a written contract is a waste of paper. If you can't trust him, a written contract is still a waste of paper.

The man who works for you is entitled to decent wages, decent working conditions—and your respect.

Money is only as good as what you do with it. The best thing you can do with your money is to keep it working to produce more and better goods and services for more people at lower prices. (J. PAUL GETTY)

The wayside of business is full of brilliant men who started out with a spurt and lacked the stamina to finish. Their places were taken by patient and unshowy plodders who never knew when to quit.(J.R. TODD)

You can tell a company by the men it keeps. (W. A. CLARKE)

Since he's become a member of the board, he just lumbers along.
(JOAN WELSH)

The closest some people ever come to reaching their ideal is when they write their resumés.

I don't believe companies can be run the way they used to be. The top boss or old bull of the woods operation is passé. The holding company concept is dead. Big companies have to be run by a lot of people given a lot of authority. (Harold Geneen)

BUSYBODY

There is a vast difference between putting your nose in other people's business and putting your heart in other people's problems.

BUYING AND DISCARDING

Anyone can buy new things, but only a strong man can throw out old things. (William Feather)

CAMPS

Summer camps and some are not. (WES KLUSMAN)

A New York youngster, who was more accustomed to man-made wonders than the marvels of nature, was treated to a vacation in the country. There he saw his first rainbow.

The attitude of the child, as he gazed upon the gorgeous display of colors in the sky, was one of wonder and perplexity.

"Mother," he finally exclaimed, "it's very beautiful, but what is it supposed to advertise?" (CONSTRUCTION DIGEST)

I'm trying something new this summer, I'm sending the dog to camp and the *kids* to obedience school!

Kid: We're going home tomorrow. Guess I'd better rumple up my pajamas and squeeze out half of my toothpaste.

By what do we gauge a successful camp program? That the camper goes home to enthusiastically report on the real sharp counselor, the good food, or the number of badges he has won?

Or by a quietly spoken statement: "Mom, I met Jesus Christ while I was at camp"? (VIVIENNE BLOMQUIST)

A camping enthusiast pays good money to do all the things he griped about in the army. (GREEN LIGHT)

During evening devotions in a boys' summer camp, a counselor was startled to hear this prayer from a 12-year-old: "O God, we thank Thee for every blessing. We are grateful for the birds and the bees and the flowers—they mean so much to those who teach us about them. Amen." (ELBERTON [GA.] STAR)

Camp counselors often end up with tents nerves. (JACK KRAUS)

CANNIBALS

There's the cannibal who ate something that didn't agree with him. His wife. (SHELBY FRIEDMAN)

CAPITALISM

The inherent vice of capitalism is the unequal sharing of blessings; the inherent vice of socialism is the equal sharing of miseries. (WINSTON CHURCHILL)

CARE

A man can be no bigger than the number of people for whom he genuinely cares. (SHERM WILLIAMS)

Nobody cares how much you know—until they know how much you care. (JOHN CASSIS)

Too many people don't care what happens so long as it doesn't happen to them. (WILLIAM HOWARD TAFT)

Life needs someone to care for so life can focus on others and not itself. The care that focuses on others keeps the vision of life clear, not beclouded with self. (C. NEIL STRAIT)

Sentimentality comes easy. But caring is hard—it involves doing.

Care is a state in which something does matter; it is the source of human tenderness. (ROLLO MAY)

CAREERS (see JOBS)

Seventy percent of those who graduate from college don't know what they're gonna do. (G. HERBERT TRUE)

CATASTROPHE

The only complete catastrophe is the catastrophe from which we learn nothing. (WILLIAM HOCKING)

CATS

One reason we admire cats, those of us who do, is their proficiency in one-upmanship. They always seem to come out on top, no matter what they are doing—or pretend they do. Rarely do you see a cat discomfited. They have no conscience, and they never regret. Maybe we secretly envy them. (BARBARA WEBSTER)

CAUTION

An anecdote which is often told of Abraham Lincoln involves General George B. McClellan, who was then Commander of the Union force and was conducting a waiting campaign. He was so careful to avoid mistakes that little headway was evident. President Lincoln wrote him a letter which said: "My Dear McClellan, if you do not want to use the Army, I should like to borrow it for a while. Yours respectfully, A. Lincoln."

CHANCES (see OPPORTUNITIES, RISKS)

If at times you feel that you have not had the same chance that others have, ask yourself what chance did Abraham Lincoln have? Remember that "it is not so much the size of the dog in the fight that counts, but the size of the fight in the dog." (SAMUEL PETTENGILL)

Now here's a linguistic quirk I note with unusual vim.
　To wit, what we call a fat chance is the same as a chance that's slim. (RICHARD ARMOUR)

CHANGE

"Time sure changes things," an airline passenger told his companion. "When I was a boy, I used to sit in a flat-bottomed rowboat in the lake down there below us and fish. Every time a plane flew over I'd look up and wish I were in it. Now I look down and wish I were fishing."

Many great civilizations have collapsed at the very height of their achievement because they were unable to analyze their basic problems, to change direction, and to adjust to the new situations which faced them by concerting their wisdom and strength. (KURT WALDHEIM)

Very often a change of self is needed more than a change of scene.
(A.C. BENSON)

Consider how hard it is to change yourself and you'll understand what little chance you have of trying to change others. (JACOB M. BRAUDE)

In our century everything seems to be changing; nothing abides. Only those who know the living God escape this threat of universal obsolescence. God abides. The divine Commandments abide. Christ's Gospel abides. And whoever abides in Him now will forever abide with Him. The cosmic process offers no enduring place to hide but God's own abiding place.   (CARL F.H. HENRY)

I have learned not to look for the greener grass on the other side of the fence. I look for a smile on the face of the cow.   (GARY GULBRANSON)

Little men with little minds and little imagination jog through life in little ruts, smugly resisting all changes which would jar their little worlds.
(MARIE FRASER)

It might be just as offensive to be around a man who never changed his mind as one who never changed his clothes.   (COUNTRY PARSON)

Change is not made without inconvenience, even from worse to better.
(RICHARD HOOKER)

To paraphrase the words of J.D. Pringle, "Magazines, like clocks, run down unless they are constantly rewound."
Success with a certain format can induce complacency. You get bogged down in a narrow pattern, fall into a rut, become typed. A time then arrives when inspiration tires, zest wanes. The performance as a whole takes on a certain weariness of tone.
One issue begins to look and read too much like another. And before you know it, the book bores its readers and wears out its welcome.
We've seen this happen to the best and brightest of magazines. The only immunity we've been able to discover against it is to be aware of this natural tendency—and combat it continually.   (ARNOLD GINGRICH)

Welcome change as a friend; try to visualize new possibilities and the blessings it is bound to bring you. If you stay interested in everything around you—in new ways of life, new people, new places, and ideas— you'll stay young, no matter what your age. Never stop learning and never stop growing; that is the key to a rich and fascinating life.
(ALEXANDER DE SEVERSKY)

When you're through changing, you're through.   (BRUCE BARTON)

We can benefit from change. Anyone who has ever really lived knows that there is no life without growth. When we stop growing, we stop living and start existing. But there is no growth without challenge, and there is no challenge without change. Life is a series of changes that create challenges, and if we are going to make it, we have to grow.
(WARREN WIERSBE)

Life is a long process of getting used to the things you started out to change.   (FRANK A. CLARK)

Change is always hard for the man who is in a rut. For he has scaled down his living to that which he can handle comfortably and welcomes no change—or challenge—that would lift him.   (C. Neil Strait)

It is very unlikely you will be able to change the personality of another person through your own dislike.   (Tom Haggai)

The world hates change; yet it is the only thing that has brought progress.   (Charles Kettering)

The people who usually get the most out of life are those who are prepared to roll with the punches . . . those who recognize the fact that they can't afford to become static and stagnant. The ability to adapt to new conditions is particularly important today. We have never lived in times when change has been more swift in almost every area of our lives.   (Leon Kulikowski)

There is a certain relief in change, even though it be from bad to worse. I have found in traveling in a stagecoach, that it is often a comfort to shift one's position and be bruised in a new place.   (Washington Irving)

For all your days prepare,
And meet them ever alike:
When you are the anvil, bear—
When you are the hammer, strike.   (Edwin Markham)

CHARACTER

There is no substitute for character. You can buy brains, but you cannot buy character.   (Robert A. Cook)

Character is simply habit long continued.   (Plutarch)

Your character is built by what you stand for, your reputation by what you fall for.   (Danville [Va.] Commercial Appeal)

Character is what you are in the dark.   (D.L. Moody)

A man's character, like rich topsoil, can erode so gradually you don't notice till it's gone.   (Country Parson)

A broken character doesn't knit easily.   (Megiddo Message)

You can't give character to another person, but you can encourage him to develop his own by possessing one yourself.   (Artemus Calloway)

Promises must be kept, deadlines met, commitments honored; not just for the sake of old-fashioned morality, but because we become what we do (or fail to do), and character is simply the sum of our performances. (HOWARD SPARKS)

The highest reward for a man's toil is not what he gets for it, but rather what he becomes by it. (AMERICAN WAY)

The way to find out about one man, I have often found, is to ask him about another. (GERARD FAY)

A scorpion, being a poor swimmer, asked a turtle to carry him on his back across a river. "Are you mad?" exclaimed the turtle. "You'll sting me while I'm swimming and I'll drown."

"My dear turtle," laughed the scorpion, "if I were to sting you, you would drown and I would go down with you. Now, where is the logic in that?"

"You're right," cried the turtle. "Hop on!"

The scorpion climbed aboard and halfway across the river gave the turtle a mighty sting. As they both sank to the bottom, the turtle resignedly said, "Do you mind if I ask you something? You said there'd be no logic in your stinging me. Why did you do it?"

"It has nothing to do with logic," the drowning scorpion sadly replied. "It's just my character." (HORIZONS)

A man's character is like a fence—it cannot be strengthened by whitewash. (MEGIDDO MESSAGE)

God is more concerned about our character than our comfort. His goal is not to pamper us physically but to perfect us spiritually. (PAUL W. POWELL)

Great occasions do not make heroes or cowards; they simply unveil them to the eyes of men. Silently and imperceptibly, as we wake or sleep, we grow strong or we grow weak, and at last some crisis shows us what we have become. (BROOKE FOSS WESTCOTT)

Character is always lost when a high ideal is sacrificed on the altar of conformity and popularity. (WAR CRY)

CHARITY

Many a man's idea of charity is to give unto others the advice he can't use himself. (HUGH MURR)

You cannot help men permanently by doing for them what they could and should do for themselves. (ABRAHAM LINCOLN)

CHEERFULNESS (see SMILES)

Assume a cheerfulness you do not feel and shortly you will feel the cheerfulness you assumed. (CHINESE PROVERB)

Lots of people get credit for being cheerful when they are just proud of their teeth. (WOODMEN OF THE WORLD)

We have absolutely no right to annoy others by our various moods. Let the prevailing mood be cheerful and serene; keep your other moods to yourself, or better still, get rid of them. (ANNE GOULD)

The best way to cheer yourself is to try to cheer somebody else. (MEGIDDO MESSAGE)

An old man surprised everyone with his cheerfulness since he seemed to have an unusual amount of trouble and relatively few pleasures. When asked the secret of his cheery disposition, he replied, "Well, you see, it's like this. The Bible says often, 'And it came to pass,' never 'It came to stay.' "

Cheerfulness is among the most laudable virtues. It gains you the good will and friendship of others. It blesses those who practice it and those upon whom it is bestowed. (B.C. FORBES)

It has been scientifically proved that worry, discord, and melancholy undermine health. Good spirits make for good digestion. Cheerfulness costs nothing; yet is beyond price. It is an asset for both business and body. The big men of today, the leaders of tomorrow, are those who can blend cheerfulness with their brains. (B.C. FORBES)

One ABC of Christianity: "Always Be Cheerful." (1 THESSALONIANS 5:16, MLB)

CHILDREN

By the time children are five, their parents will have done at least half of all that can ever be done to determine the children's future faith. (RANDOLPH MILLER)

Our kids are the most valuable things we have. The causes of delinquency are: (1) lack of love; (2) lack of discipline. . . . Don't shortchange your children for a ministry to a larger group. Don't just help others find the Lord and let your own kids go down the drain. (JIM VAUS)

The surest way to make it hard for your children is to make it soft for them. (WESLEYAN METHODIST)

The soul is healed by being with children. (FYODOR DOSTOEVSKY)

Almost every child would learn to write sooner if allowed to do his homework in wet cement.

When I approach a child, he inspires in me two sentiments: tenderness for what he is, and respect for what he may become. (LOUIS PASTEUR)

Children seldom misquote you. They more often repeat word for word what you shouldn't have said. (MAE MALOO)

There was never a child so lovely but his mother was glad to get him asleep. (RALPH WALDO EMERSON)

What's done to children, they will do to society. (KARL MENNINGER)

Father, report card in hand: "Son, it's too bad they don't give a grade for courage. You would get an 'A' for bringing this report card home."

Children very often are brought up believing they are guests in the home because they have nothing to do except live there. (G. BOWDEN HUNT)

There is a danger of overprotecting children, a tendency that parents should guard against. Take hard work for instance. The discipline of work is one of life's most important ones. Work requires certain adaptations, concentrations, and continuity of effort. Children have to learn how to work. It is a gradual process, a growing experience as a boy matures. As a young adult he's pretty liable to find the confinement of sticking to a task almost unbearable at times if he hasn't learned it earlier. (WALTER MACPEEK)

Kids are confused. Half of the adults tell him to find himself; the other half tell him to get lost.

In many cases a gifted child is defined in terms of his intelligence quotient when the intelligence quotient alone is not a sufficient measure of giftedness. Thomas Edison was labeled a slow learner, and Einstein was called a dull boy. Some children are culturally deprived and perform poorly on tests, while others possess talents which may not be revealed by the verbal symbols of an intelligence test. (CHLOE MCKEEVER)

Every child has a right to be both well fed and well led. (RUTH SMELTER)

It is the sum total of a child's experiences that determine his destiny, including his heredity as well as his home life, his friends, his education, his church, his recreation, his job, his wife or husband, plus the books and magazines he reads, the films he sees, the television he watches. Our children are a composite of all these, some of which are beyond our control. (ROBERT HASTINGS)

Children have not grown up until they can look at their parents as real people. Little children see their parents as paragons. Mother is the most beautiful woman in the world; father, the strongest man. Then comes the stage when everything is wrong with the parents. Maturity is being able to deal with parents as human beings; neither perfect nor impossible, but loved. (GEORGE SWEAZEY)

The best time to tackle a minor problem is before he grows up. (RAY FREEDMAN)

Children should be careful what they say—parents are always repeating what they hear.

Little Margaret asked her father when their new baby would talk. He told her not for two years, since little babies don't talk.
Said Margaret, "Oh, yes they do. Even in the Bible they do."
"Who did?" asked the father.
She replied, "Sister read the Bible to us this morning and I heard with my own ears that Job cursed the day he was born."

Young lad, to librarian: "Do you have anything on the parent from 30 to 35?" (VAUGHN'S VIEWPOINT)

Children are like mosquitoes—the moment they stop making noises you know they're getting into something.

What do you want your next child to be?
A grandchild.

Children can forgive their parents for being wrong, but weakness sends them elsewhere for strength. (LEONTINE YOUNG)

There are only two things a child will share willingly—communicable diseases and his mother's age. (MODERN MATURITY)

If you want your boy to follow in your footsteps, you've probably forgotten a few you took.

Children have more need of models than of critics. (JOSEPH JOUBERT)

Pretty much all the honest truth-telling in the world is done by children. (OLIVER W. HOLMES)

Thinking that three hours of any movie are harmless for the child but two hours of church and Sunday School are too much for his nervous system is just bad thinking. Giving him a nickel for the collection and a dollar for the movies not only shows a parent's sense of value but is also likely to produce a proportionate giver. (ZION'S HERALD)

Kids really brighten a household. They never turn off the lights.
(RALPH BUS)

In their eagerness for their children to acquire skills and to succeed, parents may forget that youngsters need time to think, and privacy in which to do it. (JAMES COX)

Children are a real comfort in your old age—and they make you reach it sooner too.

A father's task is many-sided, but the most important part of his work is to fit himself and his children into God's plan of family authority. Children are to be encouraged by the father's pat on the back and helped to better things when necessary by the application of the hand or stick to the seat of learning. Of course there are many other methods of discipline besides spanking, but whatever is called for must be used. To refuse to discipline a child is to refuse a clear demand of God, for a child who doesn't learn to obey both parents will find it much harder to learn to obey God. (KENNETH TAYLOR)

True parenthood is self-destructive. The wise parent is one who effectively does himself out of his job as parent. The silver cord must be broken. It must not be broken too abruptly, but it must be broken. The child must cease to be a child. . . . The wise parent delivers his child over to society. (ROBERT HOLMES)

If a child lives with criticism, he learns to condemn.
If a child lives with hostility, he learns to fight.
If a child lives with fear, he learns to be apprehensive.
If a child lives with jealousy, he learns to feel guilty.
If a child lives with tolerance, he learns to be patient.
If a child lives with encouragement, he learns to be confident.
If a child lives with praise, he learns to be appreciative.
If a child lives with acceptance, he learns to love.
If a child lives with approval, he learns to like himself.
If a child lives with recognition, he learns it is good to have a goal.
If a child lives with honesty, he learns what truth is.
If a child lives with fairness, he learns justice.
If a child lives with security, he learns to have faith in himself and those about him.

If a child lives with friendliness, he learns the world is a nice place in which to live. (SINAI SENTRY)

CHINA

Old Chinese never become senile—just disoriented.

CHINS

Keep your chin up. It helps to keep your mouth shut. (LOU ERICKSON)

It's harder to keep your chin up after you've got more than one.

CHOICES

What you do when you don't have to will determine what you'll be when you can't help it. (WILLIAM D. HERSEY)

CHRIST (see CROSS OF CHRIST, JESUS)

I read in a book that a man called Christ went about doing good. It is very disconcerting to me that I am so easily satisfied with just going about. (TOYOHIKO KAGAWA)

The lordship of Christ, if you take Him seriously, will guide you around many of the temptations and decisions over which most believers agonize. (ROBERT A. COOK)

He came to pay a debt He didn't owe because we owed a debt we couldn't pay. (DAYSPRING)

Look backward—see Christ dying for you.
Look upward—see Christ pleading for you.
Look inward—see Christ living in you.
Look forward—see Christ coming for you.

Christ companied with sinners without becoming complicated with their sins. (HOWARD HENDRICKS)

Christ on our cross is the way Calvary really reads. For He died for us— in our place. We, then, are debtors. Strange, that so often we act like we owe nothing. (C. NEIL STRAIT)

He died for us. Now He, and we, live for others. (MALCOLM CRONK)

CHRISTIANITY (see RELIGION, SPIRITUAL PROGRESS)

The Creator thinks enough of you to have sent Someone very special so that you might have life—abundantly, joyfully, completely, and victoriously. *You are important!*

People can be saved from sin and come into possession of eternal life by realizing they are sinners, believing that the Lord Jesus Christ loves them and has provided salvation through His own shed blood upon Calvary. Salvation is by grace through faith in Christ as personal Saviour and Sin-bearer, and is entirely a free gift of God. Salvation cannot possibly be achieved by man's works (John 3:14-18, 36; 5:24; 6:47; Acts 4:12; Romans 1:16-17; 3:20-26; 5:1; 8:1; Ephesians 2:8-9; Titus 3:5; 1 Peter 1:18-19; Revelation 1:5). (SCRIPTURE PRESS DOCTRINAL STATEMENT)

Why should we seek to walk on water when we can stand on the Rock? (GARY GULBRANSON)

One of the reasons people find it hard to be obedient to the commands of Christ is that they are uncomfortable taking orders from a stranger. (GARY GULBRANSON)

A Christian is not one who is *seeking* God's favor and forgiveness—he is one who has *found* them. (T. ROLAND PHILIPS)

After World War II a few bombers, which had been used for missions of destruction, were taken over for commercial service. They were called "converted bombers." The converted bomber had a new owner. It carried a new cargo. It had a new pilot. In Christian conversion, Jesus Christ delivers us from the old life and possesses us for God. He enters into the cockpit of the heart, takes over the controls, and operates the old life on a new course. (ROBERT B. MUNGER)

Christians do not become "sons of God" by their works, but it is by their works alone that they prove themselves to be "sons of God." (JOHN MACKEY)

If your Christianity doesn't work at home, it doesn't work. Don't export it. (HOWARD HENDRICKS)

Christianity is more than a storm cellar; it is a way of life. (GILBERT PETERS)

We learn, in Christian education, in exact proportion as Christ is Lord. (ROBERT A. COOK)

The Christian is a person who makes it easy for others to believe in God. (ROBERT M. MCCHEYNE)

The devil's No. 1 tool is not an active sinner, but an inactive Christian.

Many Christians have enough religion to make them decent, but not enough to make them dynamic. (KENNETH GRIDER)

I do not believe there is a Christian country anywhere in the world. They are all secular. (BILLY GRAHAM)

You don't have to have a high coefficient of gullibility to be a Christian. (VICTOR E. CORY)

A few Christians want the spiritual maturity that comes through testings; the rest want to take life easy. (HENRY JACOBSEN)

Perhaps Dean Inge was somewhat caustic when he said: "The Christian of today is a harmless little person whose chief interest in life is having a good time." There is, however, more truth than comfort in the saying, for most of us hide our Christianity quite successfully and follow the fashion of the world quite religiously. There is nothing that the majority of people dread as much as being out of fashion, and there are fashions in thought, in manners, and in practice, as well as in dress. (STEPHEN PAULSON)

Many people today can say truly (as Pilate did): "I find no fault in this Man," when referring to Jesus. Any verbal criticism of Jesus is rare. However, it is very common to find people whose actions say: "I find no fault in this Man, but I haven't been to church in years." Their actions will say, "I find no fault in this Man, but I wouldn't lift a finger, and don't, to aid the things He cared for most." (HALFORD LUCCOCK)

Many Christians are ineffective because they take their eyes off the instruments and are, as a result, flying through life upside down. (CHARLES PITTS)

The Christian's chief occupational hazards are depression and discouragement. (JOHN STOTT)

When one's view of life is fragmentized, so that Christ is in one compartment and most of the routine of living and studying is in another, it is exceedingly difficult to do one's best. (VIRGINIA MOLLENKOTT)

The trouble with many Christians is that they want to reach the Promised Land without going through the wilderness.

Let us encourage our churches to substitute salt and light for some of the sugar and spice. We need to begin again to know the sort of victory and blessing and humdrum hard work that comes from serving the poor, the widowed, the infirm, the lonely. Jesus Christ often ministered to the people nobody else wanted. (PETER E. GILLQUIST)

One of the funny things about becoming a Christian in the 20th century is that everybody looks around for some explanation other than the fact that one believes Christianity to be true, which, indeed, is the only basis on which anyone could become a Christian. A lot of my friends—old friends—regard my Christian faith as a sign of total senility. Others not so well disposed think it's due to the fact that as the capacity to engage in sins of the flesh diminishes with advancing years, one solaces himself by denouncing them. (MALCOLM MUGGERIDGE)

There are a lot of different kinds of nuts in the Lord's fruitcake.
(WALTER HEARN)

When we try to produce our own fruit of the Spirit, we come up with a pathetic synthetic. (BILL DILLON)

Christians who move the world are those who do not let the world move them. (MOODY MONTHLY)

When a Christian ceases to grow, he begins to decay. (CLATE RISLEY)

Many who saw a Man hanging on a cross almost 2,000 years ago thought: "The Christian religion is dissolved." But it was not so. It is true now as it was then. The end is the beginning. (IAN McCRAE)

All things being equal, a Christian will make spiritual progress exactly in proportion to his ability to criticize himself. . . . Some Christians hope in a vague kind of way that time will help them to grow better. They look to the passing of the years to mellow them and make them more Christlike. . . . A crooked tree does not straighten with age; neither does a crooked Christian. (ALLIANCE WITNESS)

The Christian life is not like a ship's cruise on a calm ocean, with shining sun and bracing temperature. Often it is more like the journeying of a well-built ship through rough seas and dense fogs, confronted by opposing currents, contrary winds, and broken propeller shafts.
(CHRISTIANITY TODAY)

A truck driver told about the change Christ had made in his life, and I asked him to think of some specific way in which he was different. After a pause he said, "Well, when I find somebody tailgating my truck I no longer drive on the shoulder of the road to kick gravel on him."
(BRUCE LARSON)

Christianity is either relevant all the time or useless anytime. It is not just a phase of life; it is life itself. (RICHARD HALVERSON)

We may not be able to do any great thing; but if each of us will do

something, however small it may be, a good deal will be accomplished
for God.   (D.L. MOODY)

A Christian is a *mind* through which Christ thinks, a *heart* through
which Christ loves, a *voice* through which Christ speaks, a *hand* through
which Christ helps.   (GUIDEPOSTS)

Fight the temptation to be bashful about the Christian faith. Avoid a
bashful brand of Christianity that tiptoes up to people and hesitatingly
suggests: "I may be wrong, but I'm afraid that if you do not repent after a
fashion and receive Christ, so to speak, you might be damned, as it
were."

The radiant Christian is more concerned with carrying his cross than
with complaining about his callouses. He remembers the harvests, not
the hardships. He thinks about his friends, not his failures. He talks more
about his blessings than his backaches, more about his opportunities
than his operations.   (WILLIAM A. WARD)

It is not what we do that matters, but what a sovereign God chooses to
do through us. God doesn't want our success; He wants us. He doesn't
demand our achievements; He demands our obedience.(CHARLES COLSON)

The day has now come when a Christian man who is not praying and
working for missions must first explain, then apologize, for calling himself a Christian. Mission's call to men today is not to let their Christianity
end in what it does for them, but to let it begin by doing something for
God and their fellowmen. Missions is the church of God on the errand of
God interpreting the Gospel to all nations. This is the highest expression
of Christian service and of spiritual life of the church.   (CHURCH LIFE)

Rowland Bingham was once seriously injured in a head-on automobile
crash. Next day, when he regained consciousness, he asked the nurse
what he was doing there.
   "Be very quiet," she replied. "You have been in a frightful accident."
   Dr. Bingham exclaimed, "Accident? Accident? There are no accidents
in the life of a Christian. This is an incident."   (EDWARD MILES)

When you work for the Lord the pay may not be so hot, but you can't
beat the retirement plan.

Whatever makes men good Christians makes them good citizens.
                                                        (DANIEL WEBSTER)

Remember the weekday, to keep it holy.   (DECISION)

Water and oil are more compatible than Christianity and prejudice.
(WILLIAM A. WARD)

The Christian army is unlike any other army in the world; it shoots its own wounded. (JIM SLEVCOVE)

The church is so subnormal that if it ever got back to the New Testament normal it would seem to people to be abnormal. (VANCE HAVNER)

Vision without action is visionary.
Action without vision is mercenary.
But vision with action is missionary.

A traveler once asked a man in China, "Have you ever heard the Gospel?"
"No," he replied, "but I have seen it. There is a man in our village who was the terror of his neighborhood. He had a violent temper. He was an opium smoker, a criminal, and a dangerous man. But the Gospel has made him gentle and good. He no longer smokes opium. No, I have never heard the Gospel, but I have seen it and it is very good."
(BIBLE EXPOSITOR & ILLUMINATOR)

CHRISTMAS

The Son of God became a man to enable men to become the sons of God. (C.S. LEWIS)

The coming of Christ by way of a Bethlehem manger seems strange and stunning. But when we take Him out of the manger and invite Him into our hearts, then the meaning unfolds and the strangeness vanishes.
(C. NEIL STRAIT)

Christmas—the Advent—is the first step of Calvary's journey. The coming of Christ to man was a journey no one had ever taken before—or since. But all can travel the road from man to God. (C. NEIL STRAIT)

Christmas is less than what it can be—and less than what it was intended to be—where gifts are given grudgingly, and where gifts are received without appreciation.

Christmas is like a microwave dinner. It's here before you're really ready for it. (ROBERT ORBEN)

Some businessmen are saying that this could be the greatest Christmas ever. I always thought that the first one was. (ART FETTIG)

Shopping in crowded stores gives me Santa Claustrophobia.

For the millions who have been saving for a rainy day, Christmas is the monsoon season. (THINKING OUT LOUD)

November runs into December. December runs into Christmas, and Christmas runs into money.

Christmas is the season when you buy this year's gifts with next year's money.

[For some people] Christmas is one of the worst times of the year. Suicide rates go up, more people die from "natural causes," marriages fall apart, psychiatrists' patients suffer regressions, religious communities are torn assunder, new family feuds are begun, and many alcoholics venture forth on technicolor binges. God rest you merry, gentlemen, indeed. (ANDREW GREELEY)

CHURCH

The Christian church is the only society in the world in which membership is based upon the qualification that the candidate shall be unworthy of membership. (CHARLES C. MORRISON)

Jesus started the first church picnic when He fed the 5,000 with the lad's loaves and fishes. He also pioneered the Easter sunrise breakfast when, after His resurrection, He called the fishermen to shore and fed them a broiled fish which He had prepared, plus bread. (GEORGE CRANE)

Lots of folks spend more on dog food than on the church—maybe because the dog pays them more attention. (FRANK A. CLARK)

Some churches welcome all denominations, but most prefer tens and twenties. (LARRY BONKO)

We will only be weak and stumbling believers and a crippled church unless and until we truly apply God's Word—that is, until we truly love Him and act on that love. (CHARLES COLSON)

Ed's a regular churchgoer. Never misses an Easter.

A church needed new choir robes so one Sunday the pastor asked all members who would contribute $10 to the robe fund to please stand. The alert organist began a lively rendition of "The Star-Spangled Banner," with astounding results.

The most expensive piece of furniture in the church is the empty pew. (St. John's Newsletter)

The test of a good church bulletin, like a restaurant's menu, is whether or not the establishment can deliver what is listed in the contents. (Arkansas Baptist)

A minister of a rural church took a look at the offering in the collection plate and told the congregation, "Sometimes I get the feeling that you folks are under the impression that this church is coin-operated." (Bob Talbert)

How often have you met a critic of the church who has tried to make it better? (Sunshine)

Two of the dangers which confront the church are first that her message may change, and second that her methods may *not* change. (Henry Jacobsen)

A church that is not reaching out is passing out. (Duke Barron)

The church that does not gather into its fold the drunks, the harlots, the liars, and the thieves does not deserve the right to welcome the saints. (Jack Coke)

There is nothing automatic about the survival of the church. If a car manufacturer stops making cars, the firm goes out of business. If the church ceases to be the instrument for making Christians, it disappears. (Kenneth Greet)

We are sometimes so interested in creating the machinery of the church that we let the fire go out in the boiler. (Leonard Klotz)

"Dad, can I ask you a question?"
"Sure, Son."
"When am I going to be old enough not to have to go to church either?"
The father hesitated a moment and then said, "Wait a minute, Son, and I will go with you." Without a doubt the answer was the right one. (Warren Hultgren)

As they were leaving church, the wife turned to her husband. "Did you see that new hat Mrs. Lambert was wearing?"
"No, I didn't."
"Well, did you notice the new velvet dress Mrs. Frawley had on?"
"No, I didn't notice that either."

"For goodness sake," the wife snapped, "a lot of good it does you to go to church!" (FRANCES BENSON)

A woman was giving her testimony: "Before I joined this church I just hated my brother-in-law. I hated him so much I wouldn't have gone to his funeral. Now that I am a church member, I am ready to go any day." (LEO AIKMAN)

A minister was talking to a poor lady who worked hard as a cleaning lady. He told her how glad he was to see her in her place in church every Sunday, so attentive to his sermons.

"Yes," she replied, "it is such a rest after a hard week's work to come to church, sit down on the soft cushions, and not think about anything."

One of American Christianity's most serious evils may be the sin of "sermon listening." We hear, but we do not act. God is not basically interested in our listening to sermons. He wants us to be living sermons. The church is intended to be a vibrant, redeeming community of compassion, service, love, and worship. It is not a fraternity of fans of the faith. (BEAM)

Church newsletter: Why not tackle regular attendance on a trial basis? If you don't like what you hear on any Sunday, your sins will be cheerfully refunded. (DAISY BROWN)

A new minister in a small Oklahoma town . . . spent the first four days desperately calling on the membership, begging them to come to his first services. He failed. . . . He placed a notice in the local newspaper, stating that as the church was dead, it was his duty to give it a decent Christian burial. The funeral would be held the following Sunday afternoon. Morbidly curious, the whole town turned out. In front of the pulpit they saw a high coffin, smothered in flowers. The minister read the obituary and delivered a eulogy; he then invited his congregation to step forward and pay their respects to the dearly beloved who had departed. The long line filed by. Each mourner peeped into the coffin, and turned away with a guilty, sheepish look. For in the coffin, tilted at the correct angle, was a large mirror. Everyone saw himself. (LOUIS BINSTOCK)

Folks are quick to condemn a man who does wrong—unless he's a church member and then they condemn the church. (FRANK A. CLARK)

The church is a sunny place for shady people. (OSWALD HOFFMAN)

The lowest common denominator in the multiplication of people in the church is fellowship. The highest uncommon denominator in the division of the church from the world is disobedience. (GARY GULBRANSON)

Church problems, in the first century and today:
1. Danger of losing first love (Rev. 2:4)
2. Being afraid of suffering (2:10)
3. Doctrinal defection (2:14-15)
4. Moral departure (2:20)
5. Spiritual deadness (3:1-2)
6. Not holding fast (3:11)
7. Lukewarmness (3:15-16)   (JOHN F. WALVOORD)

It is strange that sometimes the church is written off by those who know little or nothing about it. They are not involved in its process or mission. In no other field would we take the word of a bystander as a word of authority and appraisal.   (C. NEIL STRAIT)

Church signs: The competition is terrific, but we're still open on Sundays.
   Come in and get your faith lifted.
   You are not too bad to come in. You are not too good to stay out.
                                                  (JIM KELLY)

Men hold three times as many church offices as the women, but the women do twice as much of the church work as the men, according to a study in six states.   (PASTOR'S JOURNAL)

The difference between listening to a radio sermon and going to church . . . is almost like the difference between calling your girl on the phone and spending an evening with her.   (MOODY MONTHLY)

Some go to church to take a walk;
Some go to church to laugh and talk;
Some go there to meet a friend;
Some go there their time to spend;
Some go there to meet a lover;
Some go there a fault to cover;
Some go there for speculation;
Some go there for observation;
Some go there to doze and nod;
The wise go there to worship God.

CITY VS. COUNTRY

In Boston, a smart little girl got an "A" for her composition describing her vacation in the White Mountains. It began, "In the country I found that the trees are more crowded but the people are farther apart."
                                                  (BENNETT CERF)

CIVILIZATION

All that is best in the civilization of today is the fruit of Christ's appearance among men. (DANIEL WEBSTER)

Civilization is a movement and not a condition, a voyage and not a harbor. (ARNOLD TOYNBEE)

Civilization is always in danger when those who have never learned to obey are given the right to command. (FULTON SHEEN)

What is still called Western civilization is in an advanced stage of decomposition. (MALCOLM MUGGERIDGE)

Alcohol and race consciousness are two conspicuous sources of danger to Western civilization. A mixture of atheism, materialism, socialism, and alcoholism have been the cause of the decline and decay of 19 out of 21 civilizations. (ARNOLD TOYNBEE)

There are four major dangers to civilization, and the greatest is population. Stemming from that are pollution, depletion of natural resources, including food, and atomic proliferation. It's almost essential, if civilization is to survive, that we get a handle on nuclear armaments, and it should be serious disarmament, not just a ceiling on nuclear arms. (WALTER CRONKITE)

CLEANLINESS

The American mania for cleanliness is probably responsible for producing more skin disease than dirt. Deodorants for everything, twice-a-day baths, and constant handwashing upset the delicate natural balance of the skin, leaving it easy prey to germs that cause skin disease. A little dirt on a boy isn't going to hurt him. (JOHN M. KNOX)

If you go long enough without a bath, even the fleas will let you alone. (ERNIE PYLE)

CLOTHING (see FASHION)

A key to success is to copy the dress and behavior of your boss and your boss' boss. (BERKELEY PRICE)

Freedom of the press means no-iron clothes.

My wife is always complaining about her clothes. I said, "Are you kidding? There are internationally famous celebrities who don't have the wardrobe that you do."
    She said, "Name one."
    I said, "Little Orphan Annie." (ROBERT ORBEN)

My dry cleaning joint advertises that it has been doing business for 35 years on the same spot.

People seldom notice old clothes if you wear a big smile.(LEE MILDON)

COINCIDENCES

A coincidence is a small miracle where God prefers to remain anonymous. (BITS AND PIECES)

COLD

The best way to treat a cold is with contempt. (WILLIAM OSLER)

It got so cold here last night that worms were mugging caterpillars for their fur coats. (LOU ERICKSON)

COLLEGE

A Chinese student wrote home, telling his friends and relatives about American institutions. He wrote, "An American university is a vast athletic association where, however, some studies are maintained for the benefit of the feeble-bodied." (INDIANA TELEPHONE NEWS)

Sending children to college educates parents. It teaches them to do without a lot of things.

It costs as much to send a man to prison for a year as to send one to college for a year—the chief difference being that the convict customarily continues his professional education after he gets out, while the college student terminates his. (SYDNEY HARRIS)

College prof: He took my course during his first siesta.(JOHN GILLESPIE)

"This school has turned out some great men."
    "When did you graduate?"
    "I didn't graduate. I was one of those turned out."
(WALL STREET JOURNAL)

Football coach: I have a master's degree. The subject of my thesis was "What college done for me." (AL CONOVER)

The college graduate is presented with a sheepskin to cover his intellectual nakedness. (ROBERT M. HUTCHINS)

COLORS

The "warm" colors—yellow, orange, red—stimulate creativity and make most people feel more outgoing and responsive to others. "Cool" colors—blue, green, gray—have a tendency to encourage meditation and deliberate thought processes, and may have a dampening effect on both the level and the quality of communication. It has even been suggested that people should do their creative thinking in a red room and then proceed to a green one to carry out the ideas. (DON FABUN)

COMEDIANS (see HUMOR)

A comedian is a person who says things funny, as opposed to a comic who says funny things. (ED WYNN)

It seldom fails. The funniest men in the world always seem to be the brightest, the most sensitive, the most serious, and the most miserable. It's not hard to understand. First-rate wit is essentially critical, and good critics are seldom stupid, obtuse, easygoing, or satisfied. Loner-ness can be part of the package too—a particular kind of loner-ness—the kind that works in a crowd, since making people laugh is one of the neatest ways of separating yourself from them. (LOOK)

COMFORT

Rev. George Hall has grudgingly agreed to air-conditioning our church. "I suppose," he says, "it won't do any harm for our bodies to be comfortable, so long as we don't let it happen to our souls." (BURTON HILLIS)

God, it has been said, does not comfort us to make us comfortable, but to make us comforters. Lighthouses are built by ex-drowning sailors. Roads are widened by mangled motorists. Where nobody suffers, nobody cares. (W.T. PURKISER)

COMMITTEES (see WORKTEAMS)

One of the reasons why the Ten Commandments are so short and to the point is the fact they were given direct and did not come out of committees. (H.G. HUTCHESON)

Search all the public parks and you'll never find a monument to a committee.

The philosophy of most committees: I came, I saw, I concurred. (IRVINE PAGE)

Actually there is nothing wrong with committees—nothing at all—except the folks that are on them. . . . If you are indecisive, vacillating, indifferent, the committee will reflect and magnify your faults and foibles. If you are positive, determined, enthusiastic, you will have one of those committees that really goes out and gets the job done. (HAROLD DONAHUE)

COMMUNICATION

It is true . . . that there is a 12-year-old mentality in the world, and every 6-year-old has it. It's a knowing world today, and it takes hard work to present your story memorably, but it pays. (WILLIAM BERNBACH)

The constant use of long, involved words proves two things: (1) that you're learned, and (2) that you're ignorant of how best to communicate with people. (WILL CONWAY)

Sending: Are your words, thoughts, and actions designed to encourage the person to react favorably toward you?
Receiving: Do you hear what you want to hear—or do you hear what the other person is communicating?

We can communicate an idea around the world in 70 seconds, but it sometimes takes years for an idea to get through one-fourth inch of human skull. (CHARLES KETTERING)

The great challenge in communicating is to understand the mind, the background, and the thinking process of your audience. If you know these, you can prevent a lot of "communication static." (WAYNE PENNINGTON)

It's a shame when people can't communicate. When they're managers in your company, it's a catastrophe. (FORTUNE)

Inability to communicate in a true sense represents reality in our time. Though we have more communication facilities than man previously had been able to imagine, most of us are spiritually isolated from our neighbors and even our friends. We spend more hours a day listening to radio and TV and don't know how to establish or maintain satisfying relationships with members of our own households. (THEODORE NELSON)

If you master the act of communication, you will be ready for leadership. Peter Drucker says, "Leadership is not magnetic personality—that can just as well be a glib tongue. It is not 'making friends and influencing people'—that is flattery. Leadership is lifting a person's vision to higher sights, the raising of a person's performance to a higher standard, the building of a personality beyond its normal limitations." What Drucker is really saying is that leaders create responses in others; they are communicators. Communicators—if not already leaders—certainly have the potential to be. (CYNTHIA H. TYSON)

Half the world's problems are caused by poor communications. The other half are caused by good communications.

In order to communicate God we need to get close to people, understand their needs and fears and hopes and dreams, and then start at that point and preach Jesus to them, putting the story into words and illustrations they can understand. (LEIGHTON FORD)

COMMUNISM

Communism really exists nowhere, least of all in the Soviet Union. Communism is an ideal that can be achieved only when people cease to be selfish and greedy and when everyone receives according to his needs from communal production. But that is a long way off. (MARSHAL TITO)

All philosophies have sought to explain the world; our business is to change it. (KARL MARX)

Communism is not love. Communism is a hammer which we use to crush the enemy. We are always revolutionists and never reformers. (MAO-TSE-TUNG)

Communism is a religion and only as we see it as a religion, though a secular religion, will we understand its power. (ELTON TRUEBLOOD)

Sign on desk of communist leader in New York: A world to win.

Despite its fateful grip on Soviet life, Communism's weakness lies in the fact that an elite cadre of 9 million party members forces its program on 200 million people; that its naturalistic ideology is indoctrinated rather than established. (CARL HENRY, '64)

COMPARISONS

If you compare yourself with others, you may become bitter or vain, for always there will be greater and lesser persons than yourself. (MAX EHRMAN)

COMPASSION (see EMPATHY, PITY)

Compassion is your pain in my heart.

A singular quality about Abraham Lincoln . . . sets him apart from all our other Presidents . . . a dimension of brooding compassion, love for humanity; a love which was, if anything, strengthened and deepened by the agony that drove lesser men to the protective shelter of callous indifference. . . . In what he did to lift the baleful burden of racism from the American soul, Abraham Lincoln stands as a teacher—not just to his people—black and white alike—but to all humanity. (LYNDON B. JOHNSON)

Compassion is a sign of a truly great and generous heart. Compassion is understanding the troubles of others, coupled with an urgent desire to help. Man naturally is not compassionate. It is an attribute he must learn by living and by his own experiences. It is cultivating an ability to put himself in the other fellow's shoes, remembering that all facts and circumstances influencing the other fellow cannot be known to him.

(MEGIDDO MESSAGE)

Don't let the brightness of your idealism blind your compassion.

(GARY GULBRANSON)

Compassion is not a snob gone slumming. Anybody can salve his conscience by an occasional foray into knitting for the spastic home. Did you ever take a *real* trip down inside the broken heart of a friend? To feel the sob of the soul—the raw, red crucible of emotional agony? To have this become almost as much yours as that of your soul-crushed neighbor? Then, to sit down with him—and silently weep? This is the beginning of compassion. (JESS MOODY)

COMPATABILITY

Asked for her secret of getting along with her associates, one manager said, "I never deny. I never contradict. I sometimes forget."

Nothing is a greater impediment to being on good terms with others than being ill at ease with yourself. (HONORE DE BALZAC)

They get along like two peeves in a pod. (EVERYBODY'S, ENGLAND)

COMPETITORS

When you love somebody for his shortcomings, chances are he's a competitor. (FRANKLIN P. JONES)

Competition is still the essence of the American way of life. Or of anybody's way of life. We need to crawl off to a tranquil retreat now and then, but if we don't return to the fray—in fighting trim—it's only a matter of time till we're by-passed, bopped, or busted. This has been proved many times by such disparate entities as the Roman Empire, playboy prizefighters, and take-it-easy toastmasters. (WALTER HOLLAND)

Don't worry if a rival imitates you. While he follows in your tracks, he can't pass you. (UPLIFT)

Trying to keep up with the Joneses? Forget it. You might find yourself stuck with more than you bargained for. Two of the country's leading psychiatrists believe that the competitive nature of the modern urban society is leading to a rise in mental illness. (RAZIA BONDREY)

Does your competitor speak well of you? Do you speak well of him? Does he consider you his friend? Does he admire and respect you? Do you keep him on his toes without stepping on them? Do you set him an example of good competitor relations? When he sees the word "integrity," does he think of you?

COMPLACENCY

Complacency is a blight that saps energy, dulls attitudes, and causes a drain on the brain. The first symptom is satisfaction with things as they are. The second is rejection of things as they might be. "Good enough" becomes today's watchword and tomorrow's standard. Complacency makes people fear the unknown, mistrust the untried, and abhor the new. Like water, the man who is complacent follows the easiest course —downhill. He draws fake strength from looking back.

COMPLAINING (see GRIEVANCES)

Don't complain how the ball bounces after you dropped it.

(JACK BRADFORD)

Everyone must see daily instances of people who complain from a mere habit of complaining; and make their friends uneasy, and strangers merry, by murmuring at evils that do not exist, and repining at grievances which they do not really feel. (GRAVES)

When I complain, I do it because "it's good to get things off my chest"; when you complain, I remind you that "griping doesn't help anything."

(SYDNEY HARRIS)

The usual fortune of complaint is to excite contempt more than pity.

(SAMUEL JOHNSON)

We have no more right to put our discordant states of mind into the lives of those around us and rob them of their sunshine and brightness than we have to enter their houses and steal their silverware. (JULIA SETON)

Who gets punished as much as he deserves? "Why should any living mortal, or any man, offer complaint in view of his sins?"

(LAMENTATIONS 3:39, NASB)

COMPLEXITY

If the safety pin were invented today, it would have two transistors, a regulator, an off-and-on switch, and require a service check every six months. (BITS AND PIECES)

COMPLIMENTS

A person may not be as good as you tell him he is, but he'll try harder thereafter. (CROSSWORD VARIETIES MAGAZINE)

Some fellows pay a compliment like they expect a receipt.(KIN HUBBARD)

It takes courage to speak a sincere compliment. It is easy to complain and criticize because you are upset and your anger motivates you, but to stand up and call a good job a "good job" . . . is a truly rewarding pastime. You cannot possibly make another person as happy as you make yourself. (ARTHUR FETTIG)

COMPROMISES

An Arab loaded his camel heavily for a journey. He then asked the camel if he preferred to walk uphill or downhill. Said the camel, "Is the level road closed?" Perhaps the world's problems are concerned with finding a sane middle ground between two extremes. (GEORGE ARMACOST)

It had been a run-of-the-mill marital hassle until he accused her of being stubborn. She cried, "I am not stubborn. I'm always willing to compromise—except when I know I'm right."

COMPUTERS

Had there been a computer in 1872, it would probably have predicted that by now there would be so many horse-drawn vehicles, it would be impossible to clean up all the manure. (KARL KAPP)

The danger of the computer is not the science-fiction fear that machines will begin to think like men, but the more realistic apprehension that men will begin to think like machines. (ROBERT MUELLER)

There are those today who wish to see the computer disconnected through fear that it will dehumanize our society. The fact is that we cannot pull the plug on the computer, or on the communications with which it will be integrated, any more than we can return to the covered wagon or the sailing ship. (DAVID SARNOFF)

Gilb's Second Law of Computers: Any system which depends on human reliability is unreliable.

People used to joke about computers, but I have a lurking suspicion computers are now joking about people. (BURTON HILLIS)

For thinking of original thoughts, the computer is a moron; but for helping Psyche to achieve her task of coping with multitudinous problems, the computer is a Briareus with a hundred or a hundred million arms. The computer's arithmetic is a simpleton's arithmetic; it is the binary arithmetic of yes-or-no, right-or-wrong. But the simple-minded automation can make its binary calculations at the rate of millions to the split second; so the computer is strong in the very point at which the human being is weak. In the split second in which the computer can do its millions of binary sums, a human being can think an original thought that the computer could never dream of. But ask that human to apply his original thought to 50 million instances, and you will be condemning him to defeat. (ARNOLD TOYNBEE)

CONCEIT

I know a guy who's so conceited that on his birthday he sends his parents a telegram of congratulations.

I wouldn't say he's conceited, but he's absolutely convinced that if he hadn't been born, people would want to know why not.

CONCENTRATION

One great cause of failure of young men in business is the lack of concentration. (ANDREW CARNEGIE)

The secret to success in any human endeavor is total concentration. (KURT VONNEGUT)

Men give me some credit for genius. All the genius I have lies in this: When I have a subject in hand, I study it profoundly. Day and night it is before me. I explore it in all its bearings. My mind becomes pervaded with it. Then the efforts that I make are what people are pleased to call the fruits of genius. It is the fruit of labor and thought! (ALEXANDER HAMILTON)

CONDEMNATION (see JUDGING)

I marvel at the aim of some sinners when given a stone. (ANNABEL BATTISTELLA)

CONFESSION

Sometimes it helps to bare troubles rather than bear them. (JAMES 5:16)

Confession without change is just a game. (THOMAS HARRIS)

CONFIDENCE

Many people succeed when others do not believe in them. But rarely does a person succeed when he does not believe in himself. (HERB TRUE)

Confidence can change anyone's lifestyle for the better. All you have to do is believe you're a winner, and the world will get along better with you. (MARY ANN MOBLEY)

Confidence is when you care enough to send the very best, and you go yourself. (ROBERT ORBEN)

CONFORMITY

We forfeit three-fourths of ourselves in order to be like other people. (SCHOPENHAUER)

CONFUSION

Let all things proceed in orderly progression to their final confusion. (E. SPENCER)

CONSCIENCE

A man's conscience, like a warning line on the highway, tells him what he shouldn't do—but it does not keep him from doing it. (FRANK A. CLARK)

"Oh, yes," said the Indian, "I know what my conscience is. It is a little three-cornered thing in here"—he laid his hand on his heart—"that stands still when I am good; but when I am bad it turns around, and the corners hurt very much. But if I keep on doing wrong, by and by the corners wear off and it doesn't hurt anymore." (WEAPONS FOR WORKERS)

When a person feels that his thinking is getting broader, it is more likely that his conscience is stretching. (GRIT)

I value people with a conscience. It's like a beeper from God. (ROBERT ORBEN)

Conscience is that still, small voice that tells you what other people should do. (BITS AND PIECES)

Conscience gets a lot of credit that really should go to cold feet.

When a man says he has a clear conscience, it often means he has a bad memory. (BITS AND PIECES)

There's no substitute for conscience. Unless, of course, it's witnesses.
(Franklin P. Jones)

Conscience is that still, small voice
That quells a wicked thought,
Then adds this sequence,
"Besides you might get caught." (Supervision)

Conscience is what warns you that you'd better have an alibi.

When a man won't listen to his conscience, it may be because he doesn't want advice from a total stranger.

These teachers will tell lies with straight faces and do it so often that their consciences won't even bother them. (1 Timothy 4:2, TLB)

A man consulted a doctor. "I've been misbehaving, Doc, and my conscience is troubling me," he complained.
"And you want something that will strengthen your willpower?" asked the doctor.
"Well, no," said the fellow. "I was thinking of something that would weaken my conscience."

A poor memory is one requirement for a clear conscience.
(Mrs. S. Flaxman)

If it weren't for your conscience you'd probably do almost anything you wanted to right away.

A strong conscience does not keep you from sinning; it merely keeps you from enjoying your sin for long.

The kind of life a person leads is usually determined by how loud the volume control is set on his conscience.

Most of us follow our conscience as we follow a wheelbarrow. We push it in front of us in the direction we want to go. (Billy Graham)

Nothing is a better tranquilizer than a clear conscience. (Banking)

When you have a fight with your conscience and get licked, you win.
(Grit)

CONSIDERATION

There is nothing so chilling as to have a man show you consideration instead of interest. (Graeme & Sarah Lorimer)

CONSOLATION

Never allow your own sorrow to absorb you, but seek out another to console, and you will find consolation. (J.C. MACAULAY)

CONSTRUCTION

Passer-by: "I see you're putting up a new building."
Foreman: "Yes, sir. That's the only kind we ever put up."
(OKLAHOMA JOURNAL, OKLAHOMA CITY)

The prospective buyer for a new home commented to the builder, "These walls certainly don't look very sturdy."

"Of course not," said the builder. "We haven't put on the wallpaper yet."

CONSULTANTS

My greatest strength as a consultant is to be ignorant and ask a few questions. (PETER DRUCKER)

CONTEMPORANEOUSNESS

Be contemporary but do not be prisoners of the present.
(JOHN C. BENNETT)

CONTEMPT

Perhaps the greatest sin one person can exert against another is contempt. To exercise contempt is to invite contempt. Any person who looks with contempt upon another sets in motion an evil force which rarely ever stops. (CHARLES ASHCRAFT)

CONTENTMENT (see SATISFACTION)

It may be all right to be content with what you have; never with what you are. (B.C. FORBES)

Contentment comes not so much from great wealth as from few wants.
(EPICTETUS)

Contentment has few merits. It is acquired by a person who schools himself to be satisfied with what he has, but at that point ambition dies and buries progress with it. Civilization has never been advanced by contented women and men. (BURTON HILLIS)

CONTRADICTING ONESELF

If a man never contradicts himself, it is because he never says anything.
(MIGUEL DE UNAMUNO)

CONTRITION

During a long life I have had to eat my own words many times, and I have found it a very nourishing diet. (WINSTON CHURCHILL)

CONTROL

You can't control the length of your life, but you can control its width and depth. You can't control the weather, but you can control the moral atmosphere that surrounds you. You can't control the other fellow's annoying faults, but you can see to it that you do not develop and harbor provoking propensities. You can't control hard times or rainy days, but you can bank money now to boost you through. Why worry about things you can't control? Get busy controlling the things that depend on you. (IN A NUTSHELL)

CONTROVERSY (see ARGUMENTS)

When a thing ceases to be a subject of controversy, it ceases to be a subject of interest. (WILLIAM HAZLITT)

CONVERSATION (see TALKING)

A form of communication in which some men never stop to think and many women never think to stop is otherwise known as conversation. (AMERICAN MERCURY)

The person who monopolizes the conversation monotonizes it.

If you want all the conversation you can handle, put a bandage on your forehead. (BILL VAUGHN)

Conversation between Adam and Eve must have been difficult at times because they had nobody to talk about. (AGNES REPPLIER)

As a young man, William Gillette studied stenography. He was living then in a boarding house, so he decided to practice his shorthand evenings by taking down every word spoken in the drawing room. "Years later," Gillette told a friend, "I went over my notebooks, and found that in four months of incessant conversation, no one had said anything that made any difference to anybody." (NEW ENGLAND ALMANAC)

One of the reasons why so few people are to be found who seem sensible and pleasant in conversation is that almost everybody is thinking about what he wants to say himself, rather than about answering clearly what is being said to him.
The more clever and polite think it enough simply to put on an attentive expression, while all the time you can see in their eyes and train of

thought that they are far removed from what you are saying, and are anxious to get back to what they want to say. They ought, on the contrary, to reflect that such keenness to please oneself is a bad way of pleasing or persuading others, and that to listen well and answer to the point is one of the most perfect qualities one can have in conversation.
(FRANCOIS DE LA ROCHEFOUCAULD)

The true spirit of conversation consists in building on another man's observation, not overturning it.   (THE NAZARENE PREACHER)

One secret of successful conversation is learning to disagree without being disagreeable. It isn't what but *how* you speak that makes all the difference. Ben Franklin used to remark diplomatically, "On this point, I agree. But on the other, if you don't mind, may I take exception?"
(JACK HARRISON POLLACK)

The most brilliant, witty, and intellectual man in the world still finds it difficult to make talk with his own relatives; for, usually, we have the most to say to those we have the least to do with.   (SYDNEY HARRIS)

Conversation is the art of telling people a little less than they want to know.   (FRANKLIN P. JONES)

A bore is somebody who goes on talking while you're interrupting.
(SUNSHINE)

To entertain some people all you have to do is sit and listen.
(OHIO GRANGE)

The art of conversation is a most important but often neglected art. It is also allied with the art of written expression. Speaking and writing form a very large part of the whole of human activities, business as well as social. The art of oratory, in public life, is essential to the highest success. The best way to become a good talker is to learn to have something to say. Studying how to talk will improve the mind, and paying diligent attention to improving the mind will, almost unconsciously, gravitate into other forms of self-improvement.   (B.C. FORBES)

CONVERSION (see SALVATION)

Conversion is the end of the Christian life—but it's the front end!

CONVICTIONS

Every conviction was a whim at birth.   (HEYWOOD BROUN)

Beware lest we mistake our prejudices for our convictions.
(HARRY A. IRONSIDE)

He who is not open to conviction is not qualified for discussion.

People who go through life with granite-like convictions on every subject under the sun lead a cheerless existence. They miss all the fun of exploring, all the challenge of debating, and all the thrill of finding something new.   (ROYAL BANK OF CANADA MONTHLY LETTER)

COOPERATION

You cannot sink someone else's end of the boat and still keep your own afloat.   (CHARLES BROWER)

We are made for cooperation, like feet, like hands, like eyelids, like the rows of the upper and lower teeth. To act against one another then is contrary to nature, and it is acting against one another to be vexed and turn away.   (MARCUS AURELIUS)

COST OF LIVING

The cost of living keeps going higher—but it's still a bargain.

COURAGE

Courage is fear that has said its prayers.   (BITS AND PIECES)

The scars you acquire by exercising courage will never make you feel inferior.   (O.A. BATTISTA)

Courage is the mastery of fear, not the absence of fear. (MARK TWAIN)

Success is never final, and failure never fatal; it's courage that counts.
                                                                                            (GRIT)

Courage is a special kind of knowledge: the knowledge of how to fear what ought to be feared and how not to fear what ought not to be feared.   (BEN GURION)

Courage is doing what you're afraid to do. There can be no courage unless you're scared.   (EDDIE RICKENBACKER)

I am tired of hearing about public men with "the courage of their convictions"; Nero and Caligula and Attila and Hitler had the courage of their convictions—but not one had the courage to examine his convictions, or to change them, which is the true test of character.   (SYDNEY HARRIS)

Far better it is to dare mighty things, to win glorious triumphs, even though checkered by failure, than to take rank with those poor spirits who neither enjoy much nor suffer much, because they live in the gray twilight that knows not victory or defeat.   (THEODORE ROOSEVELT)

You cannot run away from a weakness; you must sometime fight it out or perish; and if that be so, why not now, and where you stand?

(ROBERT L. STEVENSON)

A dear old lady was about to have an operation for the removal of one of her eyes. Just as the surgeon was ready to administer the anesthetic, she stopped him and said: "I have a favor to ask of you, doctor." She looked up and smiled. "When you select a glass eye for me, be sure that it has a twinkle in it."

(THE SPEAKER'S TREASURY OF ANECDOTES)

He who loses wealth loses much; he who loses a friend loses more; but he that loses his courage loses all.

(CERVANTES)

COURTESY

Practice courtesy. You never know when it might become popular again.

(BILL COPELAND)

COURTSHIP

Courtship is when a young man gets tripped by a girl who's putting her best foot forward.

(FRANKLIN P. JONES)

Some girls are unmarried for the same reason some drivers run out of gas. They pass too many filling stations looking for their favorite brand.

(SUCCESSFUL FARMING)

"Fred and I both agree on a long engagement."
   "Is that so? Why?"
   "It gives each of us plenty of time to look around for someone who's more suitable."

(COLLEGE LAUGHS)

She's been dating an X-ray specialist. I wonder what he sees in her?

COWARDICE

To sin by silence when they should protest makes cowards out of men.

(ABRAHAM LINCOLN)

COWBOY

Bowlegged cowboy, completing army physical: Well, Doc, how do I stand?
   Doc: That's what I'd like to know.

CREATIVITY (see MAVERICKS, ORIGINALITY)

Creativeness often consists of merely turning up what is already there. Did you know that right and left shoes were thought up only a little more than a century ago?

(BERNICE FITZ-GIBBON)

Creativity is more than just being different. Anybody can play weird; that's easy. What's hard is to be simple as Bach. Making the simple complicated is commonplace; making the complicated simple, awesomely simple, that's creativity. (CHARLES MINGUS)

Creative minds are rarely tidy. (ABBEY PLAQUE)

The No. 1 thing that television does to kids today is to take away their creativity. (PAT HURLEY)

In my experience, the best creative work is never done when one is unhappy. (ALBERT EINSTEIN)

Creative people prefer complexity, have a more complex personality than that of ordinary people, and can keep more ideas in mind at one time than ordinary people can. They are more independent in their judgments, more self-assertive and dominant, more observant, and more open to new experiences. (EUGENE JACKSON)

When Alexander the Great visited Diogenes and asked whether he could do anything for the famed teacher, Diogenes replied, "Only stand out of my light." Perhaps someday we may know how to heighten creativity. Until then, one of the best things we can do for creative men and women is to stand out of their light. (JOHN GARDNER)

Without appearing to work as hard, the highly creative person appears to learn as much as, if not more than, the one with a high IQ. My guess is that these highly creative people are learning and thinking when they appear to be playing around. (EMMA BIRKMAIER)

Most executives agree that creativity is the most profit-producing possession their company has, and many wish they had more, but very few are doing much about it. As one candidly explained, "Sure, I'd like to have creative people around me if I didn't have to put up with all the inconveniences they cause." (STANLEY GILL)

There is a correlation between the creative and the screwball. So we must suffer the screwball gladly. (KINGMAN BREWSTER, JR.)

Creativity is so delicate a flower that praise tends to make it bloom, while discouragement often nips it in the bud. Any of us will put out more and better ideas if our efforts are truly appreciated. (ALEXANDER OSBORN)

Socrates defined the philosopher as a thorn in the flesh, and nobody is a creative thinker unless continually he has a thorn in his flesh, that is, unless he is disturbed by something. The thick-skinned people do no creative thinking; to them everything is understood; they have no problems; nothing baffles them. (F.S.C. NORTHROP)

Creativity is essentially a lonely art. An even lonelier struggle. To some a blessing. To others a curse. It is in reality the ability to reach inside yourself and drag forth from your very soul an idea. (LOU DORFSMAN)

The drug of creativeness is so powerful that people can go on and on until they die old and lonely. I have no interest in doing that.
(HOWARD HEAD)

Since there is nothing new under the sun, creativity means simply putting old things together in a fresh way. (SHERWOOD E. WIRT)

Terman's Law of Innovation: If you want a track team to win the high jump, you find one person who can jump seven feet, not seven people who can jump one foot.

Teamwork may be good for morale, but when new ideas are needed, it's best to let people work on their own. Research shows that people who were left by themselves to think about subjects they considered relevant came up with three times as many ideas as those who brainstormed in groups. Researchers believe that when people work in groups, their creativity is inhibited by fear of criticism and real or perceived pressures to conform. (HORIZONS)

The majority of businessmen are incapable of original thought because they are unable to escape the tyranny of reason. (DAVID OGILVY)

Creativity has historically been associated with serious psychological problems in this culture. Van Gogh was a psychotic, Gaugin seems to have been schizoid, Poe was alcoholic, and Virginia Woolf was seriously depressed. Obviously, creativity and originality are associated with persons who do not fit into their culture. But this does not necessarily mean that their creativity is the product of neurosis. (ROLLO MAY)

One of the most pressing problems of our country today is the urgent need for new creative talent. It is not enough that we train more engineers, scientists, or mathematicians; what is demanded is more creative individuals. (ALEXANDER WHITSON)

Man's need to create is just as powerful as his need for food and drink. And when the needs of life are more or less satisfied, this creative need is more freely fulfilled. (MARIETTA SHAGINYAN)

A child at birth has the capacity to become original. Or you can put him in a mold so that he will come out like everybody else. Observers say that we Americans put too much emphasis upon conformity and not enough on the development of true individuality. We could reverse this trend by encouraging our children to be different, to think for themselves, and to use their imaginations more originally.

(SYLVANUS AND EVELYN DUVALL)

I believe all of us subconsciously want to be creative. This is a very human trait and probably what makes the difference between us and the animals. The trouble is that for most of us imagination has been suppressed to the point where we have stopped using it. We need to stop and daydream once in awhile. We need to let our imaginations roam and give them a chance to breathe. It's never really too late for anyone to start thinking more creatively. (J.P. DUBOIS)

Creativity is not dulled by age, only by disuse. (O. ALDRICH WAKEFORD)

You cannot order people to be creative. People are creative only when they are doing the things they want to do. (HERMAN KRANNERT)

To be creative, relax and let your mind go to work, suggests Dr. Kenneth H. Gordon, Jr. When a person tries to force himself to create, "the result is usually either a copy of something he did before or reads like an army manual." The mind permitted to work by itself "performs tasks as yet undreamed of by computers. In fact, we have barely scraped the surface of man's abilities, reception, and potential." (ALTON BLAKESLEE)

To raise new questions, new possibilities, to regard old problems from a new angle requires creative imagination and marks real advances in science. (ALBERT EINSTEIN)

Perception. Desire. Both are important, but they go nowhere without a third component of creativity—Hard Work. (FRANK KENDER)

CREDIT CARDS

Credit cards have three dimensions: height, width, and debt.

(SHELBY FRIEDMAN)

His wife's credit card was stolen, but he didn't report it because he knew the thief would spend less than she did.

CREDIT UNION

Credit Union's sales pitch: See us at your earliest inconvenience.

CRIME

The crime situation would be improved if we could get more cops off TV and onto the streets. (BILL VAUGHN)

[The] bland toleration of the underworld by the respectable world is the root of the crime problem in America. (ALLAN ASHBOLT)

I've been asked many times as Sheriff, "Do you think you will ever eliminate crime?" I'm not naive enough to think that crime can ever be eliminated. There were prostitutes and pickpockets in the days of Christ. There was gambling and debauchery in the days of the prophets. There will always be some who submit to the soft, glittery pleasures and it will always be for the spiritually strong to lead those back. (RICHARD OGILVIE)

Nobody cares about prisons until a relative of his gets in. But we should care, because about 90 percent of the people in prisons come out, and 60 percent to 70 percent go back into crime. (JOHN BARLOW MARTIN)

They sent my uncle to the pen for an illegal turn. On a safe knob.
(SHELBY FRIEDMAN)

Patricia is rich. Patricia does good deeds. "But," she sighs, "money doesn't make you happy. Love for your fellowman can't be bought." So she sings. Free of charge . . . very loudly. In the local prison. And even in the county prison.
 A reporter, who heard her . . . commented, "I don't understand how they can let her sing for prisoners."
 "Oh," the wise old judge explained, "since she's been singing in the prisons there has been a marked decrease in crime all around here."
(FRANKFURTER ILLUSTRIERTE, GERMANY)

CRITICISM (see SELF-CRITICISM)

It is the peculiar quality of a fool to perceive the faults of others, and to forget his own. (CICERO)

It's 100 times easier to criticize than to create. (LLOYD CORY)

Lots of faults we think we see in others are simply the ones we expect to find there because we have them. (FRANK A. CLARK)

It is much easier to be critical than to be correct. (BENJAMIN DISRAELI)

If in doubt, take it personally. (JAN SPOELMAN)

He has a right to criticize who has a heart to help. (ABRAHAM LINCOLN)

No one so thoroughly appreciates the value of constructive criticism as the one who's giving it. (HAL CHADWICK)

When I am angry at myself I criticize others. (ED HOWE)

If the only way I can make myself look good is to criticize you, something is seriously wrong with me. (WARREN WIERSBE)

Any critic can establish a wonderful batting average by just rejecting every new idea. (J.D. WILLIAMS)

It is ridiculous for any man to criticize the works of another if he has not distinguished himself by his own performance. (JOSEPH ADDISON)

You can't clear your own fields while you're counting the rocks on your neighbor's farm. (JOAN WELSH)

No man is worse for knowing the worst of himself. (H.G. BOHN)

If you are not big enough to stand criticism, you are too small to be praised. (GRIT)

Adverse criticism from a wise man is more to be desired than the enthusiastic approval of a fool. (AMERICAN SALESMAN)

One of the surest marks of good character is a man's ability to accept personal criticism without malice to the one who gives it.(O.A. BATTISTA)

The trouble with most of us is that we would rather be ruined by praise than saved with criticism. (NUGGETS)

A thick skin is a gift from God. (KONRAD ADENAUER)

If you would be loved as a companion, avoid unnecessary criticisms of those with whom you live. (ARTHUR HELPS)

A smile in giving honest criticism can make the difference between resentment and reform. (PHILIP STEINMETZ)

The truth is that for everything that can be accomplished by showing a person where he's wrong, ten times as much can be accomplished by showing him where he's right. The reason we don't do it so often is that it's more fun to throw a rock through a window than to put in a pane of glass. (ROBERT T. ALLEN)

On facing criticism: If what they are saying about you is true, mend your ways. If it isn't true, forget it, and go on and serve the Lord.
(HARRY A. IRONSIDE)

Stones and sticks are thrown only at fruit-bearing trees. (FORBES)

It is easier to bear some abuse if I reflect, "I do not deserve this reproach but I do deserve others that have not been made."

(FRANCOIS MAURIAC)

Criticism is no doubt good for the soul but we must beware that it does not upset our confidence in ourselves.

(HERBERT HOOVER, ON HIS 90TH BIRTHDAY)

What people say about us is never quite true; but it is never quite false, either; they always miss the bull's-eye, but they rarely fail to hit the target.

(SYDNEY HARRIS)

Always keep your criticism up to date.

(CHRIS LYONS)

CROSS OF CHRIST (see CHRIST)

The Cross of Christ does not make God love us; it is the outcome and measure of His love for us.

(ANDREW MURRAY)

Christ's Cross is such a burden as sails are to a ship, or wings to a bird.

(SAM RUTHERFORD)

CRUELTY

All cruelty springs from weakness.

(SENECA)

CURIOSITY (see NOSINESS)

Life can be one dreary day after another or a Baghdad of fascinating things to keep learning. Get more out of every phase of your life—stay incurably curious.

(L. PERRY WILBUR)

A bright eye indicates curiosity; a black eye, too much.

(SUNSHINE)

CURSING (see PROFANITY)

The basics of cussing are simple. There are really only two major categories of swear words when you stop to analyze it: physiological and theological, and perhaps, a third group that might be called genealogical. The physiological can be subdivided into organic, principally dealing with orifices, but not entirely, and functional, concentrating largely on the less aesthetic biological activities and perversions thereof, but not entirely. The theological does not lend itself to quite such clear-cut division, but can roughly be said to consist of the names of deity, spiritual realms, principalities and powers, and an unseemly arrogation of sacred rights and judgments. The genealogical often overlaps the other two and is used to slash a bar sinister across one's family escutcheon. It is as simple as that.

(FRANK WOOD)

CYNICISM

Cynicism is nothing but idealism gone sour in the face of frustration.
(Buell Gallagher)

Cynics say: The past has no meaning. The present is a delusion. The future holds no hope. (Merrill Tenney)

Cynics are only happy in making the world as barren to others as they have made it for themselves. (George Meredith)

Cynicism is so much a trademark of our times that a good many of us feel downright embarrassed in the presence of constructive possibilities. (George A. Levesque)

Cynicism is criticism run amok, skepticism out of control.
(Marlin Van Elderen)

Everyone decides to live in a hovel on Cynical Street or in a mansion on Affirmative Acres. (William A. Ward)

DANGER

Wherever there is danger, there lurks opportunity; whenever there is opportunity there lurks danger. The two are inseparable; they go together. (EARL NIGHTINGALE)

Danger feared is folly; danger faced is freedom. (V. RAYMOND EDMAN)

Predicted dangers of the 20th century: Religion without the Holy Spirit, Christianity without Christ, forgiveness without repentance, salvation without regeneration, politics without God, and heaven without hell.
(GENERAL WILLIAM BOOTH)

DAYDREAMING (see DREAMS)

Daydreaming can be good for you. Most people who let themselves daydream are often refreshed, stimulated, and renewed when they come back to what they are doing. Many people work out solutions to problems while daydreaming. (FAMILY WEEKLY)

DEADLINES

The word "deadline" was supposed to have originated in a prison. It was a real or imagined line describing the limits of the prison yard. If a prisoner stepped beyond the line he would be shot dead by the tower guards. (SCHAEDLER NEWSLETTER)

Stenderup's Law: The sooner you fall behind, the more time you will have to catch up.

Victor Hugo, having some urgent work to do, made sure he would do it by cutting off half his hair and half his beard down the middle and throwing the scissors out of the window.

He couldn't very well go out in that state, and he had the work completed by the deadline. (SPUTNIK, USSR)

DEATH (see IMMORTALITY)

Death is the big flaw. Sometimes we can postpone it, lessen its physical pains, deny its existence—but we can't escape it. (HARVEST YEARS)

Death is only a horizon; and a horizon is nothing save the limit of our sight. (ROSSITER W. RAYMOND)

Everybody has got to die, but I have always believed an exception would be made in my case. *Now* what? (WILLIAM SAROYAN)

Cowards die many times before their deaths; the valiant never taste of death but once. (WILLIAM SHAKESPEARE)

A humorous old gent said he hoped to soon put all his aches in one casket.

I'm not afraid to die. I'm kinda looking forward to it. I know the Lord has His arms wrapped around this big fat sparrow. (ETHEL WATERS)

We seem to say: "I hate death; in fact I could live forever without it." (POGO)

You can't take it with you. You never see a U-Haul following a hearse. (ARNOLD GLASOW)

My grandfather would look through the obituary columns and say to me, "Strange, isn't it, how everybody seems to die in alphabetical order." (JACKIE VERNON)

During a recent gravedigger's strike this sign appeared at the entrance of one cemetery: "Due to the strike, all gravedigging for the duration will be done by a skeleton crew."

It's not that I'm afraid to die. I just don't want to be there when it happens. (WOODY ALLEN)

There are no dollar signs on tombstones. (LEWIS TIMBERLAKE)

Maybe death and taxes are inevitable, but death doesn't get worse every time Congress meets. (JOAN WELSH)

DECAY

Decay is directly proportional to how nice you've got it. (ROBERT A. COOK)

DECEPTION

Half the work that is done in this world is to make things appear what they are not. (E.R. BEADLE)

You are never so easily fooled as when you are trying to fool someone else. (FRANCOIS DE LA ROCHEFOUCAULD)

DECISIONS

When you have a serious decision to make, tell yourself firmly you are going to make it. Do not expect it will be the perfect one. Some of those "againsts" may never be canceled out. You must simply try to make the best decision you can, having taken all the "pros" and "cons" you can discover into account. Try not to be hurried by others, or by your own panic, into a snap decision, before you have weighed matters and informed yourself fully. . . . Whether we like it or not, making a choice is a part of being human and we do not think too highly of those who throw away this right—always needing someone else to make up their minds for them. (WOMAN'S WEEKLY)

There are no born decision-makers. The most successful decision-makers follow a set of rules that help them select the best alternative under the circumstances. . . . The basic rules of decision-making . . . involve six steps: (1) State the apparent problem or situation you face. (2) Gather the facts. (3) Organize and interpret the facts. (4) State the real problem or situation. (5) Develop alternative solutions. (6) Select the most appropriate alternative. (PHILIP BRUNSTETTER)

Decision is a sharp knife that cuts clean and straight; indecision is a dull one that hacks and tears and leaves ragged edges behind it. (GORDON GRAHAM)

We make our decisions, and then our decisions turn around and make us. (F.W. BOREHAM)

Not to decide is to decide. (HARVEY COX)

If you take so much time making a decision that it is too late to act, then you might just as well have whittled a stick. (CONSTRUCTION DIGEST)

Some people are so indecisive their favorite color is plaid.

She was so indecisive, she always fell apart at the "seems."

Weeds grow lushly in the soil of indecision.

Sixteen ways to dodge decisions: (1) Take flight into detail. (2) Counsel infinite delay of action. (3) Delegate the problem to a committee. (4) Look for the answer in the "book." (5) Induce the boss to commit himself on how to handle the problem. (6) Give an answer in doubletalk. (7) Delegate the problem to a subordinate. (8) Indicate that all problems must be considered in serial order. (9) Have a "study" made to "get all the facts." (10) Arrange to be called out of town. (11) Call in an expert to "make sure we're on solid ground." (12) Deny that any problem exists. (13) Take flight into illness. (14) Take flight into the bottle. (15) State the problem belongs in someone else's province. (16) Simply put on one's hat and go home. (EXECUTIVES' DIGEST)

The man who insists upon seeing with perfect clearness before he decides, never decides. (HENRI-FREDERIC AMIEL)

Every one of the effective Presidents in American history had his own method to match ways of producing the disagreement he needed in order to make an effective decision. Lincoln, Theodore Roosevelt, Franklin Roosevelt, Harry Truman—each had his own ways. But each created the disagreement he needed for "some understanding of what the decision is all about." Washington, we know, hated conflicts and quarrels and wanted a united Cabinet. Yet he made quite sure of the necessary differences of opinion on important matters by asking both Hamilton and Jefferson for their opinions. (PETER DRUCKER)

Freedom is opportunity to make decisions. Character is ability to make right decisions. It can be achieved only in a climate of freedom. For no one learns to make right decisions without being free to make wrong ones. (KENNETH SOLLITT)

DEEDS

You won't get dizzy from doing good turns. (CRACKERJACK)

DEFEAT (see LOSERS, SETBACKS)

You can learn more from your defeats than from your victories. (CHARLES BROWER)

What is defeat? Nothing but education, nothing but the first step to something better. (WENDELL PHILLIPS)

A defeat may be a victory in disguise.

People seldom want to walk over you until you lie down. (ELMER WHEELER)

Defeat is never more assured for an individual than at the moment when he resigns himself to it. (O.A. BATTISTA)

One of the greatest and most comforting truths is that when one door closes, another opens; but often we look so long and regretfully upon the closed door that we do not see the one that has opened for us. Defeat is nothing but education; it is the first step toward something better. (NUGGETS)

DELEGATION

Getting things done isn't necessarily the same as doing things.

The best executive is the one who has sense enough to pick good men to do what he wants done, and self-restraint enough to keep from meddling with them while they do it. (THEODORE ROOSEVELT)

A manager who can't delegate is about as competitive and effective as a school of guppies at a convention of barracudas. (DALE McCONKEY)

We tend to select top men for their character and capacity, then overload them according to their willingness. (CLARENCE JONES)

DEMOCRACY

Democracy is a system by which people are free to choose the man they will later blame for everything.

Remember democracy never lasts long. It soon wastes, exhausts, and murders itself. There never was a democracy that did not commit suicide. (JAMES MADISON)

When a bad thing isn't working, it is from an excess, and you need less of it; when a good thing isn't working (such as the democratic process), it is from a deficiency, and you need more of it. (SYDNEY HARRIS)

Democracy, as I understand it, requires me to sacrifice myself for the masses, not to them. Who knows not that if you would save the people, you must often oppose them? (JOHN CALHOUN)

Democracy is the worst system ever invented—except for all the rest. (WINSTON CHURCHILL)

DENOMINATIONS

It is becoming impossible for those who mix with their fellowmen to believe that the grace of God is distributed denominationally. (WILLIAM R. INGE)

DENTISTS

Dr. Jones, the dentist, said he served in the army. As a drill sergeant.
(SHELBY FRIEDMAN)

When the patient said, "I'd like to have my teeth checked," the most painful dentist in town reputedly answered, "That's strange. Most people want them white." (WALL STREET JOURNAL)

DEPARTURES

There is a time for departure even when there's no certain place to go. (TENNESSEE WILLIAMS)

DEPENDABILITY (see STABILITY)

The greatest ability of a Sunday School teacher is dependability.
(NORMAN S. TOWNSEND)

DEPRESSION

One of the bad things about depression is that it drains us emotionally and makes us unable to handle things that normally would not get us down. (BILLY GRAHAM)

Your energy level increases when you are down and decreases when you are up. You are active in the up state and use your energy, while you rest in the down state and restore your energy. This is the normal pattern in a healthy person. Thus, when you are depressed, you are in a position to restore your energy and come out of the depression spontaneously. It happens often. The inactivity of the depressed state allows you to re-build your energy reserves. In our culture, "down" is bad and "up" is good. But since "up" is tension and "down" is relaxation, this can only mean that if you accept the pain, the natural healing process will begin. (ALEXANDER LOWEN)

DESIRES (see WISHING)

We all want to be loved and respected for what we really are—well-meaning but imperfect. (BITS AND PIECES)

It was desire that brought progress to the world. Without it, we would still be living in a primitive age. Everything we have in our modern world is the result of desire. Indeed, desire is the motivating force of life itself. . . . It's the generating power of all human action and without it no one can get very far. (CLAUDE BRISTOL)

According to an American psychologist, Dr. A.H. Maslow, basic human desires can be classified into five levels. The lowest is a physiological desire, the desire to live. When this desire is adequately satisfied, the desire for safety comes to the fore. Next there appears the desire to belong and to love, followed by that for recognition by others. The highest level is a desire for self-realization.　　(KISHIDA JUN 'NOSUKE)

DESKS

If a cluttered desk is a sign of a cluttered mind, what's an empty desk the sign of?　　(JOE BAYLY)

DESPAIR (see GLOOM)

To hatch despair, just brood over your troubles.　　(MEGIDDO MESSAGE)

The main trouble with despair is that it is self-fulfilling. People who fear the worst tend to invite it. Heads that are down can't scan the horizon for new openings. Bursts of energy do not spring from a spirit of defeat. Ultimately, helplessness leads to hopelessness.　　(NORMAN COUSINS)

Despair is a part of our living. We despair when our hopes are dashed; we despair where war persists; we despair when illness lingers. Despair seems like a dead-end street where everything ends. But not a few times, answers have been found in moments of despair; ideas have sparked; hope has been etched anew. Maybe such occasions are telling us that we can use our despair creatively.

The despair that besets us when frustrations come can be of two kinds· a despair that causes us to give up; or a despair that makes us go to the depths and draw from our best resources. One kind is futile, the other is fruitful.

Despair comes uninvited, but only remains where it is entertained. If it is nurtured through depressive thoughts and fed with pessimistic attitudes, it remains. But when the soul takes flight to greater thoughts, despair flees. Hope, faith and a positive will starve despair.

Despair is not handled by giving in. It is handled best by giving out— giving out something of ourselves to others. By giving out, a person has no time for despair, so it departs.　　(C. NEIL STRAIT)

Sometimes we have to come to the end of ourselves before we can get to the bottom of things.　　(GARY GULBRANSON)

DETERMINATION

Lord, give me the determination and tenacity of a weed.
　　　　　　　　(MRS. LEON R. WALTERS)

DEVICES, LABOR-SAVING

We have so many labor-saving devices today that we go broke keeping them repaired. Everything is easier, but requires greater maintenance.
　　　　　　　　(LORNE SANNY)

The more labor-saving devices you use, the more of a slob you become.

DEVIL

If the devil could be persuaded to write a bible, he would title it, "You Only Live Once." (SYDNEY HARRIS)

DEVOTIONS

On having one's quiet time with the Lord: Cut your morning devotions into your personal grooming. You would not go out to work with a dirty face. Why start the day with the face of your soul unwashed?
(ROBERT A. COOK)

DICTIONARY

Dictionary: A malevolent literary device for cramping the growth of a language and making it hard and inelastic. (THE DEVIL'S DICTIONARY)

DIET (see FOOD)

Blessed are those who hunger and thirst, for they are sticking to their diets. (TROY GORDON)

There's a new diet that is supposed to really work. You only get to eat when there's good news.

Dieters try to dispose of their hazardous waist.

I've learned to love myself more than I love food. (LINDA EVANS)

There's a great new rice diet that always works—you use one chopstick.
(RED BUTTONS)

It takes about a ton of willpower to take off 10 pounds of excess weight. (GRIT)

All over the world people are dying of hunger, tortured and tormented by slow starvation. Famine may kill a million people this year. But all one hears about in America are this one's diet and that one's wonderful quick weight-reduction system. How can the planet's system of food intake have gotten into such a grotesque state of affairs? The rich and the poor are both obsessed with eating, but with what discrepancies.
(SIDNEY CALLAHAN)

Some people are no good at counting calories and they have the figures to prove it. (DIGEST OF WORLD READING)

My loss of weight was due to exercise, hard work, and diet, which proves that people will go to great lengths to avoid great widths.

(ERNEST BORGNINE)

Most Americans eat too much. Overeating in many cases is a consequence of personal frustration and loss of meaning. People try to fill the void in their lives by consuming food.   (PHILIP PHENIX)

DIFFICULTIES

It is not easy: to apologize,   to endure success,
                to begin over,   to profit by mistakes,
                to be unselfish,   to forgive and forget,
                to take advice,   to think and then act,
                to admit error,   to keep out of the rut,
                to face sneers,   to make the best of little,
                to be charitable,   to subdue an unruly temper,
                to avoid mistakes,   to maintain a high standard,
                to keep on trying,   to shoulder a deserved blame,
                to be considerate,   to recognize a silver lining.
But it always pays!   (FIRST BAPTIST CHURCH, OAKLAND, CALIF.)

DIGNITY

I know of no case where a man added to his dignity by standing on it.   (WINSTON CHURCHILL)

DIPLOMACY

Diplomacy is the art of letting the other fellow have your way.

(HERMAN VAN ROIJEN)

DIRECTION

The great thing in this world is not so much where we are but in what direction we are moving.   (OLIVER W. HOLMES)

I was going around in a circle until Jesus gave me a compass.

(LYNN LANGLEY)

DISADVANTAGES

The grass may be greener on the other side of the fence, but there's probably more of it to mow.   (LOIS J. CORY)

DISAGREEMENT

Just because nobody disagrees with you does not necessarily mean you are brilliant—maybe you're the boss.   (CONSTRUCTION DIGEST)

Humor Power can help us avoid arguments with others. Here is an example:

"Are you in favor of the new zoning laws?" a householder asked his neighbor.

"Well, some of my friends are for it and some of my friends are against it," the neighbor said. "I am for my friends."

In a friendly way the neighbor implied, "Let's agree to disagree."

(HERB TRUE)

God reserves the right to use people who disagree with me.

(ROBERT A. COOK)

Agreement makes us soft and complacent; disagreement brings out our strength. Our real enemies are the people who make us feel so good that we are slowly, but inexorably, pulled down into the quicksand of smugness and self-satisfaction.

(SYDNEY HARRIS)

DISAPPOINTMENTS

Something can be learned from the smallest as well as the greatest disappointments or frustrations. A child who drops his ice-cream cone and is not given the money for another will learn to be more careful next time. A man whose car runs out of fuel will learn to check his tank more closely in the future.

(CHRISTINE LINDEMAN)

DISCIPLINE

A Chinese philosopher said, "Parents who are afraid to put their foot down usually have children who step on toes."

A teacher in a school where corporal punishment is forbidden sent this note to the mother of an unruly pupil: "Dear Mrs. Jones—I regret very much to inform you that your son, Robert, idles away his time, is disobedient and quarrelsome, and disturbs other students who are trying to work. He needs a good thrashing and I strongly urge that you give him one."

This reply came back: "Dear Miss Smith—Lick him yourself. I ain't mad at him."

Discipline is demanded of the athlete to win a game. Discipline is required for the captain running his ship. Discipline is needed for the pianist to practice for the concert. Only in the matter of personal conduct is the need for discipline questioned. But if parents believe standards are necessary, then discipline is needed to attain them.

(MRS. WRIGHT W. BROOKS)

The first idea that the child must acquire, in order to be actively disciplined, is that of the difference between good and evil; and the task of the educator lies in seeing that the child does not confound good with immobility, and evil with activity, as often happens in the case of the old-time discipline. And all this because our aim is to discipline for activity, for work, for good; not for immobility, not for passivity, not for obedience. (MARIA MONTESSORI)

The undisciplined is a headache to himself and a heartache to others, and is unprepared to face the stern realities of life.
(WHEATON COLLEGE BULLETIN)

The clergyman was . . . disturbed during a sermon by some noisy persons. He did not scold or manifest any sign of anger. "I am always reluctant," he said quietly, "to expose those who misbehave during services, because of an experience I had some years ago. A young man who sat in front of me was laughing and making grimaces. I was annoyed and rebuked him severely. Later I was told that I had made a grave mistake. The man I had reproved was an idiot." The noisemakers subsided.
(WRIGHT LINE)

DISCONTENT

Discontent—there are two kinds in the world: (1) the discontent that works and gets what it wants, and (2) the kind that wrings its hands and loses what it has. There's no cure for the first but success, and there is no cure at all for the second. (C.H. CAMPBELL)

DISCOURAGEMENT

Discouragement is dissatisfaction with the past, distaste for the present, and distrust of the future. It is ingratitude for the blessings of yesterday, indifference to the opportunities of today, and insecurity regarding strength for tomorrow. It is unawareness of the presence of beauty, unconcern for the needs of our fellowman, and unbelief in the promises of old. It is impatience with time, immaturity of thought, and impoliteness to God. (WILLIAM A. WARD)

"Our spirits grow gray before our hairs," observed Charles Lamb. Discouragement does come to old and young alike. Things often go contrary to our dreams and plans. . . . The major cause of discouragement is a temporary loss of perspective. Restore proper perspective, and you take new heart. (J. FRANCIS PEAK)

DISCOVERIES (see INVENTIONS)

Discovering ideas is the most satisfying way of occupying your time, since you never know when you may be striking pay dirt. It is mental prospecting. (ROBERT CRAWFORD)

If I have ever made any valuable discoveries, it has been owing more to patient attention than to any other talent.   (ISAAC NEWTON)

People are usually more convinced by reasons they discovered themselves than by those found by others.   (PASCAL)

Discovery is not an invention and I dislike to see the two words confounded. A discovery is more or less in the nature of an accident. A man walks along the road intending to catch a train. On the way his foot kicks against something and he sees a gold bracelet imbedded in the dust. He has discovered that—certainly not invented it. He did not set out to find a bracelet, yet the value is just as great. (THOMAS EDISON)

Don't keep forever on the public road. Leave the beaten track occasionally and dive into the woods. You will be certain to find something that you have never seen before. One discovery will lead to another, and before you know it you will have something worth thinking about to occupy your mind. All really big discoveries are the results of thought.
(ALEXANDER GRAHAM BELL)

DISCUSSION

Professor: Jenkins, why don't you join in the discussions?
Jenkins: I learn more by listening. Anything I would say I already know.   (SUCCESSFUL FARMING)

DISPOSITION

A poor man with a sunny disposition will get more out of life than a millionaire grumbler.   (CONSTRUCTION DIGEST)

DISSATISFACTION

If you are dissatisfied with your lot in life, build a service station on it.   (SAMUEL BRENGLE)

Be dissatisfied enough to improve, but satisfied enough to be happy.
(J. HAROLD SMITH)

The reason for most folks' dissatisfaction in life is that they are looking for a custom fit in an off-the-rack world.   (GARY GULBRANSON)

DISTRUST (see FRIENDS)

Distrust is poison to friendship.   (CHRISTIAN CLIPPINGS)

DISUSE

Iron rusts from disuse, stagnant water loses its purity, and in cold weather becomes frozen; even so does inaction sap the vigors of the mind.

(LEONARDO DA VINCI)

DIVORCE (see ALIMONY)

If a breakup does occur, remember that you are more in the right than your partner believes and more in the wrong than you admit.

(DAVID VISCOTT)

Divorce is an easy escape, many think. But, in counseling many divorcees, I have discovered that the guilt and loneliness they experience can be even more tragic than living with their problem.   (BILLY GRAHAM)

DOCTORS (see MEDICINE)

Seventy percent of all patients who come to physicians could cure themselves if they only got rid of their fears, worries, and bad eating habits.

(O.F. GOBER)

Since many doctors refuse to make house calls, you have to have a measure of health to find out what's wrong with you.

One group of doctors who still make house calls: coroners.

(MALCOLM FORBES)

Doctor: Your trouble is that you're burning the candle at both ends.
     Patient: I know my problem. What I want you to tell me is how I can get more wax.

At the peak of a cold and virus season, a family doctor was giving a record number of penicillin injections. Tacked to the door of his inner office was this notice: "To save time, please back into office."

(JOSEPH McCLOSKEY)

Bob: I had an operation and the doctor left a sponge in me.
     Ken: Got any pain?
     Bob: No, but boy do I get thirsty.

A man was telling his friend about the wonderful doctor he has: "If you can't afford the operation, he touches up the X rays."   (HANK BRODY)

If you consider what doctors charge, the most precious stones are not diamonds and emeralds—they're gall and kidney.   (ROBERT ORBEN)

You may not be able to read a doctor's handwriting and prescription, but you'll notice his bills are neatly typewritten. (Earl Wilson)

The sick patient, conscience-stricken at having summoned his doctor past midnight, apologized profusely. "I'm sorry about the hour, Doc, and I know my house is somewhat out of your way too."
"Oh, that's all right," reassured the medico. "I have another very sick patient who lives near you, so I'll just kill two birds with one stone." (Dental Economics)

The man hadn't been feeling too well so he went to his doctor for a checkup. The doctor examined him, then opened an office window and said to the patient, "Pucker up and stick your head outside."
The man looked startled. "Why should I do a thing like that?"
The doctor replied, "To kiss the world good-bye." (James Whitehead)

The young man pumped the doctor's hand enthusiastically. "Doctor, I just dropped by to tell you how much I benefited from your treatment."
The puzzled doctor said, "I don't seem to remember you. You're not one of my patients, are you?"
"No, I'm not," the man replied. "But my uncle was, and I'm his heir." (John Williams)

DOERS

The fellow who never steps on anybody's toes is probably standing still. (Franklin P. Jones)

There's nothing I wouldn't do for him and nothing he wouldn't do for me. So we spend our lives doing nothing for each other. (Bing Crosby)

DOGMATISM

Don't be too dogmatic about a subject on which God's Word is silent. (Henry Jacobsen)

DOGS

A man seeking a hotel room for himself and his dog received the following reply from an innkeeper in Kingston, Jamaica: "I've been in the hotel business for 40 years and never had to eject a disorderly dog. Never has a dog set fire to a bed. Never has he sneaked a girl into his room. Never has a dog stolen a towel or blanket or gotten drunk. Your dog is very welcome. If he will vouch for you, you can come along as well." (Parade)

Is Ed's dog a setter or a pointer?
Neither. He's an upsetter and a disappointer.

DONATION

A guy donated a loud-speaking system to the church—in loving memory of his wife.

DOUBT

Worry affects the circulation, heart, the glands, the whole nervous system, and profoundly affects the heart. I have never known a man who died from overwork, but many who have died from doubt.

(NORMAN DOUGLAS)

The man who cannot live with doubts is a troubled person. For to have all the doubts settled is to have no mental pursuits taking place. And such a man, while of little trouble to himself, is also of little help to others.

Doubts can be valuable if they force a man to search deeper and longer for answers. For to pursue the doubts is to come upon some exciting beliefs and truths. (C. NEIL STRAIT)

Doubt makes the mountain which faith can move. (DECISION)

Give me the benefit of your convictions, if you have any; but keep your doubts to yourself, for I have enough of my own. (GOETHE)

DREAMS (see DAYDREAMING, WISHING)

When you let your dreams die, something dies within you.

(DENSON FRANKLIN)

No dream comes true until you wake up and go to work. (BANKING)

Dreams are the garbage disposal of the mind, a way to clear out all the useless information that interferes with rational thought and memory.

(FRANCIS CRICK)

Dreamy starters without enthusiasm quickly lose their steam, and end up disappointing fizzles, sputtering on the launching pad of life.

(ROBERT SCHULLER)

I dreamed I was eating spaghetti. When I woke up, my pajama string was gone! (SHELBY FRIEDMAN)

DRIVE

Two men were discussing the character of a third. "Let me describe him this way," said one to the other. "He's the kind of guy who follows you into a revolving door and comes out ahead of you." (BITS AND PIECES)

DRIVING

If a certain 20 percent of the country's drivers lost their licenses, the accident rate would go down 80 percent.   (KNOXVILLE NEWS SENTINEL)

DRUGS

Matz's Rule Regarding Medications: A drug is that substance which, when injected into a rat, will produce a scientific report.

Sometimes I'm asked by kids why I condemn marijuana when I haven't tried it. The greatest obstetricians in the world have never been pregnant.   (ART LINKLETTER)

There is no doubt about it. Almost every drug addict I've talked to said he started with marijuana.
(CHIEF JOHN ENRIGHT, FEDERAL BUREAU OF NARCOTICS AND DANGEROUS DRUGS)

We prayed a lot. . . . I'm a free man now. . . . Every once in a while I meet a youngster who knows I used to be a drug addict, as he is now. He asks what he can do to kick the habit. I tell him what I've learned: "Give God's temple, your body, back to Him. The alternative is death."
(JOHNNY CASH)

One of the most disturbing effects of psychoactive drugs is that they convince the drug user and those around him that psychological problems have chemical solutions, that relief is just a swallow away, that better psychological living can be achieved through chemistry, rather than by coping.   (J. MAURICE ROGERS)

DUTIES

Duties come from doctrines.   (RICHARD SEUME)

My first job was as important as any I ever had. It was my initiation into a man's world. Being a newsboy taught me the meaning of duty, and without a sense of duty a man is nothing.   (EDDIE RICKENBACKER)

He who does his duty is a hero, whether anyone rewards him for it or not.   (GEORGE FAILING)

EARS (see HEARING)

More than 50 percent of Americans wear glasses, which gives you some idea of how important ears are.

EATING (see DIET)

When it comes to eating, you can sometimes help yourself more by helping yourself less.   (RICHARD ARMOUR)

Eating slowly helps to keep one slim; in other words, haste makes waist.   (A.H. HALLOCK)

ECOLOGY (see POLLUTION)

When God put us on this ball of mud, He gave us an abundance of assets below ground and above. Foolishly, we have made too many withdrawals. We are indeed the last of the big spenders.   (JIM BISHOP)

Earth is a solitary spaceship with an unknown destination. It has 3.5 billion astronauts on board who are using up its resources without taking steps to replace them. We are approaching a global catastrophe. We must do something for Spaceship Earth.   (WERNHER VON BRAUN)

If nothing was done [about polluting the world's oceans], in 30, 40, 50 years it would be the end of everything.   (JACQUES YVES COUSTEAU)

The U.S. is far out of proportion to most of the rest of the world in contributing to the world's ecological problems. This contribution is not our numbers—many nations have a higher birth rate—but our technological development. (ALEXANDER UHL)

Man has mastered nature but, in doing that, he has enslaved himself to the new man-made environment that he has conjured up all around him. Man has condemned himself now to live in cities and to make his living by working in factories and offices. (ARNOLD TOYNBEE)

ECONOMICS

You cannot strengthen the weak by weakening the strong. You cannot help the wage-earner by pulling down the wage-payer. You cannot help the poor by destroying the rich. You cannot help men permanently by doing for them what they could and should do for themselves.
(ABRAHAM LINCOLN)

An economist is an expert who will know tomorrow why the thing he predicted yesterday didn't happen today.

ECONOMY

The secret of economy is to live as cheaply the first few days after payday as you lived the last few days before. (CHANGING TIMES)

EDITING

The more the words, the less the meaning, and how does that profit anyone? (ECCLESIASTES 6:11, NIV)

Life's headiest drive is not love's orgasm, or hate's dagger, but one person's need to change another person's copy. (HUGH LEONARD)

The important party in editing is not the writer but the reader.
(AUSTIN KIPLINGER)

I think the job of an editor is to put his head in a noose.
(NORMAN COUSINS)

If you ever see an editor who pleases everybody, he will be neither sitting nor standing, and there will be a lot of flowers around him.
(CAPPER'S WEEKLY)

EDUCATION (see GRADING PUPILS, SCHOOLS)

"Education" is one of the most discussed subjects of the times—yet 10 persons in a room will have at least 9 different definitions of what education consists in. (SYDNEY HARRIS)

A boy was found at the age of 12 being raised by a wolf. The boy had a remarkably high IQ. In three years he made it through grade school and high school. Two years later he graduated from college with highest honors in nuclear physics. He was destined for an extremely brilliant future—but he was killed one day trying to bite the tires of a speeding car.

Too much and too little education hinder the mind. (PASCAL)

Education is what's left over when you subtract what you've forgotten from what you've learned.

An education isn't something you've had; it's something you're always getting. (FRANKLIN P. JONES)

Education is something a person gets for himself, not that which someone else gives or does to him. (JOHN HOLT)

The chief end of higher education is not to make man dependent upon teachers but independent of them. (L.D. HASKEW)

Natural abilities are like natural plants; they need pruning by study. (FRANCIS BACON)

The great aim of education is not knowledge but action. (HERBERT SPENCER)

Abraham Lincoln had difficulty getting an education, but what do you expect from a guy who didn't play football, basketball, or baseball?

Education takes you from cocksure ignorance to thoughtful uncertainty.

What you learn with just the mind is quickly forgotten; what you learn when you are also emotionally involved remains imprinted in the nervous system; and the first task of education is involvement, not mere learning. (SYDNEY HARRIS)

We train the head and let the heart run wild. We allow culture and character to walk miles apart, stuffing the head with mathematics and languages—leaving manners and morals out of the picture. (THEODORE PALMQUIST)

America's founding fathers did not intend to take religion out of education. Many of the nation's greatest universities were founded by evangelists and religious leaders; but many of these have lost the founders' concepts and become secular institutions. Because of this attitude, secular education is stumbling and floundering. (BILLY GRAHAM)

If you think education is expensive, try ignorance. (DEREK BOK)

Education is hanging around until you've caught on. (ROBERT FROST)

From a fifth-grader's paper: Russian children go to school six days a week. This can never happen in America because Saturday is the day teachers wash their hair. (GENERAL FEATURES)

It is easy—even natural—to think of education as something that ends when one finishes school, or graduates from college, or is decorated with a doctorate. But it might be nearer to the truth to say that real education begins when formal education ends. I frequently recommend books to graduate students "to be read when you stop taking courses and begin to get an education." (CLIFTON L. HALL)

A famous athletic coach said that most people, including some athletes, are "holdouts." They always hold back. They do not invest themselves 100 percent in competition. Because of quasi self-giving they never achieve the highest degree of their capacity. Don't be a holdout. Be an all-out. Do this and life will not hold out on you. (NORMAN V. PEALE)

EGOTISM (see CONCEIT)

An egotist is a man who, when the doctor tells him he'd better have a minor operation, cries, "But think what it will do to the stock market!" (PHILNEWS)

An egotist is not a man who thinks too much of himself. He is a man who thinks too little of other people. (J.F. NEWTON)

Egotism is the anesthetic that dulls the pain of stupidity.(FRANK LEAHY)

That Texan bought a 10-gallon hat. Trouble is, he has an 11-gallon head.

One nice thing about egotists: they don't talk about other people. (LUCILLE S. HARPER)

Egotism is an odd disease. It makes everybody sick but the one who has it. (AUTOMOTIVE DEALER NEWS)

EMERGENCIES

An emergency brings out the best in men. It's everyday living that brings out the beast in them.

EMOTIONS

A good rule for going through life is to keep the heart a little softer than the head. (CHANGING TIMES)

Emotional stability depends in part on having many social roots that tie one to eternal reality. A tree with only one root can be more easily upturned in a storm than one with many sturdy roots running in all directions. Likewise, a person who figuratively carries all his emotional eggs in one basket can be devastated by the death or jilting of that cherished individual. (GEORGE CRANE)

Scientists have proved that music has a very definite relationship to the emotions. Music has the power to modify one emotion and transform it into another. In this way anger may be modified, moderated, and controlled. The greatest effects of music from the emotional point of view are in inducing rest, joy, and love; the least in inducing disgust and irritation. (EDWARD PODOLSKY)

Emotional Maturity: (1) the ability to deal constructively with reality, (2) the capacity to adapt to change, (3) a relative freedom from symptoms that are produced by tensions and anxieties, (4) the capacity to find more satisfaction from giving than receiving, (5) the capacity to relate to other people in a consistent manner with mutual satisfaction and helpfulness, (6) the capacity to sublimate, to direct one's instinctive hostile energy into creative and constructive outlets, (7) the capacity to love. (WILLIAM MENNINGER)

EMPATHY (see COMPASSION, PITY)

No matter what scales we use, we can never know the weight of another person's burdens.

When we put ourselves in the other person's place, we're less likely to want to put him in his place. (FARMER'S DIGEST)

To feel sorry for the needy is not the mark of a Christian—to help them is. (FRANK A. CLARK)

Empathy is your pain in my heart. (JESS LAIR)

EMPLOYER/EMPLOYEE (see WORK)

When the cat's away, the mice will be rats. (V. RAYMOND EDMAN)

Next to sex, spiritual consolation, and medical attention, providing someone with employment is surely one of the most personal functions one person can perform for another. It's a man's bread and butter, and it helps determine how satisfying his life will be.   (RONALD SCHEER)

A modern employer is one who is looking for men between the ages of 25 and 30 with 40 years' experience.   (CHANGING TIMES)

The better a man is the more mistakes he will make, for the more new things he will try. I would never promote into a top-level job a man who was not making mistakes, and big ones at that. Otherwise, he is sure to be mediocre. Worse still, not having made mistakes, he will not have learned how to spot them early and how to correct them. And those two qualifications are among the most important ones for a top job.

(PETER DRUCKER)

If you ever find a man who is better than you are—hire him. If necessary, pay him more than you pay yourself.   (DAVID OGILVY)

When one of the vice-presidents at a bank died, a young assistant went to his boss and inquired: "Do you think I could take his place?"

"It's OK with me," said the boss, "if you can arrange it with the undertaker."

EMPTINESS

Those psychiatrists who are not superficial have come to the conclusion that the vast neurotic misery of the world could be termed a neurosis of emptiness. Men cut themselves off from the root of their being, from God, and then life turns empty, inane, meaningless, without purpose. So when God goes, goal goes. When goal goes, meaning goes. When meaning goes, value goes, and life turns dead on our hands.   (CARL JUNG)

EMPTY NEST

No one told me that it [the "empty nest"] really means having the phone ring and it's for you. It's having leftovers in the refrigerator that you can count on. It's having hot water in the shower, ice cubes in the freezer, gas in your car. It's like being reborn.   (ERMA BOMBECK)

ENCOURAGEMENT

A pat on the back, though only a few vertebrae removed from a kick in the pants, is miles ahead in results.   (ROYAL NEIGHBOR)

Correction does much, but encouragement does more. Encouragement after censure is as the sun after a shower.   (GOETHE)

ENEMIES (see ADVERSARIES)

If you have some enemies, you are to be congratulated, for no man ever amounted to much without arousing jealousies and creating enemies.

Your enemies are a very valuable asset as long as you refrain from striking back at them, because they keep you on the alert when you might become lazy.   (DRESCH MESSENGER)

Friends may come and go, but enemies accumulate.   (JONES' LAW)

One important ingredient of success is a good, wide-awake, persistent, tireless enemy.   (FRANK B. SHUTTS)

Remember, nobody will ever get ahead of you as long as he is kicking you in the seat of the pants.   (WALTER WINCHELL)

Enemies are made, not born.

Could we read the secret history of our enemies, we should find in each man's life, sorrow and suffering enough to disarm all hostility.
                                                  (H.W. LONGFELLOW)

I have had a lot of *adversaries* in my political life, but no *enemies* that I can remember.   (GERALD FORD)

You should really cherish your enemies. At least they don't try to hit you for a loan.   (LOU ERICKSON)

The world is a spiritual jungle in which we all are traveling. In it we find that it is not the big enemies from which we stand in the greatest danger of losing our self-control, but the little things that lurk in the dark recesses of our nature: gossip, the poisoner of the blood, the temper uncontrolled, the unruly tongue which shoots out the venom of bitter words, the lust for forbidden things, the foolish or injurious word, the unholy thought, the wasted moment.   (MEGIDDO MESSAGE)

ENJOYMENT

Enjoy what you can and endure what you must.   (GOETHE)

"I always enjoy myself," snapped Groucho. "It's the other people I have trouble enjoying."

The only way to enjoy anything in this life is to earn it first.
                                                  (GINGER ROGERS)

ENTHUSIASM

Be not afraid of enthusiasm; you need it; you can do nothing effectively without it.   (FRANCOIS GUIZOT)

Every man is enthusiastic at times. One man has enthusiasm for 30 minutes—another man has it for 30 days, but it is the man who has it for 30 years who makes a success of life.   (EDWARD B. BUTLER)

Enthusiasm and persistence can make an average person superior; indifference and lethargy can make a superior person average.
                                                                (WILLIAM A. WARD)

You must have enthusiasm for life, or life is not going to have a lot of enthusiasm for you.   (J. HAROLD SMITH)

People are persuaded more by the depth of your conviction than by the height of your logic—more by your own enthusiasm than any proof you can offer.

Enthusiasm has a great cloak which can conceal lame talents, dwarfed ambitions, and mangy personalities. It has a sparkle like sunlight on rippling waters and can cause dedicated failures to be delightful.

Enthusiasm is the all-essential human jet propellant. It is the driving force which elevates men to miracle workers. It begets boldness, courage; kindles confidence; overcomes doubts. It creates endless energy, the source of all accomplishment.   (B.C. FORBES)

The worst bankrupt in the world is the man who has lost his enthusiasm. Let a man lose everything else in the world but his enthusiasm and he will come through again to success.   (H.W. ARNOLD)

All through the ages the most worthy characters have been those who were dynamically enthusiastic over some definite aim and end. The young man who is afraid to manifest enthusiasm lest his dignity suffer is not likely to have much dignity to lose by and by. Enthusiasm is the propelling force that is necessary for climbing the ladder of success.
                                                                (B.C. FORBES)

An agency executive has compiled a list of fail-safe phrases, or comments, which automatically throw the brakes on enthusiasm. You're feeling pretty fired up about some idea, he says, and then one of these phrases drops into the conversation like a policeman into a party. The list includes: "Might be better if," "I like it—it's just that," "See your point, but," "Let's look at it this way," "Our usual procedure is," "How would we justify it?" "How would it look?" And also, of course, "Yes, but," "No, but," "Maybe, but," and "Let me sleep on it."

We act as though comfort and luxury were the chief requirements of life, when all that we need to make us really happy is something to be enthusiastic about.   (CHARLES KINGSLEY)

117

Apathy can only be overcome by enthusiasm, and enthusiasm can only be aroused by two things; first, an ideal which takes the imagination by storm, and second, a definite intelligible plan for carrying that ideal into practice. (ARNOLD TOYNBEE)

Both enthusiasm and pessimism are contagious. Which one do you spread?

ENVY (see JEALOUSY)

Envy takes the joy, happiness, and contentment out of living.
(BILLY GRAHAM)

An envious man is a squinty-eyed fool. (H.G. BOHN)

If there is any sin more deadly than envy, it is being pleased at being envied. (RICHARD ARMOUR)

EQUAL RIGHTS

Equal rights for women is OK, but there sure are some inequalities in their favor. How come diamonds are a girl's best friend, but a man's best friend is a dog? (ROY CLARK)

EQUIPMENT

If you need a piece of equipment but don't buy it, you pay for it even though you don't have it. (HENRY FORD)

ERRORS (see MISTAKES)

A man who has committed a mistake and doesn't correct it is committing another mistake. (CONFUCIUS)

Anybody who profits from his mistakes has probably written a successful autobiography.

ETERNITY (see HEAVEN, HELL)

The truest end of life is to know the life that never ends. (WILLIAM PENN)

All that is not eternal is out of date. (C.S. LEWIS)

Millions long for immortality who do not know what to do with themselves on a rainy Sunday afternoon. (SUSAN ERTZ)

We have come from somewhere and are going somewhere. The great architect of the universe never built a stairway that leads to nowhere.
(ROBERT MILLIKAN)

EVALUATION

If at first you don't succeed, try, try again. If you still don't succeed, stop trying. Sit down and think it over. Persistence is a noble virtue, but it's no substitute for evaluation. (R.W. JANSSEN)

EVANGELICALISM

I am more and more impressed with the cultic kind of evangelicalism we are developing in American evangelicalism. We are evangelical faddists about food, fat, sex, eschatology, and pseudopsychology.(BERNARD RAMM)

EVANGELISM

The world has more winnable people than ever before . . . but it is possible to come out of a ripe field empty-handed.(DONALD McGAVRAN)

The evangelistic harvest is always urgent. The destiny of men and of nations is always being decided. Every generation is strategic. We are not responsibile for the past generation, and we cannot bear the full responsibility for the next one; but we do have our generation. God will hold us responsible as to how well we fulfill our responsibilities to this age and take advantage of our opportunities. (BILLY GRAHAM)

The way from God to a human heart is through a human heart. (SAMUEL GORDON)

EVIL (see SIN)

Repay evil with good and you deprive the evildoer of all the pleasure of his wickedness. (LEO TOLSTOY)

There is an evil which most of us condone and are even guilty of: indifference to evil. We remain neutral, impartial, and not easily moved by the wrongs done unto other people. Indifference to evil is more insidious than evil itself; it is more universal, more contagious, more dangerous. (ABRAHAM JESCHEL)

Of two evils, choose neither. (CHARLES H. SPURGEON)

EVOLUTION

The evolutionists seem to know everything about the missing link except the fact that it is missing. (G.K. CHESTERTON)

If evolution works, how come mothers still have only two hands? (ED DUSSAULT)

EXAGGERATION

There are people so addicted to exaggeration that they can't tell the truth without lying. (JOSH BILLINGS)

EXAMPLE

Others will follow your footsteps easier than they will follow your advice. (ADVANCE)

Example is not the main thing in influencing others. It is the only thing. (ALBERT SCHWEITZER)

EXCELLENCE

All things excellent are as difficult as they are rare. (SPINOZA)

The secret of joy is contained in one word—excellence. To know how to do something well is to enjoy it. (PEARL BUCK)

EXCUSES

Excuses are the tools with which persons with no purpose in view build for themselves great monuments of nothing.

It is easy to make excuses when we ought to be making opportunities. (WARREN WIERSBE)

Whoever wants to be a judge of human nature should study people's excuses. (HEBBEL)

When I was in Harvard, going on a hundred years ago, more or less, LeBaron Briggs was dean. One day a student explained his failure to do some assigned work by saying, "I wasn't feeling well."
Dean Briggs replied, "I think in time you may perhaps find that most of the work in the world is done by people who aren't feeling well." (PERCY WHITING)

Someone has compiled the following 10 excuses that are not recommended for ambitious men and women:
1. That's the way we've always done it.
2. I didn't know you were in a hurry for it.
3. That's not in my department.
4. No one told me to go ahead.
5. I'm waiting for an OK.
6. How did I know this was different?
7. That's his job, not mine.
8. Wait till the boss comes back and ask him.

9. I forgot.
10. I didn't think it was that important. (GRIT)

I never knew a man who was good at making excuses who was good at anything else. (BENJAMIN FRANKLIN)

EXECUTIVES (see MANAGEMENT)

A good manager is a man who isn't worried about his own career but rather the careers of those who work for him. My advice: Don't worry about yourself. Take care of those who work for you and you'll float to greatness on their achievements. (H.M.S. BURNS)

Good executives thrive on problems because it is their job to solve them calmly and efficiently. (GUY FERGUSON)

Innumerable symptoms of [executive] failure can be traced to four basic causes: (1) *Lack of drive.* This used to be attributed to laziness. More likely it is due to preoccupation, a bone-deep concern with other matters, physical and pyschological, that leave such a man powerless to concentrate on his job, unable to be motivated by it. (2) *Deficiency of imagination.* A good executive has the capacity to explore the future in fiction before he undertakes it in fact. He expects the unexpected. . . . (3) *Lack of common sense . . . and lack of perception and judgment . . .* essential to any successful human relationship. (4) *Inability to communicate.* . . . He is disorganized, unfamiliar with his audience and his material. Because he cannot express himself with clarity and precision, he cannot be understood or he is misunderstood. (ROY PEARSON)

Pampers is making earmuffs for junior executives who are still wet behind the ears. (ROBERT ORBEN)

He who is carried on another's back does not appreciate how far the town is. (A TREASURY OF AFRICAN FOLKLORE)

One of the qualities I would certainly look for in an executive is whether he knows how to delegate properly. The inability to do this is, in my opinion (and in that of others I have talked with on this subject), one of the chief reasons executives fail. Another is their inability to make decisions effectively. These two personality lacks have contributed more to executive failure than any amount of know-how lacks.

(J.C. PENNEY)

Definition of an executive: A man in any organization who has the courage to dream, the ability to organize, and the strength to execute. (EXECUTIVES' DIGEST)

A business manager in search of talent within his own organization passed out a list of questions to his younger workers. One question asked, "What is your chief reason for believing that you possess executive ability?"

Many of the answers were duplications, but one stood out unequaled. It read, "I think I would make a very successful executive because I seldom get lonesome, and would not mind working in a private office."
(WALL STREET JOURNAL)

An executive is a man employed to talk with visitors so that the other employees can keep on working. (GRIT)

Have you noticed how the company parking lot confers executive status, while the company bowling league takes it away? (BURTON HILLIS)

Doctors say one of the four leading symptoms of an impending crackup for executives is a bulging briefcase taken home too often. The other three danger signs are: irritability, indecision, and inability to delegate authority.

An executive was checking through the evaluation chart for one of the men reporting to him. As he studied the various aspects of the man's performance and abilities, a light suddenly dawned. . . . "All at once I realized that most of the criticism I have to make about Dick, I can also make about *myself.* I wonder if maybe he's just reflecting my own faults because I'm his boss?" He was absolutely right. The weaknesses—and the strengths—of the executives under him were often imitations of his own. This is true, to a very considerable extent, throughout the managerial ranks. What we are as managers—our own philosophy, our own practices, our own development—are the determining factors in the development of those who report to us. (GORDON ELLIS)

He realized he was a failure when the waiter refused to serve him a businessman's lunch. (BOB WILLETT)

Executives in their 30s and 40s are valuable because they're eager and keen and aware of what can, should, needs to be done. Executives in their 50s and 60s are valuable because they're more relaxed and experienced and often aware of what can't, shouldn't, needn't be done.
(MALCOLM FORBES)

The executive's loneliest hours are spent, not choosing between right and wrong, but between two rights or two wrongs. His most creative moments are those in which he successfully integrates values, bringing diverse ideas together into new arrangements. (NATION'S BUSINESS)

EXERCISE (see JOGGING, TENNIS, PHYSICAL FITNESS)

You can't turn back the clock, but you can wind it up again.
(BONNIE PRUDDEN)

The only exercise some people get is jumping to conclusions, running down their friends, sidestepping responsibilty, dodging issues, passing the buck, and pushing their luck.　　(BAPTIST COURIER)

Nowadays they spend $20,000 for a school bus to pick the kids right up at the door so they don't have to walk. They then spend $200,000 for a gym so they can get some exercise.　　(RED BLANCHARD)

Lack of exercise is a direct consequence of the national mania for individual transportation, and the introduction of power aids not only in industry, but everywhere in the office, and in the home, in the automobile and even in recreation and "sports," where the golfmobile and snowmobile are . . . threats to fitness. Emphasis in urban planning on proximity of parking rather than on attractiveness and safety of walking has produced the most immobile group of men in the history of the world—yet we know that exercise is vital to weight control.　　(JEAN MAYER)

You are most in need of exercise when you don't have any time for it.　　(LLOYD CORY)

Exercise stimulates many of the same adrenal responses as caffeine and nicotine—but at a rate you can live with. It also rejuvenates your blood's supplies of oxygen and releases mood-elevating chemicals in the brain. So try a few jumping jacks the next time your eyelids are at half-mast. Considering that exercise was people's way of life for eons, it should come as no surprise that depression and fatigue are often the result of not getting enough exercise.　　(EXECUTIVE FITNESS NEWSLETTER)

Often a voluntary change of activity is as good or better than a voluntary rest. When either fatigue or enforced interruption prevents us from finding a mathematical solution, it is better to go for a swim than simply sit around. Substituting demands on our musculature for those made on the intellect not only gives our brain a rest but helps us avoid worrying about the frustrating interruption. Stress on one system helps to relax another.　　(HANS DELYE)

I don't think exercise makes you nearly as hungry as thinking does. Especially thinking about food.　　(BERYL PFIZER)

You don't stop exercising because you grow old. You grow old because you stop exercising.　　(RUSS HARRIS)

A man who drops out of recreation after an active youth is committing slow suicide.   (JAMES MICHENER)

A man too busy to take care of his health is like a mechanic too busy to take care of his tools.

Activity strengthens. Inactivity weakens.   (HIPPOCRATES)

A man is as old as his arteries.   (THOMAS SYDENHAM)

In a sense walking is the best bargain in transportation, for when you step outside the door and start moving your feet forward you are exercising your leg muscles, pepping up your circulation, gaining uncomplicated privacy and time for thought and sightseeing, and all this while getting to your destination. While even the strongest advocate of physical fitness would not advise throwing away the keys to the family car, it is recommended that you keep them in your pocket more often and walk to the store for that newspaper or just take a stroll to see the wonders that nature has provided.   (WOODEN BARREL)

That person who exercises his body, but forgets the exercises of the mind and of the soul, is like a man getting all dressed up but nowhere to go. A conditioned, healthy body is good, but when it has a purpose and a mission, it is better.   (C. NEIL STRAIT)

EXPECTATIONS (see HOPE)

Expecting too little of ourselves is wasteful; expecting too much of ourselves is folly.   (WILLIAM A. WARD)

Blessed is he that expecteth nothing, for he shall not be disappointed.
                                                        (C.B. EAVEY)

Blessed is he that expecteth nothing, for he shall be gloriously surprised.
                                                  (G.K. CHESTERTON)

The more reasonable we are in our expectations, the fewer disappointments we will have in life.   (A. NIELEN)

EXPERIENCE

Experience is what you get when you were expecting something else.

Experience is what causes a person to make new mistakes instead of old ones.   (ENOS MAGAZINE)

The head learns new things, but the heart forevermore practices old experiences.   (HENRY W. BEECHER)

Experience is the best of schoolmasters, only the school fees are heavy.
(THOMAS CARLYLE)

Experience is the thing that enables you to recognize a mistake when you make it again. (BITS AND PIECES)

Some learn from experience—others recover from it. (KING CITY RUSTLER)

It's paradoxical, but cold feet are often the direct result of burned fingers. (SHAMOKIN CITIZEN)

It seems that every time you think you are ready to graduate from the school of experience, somebody thinks up a new course.
(EDUCATION DIGEST)

One reason experience is such a good teacher is that she doesn't allow any dropouts. (ILLINOIS JOURNAL OF EDUCATION)

Learn by experience—other people's if you are smart.
(ILLINOIS JOURNAL OF EDUCATION)

Experience is a comb which nature gives to men when they are bald.
(OLD PROVERB)

EXPERTS

An expert is someone who knows no more than you do, but who has it better organized and uses slides. (CRUMBLEY)

An expert is like the bottom half of a double boiler. It lets off a lot of steam, but it really doesn't know what's cooking. (HOWARD MEYERHOFF)

An expert is a person who avoids the small errors as he sweeps on to the grand fallacy. (BENJAMIN STOLBERG)

An expert is someone called in at the last minute to share the blame.
(WISCONSIN JOURNAL OF EDUCATION)

EYES

I gaze into her shining eyes
With joy my soul transcends
And yet—I wonder is it love
Or shiny contact lens? (SHELBY FRIEDMAN)

Carrots are positively good for the eyes. Have you ever seen a rabbit with glasses?

Eye contact helps people in almost any walk of life. Salvation Army bell-ringers claim they almost always get a donation if they make eye contact with pedestrians. Salespeople who use eye contact with customers generate more and larger sales. Hitchhikers stand a better chance of getting rides if they engage in eye contact with passing motorists. Managers and executives who use their eyes when talking with their staffs open communications. And parents often find eyes the most effective means of scolding children. (UNIVERSITY OF UTAH STUDY)

The best thing for your eyes is to use them, not save them, according to Dr. Albert E. Sloan, eye surgeon at the Massachusetts Eye and Ear Infirmary in Boston. Dr. Sloan also said, contrary to some belief, reading in poor light does not harm the eyes. That type of use improves the ability of the eye to use its potential to the fullest. (GRIT)

FACTS

Every man has a right to his opinion, but no man has a right to be wrong in his facts. (BERNARD BARUCH)

Facts do not cease to exist because they are ignored.
(WATCHMAN—EXAMINER)

FAILURE

You can tell a failure by the way he criticizes success. (MEL JOHNSON)

If you visualize failure, you tend to create the conditions that produce failure. (BOB FOSTER)

Ninety-nine percent of failures come from people who have the habit of making excuses. (GEORGE WASHINGTON CARVER)

Failure should be our teacher, not our undertaker. Failure is delay, not defeat. It is a temporary detour, not a dead-end street.
(WILLIAM A. WARD)

Some men learn so much from their failures they seem to go around avoiding success. (FRANKLIN P. JONES)

You may be disappointed if you fail, but you are doomed if you don't try. (BEVERLY SILLS)

Failure is something we can avoid by saying nothing, doing nothing, and being nothing. (EUGENE W. BRICE)

He who has never failed has never tried. (EMMETT LeCOMPTE)

The greatest failure is the failure to try. (WILLIAM A. WARD)

No man ever fails until he fails on the inside.

More men fail through lack of purpose than lack of talent. (BILLY SUNDAY)

People do not inadvertently stumble into failure. They think their way into it. (JOHN B. JOHNSON)

Failure is the line of least persistence. (W.A. CLARKE)

Failures can be divided into those who thought and never did, and those who did and never thought. (W.A. NANCE)

We who do less than our best have failed as surely as those who attempt nothing. The only difference is in the degree. (RICHARD MORGAN)

Haves and have-nots are the second stage. The first stage is dids and did-nots. (PEN MAGAZINE)

No man is a failure until he begins to blame somebody else.
(BITS AND PIECES)

Five Rules for job failure: (1) Do only what is required. (2) Leave it till the last minute. (3) Let the mistakes go. (4) Don't listen to your conscience. (5) Learn to be a convincing bluffer. (TRAINED MEN)

Failure is a cloud that floats between man and success, shielding him from the blistering rays of pride. (WILLIAM A. WARD)

It is a rare person who doesn't hope responsibility for his failures will fall on somebody else. It is normal to want to shift blame for our troubles. But shifting isn't easy to do. People don't fool easily. It isn't even easy to fool oneself. Besides, shifting the blame serves no practical ends. It means talking about troubles instead of remedies, about past problems instead of future plans. (NORMAN SHIDLE)

I can take any group of young people any place, and teach them to be inventors, if I can get them to throw off the hazard of being afraid to fail. You fail because your ideas aren't right. You shouldn't be afraid to fail, but you should learn to fail intelligently. By that I mean, when you fail, find out why you failed, and each time you fail it will bring you up nearer to the goal. (CHARLES KETTERING)

Constant effort and frequent mistakes are the stepping-stones of genius. (ELBERT HUBBARD)

From failure can come valuable experience; from experience—wisdom; from wisdom—mutual trust; from mutual trust—cooperation; from cooperation—united effort; from united effort—success. (WILLIAM A. WARD)

FAITH

Faith grows only in the dark. You've got to trust Him where you can't trace Him. That's faith. You just take Him at His Word, believe Him, and grip the nail-scarred hand a little tighter. And faith grows. (LYELL RADER)

Faith rests on the naked Word of God; that Word believed gives full assurance. (HARRY A. IRONSIDE)

You don't know what faith you have until it is tested. (REES HOWELLS)

No one can give faith unless he has faith. It is the persuaded who persuade. (JOSEPH JOUBERT)

If we desire an increase of faith, we must consent to its testings.

Faith comes first to the hearing ear, not to the cogitating mind. (A.W. TOZER)

Saving faith is never spoken of in relative terms, for the consequence of faith is not relative: it is a passing from death into life. One is either lost or saved, and the scale between the two conditions is not graduated. (CHRISTIANITY TODAY)

Faith is not the absence of fear or doubt, but the force that gets you safely through those long, dark, waiting-room hours. (MERRILL WOMACH)

Living without faith is like driving in a fog.

Faith is one of the most precious treasures a man can possibly possess. It is a pity that so few understand what the Bible teaches about it. Faith is often confused with presumption, optimism, determination, superstition, and imagination. Actually, it is simply *believing*. . . . Obviously faith honors God, while doubting His Word must insult and displease Him. (WEEKLY REVIEW)

Faith sees the invisible, believes the incredible, and receives the impossible. (THE FREE METHODIST)

Faith in God makes a person undaunted, unafraid, undivided, and "unflappable."
   Real faith results in active response, responsive action, and willing obedience.
   Faith is continuing to run the race, assured that you will get your second wind.
   Faith is focusing on God's promises, and cropping out the world's discouragements.
   Faith is confidently expecting miracles from the Source and Promiser of miracles. (WILLIAM A. WARD)

We live by faith or we do not live at all. Either we venture—or we vegetate. If we venture, we do so by faith simply because we cannot know the end of anything at its beginning. We risk marriage on faith or we stay single. We prepare for a profession by faith or we give up before we start. By faith we move mountains of opposition or we are stopped by molehills. (HAROLD WALKER)

Faith is like a toothbrush. Every man should have one and use it regularly, but he shouldn't try to use someone else's. (J.G. STIPE)

Faith is more than thinking something is true. Faith is thinking something is true to the extent that we act on it. (W.T. PURKISER)

Faith is not trying to believe something regardless of the evidence. Faith is daring to do something regardless of the consequences. (SHERWOOD EDDY)

Faith makes the uplook good, the outlook bright, the inlook favorable, and the future glorious. (V. RAYMOND EDMAN)

Pray for a faith that will not shrink when it is washed in the waters of affliction. (ERNEST WADSWORTH)

Never doubt in the dark what God told you in the light. (V. RAYMOND EDMAN)

To seek proof is to admit doubt, and to obtain proof is to render faith superfluous. (A.W. TOZER)

A fellow shouldn't abandon his faith when it weakens, any more than he'd throw away a suit because it needs pressing. (FRANK A. CLARK)

The late Bishop William A. Quayle used to tell of an experience during a sleepless night. After rolling and tossing far into the night, he said that he seemed to hear God's voice telling him to go on to sleep and let God run the world the rest of the night. (O. AFTON LINGER)

A famous heiress keeps her priceless collection of jewels in the vault of a large bank. One of her prize possessions is a very valuable string of pearls. It is a scientific fact that pearls lose their original luster if not worn once in a while in contact with the human body. So, once a week, a bank secretary, guarded by two plainclothesmen, wears these priceless pearls to lunch. This brief contact with the human body keeps them beautiful and in good condition.

Our faith is a lot like the pearl. It must be used in order to be useful. It must be worn out among the masses of mankind where faith and hope are needed. (UPLIFT)

The man who is ashamed of his faith ought to be ashamed of himself.
(MEGIDDO MESSAGE)

FAITHFULNESS

God has no larger field for the man who is not faithfully doing his work where he is.

Old Faithful is not the largest geyser, nor does it reach the greatest height. Nevertheless it is by far the most popular geyser. Its popularity is due mainly to its regularity and dependability. You can count on Old Faithful. Nothing in life can take the place of faithfulness and dependability. It is one of the greatest virtues. Brilliance, genius, competence—all are subservient to the quality of faithfulness. (WALLACE FRIDY)

FAME

It is said that some men are born to fame; some achieve it by their efforts, and some have it thrust upon them. Much the same could be said about obscurity; some seem to be born for it; some earn it by the quality of what they do, and some have it thrust upon them by the lack of a good press agent. (EDUCATIONAL FORUM)

Fame, like flame, is harmless until you start inhaling it.(O.A. BATTISTA)

Many a man's name appears in the paper only three times: when he's too young to read, when he's too dazed to read, and when he's too dead to read. (GRINS AND CHUCKLES)

FAMILIARITY

Familiarity breeds attempt. (PHILNEWS)

FAMILIES

Happy families are all alike; every unhappy family is unhappy in its own way. (LEO TOLSTOY)

Children learn first and best from their families. Just as by the end of the second year their language is that of the people with whom they live, so their behavior is stamped with the seal of their adult protectors.
(SADIE GINSBERG)

Every family tree has to have some sap. (ANN OMINOUS)

See how a man treats his family, and you will see what his true feelings are about mankind. (INFORMATION MAGAZINE)

In the all-important world of family relations, three words are almost as powerful as the famous "I love you." They are "Maybe you're right."
(OREN ARNOLD)

A modern home is where the TV set is better adjusted than the kids.

Successful family living strikes me as being in many ways rather like playing chamber music. Each member of the ensemble has his own skills, his own special knack with the part he chooses to play; but the grace and strength and sweetness of the performance come from everyone's willingness to subordinate individual virtuosity and personal ambition to the requirements of balance and blend. (ANNIS DUFF)

My authority in my home is exactly proportional to what I got fresh from God that day. I don't even have to talk about it—there's a heavenly aura when Dad's met God. When I backslide, everything at home falls apart.
(ROBERT A. COOK)

One of the great concerns of today is the collapse of the family as a meaningful unit in our society. It is said that the average person in the U.S.A. spends 76 percent of his lifetime at home. Yet our homes are too often split-level traps from which we want to flee. So often, each member of a family goes his separate way. Consequently, our family relationships are fractured, or frozen at best. We do not know each other. What is worse, many do not care. (WILLIAM ENRIGHT)

FANTASY

Nothing, ultimately, costs more than the upkeep on castles in the air. Reality, no matter how taxing, is never as expensive (both physically and financially) as fantasy. (SYDNEY HARRIS)

FARMING

A farmer overheard a flock of chickens in his barnyard talking together just as a football flew over the fence and landed in their midst.

The barnyard rooster waddled over, studied it, then said: "I'm not complaining, girls, but look at the work they're turning out next door."
(GENERAL FEATURES)

FASHION (see CLOTHING)

Fashion is what you adopt when you don't know who you are.
(QUENTIN CRISP)

FAT

I never laugh at fat people. One shouldn't laugh at the other's expanse.
(SHELBY FRIEDMAN)

In spring a lot of things pop up, including stuff that won't fit into my old bathing suit.

Nothing stretches slacks like snacks.

Reducing salon ad: Flabbery will get you nowhere. (SHELBY FRIEDMAN)

A fat wife had to quit exercising on a Pogo stick. It registered 6 on the Richter Scale.

She had a million dollar figure—then inflation set in. (ARNOLD GLASOW)

If someone calls me fat, I don't get angry. I just turn the other chin.
(ROBERT ORBEN)

Are chubby people more cheerful than thin ones? A study of more than 800 middle-aged people in England who were obese shows that they suffer from less anxiety and depression than those of normal weight. Dr. P. McGinnis of St. George's Hospial Medical School revealed this finding in a recent issue of the British Medical Journal. They discovered that men 20 percent overweight and women 40 percent overweight were generally less depressed than the rest of the population. How come? "There is a chemistry in obesity that is incompatible with depression and anxiety," say the researchers.

FATE

As soon as a fellow resigns himself to fate, his resignation is promptly accepted.

I do not believe in a fate that falls on men however they act, but I do believe in a fate that falls on men *unless* they act. (G.K. CHESTERTON)

It is true that when fate throws a knife at us, we can catch it by the blade and wound ourselves . . . or catch it by the handle and carve out some remaining good for ourselves. (WOMAN'S WEEKLY)

What men commonly call their fate is mostly only their own foolishness. (SCHOPENHAUER)

FATHERS (see PARENTS)

A father is a man who expects his son to be as good a man as he meant to be. (FRANK A. CLARK)

A father is someone who carries pictures where his money used to be. (LION)

Class composition written by an eight-year-old student: He can climb the highest mountain or swim the biggest ocean. He can fly the fastest plane and fight the strongest tiger. My father can do anything. But most of the time he just carries out the garbage. (SUPERVISION)

Father: How dare you! What do you mean by hugging my daughter so tightly?
   Boy: I was just carrying out the scriptural injunction, "Hold fast that which is good."

Live so that your son, when people tell him that he reminds them of you, will stick out his chest, not his tongue. (THE FURROW)

Any father who thinks he's all-important should remind himself that this country honors fathers only one day a year while pickles get a whole week. (QUOTE)

Small boy's definition of Father's Day: It's just like Mother's Day only you don't spend so much. (AUSTRALASIAN MFR.)

The best gift a father can give to his son is the gift of himself—his time. For material things mean little, if there is not someone to share them with. (C. NEIL STRAIT)

Jim Bishop describes the feeling a father had when his daughter became engaged: "This is the third of four daughters. Every time it happens, I'm obsessed with the feeling I'm giving a million-dollar Stradivarius to a gorilla."

A father is a thing that is forced to endure childbirth without an anesthetic. . . . A father never feels worthy of the worship in a child's eyes. He's never quite the hero his daughter thinks, never quite the man his son believes him to be, and this worries him, sometimes. So he works too hard to try and smooth the rough places in the road for those of his own who will follow him. . . . Fathers are what give daughters away to other men who aren't nearly good enough, so they can have grandchildren who are smarter than anybody's. Fathers make bets with insurance companies about who'll live the longest. One day they lose and the bet's paid off to the part of them they leave behind.   (PAUL HARVEY)

FATIGUE (see DEPRESSION)

Fatigue is the most frequent sign of depression and is usually accompanied by a loss of interest in normal activities. Having too little to do as well as too much can also cause fatigue.

FAULTS (see SHORTCOMINGS)

You can bear anything if it isn't your fault.   (K.F. GEROULD)

The way my wife finds fault with me, you'd think there was a reward.
(JACK LEMMON)

If we had no faults we should not take so much pleasure in noting those of others.   (FRANCOIS DE LA ROCHEFOUCAULD)

When looking for faults, use a mirror, not a telescope.
(THE GOOD SHIP GRACE)

Many people believe that admitting a fault means they no longer have to correct it.   (MARIE VON EBNER-ESCHENBACH)

Every man should have a fair-sized cemetery in which to bury the faults of his friends.   (HENRY WARD BEECHER)

Nature didn't make us perfect, so she did the next best thing. She made us blind to our faults.   (GRIT)

The easiest faults to notice are those you don't have.

Most of us can live peacefully with our own faults, but the faults of others get on our nerves.   (BANKING)

Rare is the person who can weigh the faults of others without putting his thumb on the scales.   (LANGENFELD)

Think of your own faults the first part of the night when you are awake, and of the faults of others the latter part of the night when you are asleep. (CHINESE PROVERB)

A fellow shouldn't hide his faults too carefully. Perfection in others isn't easy to admire.

A fault which humbles a man is of more use to him than a good action which puffs him up. (THOMAS WILSON)

The greatest of all faults is to be conscious of none. (THOMAS CARLYLE)

FEAR

Not all fears are bad. Many of them are wholesome, indeed, very necessary for life. The fear of God, the fear of fire, the fear of electricity, are life-saving fears that, if heeded, bring a new knowledge to life.
(C. NEIL STRAIT)

Some people are so afraid to die that they never begin to live.
(HENRY VAN DYKE)

Ungodly fear: that God will allow me to be hurt.
Godly fear: that I will do something to grieve God.

A group of university students from Toronto went up to Georgian Bay for a fishing trip. They hired a boat and a captain to take them out into the bay. Without warning, a storm broke. The captain, an old tar, sat at the helm with a worried look on his face. The students laughed at him in his fear and through their laughter declared: "We are not afraid!"
The old sea dog looked at them and said, "Yes, you are too ignorant to be afraid." (GEORGE BOWMAN)

Sign outside a London church during World War II: If your knees knock, kneel on them.

I haven't been so scared since I donated my body to a medical school—and they said they want it now. (ROBERT ORBEN)

Fear is the most destructive force in the world today. It is much easier to frighten people, and more profitable, than to persuade them.
(WALTER STONE)

Fear causes people to draw back from situations; it brings on mediocrity; it dulls creativity; it sets one up to be a loser in life. (FRAN TARKENTON)

Do the thing you fear, and the death of fear is certain. (GRIT)

To live with fear and not be afraid is the final test of maturity.
(EDWARD WEEKS)

The fears of men are more likely to center around money and careers, illnesses, and going to a dentist. The fears of women center more around love and marriage, snakes, spiders, growing old, getting fat, and staying alone at night. Women are more likely to express their fears through tears. Men are more likely to commit suicide—it might be better if they cried more. (SYLVANUS AND EVELYN DUVALL)

Psychologist E.R. Hagmen interviewed a number of mothers about their own and their children's fears. He found that mothers and their children were alike, both as to the number of fears and what they were afraid of. To teach people to control their fears, we must apparently begin with their parents. (SYLVANUS AND EVELYN DUVALL)

Things never go so well that one should have no fear, and never so ill that one should have no hope. (TURKISH PROVERB)

Keep your fears to yourself; share your courage with others.
(ROBERT L. STEVENSON)

FEELINGS (see MOODS)

When we are in high spirits, the world is a great place—your friends are the dearest, your kiddies the smartest, your employees the best, and your canary the tweetiest. But when your mood is dark, the world is bleak, your friends selfish, your children ungrateful, your boss the meanest, and even your pup, wagging his tail, is nothing but a big nuisance.
(SONJA EITELJORG)

Never apologize for showing feelings. Remember that when you do, you apologize for the truth. (BENJAMIN DISRAELI)

FELLOWSHIP

God calls us not to solitary sainthood but to fellowship in a company of committed men. (DAVID SCHULLER)

Searching for oneself within is as futile as peeling an onion to find the core: When you finish, there is nothing there but peelings; paradoxically, the only way to find oneself is to go outward to a genuine meeting with another. (SYDNEY HARRIS)

When our fellowship with the Lord is ruptured, our conscience gets dull, we blow our stacks, let the seamy side of life show through, and live like children of the devil. (MALCOLM CRONK)

FENCING

The local fencing club is looking for new blood.

FIGHTING

The human race has an enormous amount of inbred, or inborn, bellicosity. Especially the male sex. From what I can tell, fighting has been a more frequent activity than anything except agriculture in the history of man. People are always fighting somewhere. I think it has to do with identity. You don't feel like a group unless you have an enemy. That makes you feel like "us" and they are "them." People fight to give themselves a tribal identity. (BARBARA TUCHMAN)

FINANCE

"Wake up," said the office manager to the bookkeeper when he saw him, head on desk, sound asleep. "Don't you feel good?"

"Sorry," replied the bookkeeper, "but I didn't get a wink of sleep last night."

"You should try counting sheep," advised the office manager. "It works for me all the time."

"I tried it, and that's the whole trouble. I made a mistake during the first half-hour, and it took me until this morning to get it straightened out."

FINITIATIVE

One worthwhile task carried to a successful conclusion is worth half-a-hundred half-finished tasks. (B.C. FORBES)

FIRE DEPARTMENT

A not-so-bright chap was elected to the town council, where the first proposal he made was to buy a new fire engine.

"What will we do with the old engine?" another city father asked.

"Well," he offered, "we could use it for false alarms."

FISHING

An old fisherman went fishing some years ago. After a while he got a good bite. As he struggled to get the fish into the boat, his wedding ring fell off and disappeared into the watery depths.

Some three or four years later, he was fishing at the same spot and hooked on to a good-size bass. Anticipating the pleasure of having it for supper, he took it home immediately.

As he was cleaning the fish, his knife cut into something solid. It was his finger. (LEO AIKMANN)

The city fellow spotted an old New Englander fishing. "How many fish did you catch?" he asked.

"Well, Sonny, I'll tell you," he said. "If I catch this one I'm after, and two more, I'll have three." (CORONET)

First fisherman: "How are they biting today?"
Second fisherman: "On the neck and legs mostly." (CAROLINA COOPERATOR)

FLATTERY

Flattery is the art of telling a person exactly what he thinks of himself.

If you can't think of any other way to flatter a man, tell him he's the kind who can't be flattered. (CONSTRUCTION DIGEST)

Flattery is a device for getting somebody to pay attention to what you're saying. (FRANKLIN P. JONES)

FLAWS

Better a diamond with a flaw than a pebble without. (CONFUCIUS)

FLYING

If the Lord had meant us to fly, the airports wouldn't be so difficult to reach.

A landing is a controlled crash. (LEROY SCUDDER)

Orville Wright maintained the role of a modest and retiring inventor. Although, in later years, he received innumerable invitations, he rarely attended public functions, and steadfastly refused to speak on such occasions.

To a delegation of Dayton businessmen he explained: "Public speaking is not for me. I must remind you in the kingdom of the birds the parrot is the best talker—and the worst flier."

"There's one thing I don't understand," said the passenger to the pilot on the night flight. "How do you fly in the dark?"

"Well," answered the pilot, "there's a light on the left wing, a light on the right wing, and a light on the tail. All I have to do is to keep the plane between the lights." (SENIOR SCHOLASTIC)

FOLLOWER-SHIP (see LEADERSHIP)

Lord, let it not be that I follow You merely for the sake of following a leader, but let me accept You as Lord and Master of every step I take. (CHARLENE MYHRE)

FOOD (see DIET)

Mealtime is that period of the day when the kids sit down to continue eating.

When I was a kid my mother always offered me two choices at supper: Take it or leave it. (SAM LEVENSON)

The average person should cut his sugar intake by half: It's been found that sugar depresses the ability of the white blood cells to destroy bacteria by 50 percent. (U.D. REGISTER)

"My wife's cooking melts in your mouth," the young husband said. "She never thaws it long enough."

In keeping with the current terminology of ecology, housewives should no longer tell their famililes they're having leftovers for dinner but should say, "The meal has been recycled." (GRIT)

You are what you eat. For example, if you eat garlic you're apt to be a hermit. (FRANKLIN P. JONES)

I'm allergic to food. Every time I eat it breaks out in fat. (JENNIFER GREENE DUNCAN)

I want nothing to do with natural foods. At my age I need all the preservatives I can get. (GEORGE BURNS)

Americans have added a fourth meal—snacks—to their daily fare. Snacks take a big share of the family food money today—almost $2 billion was spent for snack foods in one recent year.(CAPPER'S WEEKLY)

I'm not saying my wife's a bad cook—but our garbage disposal developed an ulcer.

Middle age comes along a little sooner all the time; high cholesterol levels and arteriosclerosis, which once afflicted older people for the most part, now can be found in young adults. Young people have passed through the teenage time of eating horrible foods, when they did not want to be different by eating healthier foods. It was "kooky" to eat for nutrition. (LISA COSMAN)

We are what we eat. You can eat for happiness or sadness. Food is life, and people should have a balanced diet. . . . You can exercise for 1,000 years, and if you don't eat the right food it doesn't mean a thing. (CHARLES ATLAS)

Eat breakfast like a king; eat lunch like a prince; but eat dinner like a pauper. (O.F. GOBER)

Twenty cents out of every dollar's worth of supermarket items pays for the packages they come in. (NEWS ITEM)

I am opposed to refined, deficient, processed foods. Nowadays food is canned, bottled, vacuum-packaged, frozen, dried, dehydrated, smoked, bleached, irradiated, refined, precooked, preserved, sprayed, injected, dyed, waxed, processed, artificially flavored, conditioned, emulsified, synthesized, stabilized, pasteurized, tenderized, hydrolized, etc. Whole food is not. I don't like to eat packaged or canned foods that contain chemical additives; I try to avoid food that comes out of a factory. If you were put into a can to be eaten 12 months later, how would *you* taste? (YEHUDI MENUHIN)

Unless the underdeveloped lands learn to feed themselves, the world in this century faces more deaths by starvation than lives lost in all the combined wars of history. The stork continues to outproduce the plow. (TOM ANDERSON)

The minutes spent at the dinner table won't make you fat, but the seconds will.

A third of the food we eat keeps us alive. The other two-thirds keeps the doctors alive. (ORSON WELLES)

Never eat more than you can lift. (MISS PIGGY)

FOOLISHNESS

Mix a little foolishness with your serious plans; it's lovely to be silly at the right moment. (HORACE)

FOOLS

It is not wise to argue with a fool, because someone may come by and not be able to tell who is who. (BERNARD MELTZER)

Many a man complains he is being made a fool of, when he is only being exposed.

Let us be thankful for the fools. But for them the rest of us could not succeed. (MARK TWAIN)

No one is a fool always, everyone sometimes. It is said that the dullness of the fool is the whetstone of the wits; and that even the fool sometimes gives good counsel. (EUGENE BERTIN)

Nobody can make a fool out of a person if he isn't the right kind of material for the job. (CINCINNATI ENQUIRER)

There is a proverb from the Middle East which says: "A foolish man may be known by six things: Anger without cause, speech without profit, change without progress, inquiry without object, putting trust in a stranger, and mistaking foe for friend." (SUNSHINE)

FOOTBALL

My favorite play is the one where the player tosses the ball back to the official after scoring a touchdown. (BEAR BRYANT)

If anyone ever tells you nothing is impossible, ask him to dribble a football.

A football coach is a man smart enough to be able to get his team motivated for the game, and dumb enough to think that it is important. (EUGENE MCCARTHY)

FOOT IN MOUTH

I'm always putting my foot in my mouth. I even get my toothpicks from Dr. Scholl. (HERB TRUE)

FORCE

The more I study the world, the more I am convinced of the inability of brute force to create anything durable. (NAPOLEON I)

FOREIGN AID

Too often foreign aid is when the poor people of a rich nation send their money to the rich people of a poor nation. (BITS AND PIECES)

FORGETTING

If someone's guilty of despicable actions, especially toward me, I try to forget him. I used to follow a practice—somewhat contrived, I admit—to write the man's name on a piece of scrap paper, drop it into the lowest drawer of my desk, and say to myself: "That finishes the incident, and so far as I'm concerned, that fellow." The drawer becomes over the years a sort of private wastebasket for crumpled-up spite and discarded personalities. Besides, it seemed to be effective and helped me avoid harboring useless black feelings. (DWIGHT EISENHOWER)

FORGIVENESS (see RECONCILIATION)

Our God has a big eraser. (BILLY ZEOLI)

It's easier to get forgiven than to get permission.   (RALPH BUS)

Forgiveness from others is charity; from God, grace; from oneself, wisdom.

Friendship flourishes at the fountain of forgiveness. (WILLIAM A. WARD)

Forgiveness is better than revenge, for forgiveness is the sign of a gentle nature, but revenge is the sign of a savage nature.   (EPICTETUS)

If you are suffering from a bad man's injustice, forgive him lest there be two bad men.   (AUGUSTINE)

A Turkish soldier had beaten a Christian prisoner until he was only half-conscious, and while he kicked him he demanded, "What can your Christ do for you now?"The Christian quietly replied, "He can give me strength to forgive you."   (R. EARL ALLEN)

Forgiveness is our command. Judgment is not.   (C. NEIL STRAIT)

Forgiveness, like dimming our headlights, happens sooner when we take the initiative.

After a vigorous brotherly and sisterly disagreement, our three children retired only to be aroused at 2 o'clock by a terrific thunderstorm. Hearing an unusual noise upstairs, I called to find out what was going on. A little voice answered, "We are in the closet forgiving each other."
    (ROBERT TUTTLE)

Never does a man stand so tall as when he foregoes revenge, and dares to forgive an injury.   (J. HAROLD SMITH)

If you have a thing to pardon, pardon it quickly. Slow forgiveness is little better than no forgiveness.   (ARTHUR W. PINERO)

Forgiveness saves the expense of anger, the cost of hatred, the waste of spirits.   (MEGIDDO MESSAGE)

"You won't catch me getting ulcers," said a businessman. "For one thing, I just take things as they come. For another, I don't ever hold a grudge, not even against people who have done things to me that I'll never forgive."

We are most like beasts when we kill. We are most like men when we judge. We are most like God when we forgive.

A forgiveness ought to be like a cancelled note, torn in two and burned up, so that it never can be shown against the man. (HENRY W. BEECHER)

There's no point in burying a hatchet if you're going to put up a marker on the site. (SYDNEY HARRIS)

It is very easy to forgive others their mistakes; it takes more grit and gumption to forgive them for having witnessed your own.

(JESSAMYN WEST)

FORTUNE-TELLER

A congressman's wife sought the advice of a Washington fortune-teller. The fortune-teller prophesied, "Prepare yourself for widowhood. Your husband is about to die a violent death."

The wife sighed deeply and presented a question: "Will I be acquitted?" (GEORGE SHUFORD)

FRANKNESS

If you say what you think, don't expect to hear only what you like.

(MALCOLM FORBES)

We appreciate frankness from those who like us. Frankness from others is called insolence. (ANDRÉ MAUROIS)

FREEDOM (see LIBERTY)

Any nation that thinks more of its ease and comfort than its freedom will soon lose its freedom; and the ironical thing about it is that it will lose its ease and comfort too. (SOMERSET MAUGHAM)

Freedom decays as material society expands. (ANDRE DUMAS)

Free speech and free press are not based on the notion that everyone is going to tell the truth. From John Milton through Thomas Jefferson, and up to the present time, the right of free speech and free press is based upon the notion that if everyone is free to say and write what he pleases, then the truth has a better chance to emerge than if these processes were subject to some sort of external control, particularly control by government. (DEAN RUSK)

Let us give thanks that we live in a free country where a man can say what he thinks, if he isn't afraid of his wife, his neighbors, or his boss—and if he's sure it won't hurt his business. (CHANGING TIMES)

It is my earnest conviction that everyone should be in jail at least once in his life and that the imprisonment should be on suspicion rather than proof; it should last at least four months; it should seem hopeless; and preferably the prisoner should be sick half of the time. . . . Only by such imprisonment does he learn what real freedom is worth.

(GORDON S. SEAGRAVE)

Freedom is like a coin. It has the word privilege on one side and responsibility on the other. It does not have privilege on both sides. There are too many today who want everything involved in privilege but refuse to accept anything that approaches the sense of responsibility.

(JOSEPH SIZOO)

I have on my table a violin string. It is free. I twist one end of it and it responds. It is free. But it is not free to do what a violin string is supposed to do—to produce music. So I take it, fix it in my violin, and tighten it until it is taut. Only then is it free to be a violin string.

(RABINDRANATH TAGORE)

By the same token we are free when our lives are uncommitted, but not to be what we were intended to be. Real freedom is not freedom *from*, but freedom *for*.

(ROBERT W. YOUNG)

Both the U.S. and U.S.S.R. views of freedom look ever more unconvincing. One is based on power and privation, servitude to an all-powerful state; the other is based on affluence and self-indulgence, and an all-demanding ego.

(MALCOLM MUGGERIDGE)

Freedom is a mirage on the desert. If you reach the place it seemed to be, you will find it dry, because being free means that you are no longer needed or loved by others. It would be a death, a dusty taste in the mouth. Those who are completely free of any obligations or loyalties or responsibilities are the loneliest people on earth.

(JOSEPHINE LOWMAN)

"Born free" and "free as a bird" are common expressions—but wild animals and birds are not really free. They are confined by many laws of nature which resist them as surely as if they were caged. . . . Wild animals and birds do not go and come as they please but are controlled by environmental factors, habit, and by an invisible force which man calls instinct. When all these things are considered one must conclude that they are far from "free."

(GEORGE PURVIS)

We find freedom when we find God; we lose it when we lose Him.

(PAUL SCHERER)

FRIENDS

Life without friendship is like the sky without the sun.

(BIBLICAL RECORDER)

Friendship is one of the sweetest joys of life. Many might have failed beneath the bitterness of their trial had they not found a friend.

(CHARLES SPURGEON)

There are not many things in life so beautiful as true friendship, and there are not many things more uncommon. (MEGIDDO MESSAGE)

The greatest service one can perform is to be a friend to someone. Friendship is not only doing something for someone, but it is caring for someone, which is what every person needs. (C. NEIL STRAIT)

We can never replace a friend. When a man is fortunate enough to have several, he finds they are all different. No one has a double in friendship.

(SCHILLER)

Nothing does more to undermine the self than the absence of mutually supportive human relationships. [In business] we need competence, but also compassion. (H.B. WALKER)

Life is to be fortified by many friendships. To love and to be loved is the greatest happiness in existence. (SYDNEY SMITH)

One should keep his friendships in constant repair. (SAMUEL JOHNSON)

A real friend is a person who, when you've made a fool of yourself, lets you forget it. (BITS AND PIECES)

I don't want everyone to like me; I should think less of myself if some people did. (HENRY JAMES)

A friend in power is a friend lost. (HENRY ADAMS)

A friend that ain't in need is a friend indeed. (KIN HUBBARD)

I've already got more friends than I can use. (JACK BRADFORD)

Folks have to be friendly to live together in a small place—which the world is becoming. (FRANK A. CLARK)

Friendship is like Rome. It's not built in a day. (FRANKLIN P. JONES)

Close your eyes to the faults of others, and you open the doors of friendship. (WILLIAM A. WARD)

You can make more friends in two months by becoming interested in other people than you can in two years by trying to get other people interested in you. (DALE CARNEGIE)

A true friend is one in whom we have confidence and to whom we will listen. (K. ALVIN PITT)

Friendships should be nurtured, faithfully, lest they become fractured through neglect, or cease altogether. (C. NEIL STRAIT)

Use friendship as a drawing card, if you wish, but don't forget the deposits. (GRIT)

A friend is one to whom one may pour out all the contents of one's heart, chaff and grain together, knowing that the gentlest of hands will take and sift it, keep what is worth keeping, and with a breath of kindness, blow the rest away. (SUNSHINE)

The world is so empty if one thinks only of mountains, rivers, and cities; but to know someone here and there who thinks and feels with us, and who, though distant, is close to us in spirit, this makes the earth an inhabited garden. (GOETHE)

To enjoy a friend, I need more in common with him than hating the same people. (FRANK A. CLARK)

My best friend is the one who brings out the best in me. (HENRY FORD)

A friend is a person who does his knocking before he enters instead of after he leaves. (IRENE KEEPIN)

It's better to keep a friend from falling than to help him up. (ARNOLD GLASOW)

A true friend doesn't sympathize with your weakness—he helps summon your strength. (SURVEY BULLETIN)

A valuable friend is one who'll tell you what you should be told, even if it offends you. (FRANK A. CLARK)

A friend is one who warns you. (NEAR EAST PROVERB)

Friendship doubles our joy and divides our grief.

Iron sharpens iron, so one man sharpens the face of another. . . . Faithful are the wounds of a friend; profuse are the kisses of an enemy. (PROVERBS 27:17, 6, MLB)

Long ago I made up my mind to let my friends have their peculiarities. (DAVID GRAYSON)

Friendship will not stand the strain of very much good advice for very long.   (ROBERT LYND)

One of the best ways to lose a friend is to tell him something for his own good.

He who casts a friend aside like an old shoe is a heel without a soul.

Three men are my friends. He that loves me, he that hates me, he that is indifferent to me. Who loves me teaches me tenderness. Who hates me teaches me caution. Who is indifferent to me teaches me self-reliance.
                                                                  (PARIN)

Our friends show us what we can do; our enemies teach us what we must do.   (GOETHE)

Overheard in a refurbished tearoom in the Berkshires, one matron to another: We're trying to enlarge our circle of friends to include people we like.   (NEW YORKER)

I'm the kind of friend you can depend on. I'm always around when I need you.

There are many different kinds of friendships. They can run the gamut from fleeting social contacts in which a few pleasantries are exchanged to a complex, profound relationship in which each person gives deeply of him or herself. Friendships can be based on mutual fun, need for emotional support, warmth and love; mutual interests in sports, money, sexual conquests, intellectual pursuits and politics—as well as mutual hatred for a mutual enemy. (There are also sado-masochistic friendships which are based on upmanship and competition.) Most friendships, however, involve facets of all these characteristics and more—especially business, marital, parental, or professional friendships. To make and keep friends, it is important to realize that every friend has the freedom to end a friendship that is not healthy. Everyone needs to retain his individual identity and freedom in order to be proper friends, to others and to himself.   (THEODORE I. RUBIN)

Friendship is loyal. A real friend is loyal through thick and thin. He will stand by you in the hour of need. He will help you when you are down. He will celebrate with you when you are up. . . . Friendship is . . . patience with one's friend when he is right, patience with him even when he is wrong. . . . Friendship is rankless. One's true friends are totally without regard to station. . . . Friendship is helpful. Friendships form among people who strengthen one another.   (FRANKLIN OWEN)

FRUSTRATION

Maybe you're going around in circles because you're at the end of your rope.
(FRANKLIN P. JONES)

Life is a tender thing and is easily molested. There is always something that goes amiss. Vain vexations—vain sometimes, but always vexatious. The smallest and slightest impediments are the most piercing; and as little letters tire the eyes, so do little affairs most disturb us.
(MONTAIGNE)

Frustration is to be a lion,
Starved and captive. Then
The trap door opens, and
There's a Daniel in your den.
(RUTH SCHENLEY)

Frustration is the shirking of potentiality.
(JEANNE CAGNEY)

FUN (see PLEASURE)

Your mental health will be better if you have lots of fun outside of that office.
(WILLIAM MENNINGER)

Fun is like insurance—the older you get the more it costs.

I know of nothing more demeaning than the frantic pursuit of "fun." No people are more miserable than those who seek desperate escapes from the self, and none are more impoverished, psychologically, than those who plunge into the strenuous frivolity of night clubs, which I find a form of communal lunacy. The word "fun" comes from the medieval English "fon" meaning fool.
(LEO C. ROSTEN)

FUNERALS

The current price of funerals is enough to make you glad you're alive.
(EARL WILSON)

A funeral home is offering discount coupons for caskets, with a limit of one per customer.
(JEANNE ROBERTSON)

Where did our burial practices come from? . . . A brief look backward would seem to establish that there is no resemblance between the funeral practices of today and those of even 50 to 100 years ago. . . . On the contrary, the salient features of the contemporary American funeral (beautification of the corpse, metal casket and vault, banks of store-bought flowers, ubiquitous offices of the "funeral director") are all of very recent vintage in this country, and each has been methodically designed and tailored to extract maximum profit for the trade.

(JESSICA MITFORD)

FUTURE (see PREDICTIONS, PROPHECY)

We should all be concerned about the future because we will have to spend the rest of our lives there. (CHARLES KETTERING)

Every tomorrow has two handles; we can take hold by the handle of anxiety or by the handle of faith.

(SOUTHERN BAPTIST BROTHERHOOD JOURNAL)

Some people believe there is no time like the present, but the overwhelming majority believe there is no time like the future.

(CINCINNATI ENQUIRER)

Parents are not obligated to give their children a secure future, but they are obligated to give them a secure foundation on which to build their own futures. (SURVEY BULLETIN)

You can't have rosy thoughts about the future when your mind is full of blues about the past. (TIT-BITS)

Do not judge the future by the past. In the past may be wisdom, but in the future is life and the miracles of the living which know no end. The past has experiences, but the future has surprises. The past produces memory, but the future produces expectation and hope. . . . The past is closed, but the future is open. (BEN NATHAN)

God so mingles together adversity and prosperity that man cannot discover anything about his future (Ecclesiastes 7:14; cf. 8:7; 10:14). In view of this, Solomon recommended submission to God's sovereignty, enjoying the good times, and remembering in bad times that adversity has inscrutable purposes beyond finite human understanding (cf. 8:17).

(BIBLE KNOWLEDGE COMMENTARY)

There is a proverb, "As you have made your bed, so you must lie in it," which is simply a lie. If I have made my bed uncomfortable, I will make it again. (G.K. CHESTERTON)

Believing in fortune cookies leads to a crummy life.

The best thing about the future is that it comes only one day at a time.

(ABRAHAM LINCOLN)

Never be afraid to trust an unknown future to a known God.

(CORRIE TEN BOOM)

God wisely withholds from us the events of tomorrow. They would overwhelm us and add an extra burden to today. Thus, He wisely shows us a day at a time. Who could stand to see a whole week before it was lived? (C. NEIL STRAIT)

Things equal out pretty well. Our dreams seldom come true, but then neither do our nightmares. (C. KENNEDY)

It's a wonderful world. It may destroy itself but you'll be able to watch it all on TV. (BOB HOPE)

The final chapter of human history is solely God's decision, and even now He is everywhere active in grace or judgment. Never in all history have men spoken so much of end-time, yet been so shrouded in ignorance of God's impending doomsday. (CARL F.H. HENRY)

The future is that time when you'll wish you'd done what you aren't doing now.

GAMBLING

For those hooked on gambling, there's a new outfit you can phone. They'll give you odds they can cure you.

If the Lord never meant for us to gamble He'd never have created matrimony.

GARDENING

A garden is something most men turn over in their minds only.
(ANNA HERBERT)

In order to live off a garden, you practically have to live in it.
(KIN HUBBARD)

What a man needs in gardening is a cast-iron back, with a hinge in it. (CHARLES D. WARNER)

You can get quite a lot out of vegetable gardens if you carefully cultivate the owners. (KEN CRAFT)

Experience teaches that love of flowers and vegetables is not enough to make a man a good gardener. He must also hate weeds.
(BURTON HILLIS)

GAS, NATURAL

We're overlooking one of the biggest sources of natural gas in the country—politicians. (HERB TRUE)

GENERATION GAP (see TEENS)

Youth can measure in only one direction—from things as they are forward to their ideal of what things ought to be. They cannot measure backward, to things as they used to be, because they have not lived long enough, and they cannot measure laterally, to the condition of other societies on this earth, because they have not yet had the opportunity to know them well. Older people must add these two measurements. This is the core reason why the generation gap exists and why it will always exist. (ERIC SEVAREID)

This generation has been spoiled rotten. Parents have given kids so much in order to buy their love and respect that they've blown everything. But what's really bad is that they don't even realize there is a generation gap. The bridge can only be built with love that isn't bought. (MIKE COPE, A TEEN)

Two qualities—laughter and love—are vital to bridging the generation gap. . . . Too many of the young have forgotten how to laugh . . . and too many of their elders have forgotten how to love. (EDUCATION SUMMARY)

GENEROSITY (see GIVING)

If you are not generous with a meager income, you will never be generous with abundance. (HAROLD NYE)

The Holy Spirit is really the most determinative of all the factors in Christian giving . . . generosity [is] a matter of the heart and not the pocketbook. (FRED P. CORSON)

We're all generous, but with different things, like time, money, talent—criticism. (FRANK A. CLARK)

GENIUS

A genius is one who shoots at something no one else can see, and hits it.

Genius is an infinite capacity for taking life by the scruff of the neck. (CHRISTOPHER QUILL)

Genius is the ability to reduce the complicated to the simple. (C.W. CERAM)

Einstein was once asked how he worked. "I grope," was his reply.

Paderewski relates that a gushing listener once said to him, "Paderewski, you are truly a genius."

He answered, "Yes, madam, I am a genius; but before that I was for many years a drudge." (RICHARD BOWLES)

The hardest thing each generation has to do is to recognize the genius of its own day. We accept the work of artists of a previous generation, although their work was unacceptable at that time. (FRAYN UTLEY)

When a true genius appears in the world, you may know him by this sign, that the dunces are all in confederacy against him. (JONATHAN SWIFT)

A recent computer study shows that the human race produces "geniuses"—that is, minds and spirits that make significant contributions to the knowledge or culture of that age—at the rate of only 1 percent. It's obvious, then, that geniuses are lonely souls. That leaves 495,000 of every 500,000 of us a lot better off. (ALUMNI NEWS, U. OF ALABAMA)

GENTLEMAN

A real gentleman is a combination of gentle strength and strong gentleness. (GEORGE MONAGHAN)

GEORGE PRINCIPLE ("Let George do it.")

If only everyone else involved would do his share, then my not doing my share would have no significant effect on the outcome.

GERMS

Only kisses and money could be so full of germs and still be popular. (BERT BACHARACH)

GIVING (see GENEROSITY, PHILANTHROPIST, STEWARDSHIP, TITHING)

A man complained to his pastor, "It's getting to be just one continuous give, give, give."

Said the pastor, "You have just given one of the best descriptions of Christianity that I've ever heard." (LUCILLE GOODYEAR)

Preacher about to take offering: And now, brethren, let us all give in accordance with what we reported on Form 1040.

It is more blessed to give than to receive. And besides, you don't clutter up your attic. (FRANKLIN P. JONES)

When it comes to giving, some people stop at nothing.

If anyone is tight with the Lord, the Lord is tight with His blessings to that person. (T.J. BACH)

Money-giving is a good criterion of a person's mental health. Generous people are rarely mentally ill people. (KARL MENNINGER)

Appeal for funds: Sermon on the Amount. (DANA ROBBINS)

I have never met an unhappy giver. (GEORGE MATTHEW ADAMS)

Most people apportion their giving to their earnings. If the process were reversed and the Giver of all were to apportion our earnings according to our giving, some of us would be very poor. (WORLD VISION)

The Lord loveth a cheerful giver. He also accepteth from a grouch. (CHURCH BULLETIN)

Have you ever stopped to think that Christ never gave anyone money? The riches of the world were His for the taking, and His to give away, yet when the poor and the hungry came to Him, He didn't give them money, and He rarely gave them food; He gave them love and service and the greatest gift of all—Himself.

Some say, "I've given him the shirt off my back and now look what he has done to me," or "I've given him the best years of my life and look what I get in return." If we bestow a gift or a favor and expect a return for it, it is no gift but a trade. (GOOD READING)

The world is full of two kinds of people, the givers and the takers. The takers eat well—but the givers sleep well. (MODERN MATURITY)

We make a living by what we get; we make a life by what we give. (DUANE HULSE)

No person was ever honored for what he received. Honor has been the reward for what he gave. (CALVIN COOLIDGE)

An ungiving person does not live; he breathes, he eats, he sleeps, he gratifies his needs, but only exists until he has discovered the cleverly interwoven secret of life, giving of oneself. True giving is done without the slightest trace of expecting to receive. Is it only in giving that we ever receive? Perhaps in giving of oneself there is enough taken away to have room to receive. (ALICE R. PRATT)

It is not how many years we live, but what we do with them.
It is not what we receive, but what we give to others.

(EVANGELINE BOOTH)

GLAMOUR

Any girl can be glamorous; all you have to do is stand still and look
stupid.

(HEDY LAMARR)

GLOOM (see DESPAIR)

If you get gloomy, just take an hour off and sit and think how much
better this world is than hell. Of course, it won't cheer you up much if
you expect to go there.

(DON MARQUIS)

Telling a gloomy friend to start enjoying life is about as helpful as pointing out to a sick man that he ought to be well. The best medicine for
gloom is an active, outdoor day, followed by a fireside evening with good
friends.

(BURTON HILLIS)

GOALS (see AIMS)

To achieve happiness, we should make certain that we are never without
an important goal.

(EARL NIGHTINGALE)

Goals are not only absolutely necessary to motivate us. They are essential to really keep us alive.

(ROBERT H. SCHULLER)

We are not at our best perched at the summit; we are climbers, at our
best when the way is steep.

(JOHN W. GARDNER)

When you determine what you want, you have made the most important
decision in your life. You have to know what you want in order to attain
it.

(DOUGLAS LURTAN)

Always have a goal, whether it's becoming a company vice-president or
growing the best garden on the block, learning more about art, or upping
your bowling score. When you achieve one aim, set your sights on a new
one.

(GRIT)

The world makes way for the man who knows where he is going.

(RALPH W. EMERSON)

If you're not sure where you are going, you're liable to end up someplace
else.

(ROBERT F. MAGER)

The reason most people in business flounder is that they are goalless.

They have no personal goals at all, or their goals are undefined, too easy, or not worth the effort. (RICHARD CONARROE)

Many a person who started out to conquer the world in shining armor has ended up just getting along. The horse got tired, the armor rusty. The goal was removed and unsure. (ROBERT A. COOK)

GOD—AND PEOPLE

God is . . . a personal Father who cares, and not a God who merely wound up the world with a key and then went away to let it run by itself. God's grace is a certainty, even amid the turmoil of today's world.(SPIRIT)

To most of us it would be most convenient if God were a rascal.

Don't bother to give God instructions; just report for duty.
(CORRIE TEN BOOM)

God is a busy worker, but He loves help. (BASQUE PROVERB)

God is the only Guy I can talk to and not have to say, "You know what I mean?" He understands exactly what I mean.(ATHLETE IN FCA HUDDLE)

God often visits us, but most of the time we are not at home.
(JOSEPH ROUX)

It isn't easy to prove that there is a God. In fact, nowhere in the Bible does God attempt to prove His existence. But have you ever considered how much more difficult it is to disprove God's existence?
(C. NEIL STRAIT)

God is not greater if you reverence Him, but you are greater if you serve Him. (AUGUSTINE)

Is your God big enough? Is He big enough for your life, your problems, your needs, and your heartache? Or have you let them discourage you? . . . Our God is omnipotent. There can be no limit, boundary, or edge to His ability and His power. (PARIS REIDHEAD)

A pastor visited a family whose son had been killed in an automobile accident. He heard the mother rail out at him: "Where was your God when my boy was killed?"
He quietly said, "The same place He was when *His* Son was killed."
(ROGER LOVETTE)

Maybe the Lord lets some people get into trouble because that is the only time they ever think of Him. (NUGGETS)

You have laughed God out of your schools, out of your books, and out of your life, but you cannot laugh Him out of your death.(DAGOBERT RUNES)

If God had wanted us to have a permissive society, He would have given us the Ten Suggestions instead of the Ten Commandments.
(RABBI M.M. HERSHMAN)

Where God has put a period, do not change it to a question mark.
(T.J. BACH)

God wants us to be victors, not victims; to grow, not grovel; to soar, not sink; to overcome, not to be overwhelmed.   (WILLIAM A. WARD)

Let us recognize our inadequacy without Him—our invincibility in Him!

Don't try to defend what God does. What He does is right because He does it.   (HENRY JACOBSEN)

Is there any greater need today than that we get to grips with the living God, that we understand the discipline of God, that we learn the truth of God, that we accept the will of God, that we fulfill the purpose of God, that we know the resources of God, that we realize the power of God, and that we radiate the peace and love of God?   (TRAVERS V. JEFFERS)

God so loved mankind that He did not send a committee.
(PLAQUE IN YOUNGSTOWN, OHIO CHURCH)

What we usually pray to God is not that His will be done, but that He approve ours.   (HELGA BERGOLD GROSS)

When we ask God to do something *for* us, He generally wants to do something *in* us.

God did not write solo parts for very many of us. He expects us to be participants in the great symphony of life.   (DONALD TIPPETT)

The outward lives of God's people should be indicative of the possession of inner spiritual wealth.   (UNION SIGNAL)

One day a young man irritatedly slammed a door in Abraham Lincoln's face. Recovering himself, he said, "I am sorry, Mr. Lincoln. I am just upset today."
    Lincoln put a kindly hand on the man's shoulder and said, "Young man, why don't you stop fighting God on the inside?"
    What a student of human nature! Many times we fight God on the inside and turn to fight everyone on the outside. I have seen many a man

sign an armistice with Christ in his heart and live at peace with other people. (LOUIS H. EVANS)

Use everything as if it belongs to God. It does. You are His steward. (HOUSTON TIMES)

It was among the Parthians the custom that none were to give their children any meat in the morning before they saw the sweat on their faces. . . . You shall find this to be God's usual course: not to give His children the taste of His delights till they begin to sweat in seeking after them. (RICHARD BAXTER)

God gives us wheat, but we must bake the bread. He gives us cotton, but we must convert it into clothing. He gives us trees, but we must build our homes. He provides the raw materials and expects us to make the finished products with them. (O.A. BATTISTA)

As the sun creates your shadow, God creates your soul—but in each case it is you who determine the shape of it. (FRANK A. CLARK)

When we leave God out of our reckoning, difficulties will daunt us, temptations will triumph over us, sin will seduce us, self will sway us, the world will warp us, seeming impossibilities will irritate us, unbelief will undermine our faith, Christian work will worry us, fear will frighten us, and all things will wear a somber hue. But when God is recognized as the One who undertakes for us, then difficulties are opportunities to trust Him, temptations are the harbingers of victory, sin has no attraction, self is denied, unbelief is ignored, service is a delight, contentment sings in the heart, and all things are possible. (F.E. MARSH)

Our personal relationship with God must be right, or all else comes to naught. It is like trying to add a lot of ciphers, the sum of which is exactly nothing. (CHRISTIAN OBSERVER)

If I am not enjoying this place of maintained fellowship with the Father and with Jesus Christ, when did I depart therefrom? To that point let me return, whether it be but an hour ago or years ago, and there let me surrender at whatever cost, and do whatever God requires, however irksome it appears to be. (G. CAMPBELL MORGAN)

Muretus, a Christian scholar of the 16th century, became ill while on a trip. The doctors who were called in to treat him did not know him. He looked so much like an ordinary individual that they said, "Let's try an experiment on him, for he looks of no importance."

In the next room Muretus heard this remark, and he called to the doctors, "Call not any man cheap for whom Christ died." (CHURCH HERALD)

We cannot get away from God, though we can ignore Him. (JAMES CABOT)

Our problem today is that we are lovers of pleasure more than lovers of God. We seek pleasure as a key to happiness, whereas the only unalterable, lasting way to true happiness is through the pursuit of righteousness.   (JACK WYRTZEN)

It's more dangerous to trifle with God than to bare your chest to a blizzard, or play with a rattlesnake.   (WILBUR NELSON)

If God is kept *outside*, there's something wrong *inside.*

Contrary to our frequent assumptions, God does not exist to serve us. We exist to serve God. The universe was not put together to provide believers with a cosmic playpen. It was put together to help us discover Someone beyond ourselves.   (KENNETH L. WILSON)

God provides for us all but seems to favor the energetic.
                                                          (FRANK A. CLARK)

God gives us the nuts, but He does not crack them. (GERMAN PROVERB)

The greatest thing is, not that one shall be a scientist, important as that is; nor that one shall be a statesman, vastly important as that is; nor even that one shall be a theologian, immeasurably important as that is; but the greatest thing of all is for one human being to bring another to Christ Jesus, the Saviour.   (LYMAN BEECHER)

The hardest people to reach with the love of God are not the bad people. They know they are bad. They have no defense. The hardest ones to win for God are the self-righteous people.   (CHARLES L. ALLEN)

We should give God the same place in our hearts that He holds in the universe.

GOLF

Why don't I play? I have enough crises in my life without volunteering for 18 of them on my day off.

"Charlie plays a fair game of golf," said one player to another.
   "Yes," came the reply, "if you watch him."   (HERM ALBRIGHT)

Just because a fellow has a lot of irons in the fire doesn't mean he's successful—it may mean he's just given up golf in disgust. (GOLF DIGEST)

GOODNESS (see RIGHT AND WRONG)

On the whole, human beings want to be good, but not too good, and not quite all the time. (GEORGE ORWELL)

Goodness consists not in the outward things we *do*, but in the inward thing we are. To *be* is the great thing. (E.H. CHAPIN)

Goodness is something so simple: Always live for others, never to seek one's own advantage. (DAG HAMMARSKJÖLD)

The saintliest . . . has his foibles, and the most hardened of criminals is good to his mother. (FREDERICK NEFF)

Don't compare your goodness with that of other men; compare it with the goodness of the Man of Galilee. (MEGIDDO MESSAGE)

Most men are not as good as they pretend to be, or as bad as their enemies paint them. (MORRIS ABRAM)

GOSPEL (see CONVERSION)

I brought you what I received—something very important—that Christ died for our sins as the Bible said He would. He was buried, and He rose on the third day, as the Bible said He would.(1 CORINTHIANS 15:3-4, BECK)

Today there's a *verbiage* of the Gospel without the *power* of the Gospel. (DON HILLIS)

Man talks of the survival of the fittest, but the glory of the Gospel is that it transforms the unfit.

The Gospel is neither a discussion nor a debate. It is an announcement. (PAUL S. REES)

The world has many religions; it has but one Gospel. (GEORGE OWEN)

Some people want to hear, heed, and hoard the Gospel.(RICHARD SEUME)

GOSSIP (See RUMORS)

Gossip has never been put in the same bag as murder and assassination, but it is in the same family. Gossip assassinates a person's character. And when a character is ruined, a bit of possibility and hope are taken from a man, both of which are death to dreams and ambitions. (C. NEIL STRAIT)

A gossip is someone with a keen sense of rumor. (WALLY PHILLIPS)

Gossip is when you hear something you like about someone you don't.
(EARL WILSON)

Gossip is when you must hurry and tell someone before you find out it isn't true.

We cannot control the evil tongues of others; but a good life enables us to disregard them. (MARCUS PORCIUS CATO)

Life would be a perpetual flea hunt if a man were obliged to run down all the innuendos, inveracities, insinuations, and misrepresentations which are uttered against him. (HENRY W. BEECHER)

A gossip is someone who puts two and two together—even when they're not. Avoid gossip, lest you come to be regarded as its originator.
(DIONYSIUS CATO)

A gossip is a person who will never tell a lie if the truth will do as much damage. (OWENTON [KY.] NEWS HERALD)

Gossip is one of the so-called "little" sins that even Christians are often unable or unwilling to avoid. It is, to be sure, a common sin, but can it truly be called "little"? Gossip can destroy reputations, disrupt families, divide neighbors, and cause widespread heartbreak, and all to no purpose except the satisfaction that some find in passing on idle or malicious tales. (WILLIAM McELROY)

It seems a misnomer to call it idle gossip when it's always doing a job on somebody.

Gossips have been catalogued in three different types:
   1. Vest-button type—always popping off.
   2. Vacuum-cleaner type—always picking up dirt.
   3. Liniment type—always rubbing it in. (TABLE TALK)

The more interesting the gossip, the more likely it is to be untrue.

Gossip is always a personal confession of either malice or imbecility—shun it. (J.G. HOLLAND)

He who relates the faults of others to you will relate your faults to the other fellow. (GRIT)

When tempted to gossip, breathe through your nose. (T.N. TIEMEYER)

I would rather play with forked lightning, or take in my hands living wires with their fiery current, than speak a reckless word against any servant of Christ, or idly repeat the slanderous darts which thousands of Christians are hurling on others, to the hurt of their own souls and bodies. (A.B. SIMPSON)

Not everyone repeats gossip. Some improve it. (FRANKLIN P. JONES)

GOVERNMENT (see POLITICS)

Any man who thinks he is going to be happy and prosperous by letting the government take care of him should take a close look at the American Indian. (PERSONNEL JOURNAL)

Government is the art of trying to solve problems. Politics is the art of trying to attain power. The two meet sometimes, but not often.
(BILL MOYERS)

Man is superior to government and should remain master over it, not the other way around. (EZRA T. BENSON)

Nothing is easier than the expenditure of public money. It doesn't appear to belong to anyone. The temptation is overwhelming to bestow it on somebody. (CALVIN COOLIDGE)

Our government could stand a little more pruning and a little less grafting.

Trying to make things work in government is sometimes like trying to sew a button on a custard pie. (HYMAN G. RICKOVER)

Let's not say that Congress makes mistakes. Let's just say that it acts in haste and repeats at leisure. (LOS ANGELES TIMES)

There is no furniture more costly than a government bureau.
(ARNOLD H. GLASOW)

Just be glad you're not getting all the government you're paying for.
(WILL ROGERS)

When they call the roll in the Senate, the senators do not know whether to answer "present" or "not guilty." (THEODORE ROOSEVELT)

GRACE

I'm more aware of my need of grace. I'm afraid that I once wanted to arrive at the gate of heaven with no need of it because of my personal piety and perfection. I've given up on that. To be involved means failure, misunderstanding, and sin as well as victories and accomplishment.

Grace is not the enemy, but a friend for which I am grateful.(JAY KESLER)

Manifold simply means many folds. Manifold grace means that it is not just one blessing, but there are thousands to come, one after another. The joy you have multiplies the joys to come; the victory you have in Christ multiplies the coming conquests. (PAUL RADER)

GRADING PUPILS (see EDUCATION)
From the first day of school, there is a four-year range of mental maturity among the children, and the longer they go to school the wider the range becomes. (DWAIN ESTES)

GRAFFITI

On school chalkboard: A double negative is a no-no.

(HERM ALBRIGHT)

GRANDCHILDREN

Elephants and grandchildren never forget. (ANDY ROONEY)

Have you ever noticed that grandchildren do not carry pictures of their grandparents? (CHARLIE JARVIS)

GRANDPARENTS

Nothing makes a child as smart as having grandparents.

(FRANKLIN P. JONES)

My grandson recites the Gettysburg Address and he's only 9. Lincoln didn't say it until he was 50. (AL OKIN)

GRATITUDE (see THANKSGIVING)

Never expect gratitude. If it comes, you can be surprised and pleased. (ADRIAN SMITH)

A lady asked her physician, "Doctor, why am I seized with these restless longings for the glamorous and faraway?"
"My dear lady," he replied, "they are the usual symptoms of too much comfort in the home and too much ingratitude in the heart." (WALLACE FRIDY)

Gratitude to God makes even a temporal blessing a taste of heaven. (WILLIAM ROMAINE)

If gratitude is due from children to their earthly parents, how much more is the gratitude of the great family of men due to our Father in heaven? (HOSEA BALLOU)

He who forgets the language of gratitude can never be on speaking terms with happiness. (C. Neil Strait)

In ordinary life we hardly realize that we receive a great deal more than we give, and that it is only with gratitude that life becomes rich. It is very easy to overestimate the importance of our own achievements in comparison with what we owe others. (Dietrich Bonhoeffer)

Gratitude is a lively expectation of favors yet to come. (Ambrose Bierce)

An interesting phenomenon in children is that gratitude or thankfulness comes relatively late in their young lives. They almost have to be taught it; if not, they are apt to grow up thinking that the world owes them a living. (Fulton J. Sheen)

GREATNESS

The trouble is—before you can be a "former great" you have to be a "great." (Charlie Brown)

We are both great men, but I have succeeded better in keeping it a profound secret than he has. (Bill Nye)

One of the marks of true greatness is the ability to develop greatness in others. (J.C. Macaulay)

There is a great person who makes every person feel small. But the real great person is the person who makes every person feel great. (G.K. Chesterton)

Great men have but a few hours to be "great." Like the rest of us they must dress, bathe, and eat. And, being human, they must make visits to the dentist, doctor, and barber and have conferences with their wives about domestic matters. What makes men great is their ability to decide what is important, and then focus their attention on that. (Nylic Review)

Great souls have wills; feeble ones have only wishes. (Chinese proverb)

The first test of a truly great man is his humility. Really great men have a curious feeling that the greatness is not in them but through them. And they see something divine in every other man and are endlessly, incredibly merciful. (John Ruskin)

Greatness lies not in being strong, but in the right use of strength. (Bits and Pieces)

The really great people are very simple people. (Harvey Firestone, Jr.)

Sometime in your life you will meet a truly great man who could not care less for money or fame. Then you will know how poor you really are.

GREED (see SELFISHNESS)

Greed has three facets: love of things, love of fame, and love of pleasure; and these can be attacked directly with frugality, anonymity, and moderation. Reduction of greed will be translated into stepped-up vitality, diminished self-centeredness, and a clearer awareness of our real identity. For a permanent commitment to working with the tools of the spiritual life provides a disciplined basis for liberation from greed's tentacles.

(PAUL MARTIN)

One thing you can say for greed: It's responsible for some imaginative rationalizations.

GRIEF (see PAIN, SADNESS, SORROW)

Everyone can master a grief but he that has it. (WILLIAM SHAKESPEARE)

There is no grief which time does not lessen and soften. (CICERO)

The more grief inflicted upon you, the better fitted you are to appreciate joy. More often than not the so-called negatives are assets. There cannot be a front without a back, an up without a down, a cold without heat, a love without hate. (CADLE CALL)

It feels like being mildly drunk, or concussed. There is a sort of invisible blanket between the world and me. I find it hard to take in what anyone says. . . . Perhaps the bereaved ought to be isolated in special settlements like lepers. (C.S. LEWIS)

How one handles his grief is a personal matter. Let the one who has suffered the loss take the lead. If he feels like talking, encourage him to talk. If he prefers to sit in silence, don't intrude on his silence. Friends should call, bring food, offer to run errands, and do what needs to be done. A hug, a squeeze of the hand, a look which says, "I'm here, if you need me," conveys more than a thousand words. (ABIGAIL VAN BUREN)

GRIEVANCES (see COMPLAINING)

Most grievances are the result of many trifling annoyances compounded over a period of time. . . . Stop them, by intelligent complaint, before they take your mind off your work. (POOLE BROTHERS HANDBOOK)

GROUCHES

Grouches are nearly always pinheads, small men who have never made any effort to improve their mental capacity. (THOMAS EDISON)

GROWING

People, like trees, must grow or die. There's no standing still. A tree dies when its roots become blocked. A human being becomes mentally and spiritually, and eventually physically, dead when the circumstances of his life keep him from achieving. Psychologists and sociologists spend their lives trying to patch up individuals and institutions that have stopped growing. (JOSEPH SHORE)

GROWTH VS. LONELINESS

Men feel lonely when they do not do the one thing they ought to do. It is only when we fully exercise our capacities—when we grow—that we have roots in the world and feel at home in it. (ERIC HOFFER)

GRUDGES

The heaviest load any man carries on his back is a pack of grudges. (HIGHWAYS OF HAPPINESS)

GUARANTEE

A guarantee is what tells you how long a product will last until you need a new one. (HERB TRUE)

HABITS

Everybody should have a few bad habits so he'll have something he can give up if his health fails. (FRANKLIN P. JONES)

The unfortunate thing about this world is that good habits are so much easier to give up than bad ones. (SOMERSET MAUGHAM)

Habits are about the only servants that will work for you for nothing. Just get them established and they will operate even though you are going around in a trance. (FREDERIC WHITAKER)

Habits are like cork or lead. They tend to keep you up or to hold you down. (R & R MAGAZINE)

The chains of habit are too weak to be felt until they are too strong to be broken. (SOUTHERN BAPTIST BROTHERHOOD JOURNAL)

Habits, like fishhooks, are lots easier to get caught than uncaught. (FRANK A. CLARK)

Man's most deadly enemy is not cancer or heart disease but habit—all the routines of thinking, feeling, and doing that enable humans to get through life without living it. (LION)

The best way to break a bad habit is to drop it. (D.S. YODER)

Nothing so needs reforming as other people's habits.   (MARK TWAIN)

HAIR (see BALDNESS)

Hair is as unreliable a guide to character as it is to sex.
(ALEC DOUGLAS HOME)

Hair is a constant problem with men and women. With women it's the tint and with men it's the t'aint.   (HERM ALBRIGHT)

Don't worry about your hair falling out. Consider what would happen if it ached first and had to be pulled out like teeth.   (BARBERSHOP SIGN)

One of the nicest things about being bald is that when company comes all you have to do is straighten your tie.

HALF-TRUTHS (see LYING)

Beware of the half-truth. You may have gotten hold of the wrong half.
(SEYMOUR ESSROG)

HALITOSIS

No one blows chances quite like a person with halitosis. (BERT KRUSE)

HANDICAPS

Every single one of us is handicapped—physically, mentally, socially, and spiritually—to some degree; and although we seldom think about it, the person without faith has a far greater handicap than the person without feet.   (FRANK K. ELLIS)

If you fashion a crutch for someone, he may use it all his life. If you show him how to walk, crippled as he may be, he will learn to overcome his handicap. Many parents have forever crippled their children by an oversupply of "crutches."   (FAITH BALDWIN)

A good example of a man who turned a handicap into a blessing is Arturo Toscanini. He owed his success—or at least his chance at success—to the fact that he was very nearsighted. How could that possibly help a musician? Well, at 19, he was playing cello in an orchestra. Since he couldn't see the music on the stand, he had to memorize it. One day the orchestra leader became ill and young Toscanini was the only member of the orchestra who knew the score. So he conducted it without a score and the audience gave him a good hand for it—and audiences kept on doing it. If he hadn't been nearsighted, he might have continued playing cello in small European orchestras instead of becoming one of the greatest orchestra conductors who ever lived.
(IN A NUTSHELL)

HANDS

Learn to use your hands as well as your head. I am not belittling education. But the person educated entirely through books is only half educated. There is a kind of practical knowledge and good sense which can flow into the brain only through the use of the hands. (WILLIAM KNUDSEN)

HAPPINESS (see JOY)

Wise men and women in every major culture have maintained that the secret of happiness is not in getting more but in wanting less.

(PHILIP SLATER)

If happiness truly consisted in physical ease and freedom from care, then the happiest individual would be neither a man nor a woman; it would be, I think, an American cow. (WILLIAM LYON PHELPS)

Happiness is often the result of being too busy to be miserable.

Happiness, at best, is an illusory goal. It is not a destination; it is a manner of traveling. Happiness is not an end in itself. It is a by-product of working, playing, loving, and living. (HAIM GINOTT)

It's pretty hard to tell what does bring happiness; poverty and wealth have both failed. (KIN HUBBARD)

The happiest people are rarely the richest, or the most beautiful, or even the most talented. Happy people do not depend on excitement and "fun" supplied by externals. They enjoy the fundamental, often very simple, things of life. They waste no time thinking other pastures are greener; they do not yearn for yesterday or tomorrow. They savor the moment, glad to be alive, enjoying their work, their families, the good things around them. They are adaptable; they can bend with the wind, adjust to the changes in their times, enjoy the contests of life, and feel themselves in harmony with the world. Their eyes are turned outward; they are aware, compassionate. They have the capacity to love. (JANE CANFIELD)

Happiness comes not from having much to live on but having much to live for.

Much happiness is overlooked simply because it doesn't cost anything.

(PRISM)

We would be happier with what we have if we weren't so unhappy about what we don't have. (FRANK A. CLARK)

To be happy, add not to your possessions but subtract from your desires.

(SENECA)

Happiness? It is an illusion to think that more comfort means more happiness. Happiness comes of the capacity to feel deeply, to enjoy simply, to think freely, to risk life, to be needed.   (STORM JAMESON)

Just think how happy you'd be if you lost everything you have right now—and then got it back again.

The grand essentials to happiness in this life are something to do, someone to love, and something to hope for.   (JOSEPH ADDISON)

If one only asked to be happy, this could be easily accomplished; but we wish to be happier than other people, and this is always difficult, for we believe others to be happier than they are.   (MONTESQUIEU)

If we'd only stop trying to be happy, we could have a pretty good time.
     (EDITH WHARTON)

Happiness is doing—not having.

People will be happy in about the same degree that they are helpful.

Happiness makes up in height for what it lacks in length.(ROBERT FROST)

One is never as unhappy as one thinks, nor as happy as one hopes.
     (FRANCOIS DE LA ROCHEFOUCAULD)

Domestic happiness depends upon the ability to overlook.(ROY L. SMITH)

The happy people are those who are producing something; the bored people are those who are consuming much and producing nothing.
     (W.R. INGE)

Happiness lies in our destiny like a cloudless sky before the storms of tomorrow destroy the dreams of yesterday and last week!
     (CHARLIE BROWN)

If you don't have a little bit of heartache, how do you know when you're happy?   (JANE POWELL)

The search for happiness is one of the chief sources of unhappiness.
     (ALABAMA BAPTIST)

We cannot twist the knob to the happiness channel. Happiness is strenuously earned.   (SEMON KNUDSEN)

Those who bring sunshine to the lives of others cannot keep it from themselves.   (JAMES BARRIE)

If you stop to count the people who are fundamentally and consistently happy, I suspect you will recognize that they have two characteristics in common: They work hard at tasks that have meaning for them, and they are essentially kind in their dealings with other people. (JOHN HOWARD)

There are five things anyone can do to increase his happiness. The first is to avoid fatigue so far as possible, particularly nervous fatigue. Next . . . "avoid inflammation of the ambition"—in other words . . . content ourselves with less and get more out of what we have instead of striving vainly for something beyond our powers. Third, we should avoid "chronic dilation of conscience," and refrain from making mountains out of molehills Also, we should try for the fourth point, to avoid "prolonged infancy"- -grow up mentally and emotionally as well as physically. . . . And, finally, we should try to avoid perfectionism and adjust ourselves to the imperfections we find in every living thing.   (CHARLES ROTH)

Some cause happiness wherever they go. Some, whenever they go.
(SPOTLIGHT)

Recipe for happiness: Take equal parts of faith and courage, mix well with a sense of humor, sprinkle with a few tears, and add a helping of kindness for others. Bake in a good-natured oven and dust with laughter. Scrape away any self-indulgence that is apparent and serve with generous helpings.   (OHIO STATE GRANGE MONTHLY)

Be happy if you can, but do not despise those who are otherwise, for you do not know their troubles.   (JACOB BRAUDE)

The only true happiness comes from squandering ourselves for a purpose.   (CONSTRUCTION DIGEST)

Now that I know Christ, I'm happier when I'm sad than I was before when I was glad.   (JOHN C. WHEELER)

Happiness is to know that God loves you.

Happiness is contagious. Be a carrier!   (ROBERT ORBEN)

HARDSHIPS (see TROUBLES)

Take a real man. . . . Cripple him and you have a Sir Walter Raleigh. Bury him in the snows of Valley Forge and you have a Washington. Have him born in abject poverty and you have a Lincoln. Throw every obstacle in his path and you have a Booker T. Washington. Load him with bitter racial prejudice and you have a Disraeli. Stab him with rheumatic pains until for years he cannot sleep without drugs and you have a Steinmetz.

Make him cellist in an obscure orchestra and you have a Toscanini. Real men accept hardship as a challenge! (GOOD READING)

HATE

Hatred is self-punishment. (HOSEA BALLOU)

One of the most expensive luxuries one can possess is to hate somebody. A deep-seated grudge in one's life eats away at his peace of mind like a deadly cancer destroying a vital organ of life. (E.T. WAYLAND)

There are few things as pathetic and terrible to behold as the person who has harbored a grudge, or hatred, over the years.(DAVID JOHNSON)

Life is too short for hate—and not long enough for love.
(GEORGE PEPPARD)

I will not permit any man to narrow and degrade my soul by making me hate him. (BOOKER T. WASHINGTON)

Nearly all cases of suicide and murder are due to enormous self-hate. This self-hate is often activated by hurt pride. In suicide, the hate is usually directed inward (a desire to annihilate oneself). In murder, it is directed outward—toward someone on whom one projects a hatred of oneself. People who are severely depressed may commit suicide to rid themselves of themselves. Hysterical people may do it to get even with a supposed wrongdoer ("Then he will be sorry"). A paranoid person may strike out and kill the person felt as his oppressor, who really is the symbol of his own inner oppression and self-contempt.(THEODORE RUBIN)

I remember that when Christian teachers told me long ago that I must hate a bad man's actions but not the man, I used to think this a silly, straw-splitting distinction: how could you hate what a man did and not hate the man? But years later it occurred to me that there was one man to whom I had been doing this all my life—namely myself.(C.S. LEWIS)

It is impossible to adore God and to abhor one of His children at the same time.

When Leonardo da Vinci was working on his wonderful painting of "The Last Supper," he painted the face of a man he hated as Judas. But when he came to paint the face of Jesus he tried again and again and failed. It was only when he painted out the face of the man he hated and put another in its place that he had a clear picture of the Lord's countenance. His hatred, you see, had created a "dead spot" between him and the work he was doing, and this had to be put right before even his marvelous ability could produce the finished work. (KENNETH BUDD)

We cannot hate a person whom we know and understand.

(RAMESH CHANDRA SHAH)

HEALTH

A man too busy to take care of his health is like a mechanic too busy to take care of his tools. (SPANISH PROVERB)

The old story that it would take a mile walk to use up the calories supplied by one peanut is not the whole story. Exercise is important not so much for the calories it burns but for its effect in avoiding a high cholesterol level and arteriosclerosis, which is coming to be recognized as the main danger of obesity. . . . One who just sits and waits for death to come along will not have so long to wait. We don't wear out; we rust out. (THEODORE KLUMPP)

We have one of the unhealthiest countries in the world because of our abuse of our prosperity. We are overeating and pampering ourselves. The "life of Riley" leads to a lot of early coronary heart disease and high blood pressure. (PAUL DUDLEY WHITE)

I'm in great shape. Every artery is as hard as a rock. (ALAN ADDY)

Those of us who are the best fed and who can afford the many luxuries of life are those who most frequently ask doctors for a tonic. . . . There is an even greater tonic available that costs nothing. The tonic is an agreeable attitude, plus enthusiasm for whatever one may be doing. If you give a cheerful unqualified yes when you are asked to do something you will provide yourself with a tonic to your internal organs and increase your sense of well-being. The cheerful, pleasant, cooperative person is nice to have around. The chronically critical person is frequently the chronically tired person. (HARRY JOHNSON)

Actually, emotional upsets are good for us. All progress, personal or of the human race, comes from emotional upset. A completely stable person gets nowhere. (DONALD ROBINSON)

Everett Hale summarized the reason some people never achieve mental health in these timely words: "We should never attempt to bear more than one kind of trouble at once. Some people bear all three kinds—all they *have had*, all they *have now*, and all they *expect to have*." For some strange reason we always expect the worst. (KENNETH CARLSON)

Most breakdowns are caused by brooding and boredom rather than overwork. Doctors claim people who work hard, or even overwork, have less time to worry, to become afraid, anxious, and frustrated than those with time on their hands. (JOHN McCARTHY)

The four main requirements of good mental health as outlined by a staff member of an internationally known psychiatric hospital are: (1) A variety of sources of satisfaction in daily life. (2) Ability to demonstrate a flexibility under stress. (3) Understanding and acceptance of one's own strengths and weaknesses. (4) Understanding of others as individuals.

(KENTUCKY SCHOOL JOURNAL)

People take pills because they're lazy. They don't want to exercise or diet. They want to obtain good health by medication. (M.M. HOFFMAN)

A man's health can be judged by which he takes two at a time—pills or stairs.   (JOAN WELSH)

HEARING (see LISTENING)

A fellow told me the other day he is so poor his hearing aid is on a party line.   (JOHN GRAHAM)

HEARTS

In a normal person, the heart beats 70 times a minute, 100,000 times a day, 40 million times a year! During a single day, a ventricle pumps about 11,000 quarts, or 265 million quarts in a lifetime. If an elevator could be harnessed to this marvelous engine, you could ride from the ground floor to the fifth floor of a building in about an hour. No wonder Leonardo called it a "marvelous instrument."   (JULIUS MILLER)

The average heart specialist can usually check the condition of his patient's heart simply by sending him a bill.   (O.A. BATTISTA)

Calisthenics can build up the body. Courses of study can train the mind. But the real champion is the person whose heart can be educated.

(FRED RUSSELL)

There never was any heart truly great and generous, that was not also tender and compassionate.   (ROBERT FROST)

If he ate his heart out, it wouldn't be much of a meal. (FRANKLIN P. JONES)

A tourist was once staying at an inn in a valley in northern Italy where the floor was dirty. He thought he should advise the landlady to scrub it, when he perceived that it was made of mud and the more she would scrub it the worse it would become. So it is with our hearts; its corrupt nature will admit of no improvement; it must be made ever anew.

(WAR CRY)

HEAT

It's so hot in Texas that I saw a bird pulling a worm out of the ground—with a pot holder.

It's so hot down there that they're boiling the water—to cool it off.

The average temperature in our apartment is 70 degrees—50 in the winter and 90 in the summer.

HEAVEN (see ETERNITY)

The world has forgotten, in its concern with Left and Right, that there is an Above and Below. (GLEN DRAKE)

Our annual church meeting was rather like heaven. Many we expected to see there were absent. (KELLY FORDYCE)

He who is on the road to heaven will not be content to go there alone.

The entrance fee into the kingdom of heaven is nothing; the annual subscription is everything. (HENRY DRUMMOND)

No one gets to heaven because he is poor, or to hell because he is rich. (HENRY JACOBSEN)

It is strange how, when we imagine heaven, we think of it as somehow shadowy. We color it with the tints of moonlight, sleep, and the faces of the dead. But there are no shades there; there is the substance of joy, and the vitality of action. When we are there, and look back on earthly life, we shall not see it as a vigorous battlefield from which we have gracefully retired; we shall view it as an insubstantial dream, from which we have happily awoken. (AUSTIN FARRER)

Though Christians believe in heaven, sometimes they act as though going there were a calamity. (HENRY OR MARION JACOBSEN)

I'm not going to heaven because I've preached to great crowds of people. I'm going to heaven because Christ died on that cross. None of us is going to heaven because he's good. And we're not going to heaven because we've worked. We're not going to heaven because we pray and accept Christ. We're going to heaven because of what He did on the Cross. All I have to do is receive Him. And it's so easy to receive Christ that millions stumble over its sheer simplicity. (BILLY GRAHAM)

HECKLERS

Answering a heckler: Sir, our time is flying and you're trying to hijack it.

Answering an interrupter: Tell me, would you care to step outside and say that? Good. I'll stay here and finish my talk.

Answering a harasser: Sir, I'd like to give you a going-away present, but you've got to do your part. (ROBERT ORBEN)

HELL

The safest road to hell is the gradual one—the gentle slope, soft underfoot, without sudden turnings, without milestones, without signposts.
(C.S. LEWIS)

HELPING (see SERVICE)

Do you recall when Edmund Hillary and his native guide, Tenzing, made their historic climb of Mt. Everest? Coming down from the peak, Hillary suddenly lost his footing. Tenzing held the line taut and kept them both from falling by digging his ax into the ice. Later Tenzing refused any special credit for saving Hillary's life; he considered it a routine part of the job. As he put it: "Mountain climbers always help each other." Should the rest of us be any different? (BITS AND PIECES)

The most attractive people in the world are the ones who are interested in others—turned outward in cheerfulness, kindness, appreciation, instead of turned inward to be constantly centered in themselves.
(PAT BOONE)

We are not primarily put on this earth to see through one another, but to see one another through. (PETER DeVRIES)

He who sees a need and waits to be asked for help is as unkind as if he had refused it. (DANTE)

Sometimes nothing gives you a helping hand like receiving a kick in the pants.

Before you can help make the world right, you must be made right within. (JOHN MILLER)

Some Mennonites consider it wrong to take pay for helping another human being. Instead they say, "I will charge thee nothing but the promise that thou wilt help the next man thou findest in trouble."

HEREDITY (see PARENTS)

Did you ever notice how your belief in heredity is reinforced when one of your children does something outstanding?

HEROES AND COWARDS

We can't all be heroes because someone has to sit on the curb and clap as they go by. (WILL ROGERS)

The true hero is the man who conquers himself.

Great occasions do not make heroes or cowards; they simply unveil them to the eyes of man. Silently and imperceptibly, as we wake or sleep, we grow strong or we grow weak, and at last some crisis shows us what we have become. (GUIDEPOSTS)

HESITATION (see WAITING)

He who hesitates is sometimes saved. (JAMES THURBER)

He who hesitates is prompted, or nudged. (FRANKLIN P. JONES)

HISTORY (see PAST)

When you read history it is quite astonishing to discover that there never was a day when men thought times were really good. Every generation in history has been haunted by the feeling of crisis. (HAROLD WALKER)

The lesson of history tells us that no state or government devised by man can flourish forever. (BILLY GRAHAM)

To understand one's self, we must study man's past. To understand the past, one must examine the relationship between systems of communication, transportation, philosophy, political structure, religion, science, climate and terrain, and on and on. Life is interwoven, not compartmentalized. (HARRY KERSHEN)

Man writes histories; goodness is silent. History is, indeed, little more than the register of the crimes, follies, and misfortunes of mankind. (EDWARD GIBBON)

Anybody who thinks a poor student will never change the course of history never marked examination papers. (FRANKLIN P. JONES)

People are fond of saying that "the past is dead," but it is actually the future that is dead—and we make it come alive only by applying what we have learned from the living past to the present. (SYDNEY HARRIS)

History is the patter of silken slippers descending the stairs, and the thunder of hobnail boots moving up. (VOLTAIRE)

We Americans are the best informed people on earth as to the events of the last 24 hours; we are not the best informed as to the events of the last 60 centuries. (WILL & ARIEL DURANT)

History professor: For what was Louis XIV chiefly responsible?
 Eager beaver in front row: Louis XV, sir. (AMERICAN OPINION)

History is being made faster than we can afford it. (ARNOLD GLASOW)

When Charles A. Beard, the famous historian, was asked if he could summarize the lessons of history in a single volume, he said he could do it in four sentences:
1. Whom the gods would destroy, they first make mad with power.
2. The mills of the gods grind slowly, but they grind exceedingly small.
3. The bee fertilizes the flower it robs.
4. When it is dark enough, you can see the stars. (IMPERIAL MAGAZINE)

I think of myself as a historian more than a statesman. As a historian, you have to be conscious of the fact that every civilization that has ever existed has ultimately failed. History is a tale of efforts that failed, of aspirations that weren't realized, of wishes that were fulfilled and then turned out to be different from what was expected. So, as a historian, one has to live with a sense of the inevitability of tragedy. As a statesman, one has to act on the assumption that problems can be solved. (HENRY KISSINGER)

A bird's-eye view of the cycle of men and nations:
1. From bondage to spiritual faith.
2. From spiritual faith to great courage.
3. From courage to liberty.
4. From liberty to abundance.
5. From abundance to selfishness.
6. From selfishness to complacency.
7. From complacency to apathy.
8. From apathy to dependency.
9. From dependency back to bondage.

In his *Decline and Fall of the Roman Empire,* which he wrote in 1788, Edward Gibbon defined five basic reasons why that civilization withered and died. One wonders whether historians centuries from now will find a deadly parallel between the U.S. and Imperial Rome. Here are the flaws that Gibbon detected:
    1. An undermining of the dignity and sanctity of the home, which is the basis for human society.
    2. Higher and higher taxes, and spending public money for free bread and circuses for the populace.
    3. A mad craze for pleasure, with pastimes becoming every year more exciting, brutal, and immoral.

4. Building great armaments, although the real enemy was within—the decay of individual responsibility.

5. Decay of religion—faith fading into mere form, losing touch with life and losing power to guide the people.

HOBBIES

Dad says he has a new hobby. He collects debts. (NONNEE COAN)

It is a sad thing when a man has only a vocation, with no avocation whatsoever. An avocation can very well save the situation if we are condemned to the monotonous work which may be the by-product of some large productive process. Then our sense of creativity should be derived from our avocation or hobby. If a man can have a hobby, he can retain vigor and vitality. (HAROLD OCKENGA)

When a habit begins to cost money, it is called a hobby. (SUPERVISION)

A child who collects manhole covers will undoubtedly have a better physique than if he collects coins. (JACK KRAUS)

Everybody should have a hobby even if it's only avoiding people who want to talk about theirs. (FRANKLIN P. JONES)

HOLIDAY

A holiday is a day off generally followed by an off day.

HOLINESS (see RIGHTEOUSNESS)

A passion for personal holiness will make you a lot easier to get along with. (ROBERT A. COOK)

You can't get holy in a hurry—but you start taking steps in that direction right away. Beg God, "Put within me some holy motivation."
(MALCOLM CRONK)

HOME

I recently heard the story of a young woman who said to a real estate agent: "Why do I need a home? I was born in a hospital, educated in a college, engaged in a car, married in a hotel. I live out of a delicatessen and paper bags. I spend my mornings on the golf course, my afternoons at the bridge table, and my evenings at the movies. When I die, I'm going to be buried at the undertaker's. All I need is a garage." (JACK SPIRO)

The fellow that owns his own home is always just coming out of a hardware store. (KIN HUBBARD)

Home is where life makes up its mind. (HAZEN WERNER)

A child is a mirror. A mirror that reflects happiness, or the lack of it, in the home. To improve the image that is seen in this mirror, parents must shoulder their God-given responsibilities. Their job cannot be shifted to the church, the school, or social agencies; these organizations can assist but they cannot, and should not, supplant the work of the parents. Neither school nor counseling agency should usurp the parents' place as family head, but both organizations can work together to help family problems. (RICHARD CURTIS)

When homes have nothing to give in the early years of a child's life, it complicates the responsibilities of all other agencies. . . . Fortunate is the boy or girl who finds motivation for living in the home—where it should be. (EMMA HULBURY)

Taxes are higher. Mortgages are higher. Fuel prices are higher. Verily, in these times a man's home is his hassle. (CHANGING TIMES)

He is the happiest, be he king or peasant, who finds peace in his home. (GOETHE)

Home is the place where dad is free to do anything he pleases, because no one will pay the slightest attention to him anyway.(ARKANSAS BAPTIST)

The working girl complained to her landlord who was miserly and did not provide enough heat: "My apartment is so cold that every time I open the door the light goes on."

Robert Frost defined a home as a place where, when you come there, they have to take you in. Many people are beginning to doubt that. For too many Americans, home has become a place where the family may convene on major holidays, with just about the same kind of conviviality and the same masks to hide real feelings as one sees at business and professional conventions. (DUSTY SKLAR)

The perfect home is a drawn curtain against mistrust and discontent. It is a magnet which draws those whose duties have taken them abroad back to the heart of contentment and rest.

Home is a field where there may be grown character, nobility, and song, or where by neglect may grow the thorn tree of strife and the bramble bush of discontent.

Home is what you make it. Home is heaven or hell. It is a residence for angels or a dungeon filled with demons. (OLIVER WILSON)

The best type of home is where everything wears out but your nerves. (GRIT)

HOMETOWNS

Hometowns seem to be loved most by the people who *used* to live in them. (WILLIAM D. TAMMEUS)

HOMEWORK

On doing one's homework: God will never, in answer to prayer, help you remember something which you did not first forget. (ROBERT A. COOK)

Homework is what gives a youngster something to do while he's watching television.

HONESTY (see LEVELING WITH OTHERS)

To make your children capable of honesty is the beginning of education. (JOHN RUSKIN)

Honesty pays, but it don't seem to pay enough to suit some people. (KIN HUBBARD)

Parents shouldn't lie to their children—not even when they think it's for their own good. Even a little lie is dangerous; it deteriorates the conscience. And the importance of conscience is eternal, like love. (PABLO CASALS)

No matter how brilliant a man may be, he will never engender confidence in his subordinates and associates if he lacks simple honesty and moral courage. (J. LAWTON COLLINS)

I want you guys to tell me candidly what's wrong with our operation— even if it means losing your job. (SAM GOLDWYN)

How desperately difficult it is to be honest with oneself. It is much easier to be honest with other people. (EDWARD BENSON)

A man can build a staunch reputation for honesty by admitting he was in error, especially when he gets caught at it. (ROBERT RUARK)

Most people are so honest that they can't be induced to welsh on a contract without first consulting their lawyer. (COUNSELOR)

HONEYMOONS

I didn't get no respect even on my wedding night. My wife told me we were seeing too much of each other. (RODNEY DANGERFIELD)

HOPE

There is no medicine like hope, no incentive so great, and no tonic so powerful as expectation of something better tomorrow.(ORISON MARDEN)

In all things it is better to hope than to despair.   (GOETHE)

The world hopes for the best, but Jesus Christ offers the best hope.
(JOHN WESLEY WHITE)

Hope is the best possession. None are completely wretched but those who are without hope, and few are reduced so low as that.
(WILLIAM HAZLITT)

Hope is itself a species of happiness, and perhaps the chief happiness which this world affords.   (SAMUEL JOHNSON)

The word hope I take for faith; and indeed hope is nothing else but the constancy of faith.   (JOHN CALVIN)

Take from a man his wealth, and you hinder him; take from him his purpose, and you slow him down. But take from man his hope, and you stop him. He can go on without wealth, and even without purpose, for a while. But he will not go on without hope.   (C. NEIL STRAIT)

Other men see only a hopeless end, but the Christian rejoices in an endless hope.   (GILBERT BEENKEN)

HORSES

I hate horses—they're uncomfortable in the middle and dangerous at both ends.   (CHRISTOPHER STONE)

A farmer couldn't tell his two horses apart, so he tried cutting the tail off one horse. This didn't work because it grew right back. Then he cut the mane off the other horse. But that didn't work either because it grew right back. Finally, he measured them and found that the white horse was two inches taller than the black horse.   (SUNSHINE)

Did you hear about the riding academy that was forced to shut down because of mounting costs?   (JOSEPH MORRIS)

HOSPITALS

No patient should have to leave the hospital until he's strong enough to face the cashier.

I just got the hospital bill for a minor operation. I think I must have been in one of those expensive care units. (ROBERT ORBEN)

Why not a self-serve hospital where you can suture self?(CHARLIE LAKE)

HOSPITALITY

Hospitality is the art of making people want to stay without interfering with their departure.

HOUSEWORK

Housewife's lament: Keeping house is like threading beads on a string with no knot at the end. (CAPPER'S WEEKLY)

Housework is what a woman does that nobody ever notices unless she doesn't do it.

I'm such a bad housekeeper, people wipe their feet before they leave— and when I cook, I serve Tums for after-dinner mints. (JOAN RIVERS)

HUGS

Everybody needs a hug. It changes your metabolism. (LEO BUSCAGLIA)

HUMAN BEINGS (see PEOPLE)

Maybe the human race isn't so superior after all. Though I have seen thousands of birds crisscrossing the skies, hundreds of rabbits racing over the fields, and countless minnows in the water, all going at high speed, I have yet to see one collide with another or career into a tree or television pole. (BURTON HILLIS)

Every human being, for vitality, maturity, growth, and fulfillment, needs constant stress, constant risk, in order to reach his fullness as a creature. When you play it safe, as so many are trying to do—get a job and bury yourself in the soft, amorphous womb of industry or some giant corporation—quite often you begin to lose the qualities that make a human being great or successful. You tend to relax; you tend to stop growing. (EARL NIGHTINGALE)

HUMAN BODY

Your body is far more intricate than the federal highway system. Inside you are some 100,000 miles of nerve fibers along which messages zip at speeds of 300 miles per hour. (HAL BOYLE)

HUMAN RELATIONS

I have a friend who likes to say, "I'm very fond of the human race. All my family have belonged to it, and some of my wife's family, too." In great seriousness, God is saying, life is saying, "You must join the human race. You must learn the higher word of God—cooperation. Without cooperation, without the law of love in human relations, there is no answer to the problem of bread." (J. WALLACE HAMILTON)

Raised voices lower esteem. Hot tempers cool friendships. Loose tongues stretch truth. Swelled heads shrink influence. Sharp words dull respect. (WILLIAM A. WARD)

The degree of happiness attained by any individual is usually directly related to his ability to get along in the world. Psychologists have come up with a list of traits which seem to be common to those who have human relations problems. Here are the 10 traits which they conclude are the reasons for a person's unpopularity with other people: (1) lack of dependability, (2) a tendency to exaggerate, (3) grumpiness, (4) sarcasm, (5) a sense of inferiority, (6) bossiness, (7) a compulsion to "show off" in front of them, (8) poking fun at others behind their backs, (9) a desire to dominate others, (10) a tendency to criticize and find fault. (HEALTHWAYS)

HUMAN NATURE

He's been getting along so well he's beginning to complain.
(IHRE FREUNDIN, QUOTE TRANSLATION)

Why is it so much easier to believe something bad than something good?
(BERYL PFIZER)

HUMILITY (see MEEKNESS)

Quit trying to be so humble. You're not that great. (GOLDA MEIR)

Every person you meet is better at something than you are.
(ROBERT A. COOK)

Humility is the ability to see ourselves as God describes us.
(HENRY JACOBSEN)

Why does God want to humble any man or woman? Nobody can work for God until humility has taken hold of his life. Otherwise he magnifies himself out of all proportion to God. (PAUL RADER)

There are four occasions in a man's life when he discovers that he is no better than anybody else—when he first gets spanked, when he first gets a poke in the nose, when his face is first slapped by a woman, and when the Internal Revenue Service first slaps him with more tax on an honest return. (CARL RIBLET, JR.)

I believe that the first test of a truly great man is his humility. I do not mean by humility, doubt of his own power. But really great men have a curious feeling that the greatness is not in them, but through them. And they see something divine in every other man and are endlessly, foolishly, incredibly merciful. (JOHN RUSKIN)

HUMOR (see COMEDIANS, PUNS)

Humor is an expression in terms of the grotesque, of the appalling disparity between human aspiration and human performance.
(MALCOLM MUGGERIDGE)

When you say a person has a sense of humor, do you mean he makes you laugh or that you can make him laugh?

A well-developed sense of humor is the pole that adds balance to your steps as you walk the tightrope of life. (WILLIAM A. WARD)

A difference of taste in jokes is a great strain on the affections.
(GEORGE ELIOT)

A man with a sense of humor doesn't make jokes out of life; he merely recognizes the ones that are there. (NUGGETS)

Mark Twain observed that a sense of humor is the one thing no one will admit not having. A genuine sense of humor implies the personal perception of what is funny in situations, including one's own. (RALPH CAPLAN)

A well-developed sense of humor means a well-balanced personality. . . . The better adjusted you are, the more readily you will respond to humor in jokes, cartoons, and also everyday situations. Maladjusted people show a far greater tendency to miss the point in a joke or funny remark and to take things seriously which are meant to be funny. . . . The ability to get a laugh out of everyday situations is a safety valve, ridding you of tensions which might otherwise damage your health.
(WEEKEND)

HUNGER

It is a lot easier emotionally to handle the fact that millions of people are starving if we don't see them as individuals. (STAN MOONEYHAM)

HUNTING

I have hunted deer on occasions, but they were not aware of it.
(FELIX GEAR)

HURRY

People who don't know whether they are coming or going are usually in the biggest hurry to get there. (BITS AND PIECES)

HUSBANDS

One good husband is worth two good wives; for the scarcer things are the more they are valued. (BENJAMIN FRANKLIN)

Husband: You and your suicide attempts! Look at this gas bill!

At a retreat for pastors and wives, one session consisted of testimonies about how the Lord had blessed their lives. A young preacher's wife began nervously, "The Bible promises, 'No good thing does the Lord withhold from them that walk uprightly.' Well, my husband is one of those 'no good things'!" (JOYCE N. JURIS)

A good many husbands are utterly spoiled by mismanagement in cooking and so are not tender and good. Some women keep them constantly in hot water; others let them freeze by their carelessness and indifference. Some keep them in a stew with irritating ways and words. Some wives keep them pickled, while others waste them shamefully. It cannot be supposed that any husband will be tender and good when so managed, but they are really delicious when prepared properly.

(THE MEMPHIS COOK BOOK)

His short, unhappy life ended at 47. The widow, inconsolable at first, finally got a dog to ease her loneliness. The sorrow mellowed as she became more attached to the dog.

"She's happy because she's gotten back into her old pattern of living," reported a neighbor. "That dog is a perfect substitute for her poor husband. He's out all day, sleeps all evening, and she feeds him out of cans."

The only compliment some husbands pay their wives is to marry them.

(ARNOLD GLASOW)

HYPOCRITE (see PHONY)

A hypocrite preaches by the yard but practices by the inch.

HYSTERIC

A hysteric is a person who has discovered the secret of perpetual emotion.

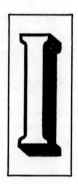

IDEALISM

I am an idealist. I don't know where I'm going but I'm on my way.
(CARL SANDBURG)

IDEALS (see VALUES)

Man generally operates a considerable distance below his ideals. Where his ideals are low, his behavior will be lower still. And the jam we are in today is in large measure caused by the fact that in recent years our mass communications and entertainment media have publicized deviation from our traditional moral standards to the point that impressionable youth imagines that deviation is the norm. (QUOTE)

IDEAS (see CREATIVITY)

A new idea is delicate. It can be killed by a sneer or a yawn; it can be stabbed to death by a quip and worried to death by a frown on the right man's brow. (CHARLES BROWER)

An idea isn't responsible for the people who believe in it. (DON MARQUIS)

History has proven that ideas are far more powerful than guns. And history has also proven that good ideas do not always prevail over evil ones. If they did, there would be no wars, no concentration camps, no inquisitions, no lynchings, no prejudice, and no crime.
(DAIRYMEN'S LEAGUE NEWS)

There's nothing more powerful than an idea whose time has come.
(VICTOR HUGO)

Great ideas need landing gears as well as wings.   (C.D. JACKSON)

Every day thousands of people bury good ideas because they are afraid to act on them.   (STANFORD LEE)

It's tough watching a good idea lose because its backers are less eloquent or have less clout than its opponents.   (LESTER CASE)

Daring ideas are like chessmen moved forward. They may be beaten, but they may start a winning game.   (GOETHE)

You can judge your age by the amount of pain you feel when you're confronted with a new idea.   (JOHN NUVEEN)

Ideas are a dime a dozen. Ideas with a solid perspective are harder to come by.   (ADVERTISING AGE)

Even the best ideas will rarely work unless you do. Many brilliant ideas have washed out simply because there just wasn't enough elbow grease and legwork put behind them.   (MILTON ROCKMORE)

Your most brilliant ideas come in a flash, but the flash comes only after a lot of hard work. Nobody gets a big idea when he is not relaxed and nobody gets a big idea when he is relaxed all of the time.
(EDWARD BLAKESLEE)

A fair idea put to use is better than a good idea kept on the polishing wheel.   (ALEX OSBORN)

Many great ideas have been lost because the folks who had them couldn't stand to be laughed at.

Some folks entertain a new thought as if it were an unwelcome relative.
(MORRIS BENDER)

I had a terrific idea this morning, but I didn't like it.   (SAM GOLDWYN)

Sometimes the best, and only effective, way to kill an idea is to put it into practice.   (SYDNEY HARRIS)

Many ideas are good for a limited time—not forever.(ROBERT TOWNSEND)

The power of ideas is concisely portrayed by this quotation of Robert

Galvin, president of the Motorola Corporation: "If you take away all of Motorola's factories, all of our inventories, and leave me with 10 scientists and engineers of ideas, we could rebuild our corporation in a few short years. But if you leave me all of our physical assets and take away all of our ideas, you leave me virtually nothing." (TOM COMELLA)

Ideas are like children—no matter how much you admire someone else's you can't help liking your own best. (ROCKMART JOURNAL)

IDENTITY CRISIS

A lot of people don't realize they have an identity crisis until they try to cash a check in a strange town. (BILL VAUGHN)

IDLENESS (see LAZINESS)

Doing nothing is the most tiresome job in the world, because you can't quit and rest.

It does a man no good to sit up and take notice—if he keeps on sitting. (ZEPHYRS)

No one has a right to live in idleness and expect to live long and be happy. The ship anchored in the harbor rots faster than the ship crossing the ocean; a still pond of water stagnates more rapidly than a running stream. Our unused minds are subject to atrophy much more rapidly than those in use. The unused cells in our brains deteriorate much faster than those which are continually exercised. Hence, to remain young we must remain active. (AMERICAN SALESMAN)

IDOLATRY (see WORSHIP)

Idolatry is worshiping anything that ought to be used, or using anything that is meant to be worshiped. (AUGUSTINE)

IGNORANCE

There is one thing to be said of ignorance—it sure causes a lot of interesting arguments. (WHEATON [ILL.] DAILY JOURNAL)

It's harder to conceal ignorance than to acquire knowledge. (ARNOLD GLASOW)

The reason there's so much ignorance is that those who have it are so eager to share it. (FRANK A. CLARK)

Ignorance is like the itch—the less you have of it the better off you are. (HARRY MENDELSON)

Everybody is ignorant—only on different subjects.   (WILL ROGERS)

To know one's ignorance is the best part of knowledge.   (LAO-TSE)

"IGNORTION"

Things do not get better by being left alone. Unless they are adjusted, they explode with a shattering detonation.   (WINSTON CHURCHILL)

ILLUSIONS

It is respectable to have no illusions—and safe—and profitable—and dull.   (JOSEPH CONRAD)

IMAGINATION (see CREATIVITY)

The soul without imagination is what an observatory would be without a telescope.   (HENRY BEECHER)

When you stop having dreams and ideals—well, you might as well stop altogether.   (MARIAN ANDERSON)

IMMATURITY

You are only young once, but you can stay immature indefinitely.(GRIT)

IMMORTALITY (see DEATH)

Washington is full of strutting people who are working furiously at the idea of achieving immortality. Somebody ought to remind them, however, that immortality is never a winner. It always arrives late—after the undertaker.   (CARL RIBLET, JR.)

Death is not a period but a comma in the story of life. (AMOS TRAVER)

I once heard a Methodist bishop say that when he was a very young minister he was called to the bedside of an elderly woman who had obviously but a few hours left for this world. The bishop admitted that he was badly frightened but the old saint was completely relaxed and radiantly happy. He tried to commiserate with her and muttered something about how sorry he was that she had to die, but she wouldn't hear any such talk. "Why, God bless you, young man," she said cheerfully, "there's nothing to be scairt about. I'm just going to cross over Jordan in a few minutes, and my Father owns the land on both sides of the river."   (ALLIANCE WEEKLY)

At the end of a monastery tour an "enlightened atheist" said to the monk guide, "If God doesn't exist, and I believe He doesn't, then you will have wasted your whole life."

The monk smiled. "If I am wrong, I will have wasted at most 50 or 70 years. If you are wrong, you will waste an eternity."

(ROBERT CLOUSTON)

Before I started working with dying patients, I did not believe in a life after death. I now believe in a life after death, beyond a shadow of a doubt.

(ELISABETH KUEBLER-ROSS)

IMPATIENCE

One of the most frequent causes for failure of able-bodied men is impatience in waiting for results.

IMPERFECTION

The only nice thing about being imperfect is the joy it brings to others.

(DOUG LARSON)

IMPORTANCE

It's nice to be important, but it's more important to be nice.

(JOHN CASSIS)

IMPOSSIBILITIES

What we need are more people who specialize in the impossible.

(THEODORE ROETHKE)

Whoever said nothing is impossible never tried to slam a revolving door.

(ROBERT ORBEN)

IMPRESSION

The best way to make an impression is by making the impression that you're not trying to make an impression.

(GEORGE HART)

IMPROVEMENT

If you forget you have to struggle for improvement you go backward.

(GEOFFREY HICKSON)

IMPS

Imps that cause trouble:
IMProvising,
IMPatience,
IMPunity,
IMPulsiveness.

INCOME

He lives on a fixed income. Spends his whole income on getting things fixed.

INCOME TAX (see TAXES)

Income tax time is when you test your powers of deduction.

(SHELBY FRIEDMAN)

Uncle claims that if he files his income tax wrong he'll go to jail, and if he files it right he'll go to the poor house. (NONNEE COAN)

INCOMPETENCE

Man cannot live by incompetence alone. (LAWRENCE J. PETER)

INDIFFERENCE

More good things in life are lost by indifference than ever were lost by active hostility. (ROBERT MENZIES)

Where the church has a record of indifference to human need, you will probably not be able to prove by your sermons that you really love your hearers. Your audience will suspect that you are only using tricks in order to manipulate them. (HARRY SPENCER)

Those who turn their backs do not see tears. (PAUL BOESE)

The opposite of love is not hate; it is something much worse than that; hate with all its negation and emotion at least takes the other into account; the opposite of love is something much colder, more pallid, and really much more cruel; the opposite of love is *indifference*. And it is real, deep-down indifference that is at the heart of most family troubles.

(WILLIAM HAGUE)

INDIVIDUALS (see COMMITTEES)

Ideas are developed by individuals. They can be refined by many people, but the basic concept is usually the product of one mind. It is difficult, for example, to imagine the "Mona Lisa" being painted by a committee. Committees are essentially, of course, for evaluation, refining, and implementation—but they must have the products of individual fertile minds to work with. (CHARLES F. JONES)

A person's worth . . . is contingent upon *who he is*, not upon *what he does*, or *how much he has*. The *worth* of a person, or a thing, or an idea, is in *being*, not in *doing*, not in *having*. (ALICE MARY HILTON)

INFERIORITY

When an individual is kept in a situation of inferiority, the fact is that he does become inferior. (SIMONE DE BEAUVOIR)

No one can make you feel inferior without your consent.
(ELEANOR ROOSEVELT)

Sign in a London employment agency waiting room: Never think of yourself as inferior. Leave this to the experts. (EVENING STANDARD)

An inferiority complex would be a blessing, if only the right people had it. (ALAN REED)

INFLATION

The only thing that goes as far as it used to 10 years ago is the quarter that rolls under the bed. (BITS AND PIECES)

Inflation is the crabgrass in your savings. (ROBERT ORBEN)

Inflation is when sitting on your nest egg doesn't give you anything to crow about.

One good thing can be said for inflation: without it there would be no football. (MARTY RAGAWAY)

Nowadays, a penny saved is ridiculous! (SHELBY FRIEDMAN)

A diner in a roadside restaurant complained bitterly to the manager when the hot dog he ordered contained meat at one end and bread at the other.
  "In high-priced, inflated times like these," the manager reasoned, "who can make both ends meat?" (JOE CREASON)

Inflation hasn't ruined everything. A dime can still be used as a screwdriver. (SUNSHINE)

INFLUENCE

Let no man imagine that he has no influence. Whatever he may be, and wherever he may be placed, the man who thinks becomes a light and a power. (HENRY GEORGE)

A man's life is like either the tumbleweed or the oak tree. Some people just grow like the weed. They are of no value in their youth and as the years of life come they break loose and become a blotch on society. They have no useful purpose in life—just drifters. Their loved ones will mourn their loss, but society will not miss them. Their influence was neither neutral nor negative. They spend their lives satisfying their selfish desires with no time for intellectual, social, or spiritual betterment.

Then there are those whose lives are like the oak. They have turned from the frivolity of this life and have invested in things that have genuine worth. Their influence for good will live on in the lives of others after they are gone. Their death is noticed because their lives were spent bettering the nation and the community. They will be missed.

(GALEN ANDERSON)

Influence: What you think you have till you try to use it. (JOAN WELSH)

The most powerful single thing you can do to have influence over others is to smile at them.

INFORMATION

As a general rule, the most successful man in life is the man who has the best information. (BENJAMIN DISRAELI)

INJURIES

If the other person injures you, you may forget the injury; but if you injure him, you will always remember. (KAHLIL GIBRAN)

INSINCERITY

The most exhausting thing in life, I have discovered, is being insincere. That is why so much social life is exhausting; one is wearing a mask.

(ANNE M. LINDBERGH)

INSTRUCTION (see TEACHERS AND TEACHING)

The wise are instructed by reason; ordinary minds by experience; the stupid by necessity; and brutes by instinct. (BALANCE SHEET)

INSULTS

Insults are the arguments employed by those who are in the wrong.

(ROSSEAU)

The only graceful way to accept an insult is to ignore it; if you can't ignore it, top it; if you can't top it, laugh at it; if you can't laugh at it, it's probably deserved. (RUSSELL LYNES)

Never insult an alligator until you've crossed the river. (CORDELL HULL)

INITIATIVE

Take a lesson from the mosquito. She never waits for an opening—she makes one. (KIRK KIRKPATRICK)

INSURANCE

The chief beneficiary of life insurance policies for young, single people is the life insurance agent. (WES SMITH)

My rich uncle took out a million-dollar insurance policy. But it didn't help—he died anyhow.

An insurance agent said to a new client: "I want to sell you this policy. But I'm not like other insurance agents. I'm not going to frighten you. I'm not going to scare you into buying it. Take the policy home. Sleep on it tonight. If you wake up in the morning, give me a call." (SCOPE)

"But, Madam, you have no claim. Your husband did not carry life insurance. He took out a policy against fire."
"That's what I claim. He's been cremated!" (JACKIE KANNON)

A fellow explained cynically why he refused to buy life insurance. "When I die I want it to be a sad day for everybody!" (EARL WILSON)

Q: When the pioneers crossed the plains, were their wagons insured?
A: Certainly—that's why they were called "covered wagons."
(SHELBY FRIEDMAN)

How about those car insurance rates? If they get any higher, it'll be easier to pay cash for the car and finance the insurance premiums.
(CURRENT COMEDY)

One nice thing about living to 100 is that insurance agents quit bothering you. (INDIANAPOLIS TIMES)

INTEGRATION

Inter-varsity graffiti: Jesus has a family in an interracial neighborhood called heaven. (DECISION)

INTELLECTUALS

Intellectual: Someone who knows when to quote what some bright fellow once said. (MIKE CONNOLLY)

President Eisenhower once defined the intellectual as "a man who takes more words than is necessary to tell more than he knows."
(SATURDAY REVIEW)

INTELLIGENCE

There are two fallacies in today's thinking. One is the fallacy of young people who think that intelligence is a substitute for experience. The other is that of older people who think that experience is a substitute for intelligence. (CONSTRUCTION DIGEST)

INTENTIONS

People judge you by your actions, not your intentions. You may have a heart of gold, but so does a hard-boiled egg. (GOOD READING)

INTERACTION

The meeting of two personalities is like the contact of two chemical substances; if there is any reaction, both are transformed.(CARL J. JUNG)

INTERESTS

It is good to have many interests, but not to dabble superficially in a host of activities while mastering none. (QUOTE)

INTUITION

Intuition is what tells a wife her husband has done wrong before he thinks of doing it.

INTERRUPTIONS

Interruptions can be viewed as sources of irritation or opportunities for service, as moments lost or experience gained, as time wasted or horizons widened. They can annoy us or enrich us, get under our skin or give us a shot in the arm, monopolize our minutes or spice our schedules, depending on our attitude toward them. (WILLIAM A. WARD)

INTOLERANCE

Intolerance is the most socially acceptable form of egotism, for it permits us to assume superiority without personal boasting.(SYDNEY HARRIS)

INTRODUCTIONS

After a flowery introduction a preacher stood up to present his address and said, "May the Lord forgive this man for his excesses, and me for enjoying them so much." (ALICE MURRAY)

INTROSPECTION
To understand the world one must not be worrying about one's self.
(ALBERT EINSTEIN)

INTROVERTS

Try to be like the turtle—at ease in your own shell. (BILL COPELAND)

INVENTIONS (see DISCOVERIES)

A study made a number of years ago said the more education a man has, the less likely he is to be an inventor. Now the reason for that is quite simple. From the time the boy, or girl, starts in school he is examined three or four times a year and, of course, it is a very disastrous thing if he fails. An inventor fails all the time and it is a triumph if he succeeds once. Consequently, if education is an inhibition to invention, it is due entirely to the form by which we rate things and not because of any intellectual differential. (CHARLES KETTERING)

Thomas Edison, the great inventor, was talking one day with the governor of North Carolina, and the governor complimented him on his inventive genius.

"I am not a great inventor," said Edison.

"But you have over a thousand patents to your credit, haven't you?" queried the governor.

"Yes, but about the only invention I can really claim as absolutely original is the phonograph," was the reply. "I guess I'm an awfully good sponge. I absorb ideas from every source I can, and put them to practical use. Then I improve them until they become of some value. The ideas which I use are mostly the ideas of other people who don't develop them themselves." (STRAWS)

Anything that won't sell, I don't want to invent. Its sale is proof of utility, and utility is success. (THOMAS EDISON)

Most people are quite sure that the major as well as the minor modern gadgets are very much worth having, but their inventors are not always of the same opinion. I have cherished the fact that Alexander Graham Bell refused to have a telephone in his house; that Alfred Sloane "sometimes regretted" the invention of the internal combustion engine; and that Robert Oppenheimer confessed to the conviction that he and some of the others responsible for the atom bomb "had known sin." . . . I have been pleased to add to this list the name of Vladimer Zworykin, said to be the man most responsible for the invention of electronic television. Asked his favorite TV program, he replied, "None." (JOSEPH KRUTCH)

Joke making the rounds in Tokyo: In January, the Americans announce a new invention. In February the Russians claim they made the same discovery 20 years ago. In March, the Japanese start exporting the invention to the U.S. (OBSERVER)

INVESTMENTS

It's not the bulls and bears you need to avoid—it's the bum steers. (CHUCK HILLIS)

JANUARY

Last month it was Jingle Bells. This month it is Juggle Bills.

JEALOUSY (see ENVY)

My wife's jealousy is getting ridiculous. The other day she looked at my calendar and wanted to know who May was.   (RODNEY DANGERFIELD)

JESUS (see CHRIST)

All that I am I owe to Jesus Christ, revealed to me in His divine Book.   (DAVID LIVINGSTONE)

Jesus says, "I love you just the way you are. And I love you too much to let you stay the way you are."   (CHRIS LYONS)

No man ever loved like Jesus. He taught the blind to see and the dumb to speak. He died on the cross to save us. He bore our sins. And now God says, "Because He did, I can forgive you."   (BILLY GRAHAM)

Jesus Christ turns life right-side-up, and heaven outside-in.
     (CARL F.H. HENRY)

Jesus Christ is God's everything for man's total need.
     (RICHARD HALVERSON)

JOBS (see CAREERS)

Consciously or unconsciously, each of us shapes his job to his own image. Often we dodge this fact. When we don't like what we see in a job, we may not be liking what we see in ourselves. (NORMAN SHIDLE)

Whatever your job, it is important if it is what God wants you to do. (HENRY JACOBSEN)

There are few, if any, jobs in which ability alone is sufficient. Needed also are loyalty, sincerity, enthusiasm, and cooperation.

"Where my brother works, he has over 500 men under him."
"Impressive. Where's he work?"
"He mows the grass in a cemetery."

JOGGING (see EXERCISE)

Jogging: Running yourself rugged. (WALL STREET JOURNAL)

Jogging is slow running that emphasizes vertical motion of the body rather than forward movement. It provides moderate to quite violent exercise, depending upon the time devoted to it and the speed at which it is done. Unlike calisthenics or isometric exercises, it can, I believe, help prevent deterioration of the heart and the circulatory system.
(HARRY JOHNSON)

Research at the University of Wisconsin at Madison revealed that exercise reduced not only the waistline, but the level of anxiety among both normal and neurotic people. The result was something of a surprise, as exercise increases the level of lactate in the bloodstream, and in earlier experiments injections of lactate had increased anxiety in subjects. Part of the explanation may be that exercise causes acidity in the body, while lactate injections cause alkalinity. So if you have troubles, keep running away from them. It just might work. (HORIZONS)

JOINERS

The greater a man's reputation for ability, the more highly he will be sought out by others and the more he will have to resist requests to get involved in tasks that waste his resources. If he is always a "good fellow," he will find he never has time to be an outstanding achiever. If we want to make a mark for ourselves, we will have to say no to many requests that would take us in other directions. (HAROLD MAYFIELD)

JOY (see HAPPINESS)

The surest mark of a Christian is not faith, or even love, but joy.
(SAMUEL SHOEMAKER)

One joy dispels a hundred cares. (ORIENTAL PROVERB)

Shortly after a snowfall a theological student saw a youngster skiing with one ski. He stopped beside the boy and said, "Son, don't you know you are supposed to have two skis?"

The lad looked up with a happy grin and replied, "I know I ought to have two, but I ain't got 'em. But, mister, you can have a lot of fun with one ski if you ain't got two." (ROBERT KAHN)

Joy is the most infallible sign of the presence of God. (LEON BLOY)

Joy is not in things. It is in us. (MEGIDDO MESSAGE)

To be able to find joy in another's joy: that is the secret of happiness. (GEORGES BERNANOS)

Joys are our wings; sorrows our spurs. (RICHTER)

Joy is not gush; joy is not jolliness. Joy is perfect acquiescence in God's will because the soul delights itself in God Himself.(H.W. WEBB-PEPLOE)

JUDGE

A judge is a law student who grades his own papers. (H.L. MENCKEN)

JUDGING (see CONDEMNATION)

Most of us are umpires at heart; we like to call balls and strikes on somebody else. (LEO AIKMAN)

It is well, when judging a friend, to remember that he is judging you with the same god-like and superior impartiality. (ARNOLD BENNETT)

Do not condemn your neighbor; you do not know what you would have done in his place. (SAYINGS OF THE JEWISH FATHERS)

Most of our suspicions of others are aroused by our knowledge of ourselves. (ILLINOIS JOURNAL OF EDUCATION)

We judge ourselves by what we feel capable of doing; others judge us by what we have done. (H.W. LONGFELLOW)

The average man's judgment is so poor, he runs a risk every time he uses it. (EDGAR HOWE)

Do not condemn the judgment of another because it differs from your own. You may both be wrong. (GRIT)

JUDGMENT

There are few things wholly evil or wholly good. Almost everything, especially of government policy, is an inseparable compound of the two, so that our best judgment of the preponderance between them is continually demanded. (ABRAHAM LINCOLN)

You only go around once in life—and after that the judgment.(DAN CORY)

A person's judgment is no better than his information.(THE OPEN DOOR)

JUNK (see ANTIQUES)

Junk is something you keep for years and then throw out two weeks before you need it.

JURIES

Why are there 12 jurors? Because there are 12 tribes of Israel, 12 months in a year, 12 inches in a foot, and 12 apostles. (QUINTIN HOGG)

JUSTICE

It is no accident that the first moral fables were written by a slave; only those who chronically suffer injustice can have a true insight into what justice consists of. (Whereas those who benefit from it have a hundred ways of rationalizing it into something else.) (SYDNEY HARRIS)

JUVENILE DELINQUENCY (see TEENS)

Many (and I am convinced most) juvenile delinquents are children who, without heroes to emulate, or outlets in imagination, or sufficient work to use up their energies, take to crime out of sheer boredom, acting out tales of derring-do suggested by comic books and televised crime stories.
(DOROTHY THOMPSON)

Six suggestions on how to curb juvenile delinquency: (1) take time with your children, (2) set your children a good example, (3) give your children ideals for living, (4) have a lot of activities planned for your children, (5) discipline your children, (6) teach them about God.
(BILLY GRAHAM)

No enemy nation could take the risk of invading us. Our juvenile delinquents are too well armed. (ARNOLD GLASOW)

KINDERGARTEN

A kindergarten teacher knows how to make little things count.

KINDNESS

Kindness makes a fellow feel good whether it's being done to him or by him.
(FRANK A. CLARK)

One can pay back the loan of gold, but one lies forever in debt to those who are kind.
(MALAY PROVERB)

We cannot hold a torch to light another's path without brightening our own.
(BEN SWEETLAND)

Be kind to dumb people.
(DON HEROLD)

To cultivate kindness is a valuable part of the business of life.
(SAMUEL JOHNSON)

Kindness has converted more sinners than zeal, eloquence, or learning.
(FREDERICK W. FABER)

Constant kindness can accomplish much. As the sun makes ice melt, kindness causes misunderstanding, mistrust, and hostility to evaporate.
(ALBERT SCHWEITZER)

Kindness is more than deeds. It is an attitude, an expression, a look, a touch. It is anything that lifts another person. (C. NEIL STRAIT)

As perfume to the flower, so is kindness to speech.(KATHERINE FRANCKE)

If someone were to pay you 10¢ for every kind word you ever spoke and collect 5¢ for every unkind word, would you be rich or poor?(NONPAREIL)

The kindness planned for tomorrow doesn't count for today.

KNOWLEDGE (see LEARNING)

A wise man, when asked how he had learned so much about everything, replied: "By never being ashamed or afraid to ask questions about anything of which I was ignorant." (FRIENDLY CHAT)

Many of us don't have to turn out the lights to be in the dark.
(ETHICAL OUTLOOK)

Some students drink at the fountain of knowledge. Others just gargle.

It is not good to know more unless we do more with what we already know. (R.K. BERGETHON)

Knowledge fills a large brain; it merely inflates a small one.

Knowing is not enough; we must apply. Willing is not enough; we must do. (GOETHE)

Knowledge is of two kinds. We know a subject ourselves, or we know where we can find information on it. (SAMUEL JOHNSON)

If men could only know each other, they would never again either idolize or hate. (BITS AND PIECES)

Knowledge is gained by learning; trust by doubt; skill by practice; love by love. (THOMAS SZASZ)

The world is governed more by appearances than by realities, so that it is fully as necessary to *seem* to know something as it is to know it. (DANIEL WEBSTER)

Knowledge is the best eraser in the world for disharmony, distrust, despair, and the endless physical deficiencies of man. (O.A. BATTISTA)

We do not know one-millionth of one percent about anything.
(THOMAS EDISON)

The trouble with the world is not that people know too little, but that they know so many things that ain't so.　　　　(MARK TWAIN)

Real intelligence is a creative use of knowledge, not merely an accumulation of facts. The slow thinker who can finally come up with an idea of his own is more important to the world than a walking encyclopedia who hasn't learned how to use the information productively.
　　　　　　　　　　　　　　　(D. KENNETH WINEBRENNER)

Intellectual affluence is just as dangerous as material affluence. With each new accumulation of knowledge there is a temptation to relax in the false assumption that because another problem has been solved there is that much less need to think. In fact every addition to our store of knowledge requires additional thought and wisdom for its use.
　　　　　　　　　　　　　　　　　　(DON ROBINSON)

Knowledge has to be improved, challenged, and increased constantly, or it vanishes.　　　　　　　　　　　(PETER DRUCKER)

The knowledge of God is far from the love of Him.　　(KEITH MILLER)

Those who think they know it all are very annoying to those of us who do.　　　　　　　　　　　　　(ROBERT K. MUELLER)

LANGUAGE (see WORDS)

A study was made . . . of 80 geniuses who became high achievers when they grew up. What had these brilliant children in common? Color of eyes? No. Weight? No. Build? No. They were neither ectomorphs nor endomorphs. Number of siblings? No. Income of parents? No. Environmental background? No. What then? It was found in every single case that the parents had great respect for the English language. They loved English, were smitten by words, used them brilliantly, precisely, imaginatively. This had rubbed off on their children, broadened their base of learning so that they were far ahead of their peers.(BERNICE FITZ-GIBBON)

We have room for but one language here, and that is the English language, for we intend to see that the crucible turns our people out as Americans and not as dwellers in a polyglot boarding house.

(THEODORE ROOSEVELT)

Our language is funny—a fat chance and a slim chance are the same thing. (J. GUSTAV WHITE)

While there are "primitive" tribes and peoples, there are no "primitive" languages; every language thus far examined by linguists is about as complex and expressive as any other, from the Australian aborigines to modern English. (SYDNEY HARRIS)

Language is the apparel in which your thoughts parade before the public. Never clothe them in vulgar or shoddy attire. (GEORGE CRANE)

If a man wore overalls at a formal dinner, his clothing would be in bad taste; if he wore them to work in his garden, the costume would be appropriate. We make changes in our vocabulary according to the impression we wish to make and the formality of the situation. If the Declaration of Independence had begun: "Listen here, we're fed up and we aren't going to take any more of this rot," it could never have achieved the effect it has had. It would be misleading to make the sweeping statement that all slang is in bad taste; the occasion, the reader, or listener, and the effect intended by writer or speaker all enter into determining whether or not the language used is in good taste.

(WORD STUDY)

When still a lad, Ben Franklin said to his mother, "I have imbibed an acephalous molluscous."

Supposing he had swallowed something poisonous, his mother forced him to take a large dose of an emetic.

When he got over the effects of the medicine he said, "I had eaten nothing but an oyster."

Then his mother thrashed him for deceiving her. Then and there Ben vowed never again to use big words when little words would do.

(ILION T. JONES)

Language is a wonderful thing. It can be used to express thoughts, to conceal our thoughts, or to replace thinking.   (KELLY FORDYCE)

LAUGHTER

A recent arrival in America from Istanbul made it clear to a friend, in spite of broken English, that what amazes her most in this country is the lack of laughter.   (MARGARET W. MARSHALL)

Scientists have been studying the effect of laughter on human beings and have found, among other things, that laughter has a profound and instantaneous effect on virtually every important organ in the human body. Laughter reduces health-sapping tensions and relaxes the tissues as well as exercising the most vital organs. . . . Laughter, even when forced, results in a beneficial effect on us, both mentally and physically. Next time you feel nervous and jittery, indulge in a good laugh. Laughter is the best medicine for a long and happy life. He who laughs, lasts.(SUNSHINE)

When a person can no longer laugh at himself, it is time for others to laugh at him.

American men dissolve their tensions and avoid nervous breakdowns by telling jokes and laughing. Men . . . competing in business, on demanding schedules . . . must adopt these friendly, joyful intermissions before they kill themselves.   (HENRIETTE VAN SPRINGEL)

With the fearful strain that is on me night and day, if I did not laugh I should die. (ABRAHAM LINCOLN)

That a man can laugh shows that he has a sense of proportion; what makes us laugh is the perception of some incongruity, of something misproportioned or grotesque. It is a sign of our sanity; and also of our solidarity. (JOHN GIFFORD)

Shared laughter creates a bond of friendship. When people laugh together, they cease to be young and old, master and pupils, worker and driver. They have become a single group of human beings, enjoying their existence. (W. GRANT LEE)

Laughter is to life what salt is to the egg. (HELEN VALENTINE)

Please feel free to laugh. Fred Allen said it was bad to suppress laughter. It goes back down and spreads your hips.

LAW

Law is the cement of civilization. When society seems to be coming apart at the seams, it is important to strengthen the rule of law. Law is the alternative to tyranny on one hand and anarchy on the other.
(THOMAS LAMBERT)

Good laws make it easier to do right and harder to do wrong.
(WILLIAM E. GLADSTONE)

Somebody figured it out—we have 35 million laws trying to enforce Ten Commandments. (EARL WILSON)

Laws too gentle are seldom obeyed; too severe, seldom executed.
(BENJAMIN FRANKLIN)

We must reject the idea that every time a law is broken, society is guilty rather than the lawbreaker. It is time to restore the American precept that each individual is accountable for his actions. (RONALD REAGAN)

If more Americans were aware of how important "due process" is in our system of justice, they wouldn't have allowed it to turn into "overdue process" (SYDNEY HARRIS)

Those who go against the grain of God's laws shouldn't complain when they get splinters. (ARKANSAS METHODIST)

Our world is fast becoming a madhouse and the inmates are trying to run the asylum. It is a strange time when the patients are writing the prescriptions, the students are threatening to run the schools, the children to manage the homes, and church members—not the Holy Spirit—to direct the churches. Such lawlessness always brings a dictator and the last of the line will be Antichrist, now in the offing awaiting his cue.

(VANCE HAVNER)

LAWS

Murphy's Law: If something can go wrong, it will.

Weiler's Law: Nothing is impossible for the man who doesn't have to do it himself.

Chisolm's Law: Anytime things appear to be going better, you have overlooked something.

Finagle's Law: Once a job is fouled up, anything done to improve it makes it worse.

Crane's Law: There is no such thing as a free lunch.

Bogovich's Law: He who hesitates is probably right.

Connor's Law: If something is confidential, it will be left in the copier machine.

LAWYERS

Lawyers are the only people in the world who can write a 10,000-word document and call it a brief. (ROUGH NOTES)

Lawyers earn a living by the sweat of their browbeating. (DAVID HUME)

The attorney's young bride bought a sewing machine. She thought she might help her husband make loopholes. (BEN BERGER)

Then there was the lawyer who instructed his son in the alleged facts of life. (DUBLIN OPINION)

If you can't get a lawyer who knows the law, get one who knows the judge. (AMERICAN SALESMAN)

Anybody who thinks talk is cheap should get some legal advice.

(FRANKLIN P. JONES)

LAZINESS (see IDLENESS, PASSIVITY)

Laziness grows on people; it begins in cobwebs and ends in iron chains.

(M. HALE)

The average American would drive his car to the bathroom if the doors were wide enough.

People who shirk, irk.

The lazier a man is the more he plans to do tomorrow.

LEADERSHIP (see FOLLOWER-SHIP)

You do not lead by hitting people over the head—that's assault, not leadership. (DWIGHT EISENHOWER)

Leadership is a matter of having people look at you and gain confidence, seeing how you react. If you're in control, they're in control.
(TOM LANDRY)

Some must follow, and some command, though all are made of clay.
(HENRY W. LONGFELLOW)

How do you spot a leader? They come in all ages, shapes, and conditions. Some are poor administrators, some are not overly bright. One clue: the true leader can be recognized because somehow his people consistently turn in superior performances. (ROBERT TOWNSEND)

A leader has been defined as one who knows the way, goes the way, and shows the way.

Anybody who throws his weight around is going to stumble sooner or later. (FRANKLIN P. JONES)

Do not trust proud, self-seeking leadership. (HAROLD L. LUNDQUIST)

The first attribute of leadership is sensitivity . . . the disposition to take cognizance of different points of view, either of individuals or groups. The sensitive leader realizes that every individual, by virtue of his background and experience, has various needs and wants, and that there are no rigid absolutes that can meet these variables. The second attribute of successful leadership is . . . a well-developed sense of responsibility. . . . The balance between sensitivity and responsibility is an exceedingly fine delineation. To be sensitive to one's followers but, at the same time to assume the responsibility of embarking upon unknown and untried paths of thought and action, is the hallmark of a true leader. To do less is to abdicate the role of leadership. (B.C. GROSS)

Leadership is the activity of influencing people to cooperate toward some goal which they come to find desirable. (ORDWAY TEAD)

There is no necessary connection between the desire to lead and the ability to lead, and even less the ability to lead somewhere that will be to the advantage of the led. (Bergen Evans)

In order to be a leader a man must have followers. And to have followers, a man must have their confidence. Hence the supreme quality for a leader is unquestionably integrity. Without it, no real success is possible, no matter whether it is on a section gang, a football field, in an army, or in an office. If a man's associates find him guilty of phoniness, if they find that he lacks forthright integrity, he will fail. His teachings and actions must square with each other. The first great need, therefore, is integrity and high purpose. (Dwight Eisenhower)

The man who follows a crowd will never be followed by a crowd. (R.S. Donnell)

You can judge a leader by the size of problems he tackles—people nearly always pick a problem their own size, and ignore or leave to others the bigger or smaller ones. (Anthony Jay)

Leadership is a serving relationship that has the effect of facilitating human development. (Ted Ward)

A prime function of the leader is to keep hope alive. (John Gardner)

A good leader takes a little more than his share of the blame, a little less than his share of the credit. (Arnold Glasow)

Congealed thinking is, in the long run, the forerunner of failure. An open mind is the mark of real leadership in top executives. Make sure that you are always receptive to new ideas. (George Crane)

No man will ever be a big executive who feels that he must, either openly or under cover, follow up every order he gives and see that it is done—nor will he ever develop a capable assistant. (John L. Mahin)

Skill in the art of communication is crucial to a leader's success. . . . He can accomplish nothing unless he can communicate effectively. (Norman Allen)

LEARNING (see KNOWLEDGE)

You never learn anything while you are telling the other person off. (Robert A. Cook)

True, a little learning *is* a dangerous thing—but it still beats total ignorance. (Abigail Van Buren)

Oh, that one could learn to learn in time! (ENRIQUE SOLARI)

Learning is acquired by reading books, but the much more necessary learning, the knowledge of the world, is only to be acquired by reading men, and studying all the various editions of them. (LORD CHESTERFIELD)

It is impossible for a man to learn that which he thinks he already knows. (EPICTETUS)

Most of us must learn a great deal every day in order to keep ahead of what we forget. (FRANK A. CLARK)

Learning teaches more in 1 year than experience in 20. (ROGER ASHAM)

One pound of learning requires 10 pounds of common sense to apply it. (PERSIAN PROVERB)

Your ability to learn depends partly on your ability to relinquish what you've held. (MILTON HALL)

We can learn from our contemporaries, even if we don't happen to like them all. I sometimes think you can learn as much, even more, from people you do not like. (FAITH BALDWIN)

To *look* is one thing.
To *see* what you look at is another.
To *understand* what you see is a third.
To *learn* from what you understand is still something else.
But to *act* on what you learn is all that really matters, isn't it?
(HARVARD BUSINESS REVIEW)

One of the reasons mature people stop learning is that they become less and less willing to risk failure. (JOHN W. GARDNER)

LECTURING (see ORATORY, SPEAKERS)

A Chinese scholar was lecturing when all the lights in the auditorium went out. He asked the members of the audience to raise their hands. As soon as they did, the lights went on again. He then said, "Prove wisdom of old Chinese saying: 'Many hands make light work.'" (JEROME BEATTY)

Lecturer: One with his hand in your pocket, his tongue in your ear, and his faith in your patience. (AMBROSE BIERCE)

LEFTIES

When Bea Wilder learned there are more than 25 million left-handed Americans, she asked if that wasn't a lot more than we really needed.

LEISURE (see RELAXATION, LOAFING)

Life lived amidst tension and busyness needs leisure. Leisure that re-creates and renews. Leisure should be a time to think new thoughts, not ponder old ills. (C. NEIL STRAIT)

One problem of more leisure time is how to keep other people from using it.

While leisure brings to us more opportunity for doing what we like, it also places in our hands a responsibility to do what we ought to do. Somewhere, leisure will force us to decide which. And the decision will make our leisure meaningful or monotonous.

Leisure time should be an occasion for deep purpose to throb and for ideas to ferment. Where a man allows leisure to slip without some creative use, he has forfeited a bit of happiness. (C. NEIL STRAIT)

When leisure becomes an end in itself, when millions begin putting fun and games before the serious business of life, when leisure activities become a form of escapism from reality, when the sole purpose for leisure activities becomes hedonism and the gratification of the senses—then a whole society is in trouble. (WILLIAM F. DANKENBRING)

Too much leisure with too much money has been the dread of societies across the ages. That is when nations cave in from within. That is when they fail. (WILLIAM RUSSELL)

LETTERS

A citizen wrote a blistering letter to a congressman, criticizing his legislative performance. The congressman replied sarcastically: "Dear Sir— This is to warn you that some crackpot is writing moronic letters and signing your name."

Weeks later the congressman returned home for a speech-making tour. Within a few days he received this note from his antagonistic constituent: "Dear Congressman—This is to advise you that some crackpot was here making idiotic speeches and using your name." (JAMES SHERLUCK)

LEVELING WITH OTHERS (see HONESTY)

On the whole, people go around not only with two faces, but with two tongues; one that speaks directly to others, and one that speaks about them. The rationalizations flow easily: "It would be unkind to be frank." "Why should I stick my neck out?" And the sophist asks: "What is the truth?" The truth is that we are frightened to behave naturally because we are scared to acknowledge the good and the bad in ourselves. "I am the only person in the world I should like to know thoroughly," said

Oscar Wilde. Behind the egocentric epigram lies the truism that only if we know ourselves can we risk being honest with others. (ALMA BIRK)

LIBERTY (see FREEDOM)

Liberty is the privilege of being free from the things we don't like in order to be slaves of things we do like.   (YORK TRADE COMPOSITOR)

Once we roared like lions for liberty; now we bleat like sheep for security! The solution of America's problem is not in terms of big government, but it is in big men over whom nobody stands in control but God.

(NORMAN V. PEALE)

LIBRARY

The librarian went over to the noisy little boy and said, "Please be quiet. The people near you can't even read."

"They can't?" the boy asked in wonder. "Then what are they doing here?"   (LEO AIKMAN)

LIES

One of the striking differences between a cat and a lie is that the cat has only nine lives.   (MARK TWAIN)

LIFE

Life can only be understood backwards, but it must be lived forwards.

(SOREN KIERKEGAARD)

Life is what happens to you while you are making other plans.

(ROBERT BALZER)

Biology defines life as "the metabolic activity of protoplasm." But there are times when it seems even worse than that.

Life isn't like a book. Life isn't logical or sensible or orderly. Life is a mess most of the time. And theology must be lived in the midst of that mess.   (CHARLES COLSON)

"My dear," Justice Brandeis once advised his impatient daughter, "if you would only recognize that life is hard, things would be so much easier for you."

The difficulties of life are intended to make us better—not bitter.(GRIT)

Life is a grindstone. Whether it grinds a man down or polishes him depends upon the kind of stuff he is made of.   (SUPERVISION)

Life is an uphill business for the guy who's not on the level.

(JOAN WELSH)

We may not prefer a world in which sorrow always seems to be so close to joy; in which heartbreak always seems so close to happiness; in which doubt always seems to be so close to faith. But this is the kind of world we're in.

(JEROLD SAVORY)

Do you ever get the feeling that life is a violin solo and you're wearing mittens?

(ROBERT ORBEN)

Life is 10 percent what you make it and 90 percent how you take it.

(IRVING BERLIN)

Life is a continual process of getting used to things we never expected.

(BITS AND PIECES)

We make a living by what we get, but we make a life by what we give.

(NORMAN MACEWAN)

The life of man is a journey; a journey that must be traveled, however bad the roads or the accommodations.

(OLIVER GOLDSMITH)

The tragedy of life is not that a man loses but that he almost wins.

(HEYWOOD BROUN)

The troublesome thing about life is not that it is rational or irrational, but that it is almost rational.

(G.K. CHESTERTON)

Life that has no faith has no foundation on which to stand when life tumbles in. And life, at some point, will tumble in. Make your first pursuit, then, the quest for faith.

(C. NEIL STRAIT)

In the game of life it's a good idea to have a few early losses, which relieves you of the pressure of trying to maintain an undefeated season.

(BILL VAUGHAN)

Life is like a taxi. The meter just keeps a-ticking whether you are getting somewhere or just standing still.

(LOU ERICKSON)

Life is easier to take than you think. All that is necessary is to accept the impossible, do without the indispensable, and bear the intolerable.

(KATHLEEN NOVIS)

We come into this world head first and go out feet first; in between, it is all a matter of balance.

(PAUL BOESE)

We dribble away our life, little by little, in small packages—we don't throw it away all at once. (ROBERT A. COOK)

Life is a hard fight, a struggle, a wrestling with the principle of evil, hand to hand, foot to foot. Every inch of the way is disputed. The night is given us to take breath, to pray, to drink deep at the fountain of power. The day, to use the strength which has been given us, to go forth to work with it till the evening. (FLORENCE NIGHTINGALE)

If you're not doing something with your life, it doesn't matter how long it is. (PEACE CORPS COMMERCIAL)

Make sure the thing you're living for is worth dying for.(CHARLES MAYES)

The great use of life is to spend it for something that will outlast it. (WILLIAM JAMES)

Life is a lot like tennis—the one who can serve best seldom loses. (AMERICAN DRUGGIST)

You have not lived a perfect day, even though you have earned your money, unless you have done something for someone who will never be able to repay you. (GOOD READING)

I have found life an enjoyable, enchanting, active, and sometimes terrifying experience, and I've enjoyed it completely. A lament in one ear, maybe, but always a song in the other. (SEAN O'CASEY)

Life is currently described in one of four ways: as a journey, as a battle, as a pilgrimage, and as a race. Select your own metaphor, but the finishing necessity is all the same. For if life is a journey, it must be completed. If life is a battle, it must be finished. If life is a pilgrimage, it must be concluded. And if it is a race, it must be won. (J. RICHARD SNEED)

When a patient completes tests at the Mayo Clinic he is frequently given a card on which is a diagram of a cross. On each arm of the cross is a word representing a main element by which a normal human being lives. The words are "work, play, love, worship." If the person examined seems to be short on one of these, it is indicated. Lopsided living is a common cause of ill health and boredom. The Mayo analysis is close to the Christian prescription for the cure of boredom. (DAVID A. MACLENNAN)

We Japanese enjoy the small pleasures, not extravagance. I believe a man should have a simple lifestyle—even if he can afford more. (MASARU IBUKA)

If your life looks cloudy, maybe the windows of your soul need washing.

Life begins when you get out of the grandstand into the game.
(P.L. DeBevoise)

The man who lives by himself and for himself is liable to be corrupted by the company he keeps.

It is but a few short years from diapers to dignity and from dignity to decomposition.
(Don Herold)

A minister, speaking to college students in their fraternity house, asked the chairman, "What are you living for?"
The student answered, "I am going to be a pharmacist."
"I understand that this is how you are going to earn your livelihood, but what are you living for?"
After thinking about the question for a moment, the young man replied with both honesty and bewilderment: "Sir, I am sorry, but I haven't thought that through."
The minister then asked the rest of the group the same question. Only 2 out of the 30 young men had seriously faced the central issue of existence: the reason for living.
(Carroll E. Word)

Some people seem to go through life standing at the complaint counter.
(Fred Propp, Jr.)

Enjoy yourself. These are the good old days you're going to miss in 2015.
(Ohio Grange)

Life becomes an exciting adventure when we expect at least one pleasant surprise each day; when we show our gratitude freely and unashamedly; when we strive to do at least one anonymous act of kindness to someone who needs it most; when we seek to discover the beauty and goodness in every person we meet.
(William A. Ward)

I can't be bitter. No one has a contract on life. (David M. Heath, dying of cancer at age 34, fulfilling lifetime ambition by earning degree in medicine)

When it comes to life the critical thing is whether you take things for granted or take them with gratitude.
(G.K. Chesterton)

Man staggers through life yapped at by his reason, pulled and shoved by his appetites, whispered to by fears, beckoned by hopes. (Eric Hoffer)

Three keys to more abundant living: caring about others, daring for others, sharing with others.
(William A. Ward)

It is faith in something and enthusiasm for something that makes a life worth looking at. (OLIVER W. HOLMES)

The measure of a life, after all, is not its duration but its donation. (CORRIE TEN BOOM)

We need not fear life, because God is the Ruler of all; and we need not fear death, because He shares immortality with us. (WARREN WIERSBE)

People need to be needed. When there is nothing to strive for, no goals, no challenges, the zest for living is gone. (ANN LANDERS)

A man's life is 20 years of having his mother ask him where he is going, 40 years of having his wife ask the same question and, at the end, perhaps having the mourners wondering too.

One life, a little gleam of time between two eternities. (THOMAS CARLYLE)

Eternal life does not begin with death; it begins with faith. (SAMUEL SHOEMAKER)

Give a man a dollar and you cheer his heart. Give him a dream and you challenge his heart. Give him Christ and you change his heart. Then the dollar and the dream become meaningful to him, and to others. (C. NEIL STRAIT)

While still a young man, I was at my workbench one day filing a piece of metal. I was working hard with vigorous strokes but very short strokes. My boss came along, saw what I was doing, and said "Both ends of that file are paid for. Don't take those short strokes with the middle of the file—use both ends."

I wonder if we don't often make that mistake in life. It is commonly acknowledged that we probably don't use more than a small percentage of the potential with which God has endowed us. By His grace, let's take broader strokes, and be more effective by utilizing *all* our time, talent, and treasure for the Lord. Let's use both ends of the file. (R.G. LeTOURNEAU)

We'll have all eternity to celebrate our victories, but only one short hour before sunset in which to win them. (ROBERT MOFFAT)

LIFESTYLE

The Old Testament does not tell us specifically whether we should buy a better car, or keep the one we have, or have no car at all. It does not tell us whether we should upgrade our lifestyle by getting a bigger house or cut it back by getting a smaller one. It does not specify exactly what our lifestyle should be. What it does do is to give us certain principles by which we must measure our lifestyle. To face these principles honestly and prayerfully is bound to lead to changes in how, in this affluent society, we are living—changes that will simplify our lives and help us be more obedient disciples of our Lord. (FRANK E. GAEBELEIN)

LIGHT

It's not necessary to blow out your neighbor's light to let your own shine. (M.R. DeHAAN)

We are told to let our light shine, and if it does, we won't need to tell anybody it does. Lighthouses don't fire cannons to call attention to their shining—they just shine. (D.L. MOODY)

LISTENING (see HEARING)

Everyone needs someone who he feels really listens to him. (C. NEIL STRAIT)

Know how to listen, and you will profit even from those who talk badly. (PLUTARCH)

One of the best ways to persuade others is by listening to them. (DEAN RUSK)

A good listener is not only popular everywhere, but after a while he knows something. (WILSON MIZNER)

Let others confide in you. It may not help you, but it surely will help them. (ROGER G. IMHOFF)

Nothing makes a person such a good listener as eavesdropping. (FRANKLIN P. JONES)

Skillful listening is the best remedy for loneliness, loquaciousness, and laryngitis. (WILLIAM A. WARD)

LITERATURE (see READERS)

In the twentieth century the U.S. produced no less than four new forms of popular literature: the movies, the comic strip, and radio. They were all criticized . . . and I don't suppose that anybody expected television to be different. The result, in any case, is that instead of a full, rich, popular literature, we have the poorest in the history of the world. (JAMES COLLIER)

LOAFING (see LEISURE)

If you're coasting, you're either losing momentum or else you're headed downhill. (JOAN WELSH)

LOGIC (see REASON)

If you're strong on facts and weak on logic, talk facts; if you're strong on logic and weak on facts, talk logic. If you're weak on both, pound on the table. (INKLINGS)

LONELINESS

It is strange to be known so universally and yet to be so lonely.
(ALBERT EINSTEIN)

One of the prominent symptoms of our times . . . is loneliness. Isn't it ironic that in an age of the greatest population explosion the world has ever known, more people are desperately lonely than ever before? . . . Even the high-rise apartments in our big cities are monuments to loneliness. There is aching loneliness behind those doors for many people. I know of those, both in the city and in the suburb, who go to the large shopping centers simply for the opportunity to talk to somebody in the store. At least the checker will speak to them as they go out. Loneliness is one of the desperate problems of our age. (PAUL E. LITTLE)

Loneliness is more of an attitude than a circumstance; more self-inflicted than outwardly caused. (QUOTE)

Loneliness is not a matter of isolation but insulation. Lonely people build walls around themselves and then complain of their loneliness. If we are in love with no one but ourselves, we soon find ourselves hating ourselves. Loneliness spurs us to give our love to others that love may return to us. (GASTON FOOTE)

He who goes walking with a lovely dream is never lonely. He may be quite alone, but the aspiring of his soul will fill his days, and the urgency of his purpose will make the journey seem short and pleasant.
(MILO ARNOLD)

Shakespeare, Leonardo da Vinci, Benjamin Franklin, and Lincoln never saw a movie, heard a radio, or looked at TV. They had "loneliness" and knew what to do with it. They were not afraid of being lonely because they knew that was when the creative mood in them would work.
(CARL SANDBURG)

There is none more lonely than the man who loves only himself.
(ABRAHAM IBN ESRA)

We are born helpless. As soon as we are fully conscious we discover loneliness. We need others physically, emotionally, intellectually; we need them if we are to know anything, even ourselves.   (C.S. LEWIS)

Loneliness is . . . spending your days alone with your thoughts, your discouragements, having no one with whom to talk and share your thoughts.
The cure for loneliness is not a pill or suicide. It is a person. The lonely needs a person, or persons. Someone with whom he can share his dreams, his dreads, his disappointments. Life is lonely until it finds such.
The lonely person cannot wait for another to enter his life and dispel the loneliness. He must first begin the journey into another's life, through service, caring, and helping. Then, chances are, he will find his loneliness vanishing. And he will probably have filled another's lonely hours too.
(C. NEIL STRAIT)

For those who are lonely and would like to do something about it, Dr. Allan Fromme gives you these rules: (1) Keep moving. Let no week go by without giving or accepting an invitation. If no one calls you, call someone. (2) Practice speaking to new people. If necessary, learn lines in advance: what to say at parties, buffet suppers, etc. (3) Remember, the easiest social skill, and the most endearing, is to know how to listen. (4) Remember that *making a habit of people* means finding every possible way to be with people, to do things with people, to become involved with people.   (JOHN GIBSON)

LONGEVITY (see AGING)

Statistical data compiled during a 13-year study on aging strongly indicate that work satisfaction and a positive attitude toward life influence the life span.   (SCIENCE NEWS)

Prominent people live longer than the average person, despite the strains of fighting their way to the top, a recent study indicates. Famous scientists rank first in longevity, followed by clergymen, educators, and military men. Executives, judges, and lawyers are farther down the longevity scale. The shortest lifespans (of successful people) are those of writers, editors, and correspondents.   (MINUTES)

If you want to live to a ripe old age, doctors say the important . . . rules are: (1) Do not overeat. (2) Eat well-balanced, reasonably adequate meals, including fresh fruit, vegetables, and dairy products. (3) When tired, irritated, or nervous, eat sparingly. (4) Eat at regular times. (5) Avoid agitation and aggravation, particularly at mealtimes. . . . (6) Keep your blood pressure down. (7) Learn to live with life as it is. Be philosophical. (8) Avoid excessive X rays unless absolutely necessary. (9) Exercise each day, if only by walking.   (LLOYD SHEARER)

LOSERS (see DEFEAT)

People just seem to feel a little more secure knowing there are some people around who are not rich, beautiful, and blissfully happy. All the world may love a lover—but they identify with a loser.

No one knows what to say in the loser's locker room.(MUHAMMAD ALI)

He's a real loser. He moved into a new neighborhood and got run over by the Welcome Wagon.   (RED BUTTONS)

A loser is a guy whose junk mail comes marked postage due.

LOST

Many people get lost while trying to find an alternate route for the strait and narrow.   (GOOD READING)

LOVE

A noted doctor has listed several emotions which produce disease in human beings. Heading the list is fear, followed by frustration, rage, resentment, hatred, jealousy, envy, self-centeredness, and ambition. The one and only antidote that can save men from these, he says, is love.
(CADLE CALL)

Love cures people—both the ones who give it and the ones who receive it.   (KARL MENNINGER)

I have decided to stick with love. Hate is too great a burden to bear.
(MARTIN LUTHER KING, JR.)

I think that love is the only spiritual power that can overcome the self-centeredness that is inherent in being alive. Love is the thing that makes life possible or, indeed, tolerable.   (ARNOLD TOYNBEE)

Love and basketball have something in common—both involve rebounds.
(SHELBY FREIDMAN)

A baby is born with a need to be loved—and never outgrows it.
(FRANK A. CLARK)

To be loved, be lovable.

Love is oceans of emotions surrounded by expanses of expenses.
(INDUSTRIAL PRESS SERVICE)

Love will find a way. Indifference will find an excuse.

Love arrives on tiptoe and bangs the door when it leaves.

(ROBERT LEMBKE)

Love is blind; friendship closes its eyes.　　(FRENCH PROVERB)

Love and a cough cannot be hid.　　(GEORGE HERBERT)

Love is the soy sauce on the chop suey of life.　　(WALLY PHILLIPS)

"Doctor Shrink, could I be in love with an elephant?"
"Of course not!"
"Where can I sell a rather large engagement ring?"

Analysis kills love, as well as other things.　　(JOHN BROWN)

God loves each of us as if there were only one of us.　　(AUGUSTINE)

If we love Christ, our devotion will not remain a secret.

Love is like the measles—all the worse when it comes late in life.

(DOUGLAS JERROLD)

We need to be loved and we need to give love. When we are thwarted in this, we suffer terribly.　　(G.H. MONTGOMERY)

If someone loves you, your battle is a lot more than half won.

(BILL COPELAND)

The sun can break through the darkest cloud; love can brighten the gloomiest day.　　(WILLIAM A. WARD)

Love and hatred are natural exaggerators.　　(HEBREW PROVERB)

Nothing raises a man to such noble peaks nor drops him into such ashpits of absurdity as the act of falling in love.　　(RIDGELY HUNT)

It is a funny thing that we should speak of "falling in love," as though coming to love were an easy or unavoidable thing to do. Actually, this is far from true. What this metaphor really describes is enchantment, not love. Love is not something you fall into.　　(JOHN KILLINGER)

What does love look like? It has the hands to help others. It has the feet to hasten to the poor and needy. It has eyes to see misery and want. It has the ears to hear the sighs and sorrows of men. That is what love looks like.　　(AUGUSTINE)

Love life and life will love you back. Love people and they will love you back. (ARTHUR RUBINSTEIN)

It is easier to love humanity as a whole than to love one's neighbor. (ERIC HOFFER)

I love mankind—it's people I can't stand! (LINUS)

Love talked about is easily turned aside, but love demonstrated is irresistible. (STANLEY MOONEYHAM)

What makes love a rare game is there are either two winners or none. (FRANKLIN P. JONES)

Love: in tennis, nothing; in life, everything. (FRANK TYGER)

I think that love is the only spiritual power that can overcome the self-centeredness that is inherent in being alive. Love is the thing that makes life possible, or, indeed, tolerable. (ARNOLD TOYNBEE)

I may be very straight doctrinally, as straight as an icicle, and just as cold—so very doctrinal, yet ineffective in my ministry because of lack of love. (T.J. BACH)

True love never runs smooth. Just like any other kind.

Pains of love be sweeter far
Than all other pleasures are. (JOHN DRYDEN)

You can always get someone to love you—even if you have to do it yourself. (TOM MASSON)

The need to love and be loved is the simplest of all human wants. Man needs love like he needs the sun and the rain. He perishes without it. His basic longing is to be the object of love and to be able to give love. No other need is quite so significant to his nature. (CHARLES GALLOWAY)

There are as many kinds of love as there are types of people. There is passionate love, and possessive love, and paternal love, and flaming infatuation, and there is love that is motivated by a need for security. The depth of our feelings can be no more or less than the kind of people we are. (FRANK W. GRAY)

The most of us want very much to be loved. Perhaps we are not concerned enough about loving. (ERWIN McDONALD)

Love is enjoying the other person's enjoyment of you. If two people want to be enjoyed by one another, the only competition will be to outlove.
(CRAIG MASSEY)

Love is only for the young, the middle-aged, and the old.

Unrequited love generally lasts longer than any other kind, because it is never forced to confront reality. (SYDNEY HARRIS)

In the arithmetic of the stomach, half a loaf may be better than none; but in the calculus of the heart, half a love is incomparably worse than none. (SYDNEY HARRIS)

"I'd die for you, my love."
"O Harold. You're always saying that, but you never do it."

Even if you had failings, I should be forbearing. It is not love when one simply draws a beautiful picture in one's soul and endows it with every perfection; rather this is love: to love people as we find them, and if they have weaknesses, to accept them with a heart filled with love.
(CHARLOTTE, TO SCHILLER)

The new minister of a small-town church was calling at several homes in an effort to secure more members for his congregation. In one home where the husband was absent, the preacher asked, "What makes you think your husband is so religious?"
"Well," she replied, "I know he loves his enemies."
"That's fine. What enemies does he have?"
"Oh, his worst ones are whiskey and wild women." (HAROLD WILLIAMS)

Love looks through a telescope; envy, through a microscope.
(JOSH BILLINGS)

Memory touches up an old love affair just as a good professional photographer touches up a portrait. (ANN SCHADE)

When a man cannot choose between two women, or a woman between two men, they should choose neither—for love is not a scale to be balanced or a slide rule to be calculated, and the very act of having to choose between the two indicates that neither is right. (SYDNEY HARRIS)

Love, it has been said, flows downward. The love of parents for their children has always been far more powerful than that of children for their parents; and who among the sons of men ever loved God with a thousandth part of the love which God has manifested to us? (HARE)

God proved His love on the Cross. When Christ hung, and bled, and died, it was God saying to the world, "I love you." (BILLY GRAHAM)

To love a person is to give him power over us. God loves us, and He has given us that terrible power over Him. We can make Him suffer terribly. We can scorn Him and ignore Him. (LOUIS EVELY)

Love is not only something you feel. It's something you do.
(DAVID WILKERSON)

You can give without loving, but you cannot love without giving.
(AMY CARMICHAEL)

When love is felt, the message is heard. (JIM VAUS)

God's love elevates us without inflating us, and humbles us without degrading us. (B.M. NOTTAGE)

We are shaped and fashioned by what we love. (GOETHE)

Whatever you love most, be it sports, pleasure, business, or God, that is your god! (BILLY GRAHAM)

The debt of love never diminishes when we pay it. (HENRY JACOBSEN)

LOYALTY

Loyalty is faithfulness, and effort, and enthusiasm. It is common decency plus common sense. Loyalty is making yourself part of an organization— making it part of you. (GOOD READING)

Some writers sacrifice their loyalties to their royalties. (SYDNEY HARRIS)

It is better to be faithful than famous. (THEODORE ROOSEVELT)

Often loyalty consists of keeping your mouth shut.

We are all in the same boat in a stormy sea, and we owe each other a terrible loyalty. (G.K. CHESTERTON)

LUCK

The chance of bread falling with the buttered side up is directly proportional to the cost of the carpet. (ARTHUR BLACK)

Luck is preparation meeting opportunity. (BITS AND PIECES)

He is so unlucky that he runs into accidents which started out to happen to somebody else. (DON MARQUIS)

LUXURY (see WEALTH)

Give me the luxuries of life and I will willingly do without the necessities. (FRANK LLOYD WRIGHT)

Luxuries are what other people buy. (DAVID WHITE)

Most of the luxuries and many of the so-called comforts of life are not only not dispensable, but positive hindrances to the elevation of mankind. (THOREAU)

Luxury is the first, second, and third cause of ruin of reputation. It is the vampire which soothes us into a fatal slumber while it sucks the life-blood of our veins. (HAMILTON MABIE)

Luxury is what excites envy in others, what you waste, not what you consume, the half of anything you throw away, rather than what satisfies you in yourself. It is fairy gold, pie in the sky, toys in the attic, leftovers in the swill bin. Nobody needs luxury. Or if anybody does, then it is no longer luxury. (ALAN BRIEN)

LYING (see HALF-TRUTHS)

A lie travels around the world while Truth is putting on her boots. (CHARLES H. SPURGEON)

A lie is the refuge of weakness. The man of courage is not afraid of the truth. (J.C. MACAULAY)

No man has a good enough memory to make a successful liar. (ABRAHAM LINCOLN)

With lies you may go ahead in the world—but you can never go back. (RUSSIAN PROVERB)

Never chase a lie. Left alone, it will run itself to death.

MAGAZINES

Aren't women's magazines funny? Half the pages list fattening recipes, the other half diets. (VAL PALMER)

MAGICIANS

Teacher: Dan, I understand your hobby is magic. What's your favorite trick?
Dan: Sawing a girl in two.
Teacher: Wonderful! Are there any other children in your family?
Dan: Yes—six half sisters.

MAIL

Fred: How do you keep your roommate from reading your personal mail?
Ned: That's easy. I hide it in his textbooks. (JOAN WELSH)

MAJORITY

Sometimes a majority simply means that all the fools are on the same side. (CLAUDE McDONALD)

MAN

Man is still the fastest and most efficient computer that can be mass-produced with unskilled labor. (WERNHER VON BRAUN)

Two marks of a real man are to dream and to dare.(J. Gustav White)

Unless a man believes in himself, makes a total commitment to his career, and puts everything he has into it, he'll never be successful at anything he undertakes. (Vince Lombardi)

God was smart when He made man. He made six holes in the head for information to go in, and only one for it to come out. (Wallace Johnson)

Man has a handicap that is difficult to overcome. We have the capacity to see the faults, sins, and mistakes of others, but we cannot see them in ourselves. (Cort Flint)

The history of man is his attempt to escape his own corruption. (Daniel Mullis)

Man's world has become a nervous one, encompassed by anxiety. God's world is other than this; always balanced, calm, and in order. (Faith Baldwin)

Like animals, man is a creature of earth; unlike them, he can become a citizen of heaven. (Henry Jacobsen)

Man is a peculiar, puzzling paradox, groping for God and hoping to hide from Him at the selfsame time. (William A. Ward)

MAN AND WOMAN (see SEXES)

To woman, man is a status symbol; to man, woman is a pleasure symbol. Pleasure and status are thus the main ingredients of our modern society. (Paul Boese)

Physical strength is the one trait in which man is superior to woman, and speaking is the one trait in which woman is superior to man. (Harry Harlow)

The ideal of the average Western man is a woman who freely accepts his domination, who does not accept his ideas without discussions, but who yields to his arguments, who resists him intellectually, and ends by being convinced. (Simone De Beauvoir)

Ask a woman how she stubbed her toe and she'll say she walked into a chair; ask a man and he'll say someone left a chair in the middle of the room. (Philnews)

The PTA meeting was becoming rather spirited as the question of male versus female teachers was being discussed.

"I say that women make the best teachers," said one large and noisy woman. "Where would man be today if it weren't for women?"

"In the Garden of Eden eating watermelon and taking it easy," a man in the back shouted.   (C. KENNEDY)

MANAGEMENT (see EXECUTIVES, SUPERVISION)

Management is a series of interruptions interrupted by interruptions.
(SUPERVISORY MANAGEMENT)

Those who command themselves are in a position to command others.

To handle yourself, use your head; to handle others, use your heart.
(DONALD LAIRD)

A good manager is a man who isn't worried about his own career, but rather, the careers of those who work for him. Take care of those who work for you and you'll float to greatness on their achievements.
(H.S.M. BURNS)

One word of praise can achieve far more than a thousand words of dressing down.

Management maxims: (1) If not controlled, work will flow to the competent personnel until they submerge. (2) The more time you spend in reporting what you're doing, the less time you have to do anything.
(PAUL DICKSON)

So much of what we call management consists in making it difficult for people to work.   (PETER DRUCKER)

"I have a philosophy," says Lee S. Bickmore, board chairman of NABISCO, "that no man should come in to his immediate supervisor *for* a decision. He should come in *with* a decision. When you give your supervisor a chance to probe, to say, 'If you do this, what effect does it have in this area?' or, 'If you do this, what will be so-and-so's reaction?' you give him a chance to examine your depth of thinking."

Middle management, it is said, is the level where you still hear the rumors, but you're not high enough to know if they're true.(SUPERVISION)

The man who is most obsequious to his superiors is usually the most arrogant to his subordinates; what he gives to the one, he takes away from the others.   (SYDNEY HARRIS)

The ideal successor for your management job should have the ability of Andrew Carnegie, the intellect of Einstein, the character of Sir Galahad, and the creativity of Michelangelo. (JOHN MEDLIN)

MANIPULATION

Manipulation is always an act of somebody else. We influence; others manipulate. We educate; others indoctrinate. We disseminate truth; others disseminate lies and half-truths. (DAVID MOBERG)

MANNERS

Anyone can be polite to a king. It takes a gentleman to be polite to a beggar.

If a man has good manners and is not afraid of other people, he will get by—even if he is stupid. (DAVID ECCLES)

MARKETING (see SALESMEN)

The mass consumer market in the U.S. has gone from a low-income to a middle-income market, the first nation in the world to have done so, and it is well on its way to becoming a high-income market.
(RICHARD OSTHEIMER)

There are more goods bought by the heart than by the head.
(GEORGE HENNINGS)

Bidwell's Law: In the marketplace, the ultimate wisdom belongs to the customer.

The customer you butter up is apt to slip away.

"What's this big item on your expense account?" asked the sales manager.
"That's my hotel bill," explained the salesman.
"Well, see that you don't buy any more hotels." (GOOD READING)

MARKETING RESEARCH

It's easier and less expensive to make the kind of product people want to buy, and then to sell it, than to make a product without specific reference to consumer desires.

The limitations of modern "market surveys" were ironically pointed up by Charles Brower, head of BBD&O advertising agency: "If Columbus had applied modern survey methods to his proposed voyage, the market test would have told him in advance that the world was flat; depth interviews with expert seamen would have revealed the hungry monsters lurking at the ocean's end; motivation studies among his crew would have shown they were interested only in money; Ferdinand and Isabella would have canceled their appropriation; America would never have been discovered, and all of us would be Indians." (SYDNEY HARRIS)

MARRIAGE (see WEDDINGS, HONEYMOON)

My wife hates to walk. When we married, she picked a church with a short aisle.

Some girls who are an armful during courtship become a handful after the wedding ceremony. (DAN BENNETT)

The times when spouses are most universally appreciated seem to be before the wedding and after the funeral.

"Where did you meet your wife?"
"At a travel bureau. I was looking for a vacation spot and she was the last resort."

Originally, a wedding ceremony amounted to no more than kidnapping a maiden. Though it has since grown to be more "civilized" many of our present customs reflect these old practices. Today's ushers and best man used to be warriors who accompanied the groom when he went to capture his bride. And the gifts the groom presented them with for helping him in his mission have become the groom's favors of today. (TODAY'S SECRETARY)

People living together without getting married are particularly disturbing to the guy who has just been arrested for fishing without a license.

A man should choose for his wife the woman he would choose as his friend, were she a man.

Wife complaining to marriage counselor: It all started with him wanting to be in the wedding photographs.

If your marriage is going to be much of a duet, you've got to face the music. (FRANKLIN P. JONES)

In rural Japan, a man's wife is chosen for him by his parents and he doesn't know who she is until after the marriage. Though the custom in America is completely different, the end result is often the same. (QUOTE)

If mates "change" after marriage, it is only in the direction they were already headed, not in the direction that the other may have hoped for. (SYDNEY HARRIS)

A manicurist married a pedicurist and they waited on each other hand and foot. (KREOLITE NEWS)

If a husband's words sometimes seem sharp, perhaps it's from trying to get them in edgewise.

My wife and I get along like cats and dogs. For Christmas we're giving each other flea collars.

There are some four-letter words which shock new brides—like cook, wash, and iron. (JOAN WELSH)

A young bride complained to her friend: "My husband and I are getting along together fairly well, but he simply can't bear children."

"Oh well," the friend consoled her, "you can't expect men to do everything." (GENERAL FEATURES)

No man is so virtuous as to marry a wife only to have children.
(MARTIN LUTHER)

One common difficulty in marriage is the disillusionment which often comes when a young couple discovers that their romantic dreams of perpetual bliss simply cannot be realized. The typical bride anticipates a continuation of the courtship, and lasting, loving attention from the man she marries. He expects the same warm response and idealized love he received during courtship. Both are disillusioned when the harsh realities of marriage begin to appear.

We begin marriage hoping for fulfillment, but often find frustration. Our own immature neurotic traits are magnified by the fact that the marriage partner has another set of neurotic tendencies. Instead of seeking fulfillment for ourselves, the primary goal should be to *fulfill the needs of one's partner*. It is thus that our own needs are met.

Adam and Eve had an ideal marriage. He didn't have to hear about all the men she could have married—and she didn't have to hear about the way his mother cooked it. (ROBERT ORBEN)

[A good] marriage is the peaceful coexistence of two nervous systems.
(EMIL KROTKY)

Many a man in love with a dimple makes the mistake of marrying the whole girl. (STEPHEN LEACOCK)

Wives are unpredictable. You never know what they are going to ask you to do as soon as you sit down.

Marriage has different attractions for different people. Those who marry for love want something wonderful and they sometimes get it. The people who marry because they want to escape something usually don't.
(CARL RIBLET, JR.)

The wife lay on her deathbed. She pleaded, "John, I want you to promise you'll ride in the same car with my mother at the funeral."
"OK," he said, "but it will spoil my whole day."

If a man works like a horse for his money, there are a lot of girls anxious to take him down the bridal path. (MARTY ALLEN)

Marriage isn't a battle that somebody is supposed to win.

Marriage is neither heaven nor hell. It is simply purgatory.
(ABRAHAM LINCOLN)

Marriage is a school of experience where husband and wife are clashmates.

Opposites attract, and that's too bad. (AL BERNSTEIN)

Society creates the myth that marriage is the proper haven for all our longings and a cure for all our shortcomings. People are programmed to believe that marriage will automatically give them individuality, identity, security, and happiness, when as a matter of fact marriage gives them none of these things unless they possess them in the first place.
(GERALD GRIFFIN)

Marriage is a union that defies management.

Wife: In most marriage ceremonies, they don't use the word "obey" anymore.
Husband: Too bad, isn't it? It used to lend a little humor to the occasion. (GENERAL FEATURES)

When we got married my wife promised to love, honor, and obey—and she does—she loves new clothes, honors her credit cards, and obeys her whims. (HUMOR ORIGINALS)

Marriage is the world's most expensive way of discovering your faults.

"My wife should be in Congress," one neighbor said to another, "because she loves to bring bills to the house." (WILFRED BEAVER)

Before marriage a man yearns for a woman. Afterward the "y" is silent.
(W. A. CLARKE)

Whether a fellow winds up with a nest egg or a goose egg depends a heap on the kind of chick he married.

Husband to friend: My wife is two hours late. She's either had an accident, been kidnapped, or she's shopping. Man, I hope she ain't shopping!
(NEWS AND VIEWS)

Marriage is like twirling a baton, turning handsprings, or eating with chopsticks. It looks so easy till you try it. (HELEN ROWLAND)

Never be so busy bringing home the bacon that you forget the applesauce.

This would be a much better world if more married couples were as deeply in love as they are in debt. (EARL WILSON)

Marriage is not for a moment; it is for a lifetime. It requires long and serious preparation. It is not to be leaped into, but entered with solemn steps of deliberation. For one of the most intimate and difficult of human relationships is that of marriage.
Infinitely rewarding at its best, unspeakably oppressive at its worst, marriage offers the uttermost extremes of human happiness and human bondage—with all the lesser degrees of felicity and restraint in between. (GINA CERMINARA)

My wife is always trying to get rid of me. The other day she told me to put the garbage out. I said to her I already put out the garbage. She told me to go and keep an eye on it. (RODNEY DANGERFIELD)

"Mommy, can I swim in the ocean?"
"No, the water's too rough."
"But Daddy's swimming."
"Daddy's insured." (CRUMBLEY, BY CRACKEY)

"When did you discover a certain chemistry in your marriage?"
"When I found arsenic in the corn flakes!"

My wife was crying because the dog ate some food she'd prepared for me. I consoled her by promising to buy her another dog.

There are certain rules about skydiving you should always keep in mind. Like, never have an argument with your wife while she's packing your chute. (CURRENT COMEDY)

A police car stopped a motorist on the highway and informed the driver that his wife fell out of the auto a mile back.

"Good!" exclaimed the motorist. "I thought I'd gone deaf."

(THE WOODEN BARREL)

When a man suffers in silence, it's apt to be his wife's.

Nothing is as binding in a marriage as the memory of a jointly committed error.

(KARLSRUHE)

When your wife is hanging on your words she probably wants to see if your story will hold together.

Marriage is a record of human relationship meant to be played in high fidelity.

Some arguing occurs in every marriage, usually about money, sex, or children. But in "fighting families" everything is the subject of a struggle. Bickering is their way of life. Quarreling couples actually follow some rules without realizing it: (1) Look upon each comment as unfriendly or having an ulterior motive. (2) Rebut it by criticism in return. (3) Recall all past criticisms. (4) Recite a litany of sacrifices made for the other. (5) Press on for control of the other, never relenting for honor is at stake. (6) If hard-pressed, storm out (he) or cry (she). (7) Resume the squabble at the earliest possible time.

(ARTHUR J. SNIDER)

Man's best possession is a sympathetic wife.

(EURIPIDES)

Classified ad in a southern New Jersey weekly: Adolph, please come back home. The children miss you, the lawn hasn't been mowed in three weeks, and the garden needs a worm like you. Your loving wife, Gretchen.

(CLIPPING)

All wives are alike in many disrespects.

(JEAN FARRIS)

I wouldn't want to say that my wife always gets her way and does everything she wants to do, but she does write her diary a week ahead of time.

(HENNY YOUNGMAN)

I hid my wife's Christmas present in the broom closet. That's one door she never opens.

He: "You don't deserve a husband like me."

She: "I don't deserve sinus trouble either, but I've got it."

(LUCILLE GOODYEAR)

"What happened to that dopey blonde your husband used to run around with?"

"I dyed my hair." (TODAY'S CHUCKLE)

To her sympathetic neighbor the unhappy wife confessed, "My husband doesn't show any interest in what I do. All he cares about is whatever it is he does at that place—wherever it is—that he works!"

Two old girls met at a class reunion. "What kind of husband do you have?" asked one.
"Well, let me put it this way," answered the other. "If he mentions Daisy in his sleep—he's definitely talking about flowers."
(PACIFIC OIL-MOTIVE MAGAZINE)

"For months," said the gadabout, "I couldn't discover where my husband spent his evenings."
"And then what happened?" asked a friend.
"Well, one evening I went home and there he was."(CLYDE MURDOCK)

My wife says when I get up in the morning, it reminds her of spring. The sap rises. (SHELBY FRIEDMAN)

My wife has three dimples. One in each chin.

You can never be happily married to another until you get a divorce from yourself! Successful marriage demands a certain death to self.
(JERRY McCANT)

In this age of unequal rights for women, a husband can't consider himself henpecked until he has to wash and iron his own aprons.
(HAROLD COFFIN)

The best way to make a marriage work is to make it play.

There is no lonelier person than the one who lives with a spouse with whom he or she cannot communicate. (MARGARET MEAD)

Happily married people live longer than do the unmarried or divorced, per insurance statistics.
And one essential reason is that they can talk out their inner tensions to each other, so their blood pressure goes down.
Besides, they can relax more by realizing they have a helping hand to come to their rescue if they are sick, so they suffer less anxiety.
(GEORGE CRANE)

People who are searching for an "ideal" mate rarely stop to ask themselves why such a paragon would be interested in them.(SYDNEY HARRIS)

To keep your marriage brimming,
With love in the loving cup,
Whenever you're wrong, admit it,
Whenever you're right, shut up. (OGDEN NASH)

Successful marriage is always a triangle: a man, a woman, and God.
(CECIL MYERS)

By all means marry. If you get a good wife, you will become very happy;
if you get a bad one, you will become a philosopher—and that is good
for any man. (SOCRATES)

MATERIALISM (see GREED, POSSESSIONS)

The most terrible thing about materialism, even more terrible than its
proneness to violence, is its boredom, from which sex, alcohol, drugs, all
devices for putting out the accusing light of reason and suppressing the
unrealizable aspirations of love, offer a prospect of deliverance.
(MALCOLM MUGGERIDGE)

The more you have to live *for*, the less you need to live *on*. Those who
make acquisition their goal never have enough. (SYDNEY HARRIS)

He is a wise man who does not grieve for the things which he has not,
but rejoices for those which he has. (EPICTETUS)

There is one advantage to having nothing—it never needs repair.
(FRANK A. CLARK)

Let us soar above our worldly possessions. The bee does not less need
its wings when it has gathered an abundant store; for if it sinks in the
honey it dies. (AUGUSTINE)

MATURITY

Maturity begins to grow when you can sense your concern for others
outweighing your concern for yourself. (JOHN MacNAUGHTON)

One of the marks of a mature person is the ability to dissent without
creating dissension. (DON ROBINSON)

Maturity is the ability to do a job whether you're supervised or not;
finish a job once it's started; carry money without spending it. And last,
but not least, the ability to bear an injustice without wanting to get
even. (FRED COOK)

Maturity begins when we're content to feel we're right about something, without feeling the necessity to prove someone else wrong.

(SYDNEY HARRIS)

It can be said without qualification that no human being can consider himself mature if he narrows the use of his efforts, talents, or means to his own personal advantage. The very concept of maturity rests on the degree of inner growth that is characterized by a yearning within the individual to transcend his self-concentration by extending himself into the lives of others. In other words, maturity is a stage in his development, when to live with himself in a satisfying manner it becomes imperative for him to give as well as to receive. (ALVIN GOESER)

Show me a man with both feet on the ground and I'll show you a man who can't get his pants on. (JOE E. LEWIS)

MAVERICKS (see CREATIVITY, MISFITS)

Corporations should try to tolerate and encourage their mavericks. The best leaders are apt to be found among those executives who have a strong component of unorthodoxy in their character. Instead of resisting innovation, they symbolize it—and companies seldom grow without innovation. (DAVID OGILVY)

MEANNESS

The end never really justifies the meanness. (E. DUANE HULSE)

MEASURING

When God measures a person He puts the tape around the heart instead of the head.

MEAT

My wife has gotten very tricky about food. For instance, I didn't know she was buying horsemeat until she served me a drumstick that was three feet long. (ROBERT ORBEN)

MEDICINE (see DOCTORS)

Medicine may be the only profession that labors incessantly to destroy the reason for its own existence.

MEDIOCRITY

Only a mediocre person is always at his best. (SOMERSET MAUGHAM)

MEEKNESS (see HUMILITY)

It's too bad that the meek haven't already inherited the earth, because the unmeek are making a real mess of it.

Meek endurance and meek obedience, the accepting of His dealings, of whatever complexion they are and however they may tear and desolate our hearts, without murmuring, without sulking, without rebellion or resistance, is the deepest conception of the meekness which Christ pronounced blessed. (ALEXANDER MACLAREN)

MEETINGS

Meetings are people. The chairman who hopes to manage his meeting must know people, understand people, like people. And because he has these qualities he will display patience and tolerate good humor even in trying situations. (GRANT HENDERSON)

Sometimes I get the feeling that the two biggest problems in America today are making ends meet—and making meetings end. (ROBERT ORBEN)

We just bought a new conference table. It's 8 feet wide, 30 feet long, and sleeps 20. (ROBERT ORBEN)

Meetings are a symptom of malorganization. The fewer meetings the better. (PETER DRUCKER)

MEMORY

I used to have trouble remembering names till I took that Sam Carnegie course. (JACK TAYLOR)

The advantage of a bad memory is that one enjoys several times the same good things for the first time. (NIETZSCHE)

No one is to be more pitied in this life than a person with an indelible memory. (O.A. BATTISTA)

You never realize what a good memory you have until you try to forget something.

The art of remembering is the art of taking an interest.

A retentive memory may be a good thing, but the ability to forget is the true token of greatness. (ELBERT HUBBARD)

There is a healing power in a selective memory. As humans we cannot forget our sins and hurts, but through forgiveness we can choose not to remember them. (GARY GULBRANSON)

That man who deposits experiences carefully in his memory will draw rich returns from his life. A flashback from such a past will be rewarding, not remorseful.

The memory can store the good things from experiences and draw dividends from them throughout life. Or, it can choose to store the horrible experiences and have only a dismal past to recall.

(C. NEIL STRAIT)

You always remember a kind deed. Particularly if it was yours.

Memory has a way of oversimplifying the past.   (COREY FORD)

He lives doubly who also enjoys the past.   (MARCUS MARTIAL)

Here are ten tips to improve your memory: (1) Intend to remember. (2) Understand what you are trying to remember. (3) Organize what you know into meaningful patterns. (4) Become genuinely interested in what you want to remember. (5) Use as many senses as possible. (6) Associate what you want to remember with what you know. (7) If you cannot find a logical association for a new fact, invent your own. (8) If you have a great deal to remember, spread it over a few days. (9) Review what you want to remember as often as possible. (10) The best time to memorize is at night before you go to bed.   (RAYMOND SCHUESSLER)

These are the things we forget most easily: things that have no meaning or interest for us; things we seldom have any need to recall; things we never learned or remembered properly in the first place; unpleasant things we deliberately "put out of" our minds; things that have no particular association for us. The human memory is a wonderful, baffling thing. The enormous assortment of facts and recollections that even a 20-year-old has had stick in his mind for instant recall would fill many hundreds of volumes if written down.   (DAVID GUNSTON)

The beauty of memory is that it still sees beauty when beauty has faded.   (PAUL BOESE)

MEN

Ever stop to think that, whereas women may marry for security, to have children or a home of their own, or to avoid being an old maid, men marry, 90 percent of the time, simply because they are in love?

(DALE CARNEGIE)

If it's true that men are such beasts, this must account for the fact that most women are animal lovers.   (DORIS DAY)

Have you noticed how no man ever tells a woman she's talking too much when she's telling him how wonderful he is?   (GOLDIE HAWN)

Some men need two women in their lives: a secretary to take everything down, and a wife to pick up everything. (F.M.W.)

No man lives by bread alone. They all need to be buttered up once in a while. (ANN OMINOUS)

An important difference between men and women is that women are smarter than men about women.

There must be some reason why a man must be convinced, while a woman must be persuaded. (ROBERT B. FLEMING)

Men are not against you; they're merely for themselves.(GENE FOWLER)

Whenever men gather, they soon turn the conversation to the subject of women and in the opinions that are given reveal themselves as divided into two categories—the men who would rather run away from women and the men who would rather run away with them.(CARL RIBLET, JR.)

Any man who says he can read a woman like a book is probably illiterate.

The young miss, who had no generation-gap problem, was having a heart-to-heart talk with her grandmother about her schoolwork, her boy-friends, etc.
"Tell me, Grandma," she said suddenly, "at what age are men the most fun?"
"Men are like record players, honey," replied the elderly lady. "They play at different speeds according to age but they are nice to have around at 33, 45, or 78."

Men are much like firecrackers; when they feel punk, you can expect them to explode very shortly. (JOAN WELSH)

The test of a man is how well he is able to feel about what he thinks. The test of a woman is how well she is able to think about what she feels. (MARY MCDOWELL)

If you think a woman driving a car can snarl traffic, you ought to see a man pushing a cart in a supermarket. (JOURNEYMAN BARBER)

Men and women are different in literally every cell of their bodies—due to male and female chromosomes—different in height, weight, figure, skeletal structure, metabolism, strength, some internal organs, ability to bear children—and temperament! It is not a matter of superiority or inferiority in any of those fields, but a matter of difference. The wise married couple learns how to appreciate and enjoy these differences. (PLAIN TRUTH)

Men have monthly rhythms too, although not much research has been done in this area since all the researchers are men. But it has been shown that men have pronounced four- and six-week mood cycles.

(GAY GAER LUCE)

Much of the trouble the country is in, is through the misapprehension of the sexual role. The U.S. is filled with fat, flabby men who think of themselves as Gary Cooper—two-fisted he-men, when actually it's a country of beer-drinking fat men looking at television. American men are the fattest in the world, incidentally, and certainly the weakest physically.

(GORE VIDAL)

The idea of masculine superiority may be just another old husbands' tale.

To summarize the advice (given to men over 40 years of age), two factors are vital: physical activity and a variety of interests: (1) you should move around, but not rush around; (2) keep an open mind and a closed refrigerator; (3) remember that variety is more than the spice of life—it's the wellspring of life. The man who pursues a variety of activities, balancing work with play, will usually stay fit long after middle age.

(TODAY'S HEALTH)

You're never too old to yearn.

(JOAN WELSH)

Some men in high positions are mighty small. Some men in low positions are mighty.

(M. DALE BAUGHMAN)

What God wants are men great enough to be small enough to be used.

MENTAL HEALTH

Mental health is the ability to accept inconsistency.

(PSYCHIATRIST, QUOTED BY BRUCE LARSON)

MENTAL ILLNESS

There are more men than women in mental hospitals, which just goes to show who's driving who crazy.

(PETER VEALE)

The mayor of a large American city was once a mental patient. So was a prominent publisher, the head of a big trade association, the board chairman of a large corporation, as well as prominent people from the writing and entertainment world. Mental illness is like any other kind of sickness. It often can be cured, permanently and completely, and it increasingly is.

(SYLVANUS AND EVELYN DUVALL)

MERCY

Mercy does not always express itself by withholding punishment.

(ERNEST M. LIGON)

MESSAGES

A message prepared in the mind reaches a mind; a message prepared in a life reaches a life. (BILL GOTHARD)

METRIC SYSTEM

When the U.S. goes metric, there are many phrases involving weights and measures which might have to be converted:
A miss is as good as 1.61 kilometers.
There isn't 0.06 gram of truth in it.
He felt 3.05 meters tall.
He was wearing a 37.86-liter hat.
First down and 9.14 meters to go.
She 2.54-centimetered her way through the crowd.
Don't hide your light under 35.24 liters. (WORLD WEEK)

If God had meant for us to have the metric system, there would have been only 10 apostles.

MIDDLE AGE

Middle age is when skin-tight isn't that accurate a description.

(ROBERT ORBEN)

Middle age is the time when a man is always thinking that in a week or two he will feel as good as ever. (DON MARQUIS)

You've reached middle age when people begin to recognize you from the rear too.

The really frightening thing about middle age is the knowledge that you'll outgrow it. (DORIS DAY)

Middle age is when everything starts to click—your elbows, knees, and neck. (ROBERT ORBEN)

Middle age is that difficult period between juvenile delinquency and senior citizenship, when you have to take care of yourself.(RON GREER)

Middle age is when a guy keeps turning off lights for economical rather than romantic reasons. (ELI CASS)

Middle age is when the only thing that can lead you down the garden path is a seed catalog. (IVERN BOYETT)

Middle age is the time when our middles get bigger, our hair gets thinner, our sights get shorter, and our faces get saggier.

Common exercises indulged in by the average middle-aged American male are running down their friends, jumping to conclusions, sidestepping responsibility, and pushing their luck.

(W. J. BOWERMAN AND W.E. HARRIS)

MINDS

You can have such an open mind that it is too porous to hold a conviction.

(GEORGE CRANE)

Merely having an open mind is nothing; the object of opening the mind, as of opening the mouth, is to shut it again on something solid.

(G.K. CHESTERTON)

When the water gets up to the neck, the mind begins to work.

(JACK HIEMAN)

Too many people just aren't equipped to attend a meeting of minds.

(EMPIRE)

Some of the narrowest minds are found in the fattest heads.

(MARJORIE M. STANLEY)

MINISTERS (see PREACHERS)

There are too many weary and frustrated ministers with that "poor me" feeling. There's simply no room for feeling sorry for oneself in the ministry. All I can say to discouraged ministers, who have given up too easily and feel put upon . . . is that God has called us to do a job for Him, and has given us the courage to be His witnesses in the world. There is no time for moaning, complaining, and getting into trouble, if the minister is about God's business. He is under orders and under discipline and, to recall Churchill's words, "He must like what he has to do." The minister, as are all Christians, is called on to lose his life in a cause in order to find it has value and meaning; and his freedom is measured by the goals to which he surrenders himself—one of which is the spread of His kingdom.

(JAMES W. KENNEDY)

If the average preacher would listen to some other preacher twice each day for two weeks, he would go home and abbreviate his messages.

(BAPTIST STANDARD)

The parson was giving his first sermon in the big new church, and he celebrated the occasion by really teeing off on the sinners. After the service he met one of his most outspoken parishioners and asked, "How did you like my sermon?"

"Well, Reverend, after raising all the money to build this new church we sorta hoped you'd quit yelling at us." (L.S. HEMBREE)

Clabe Hawkins throws light on why it takes some churches so long to get new pastors after their pulpits become vacant: "The churches is scared they'll get another preacher like the one they just had, and every prospective pastor is afeared he'll wind up with another church like the one he is trying to get loose from." (ARKANSAS BAPTIST)

MINISTRY

A ministry that is college-trained but not Spirit-filled works no miracles.
(SAMUEL CHADWICK)

MINORITY

I find more and more that it is well to be on the side of the minority, since it is always the more intelligent. (GOETHE)

MIRACLES

Anyone who doesn't believe in miracles is not a realist.
(DAVID BEN-GURION)

We couldn't conceive of a miracle if none had ever happened.
(LIBBIE FUDIM)

MISERS

The miser does no one any good, but he treats himself worst of all.
(PUBLIUS SYRUS)

A miser isn't much fun to live with, but he makes a wonderful ancestor.
(MODERN MATURITY)

MISERY

How to be miserable: (1) Use "I" as often as possible. (2) Always be sensitive to slights. (3) Be jealous and envious. (4) Think only about yourself. (5) Talk only about yourself. (6) Trust no one. (7) Never forget a criticism. (8) Always expect to be appreciated. (9) Be suspicious. (10) Listen greedily to what others say of you. (11) Always look for faults in others. (12) Do as little as possible for others. (13) Shirk your duties if you can. (14) Never forget a service you may have rendered. (15) Sulk if people aren't grateful for your favors. (16) Insist on consideration and respect. (17) Demand agreement with your own views on everything.

(18) Always look for a good time. (19) Love yourself first. (20) Be selfish at all times. This formula is guaranteed to work. (QUOTE)

It is difficult to make a man miserable while he feels he is worthy of himself and claims kindred to the great God who made him.
(ABRAHAM LINCOLN)

Sin's misery and God's mercy are beyond measure.

MISFITS (see MAVERICKS)

The greatest advantage in being a misfit is that you are not easy to replace. There may not be many square holes, but if you are a square peg you have almost a monopoly. (ALAN BRIEN)

MISFORTUNES

Sometimes we want to forget the misfortunes of life but fail to realize that the low places in life have given us stability. (RAY O. JONES)

Little minds are tamed and subdued by misfortune; but great minds rise above it. (WASHINGTON IRVING)

MISSIONARIES

Missionaries are never beggars. They are ambassadors who give us an opportunity to become partners by giving our dollars while they give their lives. (HARRY IRONSIDE)

I have but one candle of life to burn, and would rather burn it out where people are dying in darkness than in a land which is flooded with lights.
(A MISSIONARY)

If God calls you to be a missionary, don't stoop to be a king.
(JORDAN GROOMS)

The missionary was the speaker at a dinner in his honor before he embarked for a distant land. "I want to thank you for your kindnesses, and I want all of you to know that when I am out there, surrounded by ugly, grinning savages, I shall always think of you people."

MISSIONS

The Spirit of Christ is the spirit of missions, and the nearer we get to Him the more intensely missionary we must become. (HENRY MARTYN)

I look upon foreign missionaries as the scaffolding around a rising building. The sooner it can be dispensed with, the better; or rather, the sooner it can be transferred to other places, to serve the same temporary use, the better. (HUDSON TAYLOR)

We are the children of converts of foreign missionaries; and fairness means that I must do to others as men once did to me.
(MALTBIE D. BABCOCK)

Many of us cannot reach the mission fields on our feet, but we can reach them on our knees. (T.J. BACH)

God's standard for missions: The man of God, with the Word of God, in the Spirit of God, for the glory of God. (T.J. BACH)

MISTAKES (see ERRORS)

A lot of impulsive mistakes are made by people who simply aren't willing to stay bored a little while longer. (FRANK A. CLARK)

We'll do all right if we can capitalize on our mistakes. (MICKEY RIVERS)

If everybody profited by his mistakes there'd be no poverty in the world.

When we commit a gross piece of stupidity, we call it "an honest mistake"—as if most other people make dishonest mistakes. (SYDNEY HARRIS)

Just in case you find any mistakes in this magazine, please remember they were put there for a purpose. We try to offer something for everyone. Some people are always looking for mistakes.
(A CARIBBEAN AIRLINE TRAVEL GUIDE)

Don't worry about your mistakes. Some of the dullest people don't make any. (ROBERT D. HAHN)

Making mistakes isn't stupid. Disregarding them is. (JOSEPH GANCHER)

We know at least one thing about a person who never makes mistakes—he can't be very busy.

If you must make mistakes, it will be more to your credit if you make a new one each time. (CONSTRUCTION DIGEST)

More people would learn from their mistakes if they weren't so busy denying them. (HAROLD J. SMITH)

We must never overlook the untold benefits that can be derived from mistakes. A person should never hesitate to own he has been in the wrong, which is but saying in other words that he is wiser today than he was yesterday, because of his mistake. (MEGIDDO MESSAGE)

The six mistakes of man: (1) The delusion that personal gain is made by crushing others. (2) The tendency to worry about things that cannot be changed or corrected. (3) Insisting that a thing is impossible because we cannot accomplish it. (4) Refusing to set aside trivial preferences. (5) Neglecting development and refinement of the mind, and not acquiring the habit of reading and study. (6) Attempting to compel others to believe and live as we do. (CICERO)

A doctor's mistake is buried.
A lawyer's mistake is imprisoned.
An accountant's mistake is jailed.
A dentist's mistake is pulled.
A pharmacist's mistake is dead.
A plumber's mistake is stopped.
An electrician's mistake is shocking.
A carpenter's mistake is sawdust.
A teacher's mistake is failed.
A printer's mistake is redone.
And yours? (IN A NUTSHELL)

No matter what mistakes you may have made—no matter how you've messed things up—you still can make a new beginning. The person who fully realizes this suffers less from the shock and pain of failure and sooner gets off to a new beginning. (NORMAN V. PEALE)

MODERN AGE

Society today has become too impersonal. More and more of the factors shaping our lives seem to be beyond our own influence.
(MORRIS B. ABRAM)

Newspapers do our thinking for us, professional athletes play games for us, movies make love for us, and advertisements choose goods for us. All that's left for us to do is work and shell out the price. (EXAMINER)

Modern man drives a mortgaged car over a bond-financed highway on credit-card gas. (EARL WILSON)

We live in a world of invertebrate theology, jellyfish morality, see-saw religion, India-rubber convictions, somersault philosophy, and a psychology that tells us what we already know in words we don't understand.
(ROBERT G. LEE)

MODESTY

Modesty is a form of immodesty, suggesting, as it does, that you've done something worthy of praise. (FRANKLIN P. JONES)

False modesty is better than none. (VIHJALMUR STEFANSSON)

Modesty is to merit what shade is to figures in a picture; it gives it strength and makes it stand out. (JEAN DE LA BRUYÈRE)

Never trust too much in an overly modest man. A guy failing to toot his own horn may simply have a dead battery.
(CHARLESTON [S.C.] NEWS AND COURIER)

Modesty is that certain feeling that others will discover how wonderful you are. (ARGUS POSTER)

They were discussing a mutual acquaintance. "I admire the man's unusual modesty," said one.
"Yes," agreed the other, "but you must admit he has a great deal to be modest about." (JACK KYTLE)

MONDAY

Monday is a terrible way to spend one-seventh of your life.
(HOUGHTON LINE)

MONEY (see WEALTH)

If your outgo exceeds your income, then your upkeep will be your downfall. (BILL EARLE)

Modern man is frantically trying to earn enough to buy things he's too busy to enjoy. (FRANK A. CLARK)

Money can't buy health, happiness, or what it did last year.

If a person gets his attitude toward money straight, it will help straighten out almost every other area in his life. (BILLY GRAHAM)

It's peculiar how a dollar can look so big when it goes to church and so small when it goes for groceries. (GRIT)

It seems quaint to us that our ancestors used clamshells and beads for money, but then I wonder what they'd think about a walletful of little plastic cards. (BURTON HILLIS)

Most Americans are members of the debt set. (FRANK TYGER)

A "credit bureau" is an organization that turns down as a "poor risk" a man who has paid cash for everything and has never owed a penny in his life. (SYDNEY HARRIS)

One-sixth of Matthew, Mark, and Luke, and 12 of Jesus' 38 parables, have to do with money. (DAVID ALLEN)

Our economy is based upon people wanting more—their happiness on wanting less. (FRANK A. CLARK)

The way you're most apt to meet your bills these days is on every hand.

Money in the bank is like toothpaste in the tube. Easy to take out, hard to put back. (EARL WILSON)

Make money your god, and it will plague you like the devil. (HENRY FIELDING)

Nowadays money is like a New Year's resolution—you make it, but you can't keep it. (ROBERT ORBEN)

Make all you can, save all you can, give all you can. (JOHN WESLEY)

If you pay a person less than he earns, he will soon be earning less than he's paid. (DAVID L. WESTLAKE)

More than ever before, Americans are suffering from back problems—back taxes, back rent, back auto payments. (ROBERT ORBEN)

Money is in some respects like fire; it is a very excellent servant, but a terrible master. (P.T. BARNUM)

Money often costs too much. (RALPH W. EMERSON)

Never lend money to a friend. It's dangerous—it could damage his memory. (SAM LEVENSON)

Credit manager: Do you have any money in the bank?
  Applicant: Certainly.
  Credit manager: How much?
  Applicant: I don't know. I haven't shaken it lately. (H.E. MARTZ)

Easy credit is what makes people uneasy later.

Sign in finance company window: Loans—for those who have everything but haven't paid for all of it yet.

Nothing makes time go faster than buying on it.　　　(BALANCE SHEET)

Money may not bring happiness but it puts your creditors in a better frame of mind.

If you have to borrow money, borrow from a pessimist. He never expects to get it back anyhow.

A son seldom makes his money last, if his father made it first.
　　　　　　　　　　　　　　　　　　　　　　　　　　(DICK NEALE)

There are several ways to apportion the family income—all of them unsatisfactory.　　　　　　　　　　　　　　　　(ROBERT BENCHLEY)

Part of today's problem is that our paychecks are minus tax and our bills are plus.　　　　　　　　　　　　　　　　　　(JOHN RAUDONIS)

The fool who's soon parted from his money is hard to detect among the rest of us having the same problem.　　　　　(FRANKLIN P. JONES)

To figure your cost of living simply take your income and add 10 percent.

It is easy to meet your expenses these days. In fact, you meet them every time you turn around.　　　　　　　　　　　　　　　　(GRIT)

Who wants to change a friend into an enemy should lend him money.

Stop such un-American child-rearing policies as to give your child an allowance. That "allowance plan" is part of the reason why America is now in the "gimmie" mood, where even adult voters want to be promised more free favors, larger Social Security checks, and . . . boondoggling handouts. Instead of the "allowance plan," which thus creates the "dole" psychology, pay your child on a piecework basis for specific chores and other designated pay tasks.　　　　　(GEORGE CRANE)

Sign in a loan company window: Now you can borrow enough money to get completely out of debt.

It's good to have money and the things that money can buy, but it's good too to check up once in a while and make sure you haven't lost the things that money can't buy.　　　　　　　　(GEORGE H. LORIMER)

While money isn't everything, it is a pretty good cure for poverty.

You can't win. If you run after money, you're materialistic. If you don't get it, you're a loser. If you get it and keep it, you're a miser. If you don't try to get it, you lack ambition. If you get it and spend it you're a spendthrift. If you still have it after a lifetime of work, you're a fool who never got any fun out of life. (QUOTE)

Getting money is like digging with a needle; spending it is like water soaking into sand. (JAPANESE PROVERB)

Many folks think they aren't good at earning money—when what they don't know is how to use it. (FRANK A. CLARK)

We're living in a time when the only way to see daylight is to moonlight. (ROBERT ORBEN)

I may not be outstanding, but my bills are. (LLOYD CORY)

My assets are in a liquid state—everything is going down the drain. (EMIL VOSICKY)

A dollar sign has been described as a capital S which has been double-crossed. (LEO AIKMAN)

People who've always kept cash in the mattress may welcome the water bed as the ideal place to hide their liquid assets.

Pursitis: Pain on reaching for the wallet. (JACK KRAUS)

Checking account: Something that needs month-to-month resuscitation. (DANA ROBBINS)

I'm not stingy—I merely have low pockets and short arms. (SHELBY FRIEDMAN)

I have not observed men's honesty to increase with their riches. (THOMAS JEFFERSON)

Sign in a Ft. Lauderdale restaurant: If you are over 80 years old and accompanied by your parents, we will cash your check.

If he now has money to burn, you can be sure your wife will refer to him as an old flame. (HAL CHADWICK)

My wife has just one extravagance. Our checking account.

Today women often push carts through supermarkets at speeds over $65 an hour. (JOSEPH SALAK)

How did Plentyrich make all his money?
By judicious speculation and investment.
And how did Poorman lose all his money?
By gambling on the stock market.   (WOODMEN OF THE WORLD)

I don't understand why so many folks seem to want to die rich.
(FRANK A. CLARK)

Recession: when the man next door loses his job. *Depression*: when you lose your job. *Panic*: when your wife loses her job.

I don't like money actually, but it quiets my nerves.   (JOE LOUIS)

Money has never yet made anyone rich.   (SENECA)

Money will buy only things which are for sale, and happiness is not one of them. The two greatest rewards in life are love and achievement.
(F. ALEXANDER MAGOUN)

And so, in conclusion, may the Bluebird of Happiness fly over your shopping cart and stamp everything with last year's prices.
(ROBERT ORBEN)

MOODS (see FEELINGS)

On managing your moods and feelings: Quiet waiting before the Lord in prayer will give Him a chance to change your mood. A few minutes of waiting on God, coupled with honesty in laying the situation before Him, will take all the steam out of the pressure cooker. The situation may not change, but you will have changed for the better in spite of the situation.   (ROBERT A. COOK)

If you're dog-tired at night, it may be because you growled all day.
(WAR CRY)

MOONLIGHTING

A comedian once defined a moonlighter as a man who holds two jobs so that he can drive from one to the other in a better car. Today it more likely is the necessity to make ends meet—or the vision of a more comfortable life through longer work hours—that drives the multiple job-holder. But money is not the only reason why people moonlight. The man with extra work may be seeking a creative outlet or relief from the boredom of his regular job, developing a second skill as a form of "employment insurance," or merely avoiding his wife.   (TED J. RAHSTIS)

You must have heard about the rabbi seen on the street with the reverse collar, who explained: "I'm moonlighting." (RABBI SAMUEL M. SILVER)

MORALE

I've seen boys on my baseball team go into slumps and never come out of them, and I've seen others snap right out and come back better than ever. I guess more players lick themselves than are ever licked by an opposing team. The first thing any man has to know is how to handle himself. (CONNIE MACK)

Sign in a boss' office: Firing will continue until morale improves.

No man can deliver the goods if his heart is heavier than the load. (FRANK I. FLETCHER)

The best morale exists when you never hear the word mentioned. When you hear a lot of talk about it, it's usually lousy. (DWIGHT EISENHOWER)

Morale is when your hands and feet keep on working when your head says it can't be done. (BEN MOREELL)

Morale is faith in the man at the top. (EUGENE P. BERTIN)

MORALITY

Of all the lessons history teaches this one is plainest: the person who tries to achieve ends through force is always unscrupulous and is always cruel. We should remember this in an age where morality seems to be disappearing and is being replaced by politics. (EUSTACE PERCY)

MORNINGS

Do you ever have the feeling that you'd need a head start just to finish last? (ROBERT ORBEN)

Morning is so nice they ought to make it later in the day.

My luck has been so bad lately that for me every morning is the dawn of a new error. (TOM McELWEE)

The happier you are in the morning, the less healthy you're apt to be, according to a British medical journal: "People who rise with the lark and sing like a bird," says *World Medicine*, "are likely to flake off during the morning, have a gloomy afternoon, and drop off during TV at night. Fit people are so subdued by sleep that they need a little time to come back to normal." (FAMILY WEEKLY)

MORTGAGES

It's a shame Professor Einstein spent all that time on the Theory of Relativity and never found out how a mortgage can speed up the months and slow down the years at the same time.

Most new homes are being bought on the layaway plan. You pay for them until they lay you away.   (ROBERT ORBEN)

MOTHERS-IN-LAW

My mother-in-law radiates a lot of warmth. But so does an H-bomb.
(SHELBY FRIEDMAN)

My mother-in-law was dangerously ill—but now she's dangerously well again.

Behind every successful man is a surprised mother-in-law.
(HOWARD W. CLEMENT)

MOTHERS (see PARENTS)

Scotland, with her well-known reverence for motherhood, insists that an ounce of mother is worth more than a pound of clergy. (H.H. BIRKINS)

Johnny: I fell into a mud puddle.
  Mother: What? With your new pants on?
  Johnny: Yeah, I fell in so fast I didn't have time to take them off.

Whistler came home and found his mother scrubbing the kitchen floor on her hands and knees.
  "Why Mother," he exclaimed, "have you gone off your rocker?"
(SUCCESSFUL FARMING)

A teacher was telling of the hardships of the Pilgrims their first winter. In the midst of her description concerning the starving conditions, one of the first-graders raised her hand and said, "I wish my mommy had been there. She always knows just what to do."   (CHURCH AND HOME)

Though a mother stays home and keeps her house clean, it is still not a home unless she creates the right spirit in the house. It is the atmosphere created primarily by the mother that makes a home worthwhile.
(J.R. BOOKHOFF)

The commonest fallacy among women is that simply having children makes one a mother—which is as absurd as believing that having a piano makes one a musician.   (SYDNEY HARRIS)

To a mother, a son is never a fully grown man; and a son is never a fully grown man until he understands and accepts this about his mother.
(SYDNEY HARRIS)

MOTIVATION

Motivation is what gets you started. Habit is what keeps you going.
(JIM RYUN)

People are always motivated by at least two reasons; the one they tell you about, and a secret one. (O.A. BATTISTA)

The motive for a deed is never the same before, during, and after its performance; for the very act itself changes the motive, unearthing deeper aspects we were unaware of. (SYDNEY HARRIS)

A bus driver in Milan, Italy, long discouraged by passengers who ignored his constant plea, "Move to the rear of the bus, please," has resorted to psychology. It's simple and successful. "Ladies and gentlemen," he calls out, "all those with clean underwear move to the rear. The rest of you stay up front with me."

Motivation is the art of getting people to do what you want them to do because they want to do it. (DWIGHT EISENHOWER)

When you want to move or motivate someone, *whisper.*

MOTIVES

Man sees your actions, but God your motives. (THOMAS À KEMPIS)

MOUTH (see TALKING)

Mouth: the principal working part of man's own built-in self-destruct system. (JEAN FARRIS)

A closed mouth gathers no feet. (KANSAS STATE COLLEGIAN)

Institutions are a lot easier to deal with than people. Stores and offices have a closing time—mouths don't. (ROBERT ORBEN)

The mouth talks about the things that fill the heart.
(Matthew 12:34, WMS)

MOVIES

In a mere half century movies have gone from silent to unspeakable.
(DOUG LARSON)

MUSIC (see SINGING)

Mark Twain is said to have said of Richard Wagner's music: "It's not nearly so bad as it sounds."

I think of music as a menu. I can't eat the same thing every day.
(CARLOS SANTANA)

Jesus, the Rock of Ages, is the rock that doesn't roll. (LARRY NORMAN)

I studied cello 5 years in Italy, 10 years in Germany, and 15 years in vain. (MOREY AMSTERDAM)

When I was a kid, my folks were so poor we couldn't even afford electricity. I was the only boy on the block who played a kerosene guitar. (GEORGE GOBEL)

Sandy, a young Scot, went to London for a holiday. On his return a friend asked how he had fared. "All right," he said cautiously. "But they're funny folk down there."
  "How's that?"
  "Well, one night very late—it must have been about 2:00 in the morning—a man came banging on my door. He shouted and yelled and was in a nasty temper. At 2 o'clock, man!"
  "And what did you do?"
  "I didn't do anything. I just went on quietly playing my bagpipes."
(UNITED MINE WORKERS JOURNAL)

A young man was practicing his guitar in the small hours of the morning when the landlord came in. "Do you know there's a little sick lady upstairs?" asked the landlord.
  "No," answered the musician. "Hum a little of it."

The only time that our blessed Lord ever is recorded as having sung is the night that He went out to His death. (FULTON SHEEN)

"What is your position in the choir?" asked the new church member.
  "Absolutely neutral," replied the mild tenor. "I don't side with either faction." (REGINA COMMONWEALTH)

If the Lord had intended us to sing, He'd have given us feathers.
(PERCY FLAAGE)

Music is a part of us, and either ennobles or degrades our behavior.
(BOETHIUS)

Rock music sounds like an octopus making love to a bagpipe.
(DAVE GARDNER)

There was so much music in America I revolted. . . . It's even in grocery stores and at the beautician's, and the worst thing about it is that nobody is listening. (HEPZIBAH MENUHIN)

A motorist driving through the wide open spaces of the West stopped at a forlorn shack to ask directions. The occupant cheerfully supplied all the desired information.

"I presume," remarked the motorist, "that ranching is your profession?"

"No," his informant replied, "I'm a piano tuner."

"Surely you can't make much of a living at piano tuning in this unsettled region. Pianos must be mighty scarce."

"That's true," came the answer, "but I make a nice income tightening up barbed-wire fences." (GREAT NORTHERN GOAT)

Music study has great value insofar as a mastery of it enables one to live more richly and wholesomely, to be a stronger, better, happier, more cooperative individual; to succeed more fully in the great business of being *human*. (VERNON LEIDIG)

A painter paints his pictures on canvas. But musicians paint their pictures on silence. We provide the music and you provide the silence. (LEOPOLD STOKOWSKI)

One moderately talented but immoderately self-confident musician asked Franz Liszt to have a look at something he had written. Liszt returned the score with these words: "Your work contains much that is beautiful and much that is novel. It's a pity that the beautiful is not novel, and the novel is not beautiful." (SPUTNIK)

Late arrival at concert: The usher said they're playing the Fifth Symphony. That means we missed the first four!

Three dowagers arrived late at a concert in the park. One said, "This sounds like the Sextet from Lucia."

Another said, "No, I think they're playing the Quartet from Rigoletto."

The third gal didn't have a clue, so she went up front to try to find out. Returning to their bench, she said, "You're both wrong. The sign says it's the Refrain from Expectoration."

At the conclusion of the concert two ushers were applauding harder than anybody else. The audience was impressed with the fact that they were true lovers of music, and then one usher suddenly stopped applauding.

The other turned to him and said in a stage whisper, "Keep clapping, you idiot! One more encore and we're on overtime." (GOOD READING)

A little boy who loved music was bitterly disappointed because he could neither play nor sing. But Amati, the violin-maker, said: "There are many ways of making music. What matters is the song in the heart." So Antonio Stradivarius was encouraged to become the world's greatest violin-maker.   (EDGAR CHRISEMER)

Country to me is the music of the people—it tells of their work, of their loves, of their hopes and dreams, and of their religion. Country music speaks for the common hardworking man—it has its roots in the pioneering spirit.   (JOHNNY CASH)

Folk music? Why Daddy, I don't know no other kind but folk music. Did you ever hear a hoss sing?   (LOUIS ARMSTRONG)

A folksinger is someone who sings through his nose by ear.
                                                                            (PAT BUTTRAM)

Forty-three musicians with an average age of 22 were tested by Dr. Rayford Reddell of the San Francisco Hearing and Speech Center. He found that 20 percent of them had the hearing of 70-year-old men. Young people in their audiences face the same hazards. Sound levels at rock concerts and discotheques have been measured up to 130 decibels, equal to the scream of a jet fighter's engine and capable of causing irreversible damage.   (SYLVIA PORTER)

Choirmaster to choirboy: No, no, Carruthers, the hymn-writer was Wesley, not Presley.   (PETERBOROUGH DAILY TELEGRAPH)

If you have never heard the mountains singing, or seen the trees of the field clapping their hands, do not think because of that they don't. Ask God to open your ears so you may hear it, and your eyes so you may see it, because, though few men ever know it, they do, my friend, they do.
                                                                     (McCANDLISH PHILLIPS)

A song is a lot like a handshake. You have to stick it out and see if anybody grabs it.   (ROGER MILLER)

Some serious symphonies are musical compositions that you think will break out into a tune any minute, but they never do.

My son is into music. In fact, there isn't an instrument he can't play. The guitar—he can't play that. The piano—he can't play that. The trumpet—he can't play that.   (ROBERT ORBEN)

NAMES

After the baby had been christened, a neighbor asked what they had called her.

"Hazel," answered the mother.

"Lord forgive you," said the neighbor. "With all the saints' names available and you name her after a nut!" (ROBERT T. REILLY)

The new employee limped up to the foreman at the end of a long day of back-breaking work. "Boss, are you sure you got my name right?" he asked.

"It's right here—you're Joe Simpson, aren't you?" the foreman replied.

"Yeah, that's it," moaned the guy. "I was just checking—I thought maybe you had me down as Samson."

NATIONALISM

There can be no hope for humanity without a new collective identity of the people out of the various nations, languages, and races. Nationalism is one of the worst seductions. It is an instrument of domination by which one people can be incited against another. (JUERGEN MOLTMANN)

NATURE

Everybody wants to go back to nature—but not on foot. (WERNER MITSCH)

Those who contemplate the beauty of the earth find reserves of strength that will endure as long as life lasts. (RACHEL CARSON)

NEEDS (see WANTS)

Man is a wanting animal—as soon as one of his needs is satisfied, another appears in its place. This process is unending. It continues from birth to death. Man continuously puts forth effort—works, if you please—to satisfy his needs. (DOUGLAS MCGREGOR)

There are three main areas of importance to every human being, according to Earl Nightingale. They are *identity*, recognition as a person; *stimulation*, the need for change as an escape from boredom; and *security*, the opposite of anxiety.
    There are also four universal needs common to all humans. They are the needs for *a livelihood, maintaining health, getting along with other people, and getting along with oneself.* (JAMES R. FISHER)

If we have to do without things we need, we just grin and bear it. It's doing without unnecessary things we want that makes us downhearted.

Some food, some sun, some work, some fun, some-one. (E.M. WALKER)

NEGATIVISM

If I were a gravedigger, or even a hangman, there are some people I could work for with a great deal of pleasure. (DOUGLAS JERROLD)

NEIGHBORHOOD

Neighborhood: The juvenile delinquent who lives next door.
(CATHEY GARAMILLO)

NEIGHBORS

If you have an unpleasant neighbor, the odds are that he does too.
(FRANK A. CLARK)

The Bible tells us to love our neighbors, and also to love our enemies; probably because they are generally the same people. (G.K. CHESTERTON)

Somehow neighborliness seemed more natural when neighbors were miles apart rather than two doors down the block, or the hall.
(GEORGE F. WILL)

My idea of a good neighbor is one who lets his grass grow just as high as mine. (KIRK KIRKPATRICK)

It's amazing how nice neighbors become when they find out you're moving. (BITS AND PIECES)

NEPOTISM

Nepotism: The theory of relativity.　　　　(SHELBY FRIEDMAN)

NEUROTICS

Neurotics are sure that no one understands them, and they wouldn't have it any other way.　　　　(MIGNON MCLAUGHLIN)

A neurotic is a person who builds castles in the air. A psychotic is someone who moves into them. (F.G. KERNAN) (And a psychiatrist is the person who collects the rent.)

Now there's a list of the 10 most neurotic people. It's called "The Best-Stressed List."　　　　(SHELBY FRIEDMAN)

NEWNESS

If the blessings of God are new every morning, why is the language of testimony and prayer threadbare and stale?　　　　(D.G. KEHL)

NEW PRODUCTS (see PRODUCTS)

"New" seems to be a word advertisers use when they can think of nothing new to say about an old product.　　　　(FRANK A. CLARK)

Few things are created and perfected at the same moment.

A product is not good because it is new, or undeserving of marketing promotion because it is not new.　　　　(ARDITH HOOTEN)

Nothing ever gets built on schedule or within budget. (PAUL DICKSON)

The way to make a fortune is to come up with something that's low-priced, habit-forming, and tax-deductible.　　　　(SUNSHINE MAGAZINE)

A new idea is like a child. It's easier to conceive than to deliver.
　　　　(TED KOYSIS)

One of the things I learned the hard way is that you simply can't go back to what was once successful with any certainty that it will succeed again.　　　　(ARNOLD GINGRICH)

Nearly every new product failure is a failure in empathy. Someone didn't possess the ability to put himself into the buyer's shoes and see the product from *his* point of view, *his* needs or lack of needs.
　　Empathy—sometimes called taste—is probably the most valuable trait any man can possess, yet is one of the least appreciated by others—

undoubtedly because so few people are capable of getting outside their own skins and prejudices.

NEWS MEDIA

Many times I'd rather be a song-and-dance man, bring some levity to you, instead of wrack and ruin. But we are on the threshold—indeed we are in it—of a revolution calling for a redistribution of the world's resources. (WALTER CRONKITE)

What is mostly wrong with television, newspapers, magazines, and films is what is mostly wrong with the schools and colleges: mindlessness. At the heart of the problem . . . is the failure of people at every level to ask why they are doing what they are doing or to inquire into the consequences. (CHARLES E. SILBERMAN)

Negativism, frustration, anxiety, and even feelings of depression are stimulated by a concept of news which has remained with us, essentially unchanged, for four decades. The "glorification" of crime by excessive and detailed reporting in itself contributes to and creates more crime. It is crystal-clear that the overwhelming emphasis on "bad news" greatly contributes to the climate of violence which characterizes this country today. (HERBERT A. OTTO)

What a scarcity of news there would be if we all obeyed the Ten Commandments. (CONSTRUCTION DIGEST)

A boy who worked in an ice cream parlor was hired as a newspaper reporter. The editor liked the way he handled big scoops. (SHELBY FRIEDMAN)

NICENESS (see IMPORTANCE)

This would be a great world if everyone was as nice to you as the guy who's trying to sell you something. (BITS AND PIECES)

NOAH (see WEATHER)

"Just the same," chided Noah's wife, "I'd feel safer if those termites were locked up in a metal box." (SUNDAY SCHOOL TIMES & GOSPEL HERALD)

NOISE

How can Billy study with the TV going full blast? Relax, parents. Noise can actually be a memory aid, according to Peter McLean of the University of Calgary. Dr. McLean asked 160 students to concentrate on materials he gave them, placing half the students in a quiet environment and half against a noisy background. Tested right after the experiment, the students who had studied in peace scored higher; but the next day those who had studied against noise topped them in recalling the same materials. Conclusion: Noise interferes with short-term memory but enhances long-term memory—the more useful kind. (PTA MAGAZINE)

A wise man has said that noise is the ultimate insult. It belittles us. It gives us nothing at which to strike back. It kills what is left of many things that we have loved: music, beauty, friendship, hope, excitement, and the reassurance of nature. Traditionally, noise is used to ridicule, embarrass, denigrate, and curse, while silence is used for worship, respect, anticipation, and love. Do we hate each other as much as our noise level suggests? (JOHN HILLABY)

NONSENSE

No one is exempt from talking nonsense; the misfortune is to do it solemnly. (MONTAIGNE)

NORMAL AND AVERAGE

Human psychology is a funny thing. Everybody wants to be normal but nobody wants to be average. (MARY MCDONALD)

NOSE

The older you get the longer your nose grows, says a prominent North Carolina plastic surgeon. The elongation moves slowly but in some people may eventually become pronounced. . . . Dr. Carl Patterson said the process can be detected by plastic surgeons as early as the teenage years. (NATIONAL ENQUIRER)

NOSINESS (see CURIOSITY)

The motto on the first coin ever issued in the U.S. (the 1787 penny) was, Mind Your Own Business.

NOSTALGIA

Nostalgia is a release from reality, far safer than drugs and alcohol, and costs nothing. (SOCIAL STUDIES)

People seem to get nostalgic about a lot of things they weren't so crazy about the first time around. (WEBSTER'S CROSSWORDS)

A trip to nostalgia now and then is good for the spirit, as long as you don't set up housekeeping. (DAN BARTOLOVIC)

Nostalgia consists of longing for the place you wouldn't move back to. (RUSS FISHER)

OBEDIENCE

When someone demands blind obedience, you'd be a fool not to peek.
(JIM FIEBIG)

Enthusiasm is easier than obedience. (MICHAEL GRIFFITH)

It is not said that *after* keeping God's commandments, but *in* keeping them there is great reward. God has linked these two things together, and no man can separate them—obedience and power.(F.W. ROBERTSON)

Every great person has first learned how to obey, whom to obey, and when to obey. (WILLIAM A. WARD)

Only he who believes is obedient; only he who is obedient believes.
(DIETRICH BONHOEFFER)

OBESITY (see WEIGHT)

Obesity: Bad breadth. (HENRY BROWN)

Obesity is a . . . complex problem. No single remedy will meet the needs of every fat person. But for the millions of Americans who are experiencing creeping obesity, our work suggests that some of the conveniences of our affluent society must be rejected. Walk, don't ride. Take the stairs, not the elevator. Get a sufficient level of physical exercise to keep the body's hunger-satiety control mechanism functioning properly.
(DONALD THOMAS AND JEAN MAYER)

OBJECTIONS

Nothing will ever be attained if all possible objections must first be overcome.

OBNOXIOUSNESS

I don't know what makes him so obnoxious. But whatever it is, it works. (BOB GODDARD)

OBSCENITY

When I was a kid, a film was considered obscene if the horse wasn't wearing a saddle. (DANNY THOMAS)

OBSERVATION

The obscure we see eventually. The completely apparent takes longer. (EDWARD R. MURROW)

OBSTACLES

Obstacles are those frightening things you see when you take your eyes off the goal. (SUNSHINE)

When you cannot remove an object, plow around it. But keep plowing. (MEGIDDO MESSAGE)

If Columbus had turned back, no one could have blamed him, but no one would have remembered him. (FRIENDLY CHATS)

OFFICIATING

Officiating is the only occupation in the world where the highest accolade is silence. (EARL STROM)

OPENNESS

Keep an open mind, but don't keep it too open or people will throw a lot of rubbish into it.

OPINIONS

Sign in executive's office: What I am about to say represents one four-billionth of the world's opinion. (JACK WILLIAMS)

It's impossible to have a high view of someone who has a low view of you. (LESTER CASE)

Men are never so good or so bad as their opinions. (JAMES MACKINTOSH)

Public opinion is held in reverence. It settles everything. Some think it is the voice of God. (MARK TWAIN)

There is no such thing as public opinion; there is only published opinion. (WINSTON CHURCHILL)

Errors of opinion may be tolerated where reason is left free to combat it. (THOMAS JEFFERSON)

Through the centuries, controversy has been the servant of education. There can be no education without controversy. (H. ROWAN GAITHER)

Between knowledge of what really exists and ignorance of what does not exist lies the domain of opinion. It is more obscure than knowledge, but clearer than ignorance. (PLATO)

Everyone has the right to his own opinion. It's generally no use to anyone else. (DUBLIN OPINION)

There are altogether too many persons who seem to have a "Do Not Disturb" sign on their opinions. (NUGGETS)

An honest opinion does the most good when sandpapered with tact. (GLORIA PITZER)

I wonder why the fellow with the least information about a subject is so often the most opinionated. (FRANK A. CLARK)

Most of us like people who come right out and say what they think-- unless they disagree with us. (GRIT)

There are many shallow thinkers in this world, including those who have dug deeply into various subjects and come up with conclusions different from yours. (CHANGING TIMES)

Opinions expressed in this periodical are not necessarily condoned or even understood by the editorial staff. (A NEW ZEALAND PAPER)

OPPORTUNITIES (see CHANCES)

A wise man will make more opportunities than he finds. (FRANCIS BACON)

When one door closes, another opens; but we often look so long and so regretfully upon the closed door that we do not see the one which has opened for us. (ALEXANDER GRAHAM BELL)

Many of us take hold of opportunity all right, but we let go too soon (A.P. GOUTHEY)

Why is it that when an opportunity is lost, it's usually your competitor who finds it? (ROBERT ORBEN)

We are continually faced with a series of great opportunities brilliantly disguised as insoluable problems. (JOHN GARDNER)

Small opportunities are often the beginning of great enterprises. (DEMOSTHENES)

Opportunity knocks. Temptation kicks the door down. (EMPIRE)

Each day comes bearing its gifts. Untie the ribbons. (ANN SCHABACKER)

Opportunities are really never lost—they just seldom return to the person who snubs them. (O.A. BATTISTA)

Some people expect the door of opportunity to be opened with an electric eye. (HOWARD HENDRICKS)

The reason some people don't recognize opportunity is because it usually comes disguised as hard work.

Never neglect the opportunity of keeping your mouth shut. (MISSOURI PHARMACIST)

Opportunity is often missed because we are broadcasting when we should be tuning in. (NATIONAL SAFETY NEWS)

I shall pass through this world but once. Any good that I can do, or any kindness that I can show any human being, let me do it now and not defer it. For I shall not pass this way again. (STEPHEN GRELLET)

About the only golden opportunities some men can recognize are blondes. (MAYNERD BRADFORD)

The reason so many people never get anywhere in life is because, when opportunity knocks, they are out in the backyard looking for four-leaf clovers. (WALTER P. CHRYSLER)

A certain amount of opposition is a great help to a man. Kites rise against, not with, the wind. (JOHN NEAL)

OPTIMISM

Don't be too optimistic. The light at the end of the tunnel may be another train.

You'll find a lot of satisfaction in looking cheerfully on the dark side of life. (MEGIDDO MESSAGE)

Because you have an occasional spell of despondency, do not despair. After all, remember that the sun has a sinking spell every night but rises again in the morning. (L & N MAGAZINE)

You never know the other fellow's circumstances. I thought my friend had a steady job. He seemed to be well enough fixed. One reason I was led to believe this was that he was sinningly cheerful.

Running into him one day I said, "I was in a taxi yesterday and I passed you. You were at a sidewalk cafe with a girl."

He smiled back at me brightly and said, "That wasn't a girl; that was my wife. And that wasn't a sidewalk cafe; that was our furniture."
(HOWARD LINDSAY)

Experience in business teaches that people are far more likely to agree with the optimist than to disagree. Conversely, people are far more likely to offer a no to the sour, gloomy pessimist. A pessimistic man's words may be completely unheeded or inspire a lack of confidence, but a healthy, vital, optimistic man uttering the same words may rock the world. (ROBERT J. FLINT)

Optimist: A man who goes into a restaurant with no money and figures on paying for his meal with the pearl that he hopes to find in the oyster he plans to order.

Optimism is akin to faith; pessimism is akin to doubt. To which are you akin?

ORATORY (see LECTURING)

Oratory is the art of making deep sounds from the chest seem like they are important messages from the brain. (GRIT)

ORDERS

I never give orders. I sell my ideas to my associates if I can. I accept their judgment if they convince me, as they frequently do, that I am wrong. I prefer to appeal to the intelligence of a man rather than attempt to exercise authority over him. (ALFRED P. SLOAN, JR.)

ORIGINALITY (see CREATIVITY)

Originality is simply a pair of fresh eyes. (T.W. HIGGINSON)

Originality is undetected plagiarism. (WILLIAM R. INGE)

Originality is the art of concealing your source.   (FRANKLIN P. JONES)

OTHERS (see SELF AND OTHERS)

We think others are thinking of us; but they aren't. They're just like us—they're thinking of themselves.

Things are pretty well evened up in this world. Other people's troubles are never as bad as yours, but their children are a lot worse.

When you see a worthy person, endeavor to emulate him. When you see an unworthy person, then examine your inner self.   (CONFUCIUS)

We all have enough strength to endure the misfortunes of others.
(FRANCOIS DE LA ROCHEFOUCAULD)

He who wishes to secure the good of others has already secured his own.   (CONFUCIUS)

What do we live for if not to make the world less difficult for each other?   (MARIAN EVANS)

Speak well of everyone if you speak of them at all—none of us are so very good.   (ELBERT HUBBARD)

Make other people like themselves a little better and rest assured they'll like you very much.   (BITS & PIECES)

Who brings sunshine into the life of another has sunshine in his own.
(DAVID S. JORDAN)

The key people in the kingdom of heaven will be those who have unlocked their hearts to the needs of others on earth. (WILLIAM A. WARD)

The more a man takes the needs of others on his own heart, the more he must take his own heart to God.

OUTLOOK (see VIEWPOINT)

Outlook determines outcome.   (WARREN WIERSBE)

Most of us spend a great deal of effort crossing bridges to which we never come. In effect, we are pulling tomorrow's cloud over today's sunshine.   (W.T. PURKISER)

OVERREACTION

Don't treat dandruff with a guillotine.   (PAUL W. POWELL)

PAIN (see GRIEF, SUFFERING)

The real problem is not why some pious, humble, believing people suffer, but why some do not.   (C.S. LEWIS)

PARENTS (see FATHERS, HEREDITY, MOTHERS)

The Hebrew word for parents is *horim*, and it comes from the same root as *moreh*, teacher. The parent is, and remains, the first and most important teacher that the child will ever have.   (RABBI KASSEL ABELSON)

Train up a child in the way he should go—and walk there yourself once in a while.   (JOSH BILLINGS)

The trouble with being a parent is that by the time you're experienced, you're unemployed.   (KREOLITE NEWS)

If there is a measure of good parenthood, it could be when our children exceed our own achievements.   (TOM HAGGAI)

Parents are prone to give their children everything except the one thing they need most. That is time: time for listening, time for understanding, time for helping, and time for guiding. It sounds simple, but in reality it is the most difficult, and the most sacrificial task of parenthood.
                                              (EMMA K. HULBURT)

Parents have little time for children and a great vacuum has developed and into that vacuum is going to move some kind of ideology.

(BILLY GRAHAM)

Good parents do not always produce good children, but devoted, dedicated hardworking mothers and fathers can weigh the balance in favor of decency and the building of moral character. Every word and deed of a parent is a fiber woven into the character of a child, which ultimately determines how that child fits into the fabric of society.

(DAVID WILKERSON)

Never try to make your son or daughter another you; one is enough!

(ARNOLD GLASOW)

By the time we realize our parents may have been right, we usually have children who think we're wrong.

(BITS AND PIECES)

Do not handicap your children by making their lives easy.

(ROBERT HEINLEIN)

The toughest thing about raising kids is convincing them that you have seniority.

(QUOTE)

Parents must not cowardly abdicate their authority. Youths who win their independence too easily, without having had to wrest it from their resisting parents, are very poorly prepared to make use of it in life. In the struggle the child will acquire experience; he will learn how far he may resist and at what point he must submit.

(PAUL TOURNIER)

When adults realize that every human being—especially the adolescent—hungers for understanding, acceptance, and recognition, many of the problems of delinquency will be on their way to solution.

(WILLIAM A. WARD)

People always involved in broad issues generally neglect those closest to them. I have seen too many damaged children whose parents were leaders.

(BRUNO BETTELHEIM)

I am convinced one has a tendency to repeat the emotional errors of one's parents. If one is the product of divorced parents, or inharmoniously married parents—it's not whether they stay together or not but what their conflicts are that counts—you are apt to copy, quite unconsciously, their pattern.

(OLIVIA DEHAVILLAND)

Parents no longer bring children up; they finance them. (JOSEPH SALAK)

A child, like your stomach, doesn't need all you can afford to give it.

(FRANK A. CLARK)

Children begin by loving their parents; as they grow older they judge them; sometimes they forgive them. (OSCAR WILDE)

Don't be discouraged if your children reject your advice. Years later they will offer it to their own offspring.

The most important thing that parents can teach their children is how to get along without them. (FRANK A. CLARK)

Parents are the bones on which children sharpen their teeth.
(PETER USTINOV)

Who of us is mature enough for offspring before the offspring themselves arrive? The value of marriage is not that adults produce children but that children produce adults. (PETER DE VRIES)

We get our parents so late in life that it is impossible to do anything with them. (FROM A CHILD'S ESSAY, NOTTINGHAM, ENGLAND)

Teen: No wonder Monette gets straight A's in French. Her parents were born in Paris and speak French at home.
Second teen: In that case I ought to get A's in geometry. My parents are square and talk in circles.

First boy: What does PTA mean?
Second boy: I think it means Poor Tired Adults.

Rejected by the college of his choice, the teenager angrily accosted his father. "If you really cared for me, you'd have pulled some wires."
"I know," replied the parent sadly. "The TV, the stereo, and the telephone would have done for a start." (DAISY BROWN)

Wouldn't it be wonderful to be as brilliant as our children thought we were when they were young, and only half as stupid as they think we are when they're teenagers?

We were kids when everything was the kids' fault. Now we're parents when everything is the parents' fault. (FARM JOURNAL)

Insanity is hereditary. You can get it from your children.(SAM LEVENSON)

The spiritual ambiance of both our political parties was most neatly summarized by Robert Frost, when he observed: "A father is always a Republican toward his son, and a mother is always a Democrat."
(SYDNEY HARRIS)

PARTICIPATION (see WORKTEAMS)

To give people help, while denying them a significant part in the action, contributes nothing to the development of the individual. In the deepest sense it is not giving but taking—taking their dignity. Denial of the opportunity for participation is the denial of human dignity and democracy. It will not work. (SAUL D. ALINSKY)

PARTIES

At a dinner party we should eat wisely, but not too well, and talk well, but not too wisely. (SOMERSET MAUGHAM)

PASSIONS

We should employ our passions in the service of life, not spend life in the service of our passions. (RICHARD STEELE)

PASSIVITY (see LAZINESS)

Stand still and silently watch the world go by—and it will! (CONSTRUCTION DIGEST)

PAST (see HISTORY, YESTERDAY)

The past always looks better than it was; it's only pleasant because it isn't here. (FINLEY P. DUNNE)

It is never wise to live in the past. There are, indeed, some uses of our past which are helpful, and which bring blessing. . . . We should remember past failures and mistakes, that we may not repeat them. We should remember past mercies. . . . We should remember past comforts. . . . But while there are these true uses of memory, we should guard against living in the past. We should draw our life's inspirations not from memory but from hope, from what is yet to come. (J.R. MILLER)

Use the past as a springboard, not as a sofa. (NUNN WISER)

Some things should be forgotten—such as the failures and mistakes of yesterday. We've all had them, so let's learn from them and forget them. It's never wise to nurse a grudge. If someone treated you unkindly or unfairly, forget it. Easier said than done? Nevertheless, it is never wise to live with situations which should be put out of our mind. This only drains us of energy and creativity. Learn to extract what wisdom you can from the experience; then bury it. (HARRIET HALL)

You cannot change the past, and you can't always control the present, but you can push the past into its proper perspective and you can face the present realistically. (HUGH P. FELLOWS)

PATIENCE

Patience comes from two Greek words, meaning *stay under*, not always bobbing up.   (Robert A. Cook)

One moment of patience may ward off great disaster; one moment of impatience may ruin a whole life.   (Chinese saying)

A poor lady had to do her laundry by hand. She did a big washing and hung it on the line to dry. The line broke and the clean clothes fell in the mud. She washed the clothes again, and a second time the line broke. This time, however, a dog came along and walked over the clothes. When she saw the muddy clothes she didn't cry. All she said was, "Ain't it funny, that dog didn't miss a single one." That was true patience.
                                                        (Bert E. Wiggers)

How can a society that exists on frozen dinners, instant mashed potatoes, packaged cake mixes, and instant cameras teach patience to the young?

Remember that quiet patience can and does master and outlive all boisterous, stormy human discords.   (Lowell Filmore)

The key to everything is patience. You get the chicken by hatching the egg, not by smashing it open.   (Arnold Glasow)

Patience is a most necessary qualification for business; many a man would rather you heard his story than granted his request.
                                                        (Lord Chesterfield)

Patience is something you admire in the driver behind you, but not in the one ahead.   (Bill McGlashen)

Patience is a minor form of despair disguised as a virtue.

Patience often gets the credit that belongs to fatigue.

Sometimes a handful of patience is worth more than a bucketful of brains.   (Megiddo Message)

A second's patience can save you months of trouble.(Chinese proverb)

Thomas Edison was a man of patience. No test that exists today screens for that.   (Morris Stein)

He has all the patience of a grenade with its pin pulled.

Patience is the greatest of all shock absorbers. The only thing you can get in a hurry is trouble. (THOMAS R. DEWAR)

Patience is a necessary ingredient of genius. (BENJAMIN DISRAELI)

Every time we hold our tongues instead of returning the sharp retort, show patience with another's faults, show a little more love and kindness, we are helping to stockpile more of these peace-bringing qualities in the world instead of armaments for war. (CONSTANCE FOSTER)

The lovely thing about patience is that it annoys the person who is annoying you. (DUBLIN OPINION)

PAYCHECK

There are more deductions in today's paycheck than in a Sherlock Holmes tale. (RAYMOND J. CVIKOTA)

PEACE

Washington has a large assortment of peace monuments. We build one after every war. (DON MACLEAN)

Peace is that brief glorious moment in history when everybody stands around reloading.

To preserve peace, we need weapons of smaller and men of larger caliber.

The most amiable man on earth can live at peace with his neighbor only as long as his neighbor chooses.

Peace is the deliberate adjustment of my life to the will of God.

We lose the peace of years when we hunt after the rapture of moments. (BULWER)

Never, "for the sake of peace and quiet," deny your own experience or convictions. (DAG HAMMARSKJÖLD)

Universal peace sounds ridiculous to the head of an average family. (KIN HUBBARD)

When a person finds no peace within himself it is useless to seek it elsewhere. (BITS & PIECES)

When somebody gets arrested for disturbing the peace these days, I'm amazed that he found any. (RUDY MANO)

Peace is rare: Less than 8 percent of the time since the beginning of recorded time has the world been entirely at peace. In a total of 3,530 years, 286 have been warless. Eight thousand treaties have been broken in this time. (PERSONNEL JOURNAL)

PEACEMAKERS

The oilcan is mightier than the sword. (EVERETT DIRKSEN)

PEANUTS

My wife won't eat peanuts. Says she's never seen a skinny elephant.
(SHELBY FRIEDMAN)

PEDAGOGY (see TEACHERS AND TEACHING)

The teacher who makes little or no allowance for individual differences in the classroom is an individual who makes little or no difference in the lives of her students. (WILLIAM A. WARD)

Discussion leaders point out that when people listen to a speech, facts and arguments presented often go in one ear and out the other. In a discussion group, each person is more apt to listen so he or she will know what is going on when given a chance to talk.
(DAIRYMEN'S LEAGUE NEWS)

Retiring schoolteacher: Some differences between kids of today and those of 40 years ago: Kids today are better informed, but less disciplined. Parents today rely too much on the school to teach their kids.

In Leningrad when a child makes a good record at school a certificate of merit is presented to his parents for bringing up a good student.
(DON ROBINSON)

Men have often found that the basis of success in influencing a boy lies in respecting him. You have to believe in the boy and in his possibilities so wholeheartedly that you convey that idea of confidence and respect to him as you use patience and skill and understanding in dealing with him. Sure it takes faith too. (WALTER MACPEEK)

What do you say when you teach?
What do they see when you teach?
What do they do after you teach?

PEOPLE

People are the portals through which men pass into positions of power and leadership. (PAUL E. PARKER)

There are two types of people in the world: those who come into a room and say, "Here I am!" and those who come in and say, "Ah, there you are!" (FREDERICK L. COLLINS)

There may be said to be two classes of people in the world: those who constantly divide the people in the world into two classes and those who do not. (ROBERT BENCHLEY)

Running a business is about 95 percent people and 5 percent economics.

Handling people need not be so difficult—all you need is inexhaustible patience, unfailing insight, unshakable nervous stability, an unbreakable will, decisive judgment, infrangible physique, irrepressible spirits, plus unfeigned affection for all people—and an awful lot of experience. (ERIC WEBSTER)

The removal of human friction is 90 percent of the problem of handling people. (SUPERVISION)

The human race is a vicious species of potentially wonderful people. (BENJAMIN SPOCK)

Most people have never known, or have forgotten, that man was created to glorify God and enjoy Him forever. They have given themselves over, instead, to the gratification of their own selfish desires. (HENRY JACOBSEN)

I once liked clever people. Now I like good people. (SOLOMON B. FREEHOF)

A careful study of the qualities of the so-called successful man will reveal, in 9 cases out of 10, that his success depends not upon his deep and profound knowledge which puzzles the brains of ordinary men, but on simple and more commonplace qualities which please the understanding of the common folk and arouse in their hearts a feeling of sympathy. For all practical purposes, social intelligence wins over abstract intelligence, 10 to 1. Abstract intelligence knows what to do, but social intelligence knows *how* to get it done. (FRED A. MOSS)

Whatever other differences they may have, there is one unfailing identifying mark among great people—they are never solemn; they may be serious or grave, or as devout as a cathedral, but they are not solemn as others are, for they retain the gaiety and clarity of childhood that is one source of their mysterious powers. (SYDNEY HARRIS)

PERFECTION

If you expect perfection from people, your whole life is a series of disappointments, grumblings, and complaints. If, on the contrary, you pitch your expectations low, taking folks as the inefficient creatures which they are, you are frequently surprised by having them perform better than you had hoped. (BRUCE BARTON)

If you're looking for perfection, look in the mirror. If you see it there, expect it elsewhere.

If you aim at imperfection, there is some chance of your getting it; whereas if you aim at perfection, there is none. (SAMUEL BUTLER)

Stop trying to perfect your child, but keep trying to perfect your relationship with him. (DR. HENKER)

Nothing gives a man a sense of failure so often as an overdeveloped sense of perfection. This leads a person to set impossible standards for himself. He therefore does not accomplish what he would hope to. Perfectionism is good in a moderate dose, but when overdeveloped it results in feelings of guilt over failures when, by ordinary or even extra-high standards, a man would be judged a success. (GEORGE S. ODIORNE)

A perfectionist is one who takes great pains—and gives them to other people. (EDUCATION DIGEST)

You need to be a perfectionist if you want to be successful. (RICK BARRY)

Bachelors' wives and old maids' children are always perfect. (CHAMFORT)

PERFORMANCE

Only a mediocre person is always at his best (SOMERSET MAUGHAM)

PERPLEXITY

God often permits us to be perplexed so that we may learn patience and so that we may better recognize our dependence upon Him. (T.J. BACH)

PERSEVERANCE (see PERSISTENCE)

By perseverance the snail reached the ark. (CHARLES SPURGEON)

Lots of people limit their possibilities by giving up easily. Never tell yourself this is too much for me. It's no use. I can't go on. If you do you're licked, and by your own thinking too. Keep believing and keep on keeping on. (NORMAN V. PEALE)

Most people show more persistency in their first 12 months than they show later in 12 years; did they not, they never would have learned to walk. . . . Without stick-to-itiveness, no man is likely to climb to the top of the ladder—and stick. (B.C. FORBES)

The tough job that tests your mettle and spirit is like the grain of sand that gives an oyster a stomachache. After a time it may become a pearl. (EASTERN SUN)

A great oak is only a little nut that held his ground.(L & N MAGAZINE)

To get through the hardest journey we need take only one step at a time, but we must keep on stepping. (MEGIDDO MESSAGE)

The will to persevere is often the difference between failure and success. (DAVID SARNOFF)

Perseverance is failing 19 times and succeeding the 20th.(JULIE ANDREWS)

When nothing seems to help I go and look at a stonecutter hammering away at his rock perhaps 100 times without as much as a crack showing in it. Yet at the 101st blow it will split in two, and I know it was not that blow that did it, but all that had gone before. (JACOB RUS)

Perseverance is the most overrated of traits if it is unaccompanied by talent; beating your head against a wall is more likely to produce a concussion in the head than a hole in the wall. (SYDNEY HARRIS)

PERSISTENCE (see PERSEVERANCE, TENACITY)

If you're ever tempted to give up, just think of Brahms who took seven long years to compose his famous Lullaby. Kept falling asleep at the piano. (ROBERT ORBEN)

Nothing in the world can take the place of persistence. Talent will not; nothing is more common than unsuccessful men with talent. Genius will not; unrewarded genius is almost a proverb. Education will not; the world is full of educated derelicts. Persistence and determination alone are omnipotent. The slogan "Press On" has solved, and always will solve, the problems of the human race. (CALVIN COOLIDGE)

Many people fail in life because they believe in the adage: If you don't succeed, try something else. But success eludes those who follow such advice. Virtually everyone has had dreams at one time or another, specially in youth. The dreams that have come true did so because people stuck to their ambitions. They refused to be discouraged. They never let disappointment get the upper hand. Challenges only spurred them on to greater effort. (DON B. OWENS, JR.)

Consider the postage stamp: Its usefulness consists in the ability to stick to one thing till it gets there. (JOSH BILLINGS)

Edison tried more than 200 different substances in attempting to find a filament for his incandescent bulb. Someone once said to him, "You have failed more than 200 times; why don't you give up?"
His answer was, "Not at all. I have discovered more than 200 things that will not work. I will soon find one that will." (W.E. PHIFER)

Your key for personal success is persistence, for persistence produces power. Let me tell you the story about one of America's most outstanding failures. In 1831 he failed in business. In 1832 he was defeated for the Legislature. In 1833 he again failed in business. In 1834 he was elected to the Legislature. In 1838 he was defeated for Speaker; in 1840 defeated for Elector; in 1843 defeated for Congress; in 1846 elected to Congress; in 1855 defeated for Senate; in 1856 defeated for Vice-President; in 1858 defeated for Senate; in 1860 elected to President of the U.S. His name? Abraham Lincoln. (MACK R. DOUGLAS)

PERSONALITY (see TEMPERAMENT)

Personality is the reflection of your inner self which helps to distinguish one individual from another. Personality is so much a part of you that you can neither hide an unpleasant personality, nor can you imitate a good one. (VOICE OF YOUTH)

It's easy to have a balanced personality. Just forget your troubles as easily as you do your blessings. (GRIT)

To a significant degree, an individual's personality is related to his or her early life experiences. Thus, if as a child, the individual has worked out his competitive relationships with his brothers and sisters or playmates in a satisfactory fashion, then he is likely to have less difficulty in adjusting to the competition of adult life. (RAYMOND W. WAGGONER)

The most arresting advice we ever encountered was this: If you want to be popular, live so that a blind person would like you. *Lasting* popularity depends not on a pretty face or being handsome, but upon inner qualities that communicate themselves to others through media other than sight. These personality assets are expressed through such things as a gentle voice, persistent friendliness, small kindnesses, thoughtfulness of the other fellow's tender ego, deserved praise, excursions in encouragement. (WHATSOEVER THINGS)

Many human beings are like refrigerators—they slowly gather an ice formation which, if allowed to accumulate unchecked, will reduce their effectiveness considerably. These people need occasional defrosting. (J. GEORGE FREDERICK)

Blessed is the man who has a skin of the right thickness. He can work happily in spite of enemies and friends. (HENRY T. BAILEY)

Be a comfortable person so there is no strain in being with you—be an old shoe, old-hat kind of individual. Be homey. (NORMAN V. PEALE)

PERSONNEL DEPARTMENT

Formula for handling people: (1) Listen to the other person's story. (2) Listen to the other person's full story. (3) Listen to the other person's full story first. (GEORGE MARSHALL)

Never threaten to resign if you don't get a raise or promotion. Once you use this ploy, you're likely to be considered a potentially disloyal employee. (JOYCE BROTHERS)

"Why do you want to be an embalmer?"
"Because I enjoy working with people."

PERSPECTIVE (see VIEWPOINT)

Three men were hard at work on a construction job when a passerby stopped to question them about what they were doing. "I'm laying bricks," mumbled the first worker.

"I'm making $20 an hour," said the second man.

The third man, when asked the same question, answered, "I'm building a cathedral!"

An hour later the third man was fired. They were supposed to be building a delicatessen. (MORTY GUNTY)

PERSUASION (see SALESMEN)

The man who moves ahead—and stays ahead—is the man who has the talent to get others to see things his way, to convince others that they should take action along the lines he recommends.(MORTIMER FEINBERG)

If you truly mean to persuade a man, you must have his goodwill. Your approach must be disarming so that he does not assume an attitude of defense. You must not seem to be opposing your conviction to his, challenging him to a contest in which his pride is at stake. On the contrary, you must be friendly and show respect for the quality of his mind, avoiding any implication of superiority on your part. To show off your own wit is merely to discredit your wisdom. (LOUIS J. HALLE, JR.)

You cannot antagonize and persuade at the same time.(BITS AND PIECES)

People are usually more convinced by reasons they discovered themselves than by those found out by others. (PASCAL)

I would rather try to persuade a man to go along, because once I have persuaded him, he will stick. If I scare him, he will stay just as long as he is scared, and then he is gone.   (DWIGHT EISENHOWER)

One of the best ways to persuade others is with your ears—by listening to them.   (DEAN RUSK)

PESSIMISTS

A lot of pessimists got that way from financing optimists.(PARTS PUPS)

A pessimist is a person who absorbs sunshine and radiates gloom.

A pessimist is someone who thinks God created the world in six days— and on the seventh day He was laid off.   (ROBERT ORBEN)

Pessimist: one who has the discouragement of his convictions.
                    (CATHOLIC DIGEST)

A pessimist is a person who is seasick during the entire voyage of life.   (GRIT)

She not only expects the worst, but makes the worst of it when it happens.   (MICHAEL ARLEN)

Sometimes I don't think we realize how wonderful today is until tomorrow.   (JIM M. OWEN)

Two pessimists met at a party. Instead of shaking hands, they shook heads.   (CHICAGO TRIBUNE)

The pessimist is an absentee from the class of faith, a truant from the course of hope, and a dropout from the school of happiness. . . . We can gloom and doom our way through life, or we can employ and enjoy our way.   (WILLIAM A. WARD)

The prime fallacy of pessimism is that no one knows enough to be a pessimist.   (NORMAN COUSINS)

PHILANTHROPIST (see GIVING)

We think of a philanthropist as someone who donates big sums of money, yet the word is derived from two Greek words, *philos* (loving) and *anthropos* (man): loving man. All of us are capable of being philanthropists. We can give of ourselves.   (EDWARD LINDSEY)

PHILOSOPHIES

Any philosophy that can be put in a nutshell should be.(SIDNEY J. HOOK)

Philosophy is common sense in a dress suit. (SUNSHINE)

This is the precept by which I have lived: Prepare for the worst; expect the best; and take what comes. (ROBERT E. SPEER)

To make the most of dull hours, to make the best of dull people, to like a poor jest better than none, to wear a threadbare coat like a gentleman, to be outvoted with a smile, to hitch your wagon to an old horse if no star is handy—that is wholesome philosophy. (BLISS PERRY)

Two philosophers were engaged in a deep discussion as to where the sun goes when it sets. They pondered the enigma all through the night— then it dawned on them.

Good philosophy must exist . . . because bad philosophy needs to be answered. (C.S. LEWIS)

I have no general philosophy. All my life I have thought only in connection with facts that came before me. (LOUIS D. BRANDEIS)

A man's philosophy will come tumbling down like a house of cards unless he learns that the bitterness of life's no is needed not less than the sweetness of life's yes. (ALEXANDER A. STEINBACH)

Billy Bray, when he heard someone telling a long story of troubles endured and sorrowings suffered, exclaimed: "I've had my trials and troubles. The Lord has given me both vinegar and honey, but He has given the vinegar with a teaspoon and the honey with a ladle."(ROBERT G. LEE)

PHOBIAS

Claustrophobia—fear of Santa.
Hydrophobia—fear of fireplugs
Phonophobia—fear of stereos or telephones

PHONY (see HYPROCRITE)

The real phony is the guy who listens to the radio while eating a TV dinner. (FARM JOURNAL)

PHOTOGRAPHY

After several frustrated attempts to pose a lady subject, the photographer remarked, "When I try to get her to look pleasant, she doesn't look natural; and when I try to get her to look natural, she doesn't look pleasant."

Old photographers never die—they just go to the Old Focus Home.

I have a pocket camera. But who wants to take a picture of a pocket?

PHYSICAL EXAM

The executive was just buttoning up his coat after a physical examination. "Doctor, if there is anything wrong with me, don't try to hoodwink me by giving a long scientific name. Just tell me in plain English what's wrong with me."

"Well, to be perfectly frank, you are just plain lazy and need more exercise."

"Thank you, doctor. Now please give me the scientific name, so I can tell the people at the office." (HERBERT TRUE)

Doctor to patient: Let me put it this way—the softness of your muscles is exceeded only by the hardness of your arteries. (MEDICAL TRIBUNE)

PHYSICAL FITNESS (see EXERCISE)

Physical fitness. To some. . . . means being strong. To others, it means being able to play three sets of tennis. To others, it means being able to get through the day without collapsing. To scientists, it means an efficient heart and lung system as measured by the amount of oxygen the system can use per minute. The more oxygen, the more efficient. By this standard, 90 percent of American teenage boys are fit; 60 percent of adults are unfit. (EARL UBELL)

Engineers for the American Seating Company of Grand Rapids, Michigan, say that American derrieres, both male and female, have expanded nearly two inches in the past 30 years.

Many people who say they're fit as a fiddle look more like a bass drum. (JACK BRADFORD)

PHYSICAL HANDICAPS

A handicap . . . does not mean permanent prohibition from fame, fortune, and fulfillment. . . . Milton and Homer were blind. Beethoven probably never heard his last symphonies as deafness closed in upon him, Franklin Roosevelt was a four-term President in a wheelchair.
(SATURDAY REVIEW)

PHYSICS

Newton's Law: Only one fig to a cookie.

PITY (see COMPASSION)

"What kind of man deserves the most pity?" Abby Raynal asked Benjamin Franklin at a dinner party in Paris.

The American responded: "A lonesome man who does not know how to read."

PLANNING (see STRATEGY)

Plan ahead. It wasn't raining when Noah built the ark. (RICHARD CUSHING)

It is a mistake to look too far ahead. Only one link in the chain of destiny can be handled at a time. (WINSTON CHURCHILL)

When planning for a year, plant corn. When planning for a decade, plant trees. When planning for life, train and educate people.(CHINESE PROVERB)

Patton's Law: A good plan today is better than a perfect plan tomorrow.

A man who does not think and plan long ahead will find trouble right at his door. (CONFUCIUS)

Without plans we shall be jostled and confused by events. . . . We shall be like the paramecium, that lowly one-celled creature, which progresses through life by taking avoiding action. It bumps into an obstacle, backs up, and goes off in a new direction.
(ROYAL BANK OF CANADA MONTHLY LETTER)

"How far can you see, Daddy?" a small boy asked.
"Oh, I don't know—20 miles, maybe 40 on a clear day. How far can you see?"
"I can see a lot farther than that," said the boy. "I can see clear to the stars."
It is easy enough to see the things that lie in front of us in our routine work. But it is far better to see over the hills of the years to a long-range work. (EDGAR CHRISEMER)

When you're dying of thirst it's too late to think about digging a well.
(JAPANESE PROVERB)

PLEASANTNESS

You have not fulfilled every duty unless you have fulfilled that of being pleasant. (SUPERVISION)

PLEASURE (see FUN)

The greatest pleasure in life is doing what people say you cannot do.
(WALTER BAGEHOT)

The inward pleasure of imparting pleasure, that is the choicest of all.
(NATHANIEL HAWTHORNE)

Sign in a locker room: To be a winner you have to say no to pleasures that an athlete can't afford.

It is the way in which we choose our pleasures that largely determines the kinds of calamities that befall us. (SYDNEY HARRIS)

That man is the richest whose pleasures are the cheapest.
(J. HAROLD SMITH)

PODIATRIST

Sign on a podiatrist's door: Why be two feet away from happiness?

POETRY

For a man to become a poet he must be in love, or miserable.
(LORD BYRON)

POLITICIANS

In these days of the closest scrutiny of the politician, it is fitting that we list what he needs to succeed. Such a creature of the animal kingdom, besides having the ability to butt like a goat and turn like a worm, must have the eyes of a vulture, the memory of an elephant, rocks in the seat of his pants to break the feet of those who kick him, and the reactions of a skunk. (CARL RIBLET, JR.)

A smart politician is one who never throws his hat into the ring until he knows which way the wind's blowing.

Our elected representatives . . . study and analyze public attitudes by sophisticated new techniques, but their purpose has little to do with leadership. . . . Their purpose, it seems, is to discover what people want and fear and dislike, and then to identify themselves with these sentiments. They seek to discover which issues can be safely emphasized and which are more prudently avoided. This approach to politics is the opposite of leadership; it is followership. (J. WILLIAM FULLBRIGHT)

An honest politician is one who when he is bought will stay bought.
(SIMON CAMERON)

POLITICS (see GOVERNMENT)

Any 20-year-old who isn't a liberal doesn't have a heart, and any 40-year-old who isn't a conservative doesn't have a brain. (WINSTON CHURCHILL)

The voters are never long happy with the results of their voting.
(ABE WATERHILL)

Sign in car window: If Con is the opposite of Pro, what is the opposite of Progress?

The reason political party platforms are so long is that when you straddle anything it takes a long time to explain it. (WILL ROGERS)

In politics, one can never do more than decide which of two evils is lesser, and there are some situations from which one can only escape by acting like a devil or a lunatic. (GEORGE ORWELL)

One of the most perplexing questions of our time: Where do all the solutions go after a candidate gets elected? (ROBERT ORBEN)

Politics is the art of making yourself popular with people by giving them grants out of their own money. (DUBLIN OPINION)

Some go into politics not to do good, but to do well.(AMERICAN MERCURY)

A person running for political office is seeking power. Power as we know it corrupts. The excessive concentration of power in Washington is what caused all this [Watergate] mess. (DAVID BRINKLEY)

Politics is funny. When a man leaves your party and goes over to the other side, he's a traitor. When he leaves the other party and comes over to your side, he's a convert. (F.G. KERNAN)

POLLUTION (see ECOLOGY)

The oceans are in danger of dying. The pollution is general. People do not realize that all pollution ends up in the seas. The earth is less polluted. It is washed by the rain which carries everything into the oceans where life has diminished by 40 percent in 20 years.(JACQUES COUSTEAU)

These days, the only thing we have to fear is atmosphere itself.
(A NAVY CAPTAIN)

My landlord is all heart. He said he's going to do his bit to curb air pollution. This winter he won't run the furnace as often.(ROBERT ORBEN)

With the pollution in all our streams today, all bridges are over troubled waters.

My new apartment has windows on all sides, so I get cross-pollution.
(LILLIAN KOSLOVER)

The water in my town is so polluted that my waterbed is lumpy.

Every way we look, somebody is doing something about pollution—like contributing to it. (BEN BERGOR)

POPULARITY

A friend attributed the secret of his popularity to one particular word. "Years ago," he said, "upon hearing a statement with which I disagreed, I used to say, 'Baloney,' and people began to avoid me like the plague. Now I substitute, 'Amazing' for 'Baloney,' and my phone keeps ringing and my list of friends continues to grow." (CAPPER'S WEEKLY)

Always remember that popularity can do to you what too much sun can do to a plant. (O.A. BATTISTA)

Popularity means profits. To have a popular president at the head of an organization means a loyal organization. To have a popular product invariably means profits. An enterprise headed by a well-liked executive has far greater chances of succeeding in winning public goodwill than a discontented organization. (B.C. FORBES)

At school everybody hated me because I was so popular. (UKIE SHERIN)

To be popular a preacher must distinguish between important problems and trivial ones—and preach about the trivial. (FRANK A. CLARK)

POPULATION

More people are living in the world today than have died since Adam, according to Dr. M.J. Taves, University of Minnesota. He says three-fifths of all the people ever born are now alive. (WHEELER McMILLEN)

If you want to know what the world will be like in the future with 6 billion people in it, try to play a trombone in a telephone booth.

PORNOGRAPHY (see SEX)

The argument that pornography cannot be censored without destroying our civil liberties is fundamentally wrong. We have censored pornography since the nation was established, and there is no evidence of an adverse effect on our civil liberties. (WINTON M. BLOUNT)

POSITIVENESS

Say and do something positive that will help the situation; it doesn't take any brains to complain. (ROBERT A. COOK)

One positive argument bears more weight than 20 negative ones.

Don't be against things so much as for things. (COL. SANDERS)

POSSESSIONS (see MATERIALISM)

Before you set your heart on something, look around you to see how happy people are who have it. (MOODY MONTHLY)

On money and possessions: It all depends on whether you have things, or they have you. (ROBERT A. COOK)

Folks spend most of their lives accumulating what they spend the rest of their lives protecting. (COUNTRY PARSON)

Our desires always increase with our possessions. The knowledge that something remains yet unenjoyed impairs our enjoyment of the good before us. (SAMUEL JOHNSON)

POSTPONEMENT

Sometimes it is better to put off until tomorrow what you are likely to botch today. (CONSTRUCTION DIGEST)

POSTURE

I don't want to seem immodest, but you may have noticed that I have excellent posture. I don't slouch. I don't slump. I stand up tall and straight. That's what comes from years of having my back to the wall. (ROBERT ORBEN)

POVERTY

The poor live in a different world than the members of affluent America, but their awareness, hopes, and aspirations are the same as those of society as a whole. Through the media—newspapers, magazines, radio, and television—they are acutely aware of the standard which most of us take for granted. They seek the same quality of education and the same level of achievement we all do. The difference lies in the possibility of realizing their hopes and dreams. For them, there is no hope. The American Dream to the poor is still one long nightmare. (ABRAHAM RIBICOFF)

Poverty is the parent of revolution and crime. (ARISTOTLE)

Poverty is uncomfortable; but 9 times out of 10 the best thing that can happen to a young man is to be tossed overboard and be compelled to sink or swim. (JAMES A. GARFIELD)

If you gave a guaranteed income to all marginal families for a full year, almost none would have got out of poverty at the end of the year. They would be poor not because they lacked money, but because money doesn't buy skills, motivation, or hope. (JOSEPH T. ENGLISH)

Don't despise your poor relations; they may become suddenly rich someday, and then it will be awkward to explain things to them.
(JOSH BILLINGS)

Poverty is catching—you can get it from your wife.

POWER

Power tends to corrupt and absolute power corrupts absolutely.
(LORD ACTON)

I have never been able to conceive how any rational being could propose
happiness to himself from the exercise of power over others.
(THOMAS JEFFERSON)

George Washington . . . was one of the few in the whole history of the
world who was not carried away by power.   (ROBERT FROST)

The greater the power the more dangerous the abuse.(EDMUND BURKE)

The love of liberty is the love of others; the love of power is the love of
ourselves.   (WILLIAM HAZLITT)

The lust for power is not rooted in strength but in weakness.
(ERICH FROMM)

Two human attributes are, probably, responsible for more misery, death,
hopelessness, war, and starvation than everything else in the world put
together. One of these is the lust for personal power; the other is the
constant desire for easy physical security without personal responsibility.   (WALTER R. YOUNGQUIST)

The more power you acquire, the less you know; for a powerful man is
totally insulated by his subordinates, who tell him only what they think
he wants to hear or what will support their previous decisions, and not
what he should be told.   (SYDNEY HARRIS)

Worry and responsibility are part of the price of power. Real power does
not lie in documents and memos outlining terms of reference and areas
of jurisdiction; it lies in what can be achieved in practice. The boss'
secretary can wield great power, like the king's mistress, without any
real authority at all. Equally, the head of a big division or company can
be powerless, just as Lear was powerless, despite any number of theoret-
ical powers. Power lies in the acceptance of the chief's authority by
others; their knowledge that if they try to resist, they will fail and he will
succeed.   (ANTHONY JAY)

Power intoxicates men. When a man is intoxicated by alcohol he can recover, but when intoxicated by power he seldom recovers.

(JAMES F. BYRNES)

Power is not of itself good or bad but becomes what its holder makes it. Held by a Churchill it might be good; by a Hitler, bad.

(HERBERT M. BAUS AND WILLIAM B. ROSS)

We have military power but not moral power, supersonic thrusts of power but not spiritual power. The strange paradox is that we are powerful and powerless.

(JOHN W. MAY)

Your powers are dead or dedicated. If they are dedicated, they are alive with God and tingle with surprising power. If they are saved up, taken care of for their own ends, they are dead.

(E. STANLEY JONES)

PRACTICE

Practice doesn't necessarily make perfect—it just makes permanent. You have to practice doing something *right* in order to make it perfect.

PRAISE

Giving praise is much like giving love. The giver is usually the most benefited. He casts bread upon the waters and often gets back cake.

(IRVING FELDMAN)

Some people will work harder for praise than even money. Those workers in your group doing good work should be occasionally praised. It's good sense and good courtesy. Many effective employees, who know they're doing good work, expect to be recognized and appreciated. When deserved, be sure to praise your team members individually or before the group. They'll appreciate your appreciation, and most of them will work all the harder for you.

(L. PERRY WILBUR)

All of us hunger for a word of praise. Mark Twain is credited with saying, "I can live for two months on a good compliment."

(OLD AMERICAN NEWS)

Modesty is the only sure bait when you angle for praise.

(G.K. CHESTERTON)

Praise is like a shadow. It follows him who flees from it, but flees from him who follows it.

(GRIT)

Praise is warming and desirable. But it is an earned thing. It has to be deserved, like an honorary degree or a hug from a child.

(PHYLLIS McGINLEY)

The only way to escape the personal corruption of praise is to go on working. (ALBERT EINSTEIN)

We are all imbued with the love of praise. (CICERO)

I praise loudly; I blame softly. (CATHERINE II)

Praise God even when you don't understand what He is doing.
(HENRY JACOBSEN)

Prayer must commence with praise. However, some people today tend to take the expression of praise to an extreme. I personally react negatively toward bright, shiny Christians telling me they have learned to praise God for anything. How can we praise God for those things He weeps over? On earth Jesus wept at death, was angry about the hardness of people's hearts, and condemned those who exploited the weak. Perhaps what these modern "praisers" are really trying to say is that it is possible to find God in every dark situation. To see Him, high and lifted up, and to praise Him for who He is and for what He is and for what we can learn of Him in the dark circumstances is not to praise Him for the darkness itself. (JILL BRISCOE)

When you praise a child, focus on his accomplishments rather than on himself. Thus you encourage good works instead of mere egotism.
(GEORGE W. CRANE)

He who sings his own praise is seldom asked for an encore.

Why is it that the good things people say about us never give us as much permanent pleasure as the bad things they say about us give us enduring pain; and that the glow of praise quickly dims and must be continually replenished, while the barbs of dispraise rankle for an unconscionably long time? (SYDNEY HARRIS)

Direct praise of personality, like direct sunlight, is uncomfortable and blinding. It is embarrassing for a person to be told that he is wonderful, angelic, generous, and humble. He feels called upon to deny at least part of the praise. Publicly he cannot stand up and say, "Thank you, I accept your words that I am wonderful." Privately too he must reject such praise. He cannot honestly say to himself, "I am wonderful. I am good and strong and generous and humble." (HAIM G. GINOTT)

An overdose of praise is like 10 lumps of sugar in coffee; only a very few people can swallow it. (EMILY POST)

Praise undeserved is poison in disguise. (ILLINOIS JOURNAL OF EDUCATION)

You don't have to be afraid of praising God too much; unlike humans He never gets a big head. (PAUL DIBBLE)

PRAYER

Prayer is . . . talking with God and telling Him you love Him . . . conversing with God about all the things that are important in life, both large and small, and being assured that He is listening. (C. NEIL STRAIT)

Prayer is the gymnasium of the soul. (SAMUEL M. ZWEMER)

Prayer is not a substitute for work, thinking, watching, suffering, or giving; prayer is a support for all other efforts. (GEORGE BUTTRICK)

If you can't pray a door open, don't pry it open. (LYELL RADER)

Most men pray for power, the strength to do things. Few people pray for love, the quality to be someone. (ROBERT D. FOSTER)

Prayer lifts the heart above the battles of life and gives it a glimpse of God's resources which spell victory and hope. (C. NEIL STRAIT)

It is strange that in our praying we seldom ask for a change of character, but always a change in circumstances. (BITS AND PIECES)

There's something exquisitely luxurious about room service in a hotel. All you have to do is pick up a phone and somebody is ready and waiting to bring you breakfast, lunch, dinner, chocolate milkshake, whatever your heart desires and your stomach will tolerate. Or by another languid motion of the wrist, you can telephone for someone who will get a soiled shirt quickly transformed into a clean one or a rumpled suit into a pressed one. That's the concept that some of us have of prayer. We have created God in the image of a divine bellhop. Prayer, for us, is the ultimate in room service, wrought by direct dialing. Furthermore, no tipping, and everything charged to that great credit card in the sky. Now prayer is many things, but I'm pretty sure this is not one of the things it is. (KENNETH L. WILSON)

God is never more than a prayer away from you. . . . We address and stamp a letter and send it on its way, confident that it will reach its destination, but we doubtfully wonder if our prayers will be heard by an ever-present God. . . . If laser beams can cut through mountains, why should we doubt the power of prayer? Wonderful things can happen to us when we live expectantly, believe confidently, and pray affirmatively. . . . The pulse of prayer is praise. The heart of prayer is gratitude. The voice of prayer is obedience. The arm of prayer is service.

(WILLIAM A. WARD)

Prayer provides power, poise, peace, and purpose.

We carry checks on the bank of heaven and never cash them at the window of prayer. . . . We lie to God in prayer if we do not rely on God after prayer. (VANCE HAVNER)

Morning prayer: Good morning, God, I love You! What are You up to today? I want to be a part of it. (NORMAN GRUBB)

Lord, make me more like Yourself, less like myself. (LESTER CASE)

Bless us, Lord—not because we deserve it, but because we so desperately need it. And bless us for Your name's sake. (MALCOLM CRONK)

If this obstacle is from Thee, Lord, I accept it; but if it is from Satan, I refuse him and all his works in the name of Calvary. (ISOBEL KUHN)

It is good to pray for the repair of mistakes, but praying earlier would keep us from making so many. . . . When puzzled, go to prayer and listen. (J.C. MACAULAY)

Prayer should be the key of the day and the lock of the night.

(GEORGE HERBERT)

He who prays for his neighbor will be heard for himself.

(HEBREW PROVERB)

We should be as specific in our requests when in prayer to God as we are when we need a definite item at the market. (SAMUEL BRENGLE)

Don't pray to escape trouble. Don't pray to be comfortable in your emotions. Pray to do the will of God in every situation. Nothing else is worth praying for. (SAM SHOEMAKER)

Nothing can so quickly cancel the frictions of life as prayers. "Praying hearts," it has been wisely said, "are forgiving hearts." So if we find ourselves growing angry at someone, pray for him—anger cannot live in the atmosphere of prayer. (WILLIAM T. MCELROY)

One way to have fewer conflicts with our fellowman is to wrestle with God in prayer.

Don't put people down—unless it's on your prayer list.(STAN MICHALSKI)

Prayer is putting the lens of your soul on time exposure. Prayer is putting on earphones that shut out all noises but the voices of you and your God. Prayer is the recovery room after surgery and before recuperation. Prayer always has, along with its receptivity, four statements: *Thank You. I'm sorry. Teach me. Go with me.* Prayer is the frame of the bridge from weeping to doing, built across the canyon of despair.

(JAMES GILLIOM)

A British soldier one night was caught creeping back to his quarters from the nearby woods. Taken before his commanding officer, he was charged with holding communications with the enemy. The man pleaded he had gone into the woods to pray by himself. That was his only defense.

"Down on your knees and pray now!" roared the officer. "You never needed it so much!"

Expecting immediate death, the soldier knelt and poured out his soul in eloquent prayer.

"You may go," said the officer simply, when he had finished. "I believe your story. If you hadn't drilled so often, you could not do so well at review." (GOSPEL HERALD)

Pray your way through the day. You can't see around the turning of life's corners, but God can. When the alarm goes off, instead of saying, "Good lord—morning!" say, "Good morning, Lord!" (ROBERT A. COOK)

Too many people pray like little boys who knock at doors, then run away. (WAR CRY)

In prayer it is better to have a heart without words than words without a heart. (JOHN BUNYAN)

Prayer is more than verbally filling in some requisition blank. It's fellowship with God! It's communion with the Lord through praising Him, rehearsing His promises, and then sharing our needs. (BILLY GRAHAM)

Too many of us are like the old-timer who wound up a long prayer filled with complaints and petitions by saying, "Use me, O Lord, use me in Thy work—'specially in an advisory capacity." (CONSTRUCTION DIGEST)

A Christian once told his non-Christian friend, "You sure swear a lot."

The unbeliever replied, "Yeah, but I don't mean nothing by it. You sure pray a lot, but you don't mean nothing by it either."

Theological gem: And now let us pray for good luck. (LUXEMBOURG RADIO)

An efficiency expert says his prayers only once a year, New Year's Day.

The rest of the time he just jumps into bed and says, "Ditto."
(C. KENNEDY)

I am convinced that nothing in Christianity is so rarely attained as a praying heart. (CHARLES G. FINNEY)

He who fails to pray does not cheat God. He cheats himself.
(GEORGE FAILING)

Too often we forget to thank God for answered prayer. Praise is the proper punctuation mark for an answered prayer. (CADLE CALL)

Prayer becomes a flat and arduous business when we refuse to obey the leads and lights that God has given us. Prayer must be followed by the courage to act. (ERNEST T. CAMPBELL)

One night a little girl surprised her mother when she concluded her prayer for her family and friends by adding, "And now, God, what can I do for You?" (SUNDAY TIMES AND GOSPEL HERALD)

Prayer is the breath of the newborn soul, and there can be no Christian life without it. (ROWLAND HILL)

Pray as though everything depended on God. Work as though everything depended on you. (AUGUSTINE)

Nothing puts feeling into a prayer like a mighty good reason for saying it. (O.A. BATTISTA)

The Christian on his knees sees more than the philosopher on tiptoe.
(D.L. MOODY)

Small boy to friend: It may be unconstitutional, but I always pray before a test. (R & R MAGAZINE)

A day without prayer is a day without blessing, and a life without prayer is a life without power. (ALLIANCE WITNESS)

Keep praying, but be thankful that God's answers are wiser than your prayers! (WILLIAM CULBERTSON)

Let's keep our chins up and our knees down—we're on the victory side! (ALAN REDPATH)

PREACHERS (see MINISTERS)

If a pastor is good, he deserves four weeks' vacation. If he isn't good, the congregation deserves it.

Paul is the father of all preachers who use "finally my brethren" as an indication that they have found their second wind.   (W.S. TINDAL)

At last a preacher guaranteed to please all has been found. He preaches exactly 25 minutes against sin in such a gentle way he never hurts anyone's feelings.

He works from 6 A.M. till 10 P.M. in every kind of work possible. He can clean the church if necessary, helps overhaul the autos of the congregation, and is an expert in almost every field.

He always dresses in the best clothes, buys the latest books on every subject, has a well-dressed and well-behaved family, drives a late-model car at all times, gives to every charitable fund, and gives $40 to the church from his $100-a-week-salary.

He is 20 years old and has been preaching for 30 years. He has a burning desire to work with teenagers, and spends all his time with older folk.

He smiles all the time with a straight face, because he has a good sense of humor that keeps him seriously dedicated to his work. He has a glowing personality with deadened feelings and iron nerves.

(ARKANSAS BAPTIST)

Every honest minister preaches from a reservoir of guilt and grace.

(GARY GULBRANSON)

The one thing no church can stand is a pastor who really wants to be something else. The men who really want out ought to be helped out, for the Christian ministry is no place for a man who wants to be something else. It is a place for men who can give counsel, not the place for men who need counsel.   (DUKE K. McCALL)

Some people accuse us of too much emotionalism. I say we have too little. That is why we are losing church people to other interests. We need not only to capture their minds; we've got to touch their hearts. We've got to make people feel their faith.   (BILLY GRAHAM)

People expect the clergy to have the grace of a swan, the friendliness of a sparrow, the strength of an eagle, and the night hours of an owl—and some people expect such a bird to live on the food of a canary.

(EDWARD JEFFREY)

A dear woman was weeping copiously as she parted with her pastor. "Now, now," said the pastor, "don't cry; the bishop is sending you a good pastor, a much better one."

"But," she wailed, "that's what they told me the *last* time."

(ROBERT C. GRIFFITH)

The small rural church had its money troubles. Yet at the regular meeting of the board of deacons there was some talk of giving the pastor a long-delayed increase in salary.

However, the pastor opposed the idea. "Brothers," he said, "I don't want you to raise my salary any more. I'm having too much trouble raising what you are already paying me."

"Junior swallowed a coin!"
"Send him to the preacher. He can get money out of anybody."

The preacher of a little mountain town church ran off with the church funds. A deacon was sent to find him. When he returned he was asked if he had found their preacher and filed charges against him. "I found him," he replied, "but he had already spent the money so I brought him back so we can make him preach it out." (THE SCANDAL SHEET)

Today we have sermonettes, by preacherettes, for Christianettes.
(CHARLES F. TAYLOR)

Whenever I say bad things about people outside our church, or good things about people inside our church, those shaking my hand at the door tell me what a fine sermon I have just given them. (GEORGE HALL)

Every preacher who trims himself to suit everybody will soon whittle himself away. (J. HAROLD SMITH)

The average pastor wants more people in his congregation, more money in the offering, and more outreach for the Gospel through his ministry. Help him achieve one or all three and he will be your friend for life. (ROBERT A. COOK)

Clinton Locy of West Richland, Washington put all long-winded preachers to shame in February, 1955 when he preached 48 hours and 18 minutes and set a world's record for the length of a sermon. He took texts from every book of the Bible, and eight listeners stayed for the completion.

Johnny liked church pretty well except for the long pastoral prayer. So when his dad asked the visiting minister to say grace when dinner was served, Johnny was worried. But to his surprise, the prayer was brief and to the point.

Pleased, Johnny said, "You don't pray so long when you're hungry, do you?" (MIKE McCALL)

A minister was rushed to the hospital and an inexperienced nurse was assigned to him. She put a barometer in his mouth instead of a thermometer and it read, "Dry and windy." (A. Ross Williams)

Just before the minister was to deliver his sermon, an usher handed him a note. The preacher announced that someone had left a car locked with the lights on in the parking lot. He added, "The implication seems to be that the battery may run down before I do."(United Methodist Today)

A well-known preacher delivered a sermon before a congregation in which his wife was a worshiper. When the service was over, he went over to her and asked, "How did I do?"
She replied, "You did fine, only you missed several opportunities to sit down." (Asbury Lenox)

Many years ago, Dean Inge somewhat caustically declared that to try to get anything across to a congregation by preaching to it was like trying to fill a number of long-necked bottles by throwing a bucket of water over them. (J.Y. Simpson)

Two ministers of different faiths were the best of friends, but often disagreed on religious issues. One day they had been arguing a little more than usual on some theological point, when one of them said: "That's all right. We'll just agree to disagree. The thing that counts is that we're both doing the Lord's work—you in your way, and I in His." (Clyde Murdock)

If you think practicing what you preach is rough, just try preaching what you practice. (Bowen Baxter)

Card taped on pulpit: What are you trying to *do* to these people? (Howard Hendricks)

PREDICTIONS (see FUTURE, PROPHECY)

General Booth predicted there would be preaching of forgiveness without regeneration, Christianity without Christ, religion without the Holy Ghost, politics without God, heaven without hell.

PREJUDICE

An unprejudiced mind is probably the rarest thing in the world. (André Gide)

Prejudice is being down on what you're not up on.

It is with narrow-minded people as with narrow-necked bottles; the less they have in them, the more noise they make in pouring it out. (Alexander Pope)

PREPARATION

By failing to prepare, you are preparing to fail.   (BENJAMIN FRANKLIN)

Before you speak, listen. Before you write, think. Before you spend, earn. Before you invest, investigate. Before you criticize, wait. Before you pray, forgive. Before you quit, try. Before you retire, save. Before you die, give.   (WILLIAM A. WARD)

PRESENT

While you are dreaming of the future or regretting the past, the present, which is all you have, slips from you and is gone.   (HILAIRE BELLOC)

Sir William Osler says that as a young man he was a chronic worrier about his own future. One day while in medical school with an examination looming on the morrow, he succeeded in worrying himself sick, when he chanced on a sentence from Carlyle: "Our main business is not to see what lies dimly at a distance, but to do what lies clearly at hand." Applying it to himself, he saw that his main business was to make final preparation for the examination and then get a good night's sleep. This he proceeded to do. He resolved to make Carlyle's dictum his guiding principle. On that basis he lived his greatly serviceable life. "The load of tomorrow, added to that of today," he says, "makes even the strongest falter."   (FRANK H. FERRIS)

Do not look back and do not dream about the future. It will neither give you back the past nor satisfy your daydreams. Your duty, your reward—your destiny—are *here* and *now*.   (DAG HAMMARSKJÖLD)

Only one person in a thousand knows the trick of really living in the present.   (STORM JAMESON)

PRESIDENT

A man was elected president of a large company. One of the older directors said, "So now you are president!"
"So it seems," the man smiled.
"Then," said the older man, "you have heard the truth for the last time."

PRESSURE (see STRESS)

The true genius in war is the one who can do the average thing when those around him grow hysterical with emotion or fright.   (NAPOLEON)

A good leader in any field doesn't panic under pressure and spread a shock wave through his people. The tougher the going gets, the calmer he becomes, the more determined to find a sensible answer to the situation and make it work. (BITS AND PIECES)

PRETENSES

Men defend nothing more violently than the pretenses they live by.
(ALLEN DRURY)

Our greatest pretenses are built up not to hide the evil and the ugly in us, but our emptiness. The hardest thing to hide is something that is not there. (ERIC HOFFER)

PRIDE (see VANITY)

A proud man is always looking down on things and people; and, of course, as long as you're looking down, you can't see something that's above you. (C.S. LEWIS)

Swallow your pride occasionally. It's nonfattening. (FRANK TYGER)

Pride is the only disease known to man that makes everyone sick except the one who has it. (BUDDY ROBINSON)

Pride is so subtle that if we aren't careful we'll be proud of our humility. When this happens our goodness becomes badness. Our virtues become vices. We can easily become like the Sunday School teacher who, having told the story of the Pharisee and the publican, said, "Children, let's bow our heads and thank God we are not like the Pharisee." (PAUL W. POWELL)

A person who gets too big for his britches will be exposed in the end.

Pride is a vice not limited to the emperors of far-flung realms. Almost anyone, by comparing himself with those who have less talent, less success, or less popularity, can emerge with a feeling of satisfaction that is the very opposite of humility. Pride is all too common among God's people—though He warns them specifically that no one has anything to boast about, since all our gifts come from Him (1 Cor. 4:7).
(ADULT TEACHER, SCRIPTURE PRESS)

Nothing is as hard to do gracefully as getting down off your high horse. (FRANKLIN P. JONES)

PRINCIPLES

Whenever you put your practice ahead of your principle you run into problems. (GARY GULBRANSON)

In matters of principle, stand like a rock; in matters of taste, swim with the current. (THOMAS JEFFERSON)

When a man says he approves of something in principle, it means he hasn't the slightest intention of putting it into practice.

(OTTO VON BISMARCK)

It is easier to fight for one's principles than to live up to them.

(ALFRED ADLER)

Some people would have higher principles if it wasn't for their interests.

(LUCILLE S. HARPER)

PRIORITIES

The older I get the more wisdom I find in the ancient rule of taking first things first—a process which often reduces the most complex human problem to a manageable proportion.   (DWIGHT EISENHOWER)

The last thing one knows is what to put first.   (BLAISE PASCAL)

PRIVACY

Privacy is freedom from interference, freedom to grow, freedom to experience, and to control what others may know about oneself. In many ways it is the first line of defense of other freedoms in that it conditions the climate of public breathing space and reserve.(CHURCH AND SOCIETY)

Our need for privacy is being violated. As the population explodes, the dream of a place of one's own grows more urgent. Nostalgic memories of a gentler era crowd our minds as too many people crowd our lives. Poignantly one remembers lying on one's back in a summer meadow, chewing on a blade of grass and staring up at a blue sky; or, on a rainy day, curling up with *Wuthering Heights* in a secret room tucked under the eaves, or listening to homely and comforting sounds, like the creak of a porch swing and the plop of garden peas falling into a saucepan, in a house where people did different things in different rooms. . . . Today the world is too much with us.   (QUOTE)

PRIZES

All anybody needs to know about prizes is that Mozart never won one.   (HENRY MITCHELL)

PROBLEMS (see STRUGGLES)

The basic problem most people have is that they're doing nothing to solve their basic problem.   (BOB RICHARDSON)

The world now has so many problems that if Moses had come down from Mount Sinai today the two tablets he carried would be aspirin.

(ROBERT ORBEN)

A man with 50 problems is twice as alive as a man with 25. If you haven't got problems, you should get down on your knees and ask, "Lord, don't You trust me anymore?"   (JOHN BAINBRIDGE)

Problems breed problems; but problems also are the main breeding ground for success. Seldom does real success, real progress, come in any other manner.   (GERALD JAGGERS)

Let God's promises shine on your problems.   (CORRIE TEN BOOM)

A man went to a very high-priced psychiatrist and said, "Doc, I've got a problem. I hope you can help me."
   "What is your problem?" asked the doctor.
   "Well, I'm married. I've got a Jaguar, my wife has a Cadillac, we have three children all in good health, and we have a home in the country and one in the city."
   "You don't seem so bad off," replied the doctor. "What is your problem?"
   The patient said slowly, "I only make $45 a week."

The easiest way to solve a problem is to pick an easy one.
           (FRANKLIN P. JONES)

Having problems may not be so bad. We have a special place for folks who have none—it's called a cemetery.   (FRANK A. CLARK)

Adolescence and snowdrifts are about the only problems that disappear if you ignore them long enough.   (WALL STREET JOURNAL)

Said the smart little waitress, slipping up beside the customer: "I've got deviled kidney, calves' brains, pigs' feet, chicken livers, and—"
   "Forget it, sister. I've got a headache, eczema, fallen arches, corns, a bunion, three warts, and an empty stomach. Tell your troubles to someone else, and bring me some ham and eggs."

To welcome a problem without resentment is to cut its size in half. . . . Problems are challenges we can complain about, dwell on, give in to—or think through. . . . We can spend our time aimlessly licking our wounds or aggressively licking our problems. . . . Our Goliaths can be feared or fought, succumbed to or slain.   (WILLIAM A. WARD)

Most people spend more time and energy going around problems than in trying to solve them.   (HENRY FORD)

I'm afraid we have become a nation of plodders, who feel that all problems can be found in books and that the answers are on a certain page.   (CLARENCE LINDER)

Submerging problems in a sea of information is not the same as solving them.

I would much rather do nothing when confronted with a difficult situation, than do the wrong thing simply for the sake of a gesture. I admire a man who has the courage to admit that he has no snap answer to all problems. Most problems can be solved, with patience and often after prolonged study; but great harm has been done by taking quick action for the sake of appearances. (JOHN O'LONDON)

It is wise not to solve any problems that you do not have to solve. Save your time, your nerves, and your brains until you are certain that a problem exists and that you are the person who has to do the solving. Many problems, like storms, never arrive in spite of threatening skies. (EDWARD HODNETT)

Every problem contains within itself the seeds of its own solution. (BITS AND PIECES)

Total absence of problems would be the beginning of death for a society or an individual. We aren't constructed to live in that kind of world. We are problem-solvers by nature, problem-seekers, problem-requirers. (JOHN W. GARDNER)

When you have a problem you have to go where you can be alone and then talk to yourself out loud. But make sure that you're *really* alone! (BILL COSBY)

The reason some people know the solution is because they created the problem. (KELLY FORDYCE)

Charles Kettering, the inventor, had a unique method of solving problems. He would break down each problem into the smallest possible subproblems. Then he did research to find out which subproblems had *already been solved.* He often found that what looked like a huge problem had previously been 98 percent solved by others. Then he tackled what was left. (BITS AND PIECES)

A biologist one day observed an ant carrying a piece of straw which seemed a big burden for it. The ant came to a crack in the earth, which was too wide for it to cross. It stood for a time, as though pondering the situation. Then it put the straw across the crack and walked across it as a span. "What a lesson for us!" the impressed biologist said. "The burden can become the bridge for progress." (GRIT)

Sometimes the only way to solve a problem you've been working on intensely is to forget it for a while. A period of mental and physical relaxation can often do what all the concentration in the world cannot: free your mind of inhibitions and pressures that have been blocking ideas. Once the pressure is off, problem-solving ideas can occur when you least expect them—when you start to shave, finish a shower, or step into a bus. (DORIAN SHAININ)

Take a break from your problems! A highly respected and successful businessman . . . made a strong effort to set aside some time each day when he refused to think about the problems he faced. He spent the time reading, talking with associates—but not about their problems or his—or doing almost anything except thinking or worrying about problems. He considered this little time-out period as an important ingredient in his success as a businessman. I buy the theory, but putting the theory into practice is not as simple as it sounds. I've tried it and it can be done, but you have to work at it. (DICK HANSON)

The best way to forget your own problems is to help someone else solve his.

People love to complain about their problems, but are usually more stimulated than destroyed by them. If a man has no troubles to overcome, no dangers to surmount, no barriers to break through, how can he prove he's a hero? It is also better to have a choice of problems to worry about, as one problem can become too boring. (HAL BOYLE)

God doesn't always give us the wisdom to solve our problems. Sometimes He just lets us know that Jesus can solve them. (MALCOLM CRONK)

You must live with people to know their problems, and live with God in order to solve them. (PETER T. FORSYTH)

When one is seeking to know God's will, he need not concern himself primarily about his particular problem. That is the business of the Lord. Our supreme concern is our relationship to Jesus Christ. If a man in his heart is right with God, God will deal with the problem. (ALAN REDPATH)

PROCRASTINATION

If you want to make an easy job seem mighty hard, just keep putting off doing it. (OLIN MILLER)

When a man does a household job, he goes through three periods: contemplating *how* it will be done; contemplating *when* it will be done; and contemplating. (MARCELENE COX)

We are all fugitives, and the things we didn't do yesterday are the bloodhounds. (PRISM)

Procrastination is not only the thief of time; it is also the grave of opportunity. (CHRISTIAN CLIPPINGS)

Never put off till tomorrow what you can do today. There may be a law against it by then.

And then there was the chap who meant to procrastinate someday, but kept putting it off. (FRANKLIN P. JONES)

Procrastination is my sin.
It brings me naught but sorrow.
I know that I should stop it.
In fact, I will—tomorrow! (GLORIA PITZER)

PRODUCTS (see NEW PRODUCTS)

To be a success in business you must have confidence in your products. Real confidence in your products. So much confidence in your products that the first name you put on your mailing list is Ralph Nader.
(ROBERT ORBEN)

PROFANITY (see CURSING)

Profanity is the use of strong words by weak people.(WILLIAM A. WARD)

The General is sorry to be informed that the foolish and wicked practice of profane cursing and swearing, a vice heretofore little known in an American army, is growing into fashion. He hopes the officers will, by example as well as influence, endeavor to check it, and that both they and the men will reflect that we can have little hope of the blessing of heaven on our arms, if we insult it by our impiety and folly. Added to this, it is a vice so mean and low, without any temptation, that every man of sense and character detests and despises it. (GEORGE WASHINGTON)

To many people, the word "God" is a formula on Sundays and an oath on weekdays. (CHRISTOPHER MORLEY)

PROFESSIONALS (see WORK)

One of the great differences between the amateur and the professional is that the latter has the capacity to progress. (SOMERSET MAUGHAM)

A professional is one who does his best work when he feels the least like working. (FRANK LLOYD WRIGHT)

PROFESSOR, ABSENT-MINDED

"Did you hear what the absent-minded Professor Mack did yesterday?"

chortled Mrs. Green. "He sent his wife down to the bank and kissed his money good-bye."

Mr. Green sighed heavily and said, "The professor isn't as absent-minded as I thought." (C. KENNEDY)

"Will you pass the nuts, Professor?" asked the dinner guest.

"Yes," answered the prof, "I suppose so. But I really should flunk them."

PROFIT-SHARING

A company decided to solicit money-saving ideas from its employees. A worker whose suggestion was used would receive 25 percent of the money saved. First prize went to a man who suggested that the awards be cut to 10 percent.

PROGRESS

Nothing will ever be attempted if all possible objections must first be overcome. (SAMUEL JOHNSON)

Progress is knowing when to stop. (G.K. CHESTERTON)

It appears that the more technology we develop, the closer we are to extinction.

All progress is based upon a universal innate desire on the part of every organism to live beyond its income. (SAMUEL BUTLER)

Little progress can be made by merely attempting to repress what is evil. Our great hope lies in developing what is good. (CALVIN COOLIDGE)

Progress is man's ability to complicate simplicity. (THOR HEYERDAHL)

Once an organization loses its spirit of pioneering and rests on its early work, its progress stops. (THOMAS J. WATSON)

Progress is a tide. If we stand still we will surely be drowned. To stay on the crest, we have to keep moving. (HAROLD MAYFIELD)

Freedom from anxiety is not the most important goal in life. . . . The ideas, inventions, and techniques that make for social progress usually have their origin in the minds of anxious or discontented persons. The advances and improvements in the social complex generally come from those who are dissatisfied with its status, can see its shortcomings, and have the inclination and ability to devise better methods, materials, and equipment. These are the individuals who are alert and anxious about the status quo and who undertake to improve it. . . . Anxiety is necessary for progress. (CHARLES SELLERS)

If you are beginning to encounter some hard bumps, be glad. At least you are out of the rut. (CONSTRUCTION DIGEST)

Any time the going seems easier, better check and see if you're not going downhill. (MEGIDDO MESSAGE)

You may be on the right track, but if you just sit there you'll be run over. (LINK)

You will never stub your toe standing still. The faster you go, the more chance there is of stubbing your toe, but the more chance you have of getting somewhere. (CHARLES F. KETTERING)

It is much more dignified to say we're moving in cycles rather than running around in circles.

"I'm 100 percent in favor of progress," said the politician. "It's just all this change I'm against." (DENTAL ECONOMICS)·

Progress may have been all right once, but it's gone on too long.
(OGDEN NASH)

If a man will go as far as he can see, he will be able to see farther when he gets there. (BITS AND PIECES)

Don't be afraid to take a big step if one is indicated. You can't cross a chasm in two small jumps. (DAVID LLOYD GEORGE)

Restlessness is discontent—and discontent is the first necessity of progress. Show me a thoroughly satisfied man—and I will show you a failure. (THOMAS EDISON)

Psychiatrist: I want to congratulate you on the progress you've been making.
Patient: Progress? Six months ago I was Napoleon Bonaparte. Today I'm nobody. You call that progress?

Progress is impossible without pain. Whenever in social reform it seems possible to sidestep suffering, we had better be suspicious of that alternative. (HARVEY SEIFERT)

I make progress by having people around me who are smarter than I am—and listening to them. And I assume that everyone is smarter about something than I am. (HENRY KAISER)

The greatest enemy of progress is not stagnation, but false progress.

(SYDNEY HARRIS)

Our boasted "progress" has landed us, not in paradise, but in pandemonium. (VANCE HAVNER)

Some sailors had been drinking. It was late on a dark night and they wished to return to their ship. They arrived at the place where they had left their rowboat and drew out the oars. They rowed and rowed and seemed to make little progress. Finally the most sober among them discovered that they had never loosened the boat's painter from the wharf.

Through this humorous incident, we see a real truth. The Master asks of His disciples that they not only row, but also that they cut loose. The reason many of us have not grown more spiritually is that we have never cut loose from the influence of the world that binds us from the progress Christ wants us, as His disciples, to have. (A.P. BAILEY)

John D. Rockefeller . . . spent no time in the early days of Standard Oil dreaming of what it might ultimately become, but . . . he sought solely to take one step forward at a time, convinced that this was all any mortal could or should attempt. We should concentrate on doing with all our might and mind the thing that lies immediately at hand, doing our best hour by hour, day by day, fretting as little as possible about what the future may hold or indulging too much in vain regrets over the past.

(B.C. FORBES)

PROMISES

God never made a promise that was too good to be true. (D.L. MOODY)

Promises may get friends, but it is performance that keeps them.

(OWEN FELTHAM)

When a man repeats a promise again and again he means to fail you.

(ANCIENT PROVERB)

PROMOTIONS

A foreman was a hardworking, conscientious man, but had not received a promotion in 10 years. Asked if he had an explanation for his failure to advance, he replied, "Many years ago I had an argument with my superior. I won." (BITS AND PIECES)

PROMPTNESS

Nothing gives a man more leisure time than always being on time for appointments. (CONSTRUCTION DIGEST)

PROOFREADERS

The world's greatest pessimist is apparently a proofreader in Kentucky, for this is the way a weather forecast read in his newspaper: "There is less than a 5 percent chance of tonight and tomorrow."(BENNETT CERF)

PROPHECY (see FUTURE, PREDICTIONS)

The most often-mentioned event in the entire Bible is the second coming of Christ. It's referred to more than 300 times in the New Testament alone. But remember that the end of the age need not be an occasion for fear. God designed it as the consummation of all things, when the followers of Christ would enter His kingdom of joy and peace. As we near the end, how important it is that we be sure of our personal salvation. Also, that our attitude of expectation keep us very ready. (BILLY GRAHAM)

Who will be caught up in the Rapture? The believing will be leaving.
(PAUL RADER)

Ad: Due to unforeseen circumstances, no Clairvoyant meeting tonight, until further notice. (LOCKPORT, N.Y. UNION-SUN AND JOURNAL)

PROPHETS

We teachers must be prophets, for prophets are men who speak forth God's Word. The word *prophet* means "forthteller," not *foreteller.* A prophet was known not primarily for his *hind*sight or *fore*sight but for his *in*sight. He saw God's plan. He was a *seer,* one who penetrated by insight into the mysteries of God. He knew the covenant God had made with His people, and he knew the gap between God's call and His people's response. (INTERACTION)

PROSPERITY (see AFFLUENCE)

As I look with awe on America's unprecedented prosperity and at how some people are receiving it, I realize anew that the greatest calamity a person can face is to have no struggle—to get everything he wants with negligible effort. Perhaps for every one of us, a long period without "hard times" is no blessing at all. (BURTON HILLIS)

Prosperity is only an instrument to be used, not a deity to be worshiped.
(CALVIN COOLIDGE)

PROVERBS

Proverbs are short sentences drawn from long experiences.(CERVANTES)

PROVISIONS

God gives us the ingredients for our daily bread, but He expects us to do the baking. (WILLIAM A. WARD)

PSYCHIATRISTS

Is a psychiatrist called a "shrink" because that's what he does to your wallet?

A psychiatrist is one who helps you to get off your chest whatever it is you have on your mind.

Patient, lying on psychiatrist's couch: Doctor, nobody takes me seriously anymore.
Doctor: You're kidding.

Sign on a psychiatrists's door: Satisfaction guaranteed or your mania back.   (CORA SOBIESKI)

Half a psychiatrist's patients see him because they are married—the other half because they're not.   (ARNOLD GLASOW)

In the old West, nobody really had any psychological problems. A high-strung man was simply a horse thief who'd been caught.   (QUOTE)

A psychiatrist is a fellow who makes you squeal on yourself.

Psychiatrists who tell parents to spend more time with their children may be simply trying to drum up more business.

"Most people are crazy," said one psychiatrist to another. "Let me ask you some questions that I ask my patients, just to give you an example."
    Then he asked, "What has smooth curves and sometimes is uncontrollable?"
    The other psychiatrist said it was a baseball pitcher, of course.
    "Next, what wears a skirt and whose lips bring you pleasure?"
    The other doctor said the answer to that one was a man who plays a bagpipe.
    "You know the answers," said the first, "but it is amazing what strange answers my patients give me."

Anyone who goes to a psychiatrist should have his head examined.
                                                              (SAM GOLDWYN)

We're told that a patient was brought to a psychiatrist by friends, who informed the doctor that the man was suffering from delusions that a huge fortune was awaiting him. He was expecting two letters which would give him details involving the deeds to a rubber plantation in Sumatra and the titles to some mines in South America. "It was a difficult case and I worked hard on it," the psychiatrist told some colleagues

later. "And just when I had the man cured—the two letters arrived."
(THIS WEEK)

Some of the people we work with don't belong to psychiatry; they belong
to a pastor. These are the ones who know they're doing wrong. When
people come to a minister for help, they take the responsibility for their
misbehavior, but when they come to a psychiatrist they often try to
shove it off upon him. (KARL MENNINGER)

A competent psychiatrist doesn't collect the rent for anyone's dream
castles. Instead he helps his patient to find a dwelling he can actually
live in. And his fee is more appropriately the cost of moving.
(LETTER TO DEAR ABBY)

Whether the patient thinks he is Napoleon, is running berserk, or has
nervous headaches, the common cause is inability to fulfill the two essential needs: (1) to love and be loved, and (2) to feel worthwhile to
ourselves and others. Those who for one reason or another are unable to
fulfill these needs are irresponsible. . . . Little good and much harm come
from delving into the patient's history—the past cannot be changed or
allowed to be used as an excuse for present irresponsibility. Morality
and discipline have a definite place in reality therapy.(WILLIAM GLASSER)

PSYCHOLOGY

To see ourselves as others see us is not necessarily to see ourselves as
we are. Rather, it is to see how we appear when viewed through the
lenses of different outlooks and when judged in terms of values different
from our own. (BRYANT WEDGE)

Modern psychology tells us it's too bad to be an orphan, terrible to be an
only child, damaging to be the youngest, crushing to be in the middle,
and taxing to be the oldest. The only way out: be born as an adult.

PSYCHOPATHOLOGY

Following a university lecture on psychopathology, a student raised his
hand for permission to ask a question. "Professor," he said, "you have
told us about the abnormal person and his behavior, but what about the
normal person?"
  "If we ever find him," answered the professor, "we'll cure him."
(ORLANDO SENTINEL)

PUBLICITY

All publicity is good, except an obituary notice. (BRENDAN BEHAN)

PUBLISHING

Millions of people today are hearing messages and asking, "What did he say?" The principle reason . . . is that the people who are doing the writing, the talking, the speaking, the producing, the broadcasting, the printing, the publishing should be doing more listening themselves—should become more sensitive, should learn more about the people they are trying to reach. (WILLIAM A. NAIL)

Book publishing is a business, resembling somewhat the horse-racing business. (J. RANDALL WILLIAMS)

Once one could write a book and it would be published three months later. Now publishers are like pregnant women—it takes them at least nine months to produce a book. (ERIC LINKLATER)

He's the type who likes to bug people. Like yesterday he wrote to the *Encyclopaedia Brittanica* people and asked them when it was coming out in paperback. (ROBERT ORBEN)

PUNCTUALITY

Punctuality is a nasty habit that some people have to make you think you're late.

Punctuality is something that if you have it, there's often no one around to share it with you. (HYLDA BAKER)

There is at least one good thing you can say about punctuality—it is a sure way to help you enjoy a few minutes of complete privacy. (O.A. BATTISTA)

People who are late are often so much jollier than the people who have to wait for them. (EDWARD V. LUCAS)

PUNCTUATION

Punctuation is troublesome for most people. According to old legends, typesetters used to follow a simple rule: Set type as long as you can hold your breath without getting blue in the face, then put in a comma. When you yawn, put in a semicolon, and when you want to sneeze, that's time for a paragraph. (GOOD READING)

A college English professor wrote the words, "Woman without her man is a savage" on the board, directing the students to punctuate it correctly. He found that the males looked at it one way and the females another:

The males: "Woman, without her man, is a savage!"
The females: "Woman! Without her, man is a savage."

PUNISHMENT

There are two great injustices that can befall a child. One is to punish him for something he didn't do. The other is to let him get away with doing something he knows is wrong. (ROBERT GARDNER)

Perhaps it's cruel for parents not to spank some children, making them feel they haven't done a very good job of being bad.(FRANKLIN P. JONES)

The whole trouble with punishment is that only those who need it least are capable of profiting from it; for the unredeemable, punishment only provokes more anger, more resentment, more desire to return the injury in kind. (SYDNEY HARRIS)

Capital punishment would be more effective as a preventive measure if it were administered prior to the crime. (WOODY ALLEN)

PUNS (see HUMOR)

I never knew an enemy to puns who was not an ill-natured man.
(CHARLES LAMB)

A pun is the lowest form of humor—when you don't think of it first.
(OSCAR LEVANT)

PURPOSE

Every life should have a purpose to which it can give the energies of its mind and the enthusiasms of its heart. That life without a purpose will be prey to the perverted ways waiting for the uncommitted life.
(C. NEIL STRAIT)

QUALITY

Quality isn't something that can be promised into an article. It must be put there. If it isn't put there, the finest sales talk in the world won't act as a substitute. (C.G. CAMPBELL)

Quantity is what you can count.
Quality is what you can count on.

When a customer buys a low-grade article he feels pleased when he pays for it and displeased every time he uses it. But when he buys a well-made article, he feels extravagant when he pays for it and well-pleased every time he uses it. (HERBERT N. CASSON)

QUARRELS (see ARGUMENTS, CONTROVERSIES)

When one will not, two cannot quarrel.

One of the little-mentioned but considerable advantages of rural living is that family quarrels can't be overheard. (SYDNEY HARRIS)

QUARTERBACKS

Old quarterbacks never die. They just pass away.

QUESTIONS

It is harder to ask a sensible question than to supply a sensible answer.
(PERSIAN PROVERB)

When somebody says, "That's a good question," you can be pretty sure it's a lot better than the answer you're going to get. (FRANKLIN P. JONES)

Don't be afraid to ask dumb questions. They're easier to handle than dumb mistakes. (SUPERVISION)

No man really becomes a fool until he stops asking questions.
(CHARLES P. STEINMETZ)

An important use of questioning is to expose difficulties, so that these may be resolved. But the technique can also be employed to test learning, to provide a change from other work, to expose gaps in knowledge, and to rectify misconceptions. Oral questions frequently have a disciplinary value in class in keeping up attention and preventing misbehavior.
(R.L. BOWLEY)

QUITTERS

Worse than a quitter is the man who is afraid to begin.

The agent was asked why he left his last position.
"Well," he said, "I just couldn't take the way the manager and the assistant manager were always fighting."
"They fought all the time?"
"Yes, if it wasn't the manager and me, it was the assistant manager and me. One of 'em was always fighting." (LOCOMOTIVE)

QUOTATIONS

He who never quotes is never quoted. (CHARLES H. SPURGEON)

I'm counting on you to quote me incorrectly. It makes me sound much wittier than I am. (GREER GARSON)

People fond of reading maxims and epigrams are always fonder of quoting those that are applicable to other people than of taking to heart those that apply to themselves. (SYDNEY HARRIS)

I quote others only the better to express myself. (MONTAIGNE)

When you quote: At this point I'd like to say a few appropriated words.
(ROBERT ORBEN)

RACISM

Racism involves the idea that there are superior and inferior races. This does not jibe at all with the truth. People individually have different patterns of potentialities; no person is generally inferior to another. A person who may be regarded as a half-wit may have a more serviceable stomach or liver than I have. Since every race is spotted with a great variety of individuals, each with a distinctive pattern of potentialities, how could we speak of a superior race? Superior for what? Mental abilities are always spotted. . . . There are many ways in which we can be sharp or dull, and each of us has a pattern of his own. Each race contains *individuals*, each of whom has his own distinctive characteristics. (ROGER J. WILLIAMS)

Racism is an idolatry, a worship of pink skin. . . . It is a sick belief that people who are white are congenitally superior to black people. . . . It kills black people by locking them out of respect, and making them feel inferior, and killing their spirit. (JESSE JACKSON)

In teaching race pride, it will be disastrous if we teach a false distinction and a false superiority. We do not correct white racism by erecting black racism. (ROY WILKINS)

RADICALS

If a man is right, he can't be too radical; if he is wrong, he can't be too conservative. (JOSH BILLINGS)

RAIN

Rain is caused by high-pressure areas, cold fronts, warm moist air, and weekends. (PAUL SWEENEY)

It ain't no use to grumble and complain,
    It's just as cheap and easy to rejoice;
When God sorts out the weather and sends rain,
    Why rain's my choice. (JAMES WHITCOMB RILEY)

RATIONALIZATION

Rationalization is a mental technique which allows you to be unfair to others without feeling guilty.

READERS (see LITERATURE)

Reading is to the mind what exercise is to the body. (RICHARD STEELE)

I divide all readers into two classes: those who read to remember and those who read to forget. (WILLIAM LYON PHELPS)

I did some heavy reading last night—my bathroom scale.
(ROBERT ORBEN)

Negative feelings move us much more than positive feelings; we can read a dozen columns we enjoy and agree with, and not signify our approval; but one column we disagree with will evoke an angry letter to the author. . . . People become more aroused over trivialities than over fundamentals, and the amount of response is often in inverse ratio to the profundity of the issue. (SYDNEY HARRIS)

The hours spent reading are investments in tomorrow. For reading sends us into the future with a great reservoir of knowledge from which we can draw at various times.
    Reading is a good way to keep boredom from closing in upon life. Reading introduces new people, new ideas, and new events into life. And boredom is a stranger to the new, exciting things. (C. NEIL STRAIT)

No matter how busy you may think you are, you must find time for reading, or surrender yourself to self-chosen ignorance.
(ATWOOD H. TOWNSEND)

If time for reading were budgeted like time for sleep, work, and meals, then everyone would read enough. But reading is done in odd moments or at the sacrifice of giving up something else. But people interested in their own self-development will read. Somewhere they'll find the time.
(LUCILLE S. HARPER)

After Mary, a first-grader, heard her older brother and friends discuss hints on how to read quickly, she volunteered some advice herself: "I've found you can read a lot faster if you don't stop to color the pictures."

One half who graduate from college never read another book.

(HERBERT TRUE)

REAL ESTATE

Property dispute: ground beef.   (TOM MCELWEE)

A housing development is where they cut down all the trees and then name the streets after them.

REALITY

Reality. What someone thinks is, is sometimes more real than what really is.   (MALCOLM S. FORBES)

Never, no, never face reality at breakfast. Keep it at bay. If it so much as dances on the doorstep, thwack it. Should it poke its head in at the window, draw the blind. No measures can be too harsh. It is a scourge to be met only in the full armor of the day.   (JEANINE LARMOTH)

Things . . . are never as ugly as you fear, nor as lovely as you hope.

(LUIGI BARZINI)

Reality is only one door—a narrow one—but it leads to life.

(PAUL FROMER)

We sing "Sweet Hour of Prayer" and content ourselves with five or ten minutes of prayer a day. We sing "Onward Christian Soldiers" and wait to be drafted into His service. We sing "O for a Thousand Tongues" and don't use the one we have. We sing "There Will Be Showers of Blessing" but do not come to church when it's raining. We sing "When They Ring Those Golden Bells" but seldom seem to hear the call of the church bells. We sing "Hiding in Thee" and then go and hide from Thee. We sing "Blest Be the Tie" and let the slightest offense sever it. We sing "Serve the Lord with Gladness" and gripe about all we have to do. We sing "We're Marching to Zion" but fail to march to the church service on Sunday. We sing "I Love to Tell the Story" and never mention it all year. We sing "Cast Thy Burden on the Lord" and worry ourselves into nervous breakdowns. We sing "O Day of Rest and Gladness" and wear ourselves out traveling, doing Sunday chores, or playing golf. We sing "Throw Out the Lifeline" and content ourselves with throwing out a fishing line.   (GREATER CHICAGO SUNDAY SCHOOL ASSN. MEMO)

REALIZATION

Sometime you'll find yourself—and you'll be very disappointed.

REASON (see LOGIC)

If the animals had reason, they would act just as ridiculous as we men-folks do. (JOSH BILLINGS)

REASONS

There's a difference between good, sound reasons and reasons that sound good.

A man always has two reasons for doing anything—a good reason and the real reason. (J. PIERPONT MORGAN)

When a man has not a good reason for doing a thing. He has one good reason for letting it alone. (GRIT)

RECONCILIATION (see FORGIVENESS)

Brothers, repudiate and denounce with all the energy of your being the idea that Christ reconciles God to the world. But proclaim in all the tones that can melt the heart, that His great mission to the world was to reconcile humanity to Himself. (DAVID THOMAS)

RECREATION

There isn't much fun in medicine, but there's a great deal of medicine in fun. (PRESCOTT COURIER)

I have always said that if a recreational activity is going to do any good for a person, he had to take it seriously and really work at it—in contrast to being a dilettante. (WILLIAM C. MENNINGER)

Recreation is nothing but a change of work—an occupation for the hands by those who live by their brains, or for the brains by those who live by their hands. (DOROTHY THOMPSON)

REFLECTION

Reflect upon your present blessings, of which every man has plenty, not on your past misfortunes, of which all men have some.
(CHARLES DICKENS)

Don't act while you're excited. Wait! More often than not, reflection counsels calming down hot, explosive retorts. Impulse often inspires imprudence. Temptation incites intemperance. Second thought, I have

discovered, often is wiser than first impetuous thought. When excited, wait!
(B.C. FORBES)

REFORM

Many persons use mighty thin thread when mending their ways. (GRIT)

Men and nations can only be reformed in their youth; they become incorrigible as they grow old.
(ROUSSEAU)

REFORMER

A reformer is one who insists on his conscience being your guide.
(PARTS PUP)

REFUSALS

To know how to refuse is as important as to know how to consent.
(BALTASAR GRACIAN)

REGRETS

Regret is an appalling waste of energy; you can't build on it; it's only good for wallowing in.
(KATHERINE MANSFIELD)

REJECTION

Want rejection? Everything about you—your tone of voice, your posture, the way you enter a room—tells people who you are and how you want them to treat you. Therefore, you must weed out of your image any appealing qualitites that might encourage people to accept you. Try to be as apologetic, boring, critical, complaining, impatient, irritable, jealous, nervous, suspicious, and wishy-washy as prudence will allow. Always hang back and wait to be coaxed to participate in a group activity when everybody else just joins in of his own accord. Be sloppy about personal hygiene. Forget people's names. Nurse grudges. Sulk. Never do what anybody else wants to do. Take yourself very seriously. Be a bad sport. Be impossible to please. If anyone should act enthusiastic about anything, be a wet blanket. When with a proud parent or pet owner confess your aversion to children or animals. Remember: sometimes you must first appear to reject in order to be rejected.
(DAN GREENBERG)

RELATIONSHIPS

It's when you rub elbows with a man that you find out what he has up his sleeve.

RELATIVES

It is my relations with my relations that I sometimes find embarrassing.
(SAMUEL BUTLER)

RELAXATION (see LEISURE)

Only when a man is at peace with himself can he find the inclination to relax. It is inner security, not the golf course or the vacation paradise, that releases a man from the tension of the daily round.

(ELLSWORTH KALAS)

The time to relax is when you don't have time for it. (SYDNEY HARRIS)

There is nothing unvirile about resting between sets of tennis when you are in the 40s, whereas in your 30s it would be a minor sort of disgrace. Indeed, not until middle age in America is leisure likely to become anything less than frantic relaxation conducted at a tempo far faster than most work. (RUSSELL LYNES)

It is necessary to relax your muscles when you can. Relaxing your brain is fatal. (STIRLING MOSS)

RELIEF

For fast-acting relief, try slowing down. (LILY TOMLIN)

RELIGION (see CHRISTIANITY)

John Wesley said that sour godliness is the devil's religion. It does not owe its inception to truly spiritual people. I suspect that sour godliness originated among unhappy, semi-religious people who had just enough religion to make them miserable, but not enough to do them good.

(EDWARD L. PEET)

A young girl was asked, "Whose preaching brought you to Christ?"
  She replied, "It wasn't anybody's preaching—it was Aunt Mary's *practicing.*" (MEGIDDO MESSAGE)

My wife, wanting to impress the five-year-olds in her Sunday School class about the importance of living their Christianity as well as believing it, started by asking, "I suppose you children all want to go to heaven, don't you?"
  "Well," said Jackie, in prompt response, "what do you think I put a nickel in the collection for?" (HAL CHADWICK)

Just because people are religious it does not make them any more saintly. (SISTER JOSEPHINE, MEDSTEAD, ENGLAND)

Men never do evil so completely and cheerfully as when they do it from religious conviction. (BLAISE PASCAL)

Charlie was walking down the street with a Bible under his arm when he met his pal, Archie. "Where are you going?" asked Archie.

"Well," replied Charlie, "I've been hearing so much about Miami: pretty girls, great shows, dog races, and so on, I'm going down there to try it out."

"What's the idea of the Bible?" asked Archie.

"If it's as good as they say it is," said Charlie, "I might stay over Sunday." (SALES MANAGEMENT)

Religions are man's search for God; the Gospel is God's search for man. There are many religions, but one Gospel. (E. STANLEY JONES)

You never will be saved *by* works; but let us tell you most solemnly that you never will be saved *without* works. (THEODORE L. CUYLER)

REPENTANCE

Repentance may be old-fashioned, but it is not outdated so long as there is sin. (J.C. MACAULAY)

Sleep with clean hands, either kept clean all day by integrity or washed clean at night by repentance. (JOHN DONNE)

If your sorrow is because of certain consequences which have come on your family because of your sin, this is remorse, not true repentance. If, on the other hand, you are grieved because you also sinned against God and His holy laws, then you are on the right road. (BILLY GRAHAM)

It is much easier to repent of sins that we have committed than to repent of those we intend to commit. (JOSH BILLINGS)

"Repent" is the translation of a Greet verb *metanoeo*, meaning *to have another mind, to change the mind*, and is used in the New Testament to indicate a change of mind in respect to sin, God, and self. This change of mind may, especially in the case of Christians who have fallen into sin, be preceded by sorrow (2 Corinthians 7:8-11); but sorrow for sin, though it may cause repentance, is not repentance. The son in Matthew 21:28-29 illustrates true repentance. Repentance is not an act separate from faith, but saving faith includes and implies that change of mind which is called repentance. (FOOTNOTE TO ACTS 17:30, SCO)

REPETITION

John Wesley used to recall that as a youth his behavior often displeased his father. His mother was more forebearing. "How can you have the patience," exploded the elder Wesley, "to tell that blockhead John the same thing 20 times over?"

"Why," replied Mrs. Wesley, "if I had told him but 19 times I had wasted my breath."

REPUTATION

Men are not always what they seem—but seldom better.   (LESSING)

A reputation may be repaired, but people always keep their eyes on the place where the crack was.

Many a man's reputation would not know his character, if they met on the street.   (ELBERT HUBBARD)

The reputation of a man is like his shadow: It sometimes follows and sometimes precedes him; it is sometimes longer and sometimes shorter than his natural size.   (FRENCH PROVERB)

Associate with men of good quality, if you esteem your own reputation; it is better to be alone than in bad company.   (MEGIDDO MESSAGE)

What people say behind your back is your standing in the community.   (EDGAR WATSON HOWE)

Reputation is character minus what you've been caught doing. (SUNSHINE)

Reputation is what you are in your own home, entertaining friends; character is what you are when you're behind the steering wheel of your car, driving down the highway.   (LEO AIKMAN)

A good reputation is being well thought of; a good conscience is thinking well of yourself.   (WILLIAM A. WARD)

It takes a very short time to lose a good reputation but a long, long time to get another one.   (MUNCIE EVENING PRESS)

RESEARCH

I see the research man as the fellow you keep in the crow's nest to see beyond your horizon, to tell you where there is another prize ship to be taken or a man-o'-war to be avoided.   (CHARLES F. KETTERING)

Research is a high-hat word that scares a lot of people. It needn't. Essentially, it is nothing but a state of mind—a friendly welcoming attitude toward change. Going out to look for change, instead of waiting for it to come to you. It is the problem-solving mind as contrasted to the let-well-enough-alone mind. It is the composer mind, instead of the fiddler mind. It is the "tomorrow" mind instead of the "yesterday" mind.
     (CHARLES F. KETTERING)

Intelligent ignorance is the first requirement in research.

(CHARLES F. KETTERING)

Basic research is what I am doing when I don't know what I am doing.

(WERNHER VON BRAUN)

If only there were a million more boys being taught what it takes to be a researcher, what a world this could be! Think of the poor kids. They're examined three or four times a year, and if they flunk, it's a disgrace. If they fail once, they're out. In contrast, all research is 99.9 percent failure and if you succeed once, you're in. Here's what we ought to teach them: The only time you don't want an experiment to fail is the last time you try it.

(CHARLES A. BUCHER)

A little knowledge, the saying goes, is a dangerous thing. So is a little research. The field is too complicated and too full of pitfalls for casual flirtation. Businesses are far better off to ignore attitude research completely than to approach it with a let's-try-it-out attitude. Like so many other of the most rewarding aspects of business life, such as advertising and public relations, attitude research is worth doing on a long-term basis or not at all.

(ROBERT GOLDBERG)

It is a popular conception that to make rapid fundamental progress it is only necessary to concentrate large quantities of men and money on a problem. Years ago when we were developing the first electrically operated cash register I ran into this type of thinking. My boss was going to Europe and wanted the job finished before he took off. "Give Kettering twice as many men so he can finish it up in half the time." When I objected to this idea he asked, "Why can't you? If 10 men can dig 10 rods of ditch in a day, then surely 20 men can dig 20 rods."

I replied, "Do you think if one hen can hatch a setting of eggs in three weeks, two hens can hatch a setting in a week and a half? This is more a job of hatching eggs than digging ditches." (CHARLES F. KETTERING)

A child-study institution has . . . completed research on youngsters who suck their thumbs and has issued a report that such children have a distinct tendency toward one clean thumb. (D.O. FLYNN)

Warning against turning ourselves "away from the stars to the sewers": We realize there are other pressing needs in this country. But research and development is not the kind of thing that can be turned on and off like a faucet.

(WERNHER VON BRAUN)

It is not the privilege of every creative man to question and doubt research. It is his duty. It is only his personal point of view that can change the charts and the graphs and the percentages into palatable, appealing advertising.

(CLEO HOVEL)

RESENTMENT

Don't resent the fact that people check on you; if you weren't worth anything, they wouldn't bother. (ROBERT A. COOK)

RESISTANCE

Expect resistance, but pray for miracles. (CORRIE TEN BOOM)

RESPECT

A child who is allowed to be disrespectful to his parents will not have true respect for anyone. (BILLY GRAHAM)

Don't always try to be popular. It isn't possible for everyone to like you. It's far more important for you to like yourself. And when you respect yourself, strangely, you get more respect than if you court it from others. (JOYCE BROTHERS)

If you wish others to respect you, you must show respect for them. For 20 days, approach everyone you meet, irrespective of his station in life, as if he or she were the most important person in the world. Everyone wants to feel that he counts for something and is important to someone. Invariably, people will give their love, respect, and attention to the person who fills that need. Consideration for others generally reflects faith in self and faith in others. (ARI KIEV)

A man who does not respect his own life and that of others robs himself of his dignity as a human being. (DALIP SINGH)

I get no respect from my dog. The other day, the dog went to the door and started to bark. I went over and opened it. The dog didn't want to go out; he wanted me to leave. (RODNEY DANGERFIELD)

RESPONSE

It is not what happens to us that counts; it is how we respond.

RESPONSIBILITY

Few things help an individual more than to place responsibility upon him, and to let him know that you trust him. (BOOKER T. WASHINGTON)

If you want your children to keep their feet on the ground, put some responsibility on their shoulders. (ABIGAIL VAN BUREN)

When your shoulders are carrying a load of responsibility, there isn't room for chips.

A man who enjoys responsibility usually gets it. A man who merely likes exercising authority usually loses it.   (MALCOLM S. FORBES)

Some people grow under responsibility—others merely swell.
                                                              (MEGIDDO MESSAGE)

Being on time is a prime characteristic of responsible people. And responsible people are what business and industry need most.
                                                              (NORMAN G. SHIDLE)

REST

Take rest; a field that has rested gives a bountiful crop.   (OVID)

RESULTS

Judge people who work for you on results, not on their personality traits.

RETARDATION

Statistics indicate that 75 percemt of all retardation is traceable to a lack of emotional development. By the same token, the parents of slow children serve them well when they offer patient and loving stimulation. Your child is an individual. Treat him as such. Love him as such. And judge him as such—not by charts and certainly not by other children.
                                                              (MINER C. HILL)

RETIREMENT

Nobody ever raises questions about the after-65 competency of doctors, lawyers, or merchants who are their own bosses. Just those people who work for somebody else.   (PAUL HIGHTOWER)

Aging is not only biological; it is also sociogenic. The role of oldness is not biologically fixed; it is something prescribed by society, and our society prescribes it fully. This country by reason of its big immigrant population has always been a youth-oriented culture, and never more than now. If you decree that once achievement is over, so is worth; if you prescribe that older citizens must retire at an arbitrary age and condemn them to poverty, and if you then repeat often enough that older people are ineducable, unemployable, asexual, unintelligent, and as the Greeks say "a burden to the soil," you will generate some of the problems which the older citizen now faces. It is no wonder that the over-65 group have come in America to resemble an underprivileged minority— but this is a minority we are all going to join.   (ALEX COMFORT)

The fellow who can't figure out what to do with a Sunday afternoon is often the same one who can't wait for retirement.

Retirement can be a catastrophe or a commencement, a rocking chair or a launching pad.

Don't think of yourself as a senior citizen. Think of yourself as a dropout from the school of hard knocks.

Business expert: How many employees do you have approaching retirement?
Personnel director: Well, we haven't got anybody going the other way.

People need to have experiences which are rewarding and challenging to their particular needs, and this need does not stop when we retire.
(JAMES BOSTIC)

What elderly workers need in this country is a choice between retirement and something they can afford. (FRANKLIN P. JONES)

With retirement, one should have on hand two or three jobs that ought to be done, and that he wants to get done, but which do not have to be done today. Once these are provided, he can experience the true joys of procrastination. (WHEELER MCMILLEN)

Work is the recreation of the retired. (ROBERT ORBEN)

Retirement can be a joy if you figure out how to spend time without spending money.

It is by no accident that, when someone meets someone for the first time, "How do you do?" is usually closely followed by "What do you do?" Since most working people describe themselves by the company or organization to which they belong, work makes them "somebody"; unemployed people become "nobodies."
The importance of this job-related identification shows up when a person retires. Scientists attribute much of the trauma associated with retirement to a sudden loss of identity.

If retirement is a part of your future, no matter how far in the future it may be, plan now to retire not *from* something but *to* something. It's a state of mind, and there are extra years of zest ahead.(BETTY ZACHOW)

My admonition from my mother was, "Wear out; don't rust out." I don't think anyone should stop working. My friends who have stopped working deteriorate fast, and I think men should be kept active as long as they are able to go. (CHARLES H. KELLSTADT)

The worst thing about retirement is to have to drink coffee on your own time. (CPA JOURNAL)

When some people retire, it's going to be mighty hard to be able to tell the difference. (VIRGINIA GRAHAM)

If you want a carefree life, retire—and forget to tell your wife. (EUGENE P. BERTIN)

REVENGE

Revenge is a deceiver—it looks sweet but is most often bitter.

It costs more to revenge injuries than to bear them. (THOMAS WILSON)

You can't win by trying to even the score.

If I were a gravedigger, or even a hangman, there are some people I could work for with a great deal of pleasure. (DOUGLAS JERROLD)

The only people with whom you should try to get even are those who have helped you. (JOHN E. SOUTHARD)

REVOLUTIONARIES

Today's revolutionaries are tomorrow's tyrants.

REWARDS

Any business or industry that pays equal rewards to its goof-offs and its eager beavers sooner or later will find itself with more goof-offs than eager beavers. (MICK DELANEY)

There are no crown-wearers in heaven that were not cross-bearers here below. (CHARLES H. SPURGEON)

RICHES

A man is rich in proportion to the number of things he can afford to let alone. (HENRY THOREAU)

Don't knock the rich. When was the last time you were hired by somebody poor? (ROBERT ORBEN)

RIDICULE

Every nation ridicules other nations, and all are right. (SCHOPENHAUER)

RIGHTEOUSNESS (see HOLINESS)

You can always tell when you are on the road of righteousness—it's uphill. (ERNEST BLEVINS)

RIGHT AND WRONG (see GOODNESS)

Right is right, even if everyone is against it; and wrong is wrong, even if everyone is for it. (WILLIAM PENN)

It is better to be despised for the right than praised for the wrong. (MEGGIDO MESSAGE)

It seems to me these days that people who admit they're wrong get a lot farther than people who prove they're right. (BERYL PFIZER)

He's a very forthright character. He's right about a fourth of the time. (GENE BROWN)

When you are so devoted to doing what is right that you press straight on to that and disregard what men are saying about you, there is the triumph of moral courage. (MEGIDDO MESSAGE)

RISKS (see CHANCES)

Progress always involves risks. You can't steal second and keep your foot on first. (FREDERICK WILCOX)

Taking chances is a fact of economic life. Business must risk to grow. Fear of what may or may not happen is no excuse for avoiding challenges. (EDWARD TELLING)

Why *not* go out on a limb? Isn't that where the fruit is? (FRANK SCULLY)

You cannot grow, in whatever dimension, without taking risks, and if you have stopped growing you might as well be dead. You cannot know people without loving them, which brings its attendant risks of loss and pain. You cannot climb Mt. Everest without risking your neck, and nothing can be achieved without risking time, effort, and reputation. (EVA FIGES)

ROUTINE

Most of life is routine—dull and grubby—but routine is the momentum that keeps a man going. If you wait for inspiration you'll be standing on the corner after the parade is a mile down the street. (BEN NICHOLAS)

RULES

The young man knows the rules, but the old man knows the exceptions. (OLIVER W. HOLMES)

There are no exceptions to the rule that everybody likes to be an exception to the rule. (MALCOLM FORBES)

RUMORS (see GOSSIP)

Trying to squash a rumor is like trying to unring a bell.

(SHANA ALEXANDER)

Why is it so much easier to believe something bad than something good? (BERYL PFIZER)

Nothing can stir up more mud than a rumor that is groundless.

(O.A. BATTISTA)

If there is a rumor in the air about you, you'd better treat it as you would a wasp: either ignore it or kill it with the first blow. Anything else will just stir it up. (JAMES THOM)

There is no such thing as an "idle" rumor. Rumors are always busy.

(F.G. KERNAN)

Rumors are a lot like rabbits. It doesn't take much to get them started. They multiply quickly. And if they spread unchecked, they can cause man much grief. (SALES MANAGEMENT)

RUSH HOUR

The rush hour is when traffic is at a standstill.

RUSSIA (see ZOO)

I cannot forecast to you the action of Russia. It is a riddle wrapped in a mystery inside an enigma. (WINSTON CHURCHILL)

We have a strange trade agreement with the Russians. We give them a bushel of wheat and they give us a peck of trouble. (ROBERT ORBEN)

The first characteristic of the Soviet Union is that it always adopts the attitude of bullying the soft and fearing the strong. The second characteristic of the Soviet Union is that it will go in and grab at every opportunity. (TENG HSIAO-P'ING)

First Russian: What was the nationality of Adam and Eve?
Second Russian: There can be no doubt but that they were citizens of the Soviet Union. They had nothing to wear, nothing to eat but an apple—and yet they were told they were living in paradise. (C. KENNEDY)

Soviet children are naturally saturated with the standards and values of Soviet society. . . . Kornei Chukovsky's four-year-old daughter, when he told her of his being taken to church as a child, queried, "Daddy, is it possible that you were born so long ago—when there was still a God?"

Another parent, explaining day and night, said to her small child, "When it is day here, it is night in America."

His reply: "Serves them right, those capitalists!" (KATHERINE TAYLOR)

I have made a great mistake. Our main purpose was to give freedom to a multitude of oppressed people. But our method of action has created worse evils and horrible massacres. You know that my deadly nightmare is to feel that I am lost in this ocean of blood, coming from innumerable victims. It is too late to turn back now, but in order to save our country, Russia, we should have had 10 men like Francis of Assisi. With 10 such men we would have saved Russia. (ALLEGED LAST WORDS OF V.I. LENIN)

RUTHLESSNESS

A lot of people tell me I'm not tough enough. Listen, there are enough tough people in the world. (HUBERT HUMPHREY)

SACRIFICE

During a visit to Korea two American businessmen were highly amused to see a young farmer pulling a plow, guided by his father. On recounting the story to a missionary they learned this father and son were Christians who sold their only ox and contributed the money to their church for a new building.

Responded one of the men in an awed voice, "What a stupendous sacrifice!"

The missionary replied, "They did not feel that way about it. They counted it a great joy that they had an ox to give to the Lord's work."

(WALTER SCHLICHTING)

SADNESS (see GRIEF)

I love everything in life, even to be sad. (ARTUR RUBENSTEIN)

SAFETY (see SECURITY)

City chap, crossing a pasture: Say there, is this bull safe?
Farmer: He's a lot safer than you are.

I have never liked to use the word "safe" in connection with Eastern Air Lines or the entire transportation field; I prefer the word "reliable." For whenever motion is involved, there can be no condition of absolute safety. The only time man is safe is when he is completely static, in a box underground. (EDDIE RICKENBACKER)

It is when we all play safe that we create a world of utmost insecurity.

(DAG HAMMARSKJÖLD)

SAINTS (see CHRISTIANITY)

Saints are persons who make it easier for others to believe in God.

(NATHAN SÖDERBLOM)

Saints are often sinners who became famous by admitting their sins in public.

(O.A. BATTISTA)

SALARY

Now's the time to ask the boss for a raise. Tell him several companies are after you: the electric company, the finance company, the gas company.

(LOU ERICKSON)

SALESMEN (see PERSUASION)

I deal with a salesman who's going to go far. This morning we were playing golf, and I was in a sand trap 200 feet from the green—and he conceded the putt.

(ROBERT ORBEN)

A good salesman is someone who has found a cure for the common cold shoulder.

He who works with his *hands* is a laborer.
He who works with his *hands* and his *head* is a craftsman.
He who works with his *hands*, his *head*, and his *heart* is an artist.
He who works with his *hands*, his *head*, his *heart*, and his *feet* is a salesman.

The old fashioned salesman is often pictured as a fast talker, a fly-by-night operator who peddled wares of doubtful merit, a nimble-witted sharper not far removed from bunko artist. Whatever the salesman of the past may have been, today's successful salesman is a different breed. He is a man who knows his product and his company, has faith in it, and wants to let the world know how good he thinks that product is.

(ROBERT C. MOOT)

A salesman had been trying to sell a particularly tough prospect and was getting nowhere. Each time he left the prospect's office, he commented, "I wish I had 10 like you."

At the end of a fruitless encounter, the unyielding prospect's curiosity got the better of him, and he inquired, "Why do you always say, 'I wish I had 10 like you'?"

The salesman replied, "I have 100 like you. I wish I had just 10."

(GRIT)

Actually there are only four primary sales appeals to persuade others to action. They are the four Ss: *Sex* (to make a favorable impression on the other sex); *Snob* (to keep up with the Joneses); *Self* (to improve one's status in life); *Soul* (to be at peace with God.)   (ADVERTISING AGE)

In England, the president of a vacuum cleaner company was explaining his talent for hiring top salesmen. "I give the new applicant a special test. I send him out to rent a flat while carrying a tuba." (FUNNY WORLD)

I try to find excuses for our salesmen. Maybe we have such a great product they hate to part with it.   (ROBERT ORBEN)

A salesman always kept his hat on while doing "desk work" at the office. When kidded about it, he answered, "That's to remind me I really ought not to be here."   (AMERICAN SALESMAN)

A salesman for a key-making machine entered a hardware store and gave the shopkeeper a demonstration. "Isn't it a wonderful machine?" he asked.
    "Yes, it is."
    "It would be a marvelous investment and a great time-saver, wouldn't it?"
    "Yes."
    "Don't you think every hardware store ought to have one?"
    "Yes."
    "Well, why don't you buy it?"
    "Well," said the shopkeeper, "why don't you ask me to?"
    Isn't it just there that so much of our Christian preaching and witness is weak? We talk, describe, illustrate, and theologize, but often fail to thrust home the direct personal challenge.   (DAVID A. MACLENNAN)

The sales manager told his crew, "You fellows don't make enough calls. If you'd make more calls, you'd sell more merchandise."
    At the next sales meeting one bright young fellow raised his hand and said, "I made 47 calls yesterday."
    "That's fine," said the sales manager. "I commend you."
    "I would have made more," the young man continued, "but some fool stopped me and asked what I was selling."   (LEO AIKMAN)

What successful salesmen need: Curiosity of a cat. Tenacity of a bulldog. Determination of a cab driver. Diplomacy of a wayward husband. Patience of a self-sacrificing wife. Deductive powers of a Sherlock Holmes. Persuasiveness of a job-hunting politician. Enthusiasm of a radio announcer. Alertness of a fox terrier. Self-assurance of a seminary graduate. Tireless persistence of a bill collector.   (AMERICAN SALESMAN)

SALT

You can't be the salt of the earth without smarting someone.

SALVATION (see GOSPEL)

If salvation could be attained only by working hard, then surely horses and donkeys would be in heaven. (MARTIN LUTHER)

I came to Georgia to convert the Indians, but oh, who will convert me? (JOHN WESLEY)

When he abandoned all attempt to save himself, Jesus Christ saved him. This was all he knew about it. And more, this was all there was about it. (ICHABOD SPENCER, OF A FRIEND)

God doesn't just patch—He renews.
God doesn't just salve sins—He saves.
God doesn't just reform—He transforms men by His power.
(MERRILL C. TENNEY)

There are too many grandchildren of Christ in the world, those whose parents were Christians but they aren't. Nowhere in the Bible does God claim grandchildren—just children, born again by faith in Christ.
(BOB PIERCE)

Unless a man is ready to work for the salvation of others, it may be questioned whether he himself is saved. He who wants only enough religion to save himself is not likely to have even that much.
(HENRY CLAY TRUMBULL)

Salvation is moving from living death to deathless life. (JACK ODELL)

SAMSON (see NAMES)

Samson died from a case of fallen arches.

SATISFACTION (see CONTENTMENT)

Most of us learn too late that it is just as easy, under most conditions, to be satisfied as it is to be dissatisfied. And it's much more healthful.
(WOODMEN OF THE WORLD)

The stomach is the only part of man which can be fully satisfied. The yearning of man's brain for new knowledge and experience and for more pleasant and comfortable surroundings never can be completely met. It is an appetite which cannot be appeased. (THOMAS EDISON)

A man who is always satisfied with himself is seldom satisfied with others. (FRANCOIS DE LA ROCHEFOUCAULD)

The business that is satisfied with itself—with its product, with its sales, that looks upon itself as having accomplished its purpose—is dead. (JOHN H. PATTERSON)

I've never been satisfied with anything we've ever built. I've felt that dissatisfaction is the basis of progress. When we become satisfied in business we become obsolete. (J. WILLARD MARRIOTT, SR.)

Show me a thoroughly satisfied man and I will show you a failure. (THOMAS EDISON)

SAVINGS (see MONEY)

The more you learn to live without, the more you'll have to live with. (FRANK A. CLARK)

SCHOOLS (see EDUCATION, UNIVERSITIES)

Eight-year-old Susie was crazy about school, while her six-year-old sister was less enthusiastic. "Let's play school," suggested Susie one day.
    "All right," agreed the younger one grudgingly, "but let's play I'm absent today." (CONSTRUCTION DIGEST)

A boy had been pawing over a stock of greeting cards for a long time when a clerk asked him, "Can I help you find what you're looking for, son?"
    "You got anything in the line of blank report cards?" he asked wistfully.

Studies are pursued but never overtaken. As one [student] remarked, "I'm getting along fine in everything but my courses."(EUGENE P. BERTIN)

September is when millions of bright, shining, happy, laughing faces turn toward school. They belong to mothers.

I ask only one thing of my kids when they go to school: Don't hang out with the troublemakers—because birds of a feather flunk together. (ROBERT ORBEN)

If Adam hadn't sinned, would we have to go to school? (PAM FELSKE)

Remember that "average" is simply the best of the poorest, and the poorest of the best. (GOOD READING)

Schools are a bad scene for boys, proclaims Patricia Sexton, New York University educator. Mrs. Sexton maintains that the male suffers from a home stacked against masculine aggression, masculine restlessness, and masculine activity. The prejudice begins at home, she says, where Mother is usually the visible partner, and continues into the "feminized schools of this country, and the few male administrators tend to be top-sergeant types, not likely to win admiration." (ALEX L. PICKENS)

One of the biggest jobs that schools face is getting money from the taxpayers without disturbing the voters. (EDUCATION DIGEST)

School is a building that has four walls—with tomorrow inside. (LON WATTERS)

"You say there's a lot of violence at the school your kid attends?"
"I'll put it this way. The required supplies are paper, pencil, and Blue Cross policy."

Once when children didn't go to school, the truant officer went after them. Now the school board holds a hearing to see whether the curriculum is meeting the felt needs of the under-endowed. (CONSTRUCTION DIGEST)

School is the mouse race that equips you for the rat race. (TIES)

Horace Fitley says nothing today is like what he was taught when he went to school and that it would have been worse than a waste of time if he hadn't forgotten it all by now. (FRANKLIN P. JONES)

Everyone favors a 12-month school year except for two groups—the students and the teachers. (GENE YASENAK)

Paying no attention to the red traffic light, the speeding cars, or the policeman's blast on a whistle, the little old lady marched primly across the street.
The policeman strode angrily up to her. "Say, lady," he growled, "didn't you see my hand raised? Don't you know what that means?"
"Well, I should hope I do," snapped the lady, "I've been teaching school for 40 years!"

SCIENCE

With every new answer unfolded, science has consistently discovered at least three new questions. (WERNHER VON BRAUN)

Modern technology has developed a soft drink can which, when discarded, will last forever—and a $12,000 car which, when taken care of, will rust out in five years. (GLORIA PITZER)

We live in an era when, for the first time in history, it is no longer practically possible to pursue simultaneously all the avenues for scientific research that are open to us. There are just too many of them. (BERNARD LOVELL)

A true scientist is known by his confession of ignorance. (A.O. FOSTER)

Though I love science I have the feeling that it is so greatly opposed to history and tradition that it cannot be absorbed by our civilization. The political and military horrors and the complete breakdown of ethics which I have witnessed during my lifetime may not be a symptom of an ephemeral social weakness but a necessary consequence of the rise of science—which in itself is among the highest intellectual achievements of man. (MAX BORN)

Disillusioned by the uses men made of science, Albert Einstein said not long before his death that if he could live again, he would choose to be a plumber rather than a physicist. (ATLANTA CONSTITUTION)

A nervous citizen asked a prominent scientist if it were possible for an atomic bomb to destroy the earth.
"Suppose it does," replied the scientist, with a shrug. "It isn't as if the earth were a major planet."

Many scientists have quit wondering how old the earth is and have begun pondering how much older it will get. (GRIT)

The probability of life originating from accident is comparable to the probability of the unabridged dictionary resulting from an explosion in a printing shop. (EDWARD CONKLIN)

Modern man is far more interested in what scientists believe about God than he is in what God thinks about scientists.

Science has nothing to say to the deepest levels of human experience. What can science say to a heart being chilled by loneliness? What can science say to a heart broken by grief? What relief can science give to a life being turned prematurely gray by unforgiven sin and guilt? (ALAN WALKER)

SCOTLAND

Excavators in Aberdeen have come across a Scottish penny dated 1588. A few feet away, as they continued to dig, they unearthed three skeletons—all on their hands and knees. (AMERICAN OPINION)

SECRETARIES

When you want something done properly and promptly, give the job to the busiest man you know. He'll have his secretary take care of it.

The secretarial occupation is 5,000 years old. The earliest [known] secretaries were Babylonian scribes who took dictation on clay tablets.
(SUNSHINE)

Newly hired secretary, to boss: Do you want double spacing on the carbons too, sir? (ROCK HILL, S.C. HERALD)

The ideal secretary . . . was described in a . . . U.S. Department of State newsletter: "She should be young enough to start at the lowest salary, thus leaving room for promotion; but near enough to retirement age so no other office will try to take her away; able to spell the words I use, but not those of anyone else; efficient and accurate enough so she does all my work perfectly, but backward enough so that she does not do good work for anyone else; attractive and cheerful enough so she brightens up the office, but not so much that some guy will come along and marry her; sensible enough so that she uses good judgment in all her duties, but foolish enough so that—if she does marry—she chooses a man she has to support and so stays on the job." (EXECUTIVES' DIGEST)

Sign on a secretary's desk: I type the way I live—fast, with a lot of mistakes. (KATHIE JOYE)

SECRETS

A secret is what you tell someone else not to tell because you can't keep it to yourself. (ARTHUR ORLOFF)

Another person's secret is like another person's money: you are not as careful with it as you are with your own. (E.W. HOWE)

Few secrets last long. Either they're too good to keep or not worth keeping anyway. (BITS & PIECES)

SECURITY (see SAFETY)

There is no security on this earth. Only opportunity.
(DOUGLAS MACARTHUR)

No one can build his security upon the nobleness of another person.
(WILLA CATHER)

There is plenty of security in a jail cell, but I have never heard of anybody beating down the doors to get in.   (WILLIAM S. BROOMFIELD)

When God made the oyster He guaranteed it absolute economic and social security. He built the oyster a house, his shell, to shelter and protect him from his enemies. When hungry, the oyster simply opens his shell and food rushes in for him. He has freedom from want.
   But when God made the eagle He declared: "The blue sky is the limit—build your own house!" So the eagle builds on the highest mountain. Storms threaten him every day. For food he flies through miles of rain and snow and wind. The eagle, not the oyster, is the emblem of America.   (JOHNSON JOURNAL)

SELF

A man needs self-acceptance or he can't live with himself; he needs self-criticism or others can't live with him.   (JAMES A. PIKE)

The greatest burden we have to carry in life is self; the most difficult thing we have to manage is self.   (HANNAH WHITALL SMITH)

I have more trouble with D.L. Moody than with any other man I ever met.   (DWIGHT L. MOODY)

You have an ego—a consciousness of being an individual. But that doesn't mean that you are to worship yourself, to think constantly of yourself, and to live entirely for self.   (BILLY GRAHAM)

SELF-AMBITION

One of the liberating aspects of the later years of life is freedom from ambition. Some of the noblest examples of human character appear when the drive for success has become obsolete. It is chiefly in being good persons ourselves that we help others.   (ELTON TRUEBLOOD)

SELF-APPRAISAL (see SELF-CRITICISM)

You damage yourself and your relations with other people if you think either too much or too little of yourself. Take a modest, realistic view of yourself. And don't wear a false front because you want to seem to be what you're not.   (MARION LEACH JACOBSEN)

SELF-BLAMERS

The quickest way to take the starch out of a fellow who is always blaming himself is to agree with him.   (JOSH BILLINGS)

SELF-CENTEREDNESS

A self-centered life is totally empty, while an emptied life allows room for God. (Tom Haggai)

Self-centeredness and happiness do not go hand in hand.
(Footnote, 1 Kings 21:4, MLB)

SELF-CONFIDENCE

Supreme confidence in one's ability to "deliver" in times of crisis or need is a quality much to be desired. It is possessed by all too few of us. Our tendency is to yield, to retreat, or to crack up when the going gets too tough. Each of us has his or her "breaking point," dependent upon the degree of courage and faith and resolution . . . built into our lives. Where one person gives up, another person may be just beginning. If you are not going forward, you are going backward. Nothing stands still in life. You must keep on putting forth the best efforts of which you are capable to maintain the position you have gained. (Harold Sherman)

SELF-CONSCIOUSNESS

We would worry less about what others think of us if we realized how seldom they do. (Ethel Barrett)

SELF-CONTROL

How shall I be able to rule over others when I have not full power and command over myself? (Rabelais)

He who smiles rather than rages is always the stronger.
(Japanese wisdom)

A man bumped into an acquaintance in a bar, and remarked, "I thought you'd given up drinking. What's the matter—no self-control?"
"Sure, I've got plenty of self-control," he replied. "I'm just too strong to use it." (Machinist)

SELF-CRITICISM (see CRITICISM, SELF-APPRAISAL)

The man who makes a habit of selling himself short, of talking people out of paying him a compliment, is giving the world a false picture of himself. Friends may argue a little with him when he makes a disparaging remark about himself or his business, but the remark will stick. By and by even his best friends will gather the idea from his own attitude that he is pretty much of a second-rater.
(Royal Bank of Canada Monthly Letter)

SELF-DELUSION

The men who really believe in themselves are all in lunatic asylums.

(G.K. CHESTERTON)

SELF-DENIAL

If you begin by denying yourself nothing, the world later is apt to do your denying for you. Deny yourself, or be denied. (B.F. FORBES)

Toward the end of his heroic, tragic life, General Robert E. Lee attended the christening of a friend's child. The mother asked him for a word that would guide the child along the road to manhood. Lee's answer summed up the creed that had borne him, through struggle and suffering, to a great place in American history. "Teach him," he said simply, "to deny himself."

SELF-DESTRUCTION

Many people go throughout life committing partial suicide—destroying their talents, energies, creative qualities. Indeed, to learn how to be good to oneself is often more difficult than to learn how to be good to others. (JOSHUA LIEBMAN)

SELF-DISCOVERY

Many people seem to get along quite happily without exploring their inner life or even paying much attention to it. Isn't the inner life an affair for artists, mystics, psychoanalysts—those breeds of queer fish—to dabble in? Self-discovery is the most important of all human discoveries.

(C. DAY-LEWIS)

Seven rules for self-discovery. We may be known by the following: (1) What we want most. (2) What we think about most. (3) How we use our money. (4) What we do with our leisure time. (5) The company we enjoy. (6) Whom and what we admire. (7) What we laugh at. (A.W. TOZER)

If we could see ourselves as others see us, we'd probably have our eyes examined. (FRANKLIN P. JONES)

SELF-DISLIKE

What makes people unhappy with themselves? Sometimes it's a sense of guilt about a wrong done to someone else or a dislike felt toward a close relative such as a parent, a brother, or sister. Sometimes it's a feeling of failure and frustration in their work or their personal relationships. But in many cases self-dislike can be traced to our early years of life, when we are forming a self-image. If a child gets frequent criticism, scolding, nagging, or if he feels that his brothers or sisters are preferred over him, he will develop a sense of unworthiness that can lead to self-dislike.

(GRETTA BAKER)

SELF-ESTEEM

I never get down on myself. I am [a] very good friend of mine.

(GUILLERMO VILAS)

SELF-EVALUATION

Most of us do not like to look inside ourselves for the same reason we don't like to open a letter that has bad news.   (FULTON J. SHEEN)

If you can see yourself as others see you and not get mad, you're a philosopher.   (ROUGH NOTES)

Forget what people think of you. You're people. What do *you* think of you?

You're in for a great deal of pain if you take yourself too seriously.

(PAUL NEWMAN)

You've no idea what a poor opinion I have of myself, and how little I deserve it.   (W.S. GILBERT)

SELF-GROWTH

The first step toward growing up, instead of out, is learning to like ourselves. More than half the hospital beds are filled with people who haven't been able to come to terms with themselves. Granted, it isn't always easy to do because it involves taking a good look at our weaknesses (and few of us like to do that) as well as our strengths. There is nothing wrong with having deficiencies. It's what we do about them that counts. Better expend our energies improving, rather than deploring. To work at overcoming weaknesses and reinforcing strengths is the way we grow.   (DORIS DICKELMAN)

SELF-IMAGE

If you don't matter to you, it's hard to matter to others. (MALCOLM FORBES)

Our self-image is determined by what others think of us. If they think of us as inferior, we also consider ourselves inferior. Those who suffer from low self-esteem are the ones most likely to be flattened by life's hammer blows.   (FLORA SCHREIBER AND MELVIN HERMAN)

SELF-IMPORTANCE

No man is as important as he sounds at his alumni banquet.

(WALL STREET JOURNAL)

SELF-IMPROVEMENT

Failure to hit the mark is never the fault of the target. To improve your aim, improve yourself. (CONSTRUCTION DIGEST)

SELFISHNESS (see GREED)

We seldom think of what we have but always of what we lack. (SCHOPENHAUER)

Every single ancient wisdom and religion will tell you the same thing: Don't live entirely for yourself; live for other people. Think what it means in concrete terms. Don't get stuck inside your own ego, because it will become a prison in no time flat—and . . . don't think that "self-realization" will make you happy. That is the way you will end in . . . your own hell. (BARBARA WARD)

Stop justifying selfishness because "the world is a jungle." It can also be a garden, depending on whether one wants to plant and water, or to plunder and uproot. (SYDNEY HARRIS)

Selfishness is the greatest curse of the human race. (W.E. GLADSTONE)

SELF-KNOWLEDGE

If you don't know you are a contradiction, whatever else you think you know about yourself is based upon a fiction. (SYDNEY HARRIS)

Only as you know yourself can your brain serve you as a sharp and efficient tool. Know your own failings, passions, and prejudices so that you can separate them from what you see. (BERNARD BARUCH)

SELFLESSNESS

A man asked Dr. Karl Menninger, "What would you advise a person to do, if he felt a nervous breakdown coming on?"

Most people expected him to reply, "Consult a psychiatrist." To their astonishment he replied, "Lock up your house, go across the railway tracks, find someone in need, and do something to help that person."

SELF AND OTHERS (see OTHERS)

A leader can best improve the efficiency of his followers by improving himself. Or, as one author put it, "The man who makes himself better makes everyone he comes into contact with better as well."

SELF-LOVE

Many . . . take the Lord's command to "love your neighbor as yourself" and totally reverse the focus so that it becomes a command to love oneself. Jesus was simply recognizing a fact of humanity. We do love ourselves very much. That is our natural orientation. The problem is to love our neighbor. Yet I am told that if I have trouble loving my neighbor, it is probably because I don't love myself enough. I suspect the *real* problem is that I already love myself too much.   (DAN DENK)

SELF-PITY

If you are feeling sorry for yourself, you are building a wall which shuts you out from the things you desire.   (EDWARD E. HALE)

Sometimes I get the feeling that the whole world is against me—but deep down I know that's not true. Some of the smaller countries are neutral.   (ROBERT ORBEN)

What poison is to food, self-pity is to life.   (OLIVER G. WILSON)

Self-pity is when you begin to feel that no-man's-land is your island.   (DANA ROBBINS)

Regardless of what you think of self-pity, it's at least sincere.   (MAURICE SEITTER)

A man busy nursing his own wounds has no time to inflict them on others.   (PETER DE VRIES)

SELF-PRAISE

People who sing their own praises usually do so without accompaniment.   (TOWN STUFF)

SELF-RESPECT

Nothing is a greater impediment to being on good terms with others than being ill at ease with yourself.   (HONORÉ DE BALZAC)

SELF-RESTRAINT

People who are proud of their "energy" usually use it in behalf of their self-assertiveness; they seem unaware that as much energy (and some might say a superior kind) is involved in exercising self-restraint.
          (SYDNEY HARRIS)

SELF-REVELATION

The circumstances of life, the events of life, and the people around me in life do not *make* me the way I am, but *reveal* the way I am.
(SAM PEEPLES, JR.)

SELF-RIGHTEOUSNESS

I've noticed that a self-righteous person may have a more shriveled soul than one who has succumbed to some of life's temptations.
(ELEANOR ROOSEVELT)

SELF-VICTORY

The hardest victory is victory over self.　(CONSTRUCTION DIGEST)

SELLING (see SALESMEN)

Sell results, not products.　(PETER OTTERSTROM)

SENIORITY (see AGING)

The trouble with seniority is that it's too close to senility.
(AL BERNSTEIN)

SENSE AND NONSENSE

In any conversation, and especially one that verges on a debate, both parties usually utter some sense and some nonsense. Typically, we are impressed with and we remember our own sense and the other fellow's nonsense.　(DON ROBINSON)

SENTIMENT

Sentiment is the main opponent of spirituality.　(ART GLASSER)

SECRECY

A woman's idea of keeping a secret is refusing to tell who told it to her.　(CONSTRUCTION DIGEST)

SERVANTHOOD

God did not save you to be a sensation. He saved you to be a servant.
(JOHN E. HUNTER)

SERVICE (see HELPING)

Length of service is not as important as breadth of service.(ROTAGRAPH)

Someone asked a famous conductor of a great symphony orchestra which orchestral instrument he considered the most difficult to play. The conductor thought a moment, then said: "Second fiddle. I can get plenty of first violinists. But to find one who can play second fiddle with enthusiasm—that's a problem. And if we have no second fiddles, we have no harmony!" (GRIT)

If the world is cold, make it your business to build fires.

(HORACE TRAUBEL)

The best exercise for strengthening the heart is reaching down and lifting people up. (ERNEST BLEVINS)

An old Quaker, passing along the street, saw a cartman's horse suddenly fall dead. It was a serious loss, for the horse was the man's livelihood. The bystanders shook their heads and clucked sympathetically. The Quaker took off his broad-brimmed hat, placed a bank note in it, and said, "Friends, I am sorry for this man ten dollars' worth. How sorry are you?" (MEGIDDO MESSAGE)

The service we render for others is really the rent we pay for our room on this earth. (WILFRED GRENFELL)

Obedience to our Heavenly Father starts with our loving service to a needy brother. (WILLIAM A. WARD)

Find out where you can render a service; then render it. The rest is up to the Lord. (S.S. KRESGE)

If you wish to be a leader you will be frustrated, for very few people wish to be led. If you aim to be a servant you will never be frustrated.

(FRANK F. WARREN)

At the close of life, the question will be not, how much have you got? but how much have you given? Not how much have you won? but how much have you done? Not how much have you saved? but how much have you sacrificed? It will be how much have you loved and served? not how much were you honored? (NATHAN C. SCHAEFFER)

SETBACKS (see DEFEAT)

Setbacks pave the way for comebacks. (PRISM)

SEX

Adolescents are much concerned about sex, morality, and behavior, and they seek help in finding answers and making the right choices. Would it help them to know and understand themselves better to know that, in general, girls are "in love with love" and will sometimes use sex to obtain "love"? And to know that boys, having stronger and more easily stimulated sexual urges, are "in love with sex" and may use "love" to obtain sex? (MARIE A. HINRICHS AND ROBERT KAPLAN)

The satisfaction of man's instinctual, biological animal needs is not sufficient to make him happy; they are not even sufficient to make him sane. (JACK WEINBERG)

SEXES (see MAN AND WOMAN)

A man should never judge by appearances. A woman who looks like a dumb blonde may really be a bright brunette. (NATIONAL SAFETY NEWS)

The first woman had to take a rib from a man—and women have been taking ribs from men ever since. (CY N. PEACE)

Arguing with a woman is like trying to shoot pool with a hockey stick. Being naturally clear-headed and logical, you may try to rely upon reason. This is a mistake. A woman uses only naked emotions, weapons she can handle far better than you. (SHEPHERD MEAD)

Men walk from the knee, women from the hip. Men strike matches toward themselves, women away. . . . Men look at the fingernails by cupping their palms and bending their fingers toward themselves; women extend their fingers palm outward. Men nag their wives for what they do; women nag their husbands for what they don't do. (KENNETH COLBY)

SHADOWS

Never fear shadows. They simply mean there's a light shining somewhere. (RUTH E. RENKEL)

SHORTCOMINGS (see FAULTS)

It is better to hold up your own shortcomings before your own eyes than other people's before theirs. (7-STAR DIARY CALENDAR)

SHYNESS (see ALONENESS, SOLITUDE)

One of the best tools to overcome shyness is your ability to smile. A warm smile radiates more heat when it has a little shyness tucked at the corners of the mouth. (TOM HAGGAI)

Shyness is . . . really an excessive preoccupation with yourself. There's an element of narcissism in it as shy people perceive others as their judges and enemies. It's "If people knew the real me, they wouldn't want me." . . . Shyness is something that prevents people from making the human connection . . . People-phobia can be hard to avoid. . . . If shyness is a social occurrence, one of the best ways to overcome it is to be concerned about others. It's a modification of the Golden Rule: "By doing unto others, you're going to be less concerned about yourself."

(SHYNESS, HARCOURT BRACE JOVANOVICH)

SICKNESS

Illness, like war, is 10 percent fear and pain, and 90 percent frustrating boredom. (CORNELIA AND GEORGE KAY)

Doctors say that cheerful people resist disease better than gloomy people. In other words, it's the surly bird who catches the germ.

(EXECUTIVES' DIGEST)

Just because your doctor has a name for your condition doesn't mean he knows what it is.

SILENCE

Ten persons who speak make more noise than 10,000 who are silent.

(NAPOLEON I)

Silence, along with modesty, is a great aid to conversation.(MONTAIGNE)

I sometimes suspect that half our difficulties are imaginary and that if we kept quiet about them, they would disappear. (ROBERT LYND)

The greatest ideas, the most profound thoughts, and the most beautiful poetry are born from the womb of silence. (WILLIAM A. WARD)

We all have a deep inner need for some silence, to be silent ourselves, to enjoy silence itself; an increasing need in an ever-noisier world. Psychiatrists are trying to impress that fact upon us, to convince us of the virtues of silence and of its value in living fully today.

We are . . . familiar with people beset with the urge to talk for talk's sake; most of us do just that far more often than we probably realize. . . . So we say *something*, when silence would be preferable—and wiser.

(DAVID GUNSTON)

A shut mouth never has to eat crow.

People fighting their aloneness will do almost anything to avoid silence.

There are three times when you should never say anything important to a person: when he is tired, when he is angry, and when he has just made a mistake. (QUOTE)

Sometimes silence is golden—other times it's just yellow.

Silence gives consent—or that horrible feeling that nobody's listening.
(GRIT)

Silence is the unbearable repartee. (G.K. CHESTERTON)

Silence and egotism go together more commonly than we suspect; the chatterbox merely hopes to be liked for what he expresses; the taciturn demands to be respected for what he contains. (SYDNEY HARRIS)

SIN (see WRONGNESS AND RIGHTNESS, WICKEDNESS)

Our age speaks of such things as error, mistake, superstition, delusion, but it does not admit such a thing as sin. (CATHOLIC MESSENGER)

Our sense of sin is in proportion to our nearness to God.
(THOMAS D. BERNARD)

Sin as a caterpillar is dangerous, but sin as a butterfly is a thousand times worse. If sin in its ugliest form is dangerous, who can know its unmeasured power and influence when it puts on robes of beauty!
(MEGIDDO MESSAGE)

A lot of folks would rather expose sins than prevent them.
(FRANK A. CLARK)

Sin may be clasped so close we cannot see its face. (RICHARD TRENCH)

If we give soft names to sin we depreciate the value of the blood which was shed to save us from sin.

The unforgivable sin is the sin of rejecting forgiveness.(HENRY JACOBSEN)

The difference between youth and age is measured in the way we sin. Youth goes out to sin boisterously. Age sins quietly and with more finesse, to prolong the pleasure because it knows that all too soon it can sin no more. (CARL RIBLET, JR.)

You cannot play with sin and overcome it at the same time.
(J.C. MACAULAY)

We are too Christian really to enjoy sinning, and too fond of sinning really to enjoy Christianity. Most of us know perfectly well what we ought to do; our trouble is that we do not want to do it.(PETER MARSHALL)

Sin is the irrational in human consciousness. It is the failure of free will to act reasonably. (CHARLES DAVIS)

Sin: putting worst things first.   (JOSEPH GANCHER)

No one ever became very wicked all at once.   (JUVENAL)

In the last analysis, we sin not because we *have* to but because we *want* to.   (HENRY JACOBSEN)

There is no man so good, who, were he to submit all his thoughts and actions to the laws, would not deserve hanging ten times in his life.
                                                               (MONTAIGNE)

The ladder of life is full of splinters that we don't feel till we backslide.

God may forgive your sins, but your nervous system won't.
                                                               (ALFRED KORGYBSKI)

A preacher who recently announced that there are 726 sins has been besieged for copies of the list.   (CRUMBLEY)

Sin would have few takers if its consequences occurred immediately.
                                                               (W.T. PURKISER)

Sin does not serve well as gardener of the soul. It landscapes the contour of the soul until all that is beautiful has been made ugly; until all that is high is made low; until all that is promising is wasted. Then life is like the desert—parched and barren. It is drained of purpose. It is bleached of happiness. Sin, then, is not wise, but wasteful. It is not a gate, but only a grave.   (C. NEIL STRAIT)

SINCERITY

Sincerity is an openness of heart; we find it in very few people.
                                            (FRANCOIS DE LA ROCHEFOUCAULD)

Young people prize sincerity above almost any other quality. One of their most frequent complaints against adults is that they are phony. But sincerity is not an easy matter to achieve, and conscious attitudes are not necessarily real attitudes. The greatest liars often consider themselves sincere because they are completely successful in lying to themselves.   (ELIZABETH CHRISTMAN)

SINGING (see MUSIC)

The woods would be very silent if no birds sang there except those who sang best.   (AUDUBON)

I took a prize once in a singing contest, but they caught me and I had to return it.

SINGLES

The general society holds that normal people are either married or wish to be . . . [but] single status is an appropriate option to marriage. . . . Singles may have been a greater object of neglect than our families. . . . The church ought to draw singles into the life of the church. Singles should be accepted. . . . All persons live for a time as singles—so it must be a normal state. . . . Happy married people *were* happy single persons.

(MARK LEE)

According to statistics, more Americans are going through life as singles. All it means is that more of us can go to our graves without getting a candid appraisal of our faults.

SINS OF OMISSION

Testing a Sunday School class, his reverence asked, "What are sins of omission, my child?"

Little Cicely replied, "They're the sins we ought to commit and don't."

(NUGGETS)

SITTING

The trouble with sitting a lot is you're apt to have a lot more to do it with.

SKIING

Novice skiers burn their britches behind them.

SLANDER

Slander is a vice that strikes a double blow, wounding both him that commits, and him against whom it is committed.   (SAURIN)

SLANG

Slang is a language that takes off its coat, spits on its hands, and goes to work.   (CARL SANDBURG)

SLAVERY

African slavery and the slave trade were not initiated by the British or any other European people. They were an African institution long before the sails of any European trader were seen in the Gulf of Benin. In Africa, as in every part of the world, slavery and trade in slaves are as old as commerce. In Africa, as elsewhere, it was the practice of primitive tribes to war against one another and, when victorious, to massacre or enslave the conquered. And from the latter process arose the practice of trading in and transporting slaves, buying from those who had enslaved them, and selling to those who had economic use for them.

(ARTHUR BRYANT)

It isn't always others who enslave us. Sometimes we let circumstances enslave us; sometimes we let routines enslave us; sometimes we let things enslave us; sometimes, with weak wills, we enslave ourselves. Sometimes we partake of detrimental things that we think will soothe our nerves, minds, or imaginations—things we think will help us to escape from reality. But no man is free if he is running away from reality. And no man is free if he is running away from himself.

(GOOD READING)

It may come as a shock to some, but slavery exists in some 30 countries, and is apt to continue to survive in many of them for a long time to come. (NOEL MOSTERT)

SLEEP

People who snore always fall asleep first. (BITS AND PIECES)

I slept like a top and woke up with my head spinning. (FRANKLIN P. JONES)

It is a common experience that a problem difficult at night is resolved in the morning after the committee of sleep has worked on it.

(JOHN STEINBECK)

Long sleepers (nine hours or more) are likely to be anxious, mildly depressed, chronic complainers about minor aches and pains, and not very sure of themselves. Short sleepers (six hours or less) are likely to be energetic, ambitious, decisive, socially adept, and satisfied with life. These are characteristics of males studied in psychological tests at the sleep laboratory of Boston State Hospital. (SCIENCE DIGEST)

If you have trouble sleeping, don't count sheep. Talk with the Shepherd.

SLIPPED DISKS

My uncle landed in jail because of slipped disks. He was caught slipping them out of a record shop. (SHELBY FRIEDMAN)

SMELLS

If you are an ordinary, average person, you should be able to smell 2,000 different odors. With a little training and persistence, you can learn to differentiate about 4,000 different smells. (RUSSELL C. ERB)

SMILES (see CHEERFULNESS)

A smile is a carnation in the buttonhole of life.

A smile is the welcome mat at the doorway of kindness.
(WILLIAM A. WARD)

The best face-lift is a smile.

Once when I was about six years old I was crying and miserable. What brought it on, I do not remember. My grandmother was sympathetic—and wise. "Go to the mirror," she said, "and smile with your face. Soon you will be smiling all over." Curiously enough it worked—and was less stressful than pounding my head against a wall. (J.D. RATCLIFF)

Smile and rest your wrinkles.

A smile increases your face value.

A smile costs nothing but creates much. It enriches those who receive without impoverishing those who give. It happens in a flash and the memory of it sometimes lasts forever. None are so rich they can get along without it and none so poor but are richer for its benefits. It creates happiness in the home, fosters goodwill in a business, and is the countersign of friends. It is rest to the weary, daylight to the discouraged, sunshine to the sad, and nature's best antidote for trouble. Yet it cannot be bought, begged, borrowed, or stolen, for it is something that is no earthly good to anybody until it is given away. Nobody needs a smile so much as those who have none left to give.
(NOTEBOOK OF SOLOMON HUBER)

Most smiles are started by another smile. (FRANK A. CLARK)

Few of us are like Mona Lisa. She keeps smiling when her back's to the wall. (SHELBY FRIEDMAN)

SMOKING

The Earth people have an odd practice. They light a fire at the end of a poisonous substance and then suck the smoke into their body. This results in much sickness and even death. The habit is also very expensive. Strange, those Earth people! (A MARTIAN'S REPORT)

When someone smokes in my presence, his vice is not private. His foul emanations find their way into my lungs and bloodstream. His stench becomes my stench and clings to me. And he raises my chance of heart disease and lung cancer. . . . Let's put it this way: your freedom to smoke ends where my lungs begin. (ISAAC ASIMOV)

SNAILS

If common garden snails are getting your vegetables, it is no wonder. Snails have 135 rows of teeth located in their tongues, and each row contains 105 teeth. This comes to a total of 14,175 teeth, according to the National Wildlife Federation. (VFW)

SNOBS

A snob is anyone who looks down on us for a quite different reason than we look down on somebody else. (SYDNEY HARRIS)

SNORING

The next time your spouse accuses you of snoring, you might try explaining patiently that it's simply a matter of your soft palate vibrating plangently against your posterior pharyngeal wall when you are relaxed in sleep. (BITS AND PIECES)

Each night, 23 million Americans settle back on their beds and snore. One out of every eight Americans snores. A number of cases of snoring can be helped or cured. Some cases of children's snoring can be remedied by removal of enlarged adenoids and tonsils. Antihistamines may stop the cold snorer from snoring. People who snore while sleeping on their backs can usually be quieted by moving them on their sides. Women snore as much as men. The frequency of the vibrations and thus the loudness depends on the size, density, and elasticity of the affected tissues and on the force of the air flow.(AMERICAN MEDICAL ASSOCIATION)

SNOW

In the final analysis, more people depend on solar energy for snow removal than any other method. (JAMES H. McGAVRAN)

SOCIALISM

There are two places only where socialism will work; in heaven where it is not needed, and in hell where they already have it.(WINSTON CHURCHILL)

There is always free cheese in a mouse trap.
(KALAMAZOO VEGETABLE PARCHMENT PHILOSOPHER)

SOCIALIZING

Men of genius are often dull and inert in society; as the blazing meteor, When it descends to earth, is only a stone. (HENRY W. LONGFELLOW)

SOLDIERS

If you think old soldiers just fade away, just try to get into your old uniform. (JACKIE GLEASON)

SOLITUDE (see ALONENESS, SHYNESS)

Solitude is a necessary part of Christian experience . . . but the man who spends his time doing just that soon has a shriveled soul not worth cultivating. Nothing develops a man's own spiritual life as sharing his blessings with others. A reasonable amount of time alone is indispensable, but it is to be spent preparing him to return to the battle.

(VANCE HAVNER)

Solitude brings out the best in me. For example, when I'm alone, I'm never shy. (WOODY ALLEN)

Solitude is painful when one is young, but delightful when one is more mature. (ALBERT EINSTEIN)

We have developed a phobia of being alone. We prefer the most trivial and even obnoxious company, the most meaningless activities, to being alone with ourselves; we seem to be frightened at the prospect of facing ourselves. (ERICH FROMM)

Many of our modern inventions and devices seem designed to keep people from the calamity of ever being alone. . . . Portable radios . . . portable television sets . . . will save us from the necessity of ever having to rub two thoughts together to make a luminous friction in our minds.

(HALFORD E. LUCCOCK)

Solitude: to the simple, prison; to the thinker, a paradise. . . . Practice the art of "aloneness" and you will discover the treasure of tranquility. Develop the art of solitude and you will unearth the gift of serenity.

(WILLIAM A. WARD)

I love to be alone. I never found the companion that was so companionable as solitude. (HENRY D. THOREAU)

We need society, and we need solitude also, as we need summer and winter, day and night, exercise and rest. (PHILIP G. HAMERTON)

SOLUTIONS

There's no such thing as the perfect solution. Every solution, no matter how good, creates new problems. (BITS AND PIECES)

SORROW (see GRIEF, TROUBLES)

The deeper the sorrow, the less the tongue has to say. (TALMUD)

Botanists say that trees need the powerful March winds to flex their trunks and main branches, so that the sap is drawn up to nourish the budding leaves. Perhaps we need the gales of life in the same way, though we dislike enduring them. A blustery period in our fortunes is often the prelude to a new spring of life and health, success, and happiness, when we keep steadfast in faith and look to the good in spite of appearances.　　　　　　　　　　　　　　　　　　(JANE TRUAX)

In sorrow problems are likely to seem even larger than they are, and people are likely to lose perspective—all of which points up the importance of patience, of understanding, of self-control, and of sensitivity to the feelings of others, sensitivity to situations.　　(RICHARD L. EVANS)

All sorrow and suffering are designed to teach us lessons we would not or could not learn in any other way.　　　　　　　(MAX HEINDEL)

Sorrow is a fruit; God does not make it grow on limbs too weak to bear it.　　　　　　　　　　　　　　　　　　　　(VICTOR HUGO)

Sorrow, like rain, makes roses and mud.　　　　(AUSTIN O'MALLEY)

Believe me, every heart has its secret sorrows, which the world knows not; and oftentimes we call a man cold when he is only sad.
(HENRY W. LONGFELLOW)

Even if you can't prevent another's sorrow, caring will lessen it.
(FRANK A. CLARK)

SOULS

My soul is like a mirror in which the glory of God is reflected, but sin, however insignificant, covers the mirror with smoke.(THERESA OF AVILA)

Souls are not for walking on.

SOUL-WINNING (see WITNESSING)

Soul-winning is not the art of bringing people from down where they are up to where you are. It is bringing them to Christ.　(GEORGE L. SMITH)

The best tact in soul-winning is contact.

When a Christian is winning souls, he isn't messing around with sin.
(GEORGE L. SMITH)

If someone were to offer me a thousand dollars for every child that I might try to win to Christ, would I endeavor to lead any more to Him than I am endeavoring to reach now?

SOUVENIRS

Keep some souvenirs of your past, or how will you ever prove it wasn't all a dream? (ASHLEIGH BRILLIANT)

SOWING WILD OATS

If you want to get a sure crop, and a big yield, sow wild oats.
(JOSH BILLINGS)

SPACE

One thing you can say definitely about outer space is that we're not apt to run out of it. (FRANKLIN P. JONES)

SPEAKERS (see LECTURING, SPEECH)

The other night I spoke to a tiny crowd. The chairman apologized for bringing a man of my stature before such a small turnout, explaining that he had tried to get a speaker with less talent, but couldn't find one.

What most banquets need is an express podium—for speakers with six thoughts or less. (ROBERT ORBEN)

A good speaker leaves the listeners more informed and a little better off than they would be if he had kept quiet. Abraham Lincoln said, "I am never more embarrassed than when I have nothing to say." Speaking for personal recognition is wasteful; speaking to provide a service to others is honorable. The best advice here is to have something to say and know what you're saying, or keep quiet. (W.F. WEAVER)

After the speaker finished, a woman came up and said, "You were much better than the speaker we had at our last meeting. He spoke for an hour and said nothing."
"Thank you," the speaker replied.
"Yes," she continued, "and you did it in 15 minutes." (LEO AIKMAN)

A great many of our speeches and sermons are of the cotton candy variety: colorful, sweet, harmless, and a bit short of content. (QUOTE)

What this country needs is less public speaking and more private thinking. (HAROLD COFFIN)

The mouth talks about the things that fill the heart.(MATTHEW 12:34, WMS)

SPECIALIZATION

Specialists are called narrow. Well, an arrow is narrow. (C.H. BARR)

Better to master one mountain than a thousand foothills.

(WILLIAM A. WARD)

Since the 17th century the amount of potential knowledge has increased far beyond the quantity that can become actual knowledge in a single human mind. Dante did know virtually everything that was to be known in Western Christendom in the year 1300. Goethe knew the greater part of what there was to be known in the year 1800. But since 1831, the date of Goethe's death, it has become impossible even for the most powerful intellect of the most industrious temperament to master more than a fraction of what there is to know. If a student is to acquire knowledge with sufficient thoroughness to be able to use it in professional practice, he now has to specialize. But the price of specialization is a myopic and distorted view of the universe. An effective specialist makes, all too often, a defective citizen and an inadequate human being.

(ARNOLD TOYNBEE)

A specialist is someone who has focused all of his ignorance onto one subject.   (ROBERT ORBEN)

SPECTATORITIS (see TELEVISION)

As a nation we do too much watching and not enough participating.

(NORMAN HARRIS)

SPECTATORS

The number of people watching you is directly proportional to the stupidity of your action.

SPEECH (see SPEAKERS)

We make more enemies by what we say than friends by what we do.   (JOHN C. COLLINS)

In speech-making: Make eye contact with three people before you say a single word. What that does: Gets the audience's attention. Makes you appear in control. Telegraphs that you're a direct, believable person.

(N. FLACKS AND R. RASPBERRY)

We spend only about 25 minutes a day in articulated speech. The rest of the time we communicate by waving, grimacing, grunting, frowning, shrugging, or long memos.   (HAL BOYLE)

A bishop . . . asked David Garrick, the great actor, how it was possible to take fiction and produce such a tremendous effect on his audience. Garrick replied, "Because I recite fiction as if it were truth, and you preach truth as if it were fiction."   (WALTER L. LINGLE)

When making a speech, pick out one person in the audience—not the smartest person there—and try to get your message across to him. If you can "sell" him on your ideas, can convince him of the desirability of what you are trying to do, then you will convince others.

(SLATTERY'S PEOPLE)

Three things matter in a speech: who says it, how he says it, and what he says . . . and, of the three, the last matters the least. (LORD MORLEY)

Each of us here has a job to do in this hour. Mine is to talk and yours is to listen. My hope is that you will not finish your job before I finish mine. (CARL W. McGEEHON)

To be ready to make a speech and not be asked to speak is even worse than being asked to speak when you are not ready. (JACK HERBERT)

Amateurs and egotists usually share one fault in common when making a talk. They try to impress rather than express.

The easiest way to stay awake during an after-dinner speech is to deliver it. (HERMAN "PAT" HERST, JR.)

Criminologists claim few acts of violence are committed after a hearty meal. This prolongs the life of speakers. (PIC LARMOUR)

It is better to speak from a full heart and an empty head than from a full head and an empty heart. (DUBLIN OPINION)

The difficulty of speeches is that you are perpetually poised between the cliché and the indiscretion (HAROLD MACMILLAN)

Introducing a speaker: His [speech] instructor took a leaf out of the story of Demosthenes, who practiced his speech with pebbles in his mouth. At the beginning of the course, each student was given a mouthful of marbles. Every day the instructor reduced the number by one marble. The student became a public speaker when he had lost all his marbles. (QUOTE)

Civilization is built on understanding, which comes through communication. . . . The use we make of words, our tools for communication, is of inestimable importance. Mrs. Einstein was asked one day if she understood her husband's theories. She replied, "I understand the words, but I don't always understand the sentences." (RALPH C. SMEDLEY)

An ancient king once commanded his wise court jester to prepare him the finest dish in the world. He was served a dish of tongue.

Then the king demanded the worst dish in the world, and again was served a dish of tongue.

The king asked the reason and the wise man said: "The tongue is the greatest of blessings when wisely and lovingly used, but becomes the greatest curse when it is unkindly and dishonestly used."

(A. PURNELL BAILEY)

Many a speaker exhausts his audience before he exhausts his subject.

(CAREY WILLIAMS)

A speech should be so short that when it's over you can still remember the beginning.

(AUSLESE [FRANKFURT])

I have discontinued long talks on account of my throat. Several members have threatened to cut it.

(LIONS)

Let thy speech be better than silence, or be silent. (DIONYSIUS THE ELDER)

"How was the applause after your speech?" asked the fond wife, when her husband returned after an evening engagement.

"Terrible," he moaned. "It sounded like a caterpillar in sneakers romping across a Persian rug."

(SUPERVISION)

In some respects a speech is like a love affair. Any fool can start one, but to end it requires considerable skill.

(LORD MANCROFT)

Some basic rules: (1) Know what you're going to say in advance. . . . (2) Look your listeners in the eye. . . . (3) Take your time. Talk clearly, concisely, and deliberately. . . . (4) Use an outline instead of memorizing a speech. . . . (5) Be constructive. Stress the merits of your viewpoint, not the flaws in someone else's. . . . (6) Use visual aids to engage your audience's eyes as well as ears, and capitalize by using gestures to emphasize important points. . . . (7) Go beyond self-interest. Showing the audience how you can help them achieve what they want is much more effective than putting yourself in the limelight. . . . (8) Be specific. . . . (9) Be yourself. You can learn from others, but don't make the mistake of trying to imitate a successful orator. . . . (10) Use a positive approach. . . . (11) Stop at the right time. When you sense that you have scored your points and that the audience gets the message, stop talking.

(HEALTHWAYS)

A friend of my father's once told me: "Say what you have to say and when you come to a sentence with a grammatical ending, sit down."

(WINSTON CHURCHILL)

SPEED

Boss to employee: You may march to a different drummer, but I want the beat speeded up. (DALE McFEATTERS)

SPELLING (see WORDS)

A young student from Europe grew upset over the difficulty in learning the English language. He said, "How can you explain the pronunciation rules of a language when it has six words that are all spelled alike and all sound completely different from each other—*plough, rough, cough, dough, through,* and *hiccough?*"

There are 14 different English spellings for the sound of *sh,* typified by *shoe, issue, mansion, mission, nation, suspicion, ocean, nauseous, conscious, chaperon, schist, fuchsia,* and *pshaw.* That's only 13. The other is *sugar.* Somebody once told Thomas Hardy that *sugar* is the only word that delivers the sound *sh* with the spelling *su.* Upon which Hardy replied, "Are you *sure?*"

SPIRITUAL PROGRESS (see CHRISTIANITY)

Your birthdays tell how long you've been on the road, but they don't tell you how far you've traveled. The same is true of spiritual birthdays. (ROY GUSTAFSON)

It's a strange and tragic truth that spiritual things can be unlearned. (ART GLASSER)

Spiritual blindness sets in when we cease to lift our eyes to Him.

The spiritual eyesight improves as the physical eyesight declines. (PLATO)

SPIRIT, WORK OF

We must not conceive of the Spirit as filling our hearts as water would fill a bottle. The Holy Spirit is not a substance to fill an empty receptacle, but a Person to control another person.

The Holy Spirit longs to reveal to you the deeper things of God. He longs to love through you. He longs to work through you. Through the blessed Holy Spirit you may have: strength for every duty, wisdom for every problem, comfort in every sorrow, joy in His overflowing service. (T.J. BACH)

To put sin out of the life, or to live a separated life, are humanly impossible tasks. That is the work of the Spirit. It is not a matter of human repression of sin, but of divine expulsion. (KENNETH WUEST)

SPORTS (see TEAMS)

Sports do not build character. They reveal it.   (HEYWOOD BROUN)

The trouble with being a good sport is that you have to lose to prove it.   (BITS AND PIECES)

I have never felt that football built character. That is done by parents and church. You give us a boy with character and we will give back a man. You give us a character—and we will give him right back to you.   (JOHN MCKAY)

The meaning of the word amateur comes from the Latin word, *amator*, meaning lover. Strictly speaking, an amateur in sports is one who participates not for financial gain, but for the pure love of it.

A small college at an athletic meet had a cross-eyed javelin thrower. He didn't win any medals but he sure kept the crowd alert.

I wasn't much of an athlete in school. In fact, one time during a 100-yard dash, a cop arrested me for loitering.   (ROBERT ORBEN)

A college grid coach had just lost his outstanding freshman prospect by way of academic dismissal. "It's going to be quite a loss to the team," commented a sympathetic sports writer.
"It sure is," replied the coach, mournfully. "Why that boy could do everything with a football—except autograph it."
     (CANADIAN [TEXAS] RECORD)

You can observe a lot just by watching.   (YOGI BERRA)

He's such a nice guy he plays goodminton.   (SHELBY FRIEDMAN)

Children who don't learn how to play some lifetime sport aren't fully educated. Adults who can't, or won't, participate regularly in some sports activity may be headed to a fast grave at a slow pace.
     (EDWARD GREENWOOD)

Sports like baseball, football, basketball, and hockey develop muscles. That's why Americans have the strongest eyes in the world.
     (ROBERT ORBEN)

SQUARES

Back in Mark Twain's day the word "square" was one of the finest words in our language. You gave a man a square deal if you were honest. And you gave him a square meal when he was hungry. You stood four-square for the right as you saw it, and square against everything else. When you got out of debt you were square with the world. And that was when you could look your fellowman square in the eye.

Then a lot of strange characters happened to get hold of this honest, wholesome word, bent it all out of shape, and gave it back to our children.

Convicts gave it the first twist. To them a square was an inmate who would not conform to the convict code. From the prisons it was flashed across the country on the marijuana circuit. . . .

Now everyone knows what a square is. He is a man who never learned to get away with it. A Joe who volunteers when he doesn't have to. A guy who gets his kicks from trying to do something better than anyone else can. A boob who gets so lost in his work that he has to be reminded to go home. A guy who doesn't have to stop at a bar on his way to the train at night because he's all fired up and full of juice already.

The square isn't thriving too well in the current climate. He doesn't fit too neatly into the current group of angle-players, corner-cutters, sharp-shooters, and goof-offs. He doesn't believe in opening all the packages before Christmas. He doesn't want to fly now and pay later. He's burdened down with old-fashioned ideas of honesty, loyalty, courage, and thrift. And he may already be on his way to extinction.

(CHARLES H. BROWER)

STABILITY (see DEPENDABILITY)

Flash powder makes a more brilliant light than the arc lamp, but you cannot use it to light your street corner because it doesn't last long enough. Stability is more essential to success than brilliancy. (ROTAGRAPH)

STATISTICS

Facts are stubborn things, but statistics are more pliable.

(ARNOLD GLASOW)

If a man stands with his right foot on a hot stove and his left foot in a freezer, some statisticians would assert that, on the average, he is comfortable. (ORAL HYGIENE)

Statistics can be used to support anything—including statisticians.

(GOOD READING)

Children are very adept at comprehending modern statistics. When they say, "Everyone else is allowed to," it is usually based on a survey of one. (PAUL SWEENEY)

Statistics are no substitute for judgment. (HENRY CLAY)

STATUS QUO

When you have got a thing where you want it, it is a good thing to leave it where it is. (WINSTON CHURCHILL)

STEWARDSHIP (see GIVING)

Plenty of people are willing to give God credit, yet few are willing to give Him cash.

STRATEGY (see PLANNING)

Strategy is when you run out of ammunition but keep firing anyway.

STREETS

They're not really fixin' the streets. They're just movin' the holes so the motorists can't memorize 'em. (HERB SHRINER)

STRENGTH

Strength is born in the deep silence of long-suffering hearts, not amid joy. (FELICIA HEMANS)

Strength is the capacity to break a chocolate bar into four pieces with your bare hands—and then eat just one of the pieces. (JUDITH VIORST)

It is truly said: It does not take much strength to do things—but it requires great strength to decide what to do. (CHING CHOW)

Strong people make as many and as ghastly mistakes as weak people. The difference is that strong people admit them, laugh at them, learn from them. That is how they became strong. (RICHARD NEEDHAM)

It is a sign of strength, not of weakness, to admit that you don't know all the answers. (JOHN P. LOUGHNANE)

Strange, but it seems to be true: Charm is a woman's strength, while strength is a man's charm. (SUNSHINE)

Only once in the history of Scotland was the Old Edinburgh castle captured. This is how it happened. The castle had a weak spot which defenders guarded. But it was thought the steepness of the castle made it inaccessible, impregnable, so no sentries were put there. An attacking party crept up that unguarded slope and surprised the garrison into surrender. . . . Where the castle was strong, there it was weak.
That is so often the story of human life. Whenever a man falls, it is usually at the point where he thinks he is strong. (HAROLD PHILLIPS)

Knowing your strength makes you confident; forgetting your weakness makes you vulnerable. (GRIT)

Do not pray for easy lives. Pray to be stronger men. Do not pray for tasks equal to your powers. Pray for powers equal to your tasks. (PHILLIPS BROOKS)

STRESS (see PRESSURE, TENSION)

Stress is really an integral part of life. We set our whole pattern of life by our stress end-point. If we hit it exactly we live dynamic, purposeful, useful, happy lives. If we go over, we break. If we stay too far under, we vegetate. (H.M. MARVIN)

Relationships without stress are either nonexistent, shallow, or sick. (HOWARD BUTT)

To avoid stress, Rule No. 1 is, don't sweat the small stuff. Rule No. 2 is, it's all small stuff. And if you can't fight and you can't flee, flow. (ROBERT ELIOT)

Stress is an important part of business life, and it has its good side: it stimulates people, gets the energy flowing, and helps to keep people alert and productive. Yet too much stress can cause burnout, low productivity, high rates of absenteeism, and health problems. Some estimates place the cost of stress at more than $100 billion a year, and one study indicates that 83 percent of all working people suffer from job-related stress. . . . Much of this stress could be avoided by better communications between bosses and their subordinates about such things as work assignments, mutual expectations, and performance. The sensitive manager is on the lookout for telltale signs of stress which may include irritability, long amounts of time spent on breaks, increased absenteeism, and slowed performance. Even fast-paced businesses can benefit greatly from a spirit of empathy, mutual support, and respect for human values. (HORIZONS)

Stress is the spice of life. Since it is associated with all types of activity, we could avoid it only by never doing anything. Who would enjoy a life consisting of "no runs, no hits, no errors"? (QUOTE)

Each of us has an optimal stress level. To keep stress from becoming distress, we must have not only the right amount but the right kind for the right duration. Distress often results from prolonged or unvaried stress, or from frustration. (QUOTE)

STRIKES

Why did the bees go on strike? Because they wanted shorter flowers and more honey.

STRUGGLES (see PROBLEMS)

No church or other association truly thrives unless struggles and differences are alive within it. (G.M. TREVELYAN)

The struggles of mankind as a whole produce the possessions of mankind as a whole. Something for nothing is not to be found on the earth. (GRIT)

STUDENTS

Some people will pay their tuition, and then *defy* you to give them an education. (ROBERT A. COOK)

STUMBLING BLOCKS

If some people would be a little more careful about where they step, those who follow them wouldn't stumble so much.

STUPIDITY

Tell a man something is bad, and he's not at all sure he wants to give it up. Describe it as stupid, and he knows it's the better part of caution to. listen. (DAVID SEABURY)

SUBMARINES

The nearsighted whale fell in love with a U.S. submarine and followed it all over the world. Every time the sub fired a torpedo, the whale would pass out cigars. (IMP)

"So you are on a submarine," gushed the lady. "What do you do?"
The sailor replied politely, "Oh, I run forward, ma'am, and hold her nose when we want her to dive." (ORAL HYGIENE)

SUBSTITUTES

The scientists have discovered so many substitutes that it's hard to remember what was needed in the first place. (ROBERT GODDARD)

SUCCESS (see FAILURE)

Success is being able to hire someone to mow the lawn while you play tennis for exercise.

If you don't have any time for yourself, any time to hunt or to fish, that's success. (JOHNNY CASH)

Most successes are built on failures. (CHARLES GOW)

If at first you do succeed, try something harder.   (BITS AND PIECES)

Many who are climbing the ladder of success have their ladders leaning against the wrong walls.   (IRWIN LUTZER)

When I was young I observed that 9 out of every 10 things I did were failures, so I did 10 times more work.   (GEORGE B. SHAW)

He was one of those men who struggle for success long after they have it, who are still making touchdowns when the stands are empty, the other team long gone, and the shadows lengthening toward them. Like most of us, he was seeking happiness, and was baffled that success had not brought it. But success itself is a sort of failure. You reach the end of the rainbow, and there's no pot of gold. You get your castle in Spain, and there's no plumbing.   (CHARLES BROWER)

Someone has defined success as the art of making your mistakes when nobody is looking.   (ALEXANDER COOPERATOR)

Success consists of getting up just one more time than you fall.   (OLIVER GOLDSMITH)

Four-word recipe for success: Make yourself more useful.

I cannot give you the formula for success, but I can give you the formula for failure: Try to please everybody.   (HERBERT BAYARD SWOPE)

Nothing conceits like success.   (AL BERNSTEIN)

Success is getting what you want; happiness is wanting what you get.

The road to success is dotted with many tempting parking places.   (BENDIXLINE)

One of the first steps a modern man must take to climb the ladder of success is to turn off the television.   (O.A. BATTISTA)

People learn from their mistakes, but grow from their successes.

We've all heard that we have to learn from our mistakes, but I think it's more important to learn from successes. If you learn only from your mistakes, you are inclined to learn only errors.   (NORMAN V. PEALE)

A minor success can help a fellow forget an awful lot of his mistakes.   (FRANK A. CLARK)

If at first you don't succeed, that makes you just about average.

If at first you don't succeed, you'll get a lot of advice.

If at first you don't succeed—so much for skydiving. (HENNY YOUNGMAN)

Most of us will be remembered more for our successes than our failures; but we tend to be more haunted by our failures than comforted by our successes. (TOM HAGGAI)

The president of a highly rated company was asked the secret of his success. "It's really simple," he said, "I always apply the Rule of the 3 D's: Do it, Delegate it, or Ditch it." (BITS AND PIECES)

The way to get on in this world is to do whatever work you are doing well; then you will be picked to do some other job that is not being done well. (SAMUEL VAUCLAIN)

Character is more important than intelligence for success. (GILBERTE BEAUX)

Success depends upon the functioning of the glands—the sweat glands. (J. HAROLD SMITH)

Success, real success in any endeavor, demands more from an individual than most people are willing to offer—not more than they are capable of offering. (JAMES M. ROCHE)

Success in life is a matter not so much of talent as of concentration and perseverance. (C.W. WENDTE)

Successful people are not gifted; they just work hard—then succeed on purpose. (G.K. NIELSON)

If you look forward to Monday with more enthusiasm than you did to Friday, you're in danger of becoming successful. (SUPERVISION)

We children knew every track up the mountains. . . . Once on one of the long marches . . . I was feeling tired. "I cannot go on," I said. "I'm too tired."
My father looked at me. . . . "See yourself at your destination," he said. "Extend your mind to seeing yourself there."
I didn't understand at the time, but now I do. Project the thought of success and half the battle is won. (SYBIL LEEK)

Men never plan to be failures; they simply fail to plan to be successful. (WILLIAM A. WARD)

A successful man will never see the day that does not bring a fresh quota of problems, and the mark of success is to deal with them effectively.
(LAURIS NORSTAD)

Doing God's will may not always lead to increased popularity, sales, and profits. It didn't in Bible days. (LLOYD CORY)

A man's success may depend upon his willingness to make some unpleasant decision. (FRANK A. CLARK)

When a man blames others for his failures, it's a good idea to credit somebody else with his successes. (KROEHLER NEWS)

Success is defined as luck if it happens to the other fellow—insatiable persistence and hard work if it happens to you. (O.A. BATTISTA)

Many people succeed when others do not believe in them. Rarely does a person succeed when he does not believe in himself. (HERB TRUE)

Success is often hard to take—especially when it's the other fellow's.

No rule for success will work, if you don't.

When success turns one's head it usually wrings his neck.

The common idea that success spoils people by making them vain, egotistic, and self-complacent is erroneous; on the contrary, it makes them, for the most part, humble, tolerant, and kind. Failure makes people cruel and bitter. (SOMERSET MAUGHAM)

History is loaded with cases of "successful" men, including many a conqueror and business tycoon, who were not good at all but thought they were. (BERNARD HALDANE)

I would rather fail in a cause that will ultimately succeed than succeed in a cause that will ultimately fail. (WOODROW WILSON)

Failure is not fatal; victory is not success. (TONY RICHARDSON)

The quickest and shortest way to crush whatever laurels you have won is for you to rest on them. (DONALD P. JONES)

To have been once brave men is not sufficient; it is harder to hold what you have gained than to gain it. (CYRUS, KING OF PERSIA)

The toughest thing about success is that you've got to keep on being a success. Talent is only a starting point in business. You've got to keep working that talent. (IRVING BERLIN)

Lefty Gomez, asked the secret of his remarkable World Series pitching record (six wins, no losses), said, "Clean living and a fast outfield." No man ever succeeds by himself. (ROBERT W. YOUNG)

Are you looking for a sure-fire formula for success? . . . "Surround yourself with people smarter than you are."
(SUNDAY SCHOOL TIMES & GOSPEL HERALD)

It is impossible to gain a toehold on success by acting like a heel.
(WILLIAM A. WARD)

All you have to do to be successful is follow the advice you give to others.

If you want to know how long it will take to get to the top, consult a calendar. If you want to know how long it takes to fall to the bottom, try a stopwatch. (CONSTRUCTION DIGEST)

What is success? It is a toy balloon among children armed with pins.
(GENE FOWLER)

Success is a different thing to every man. (WILLIAM FEATHER)

When we are young—and some of us never get over it—we are apt to think that applause, conspicuousness, and fame constitute success. But they are only the trappings, the trimmings. Success itself is the work, the achievement that evokes these manifestations. The man or woman who values the applause more than the effort necessary to elicit it is not apt to be deafened—at least not for any length of time. Concentrate on your work and the applause will take care of itself. (B.C. FORBES)

How to improve your luck: Develop your bump of curiosity. Acquire a little streak of recklessness. Sharpen your imagination. Be willing to change your mind. (HAMILTON [TEXAS] HERALD)

The sense of success is to: (1) set a long-range goal and (2) be able to relate daily work to it. Too many of us have only a vague idea of what we ultimately want. Even when we do, we do not know how to translate this desire into the necessary short-range steps which will get us there.

Qualifications for success: (1) A big wastebasket—you must know what to eliminate. (2) It is important to know what to preserve. (3) It is important to know when to say no. For developing the power to say no gives us the capacity to say yes. (A.P. GOUTHEY)

Ten rules for successful living: (1) Find your own particular talent. (2) Be big. (3) Be honest. (4) Live with enthusiasm. (5) Don't let your possessions possess you. (6) Don't worry about your problems. (7) Look up to people when you can—down to no one. (8) Don't cling to the past. (9) Assume your full share of responsibility in the world. (10) Pray consistently and confidently. (CONRAD HILTON)

A career, no matter how successful, is meaningless unless someone you care about deeply is able to share that success with you.(MARTIN LANDAU)

The trouble with success is that the formula is the same as the one for a nervous breakdown. (EXECUTIVES' DIGEST)

Nothing is more vulnerable than entrenched success. (GEORGE ROMNEY)

There is never enough success in anybody's life to make one feel completely satisfied. (JEAN ROSENBAUM)

A gauge of success is not whether you have a tough problem to handle, but whether it is the same problem you had last year.
(PERSONNEL JOURNAL)

SUFFERING (see PAIN, TORMENT)

Suffering is a misfortune, as viewed from the one side, and a discipline as viewed from the other. (SAMUEL SMILES)

There will be no major solution to the suffering of mankind until we reach some understanding of who we are, what the purpose of Creation was, what happens after death. Until these questions are resolved we are caught. (WOODY ALLEN)

Suffer and bear. Better days will come. Everything must serve those who stand firm. Heart, old child, suffer and bear. (CHRISTIAN MORGENSTERN)

No pain, no palm; no thorns, no throne; no gall, no glory; no cross, no crown. (WILLIAM PENN)

Nine-tenths of our suffering is caused by others not thinking so much of us as we think they ought. (MARY LYON)

Often it is just lack of imagination that keeps a man from suffering very much. (PROUST)

SUICIDE

Suicidal psychology can be charted by a triangle with these three corners: (1) all alone, (2) inactive, (3) indulging in self-pity. Change any one of these corners of that "suicide triangle" and you can prevent the most common cause of death among college students.   (GEORGE W. CRANE)

According to statistics, suicide by jumping from buildings has fallen off.   (JOSEPH F. MORRIS)

Taxi driver: Where to?
 Passenger: Drive off a cliff—I'm committing suicide.(SHELBY FRIEDMAN)

SUMMER

Summer is when the kids slam the doors they left open all winter.

SUN

If the sun is really putting out all that energy, how come we get so lazy when we sit out under it?   (BILL VAUGHAN)

SUN BELT

So many people are moving to the Sun Belt that they may have to let it out a notch.

SUNDAY

There are many persons who look on Sunday as a sponge to wipe out the sins of the week.   (H.W. BEECHER)

SUNDAY SCHOOL

Every Sunday School teacher is just as much called of God as a missionary to the heart of Africa. He needs to prepare just as diligently—he needs to labor just as earnestly—as if he were carrying the Gospel to the most remote spot on the globe.   (BILLY GRAHAM)

Sunday School is as American as crab grass. People, churches, theorists, have done their level best to get rid of it, and it endures and comes back strong. For all its defects, it is the most effective agency that we have ever had for Christian education or that is now in sight.
                                                 (D. CAMPBELL WYCKOFF)

The youngster had attended Sunday School for the first time, and he returned home almost in tears. His mother questioned him to find out what was disturbing him.

"I'm never going again," he said, bursting into sobs. "The first thing they did was march us into a dark basement and take our money away!"   (GENERAL FEATURES)

What does the story of David and Goliath teach?

A Sunday School student answered, "To duck!"

Teacher: Not only is he the worst behaved child in my class but he also has a perfect attendance record.   (ANDERSON [S.C.] INDEPENDENT)

SUPERIORITY

It is hard for a "superior" person to be used of the Lord.
(RICHARD HALVERSON)

The superiority of some men is merely local. They are great because their associates are little.   (SAMUEL JOHNSON)

SUPERMARKETS

One of life's hardest decisions is which line to stand in at the supermarket.   (ARNOLD H. GLASOW)

SUPERVISION (see MANAGEMENT)

Hard work never kills anybody who supervises it.   (HARRY BAUER)

Good supervision is the art of getting average people to do superior work.   (SUPERVISION)

SURGEONS (see DOCTORS)

The local doctor says he doesn't believe in unnecessary surgery. He won't operate unless he really needs the money.   (QUOTE)

We knew the eminent lady surgeon as an imperious, aloof type of person, but were surprised when she left her husband.
He was suffering from a serious internal complaint and had undergone a series of difficult operations at the hands of a team of other eminent surgeons.

She left him after the fifth operation, explaining, "I'm heartily sick of other people opening my male."   (DIGEST OF WORLD READING)

SURVIVAL

The human race's prospects of survival were considerably better when we were defenseless against tigers than they are today when we have become defenseless against ourselves.   (ARNOLD TOYNBEE)

SUSPICION

Suspicion is far more apt to be wrong than right; oftener unjust than just. It is no friend to virtue, and always an enemy to happiness. Nothing makes a man suspect more than to know little.   (MEGIDDO MESSAGE)

Suspicion in human relationships leads to alienation. No one loves those of whom they must be suspicious. It creates an atmosphere of artificiality and tension.   (WATCHMAN-EXAMINER)

SWIMMING INSTRUCTION

A swimming instructor at the summer camp pool was explaining the "buddy system" to some beginners. He asked, "Does anyone know what a buddy is?"

After a moment of silence, one youngster replied, "It's someone who drowns with you."   (SUCCESSFUL FARMING)

SYMPATHY (see COMPASSION)

Sympathy, when expressed in words, soothes the troubled heart; but sympathy, when expressed in action, takes the trouble away from the heart.   (HORSESHOE PROGRESS)

Sympathy sees, and says, "I am sorry." Compassion feels, and whispers, "I will help."

TACT

Tact is the ability to give a person a shot in the arm without letting him
feel the needle. (O.A. BATTISTA)

Tact is the ability to describe others as they see themselves.
(ABRAHAM LINCOLN)

Some people have tact; others just tell the truth. (LESTER CASE)

Cultivate tact, for it is the mark of culture . . . the lubricant of human
relationships, softening contacts and minimizing friction.
(BALTASAR GRACIAN)

Tact is remembering any person's birthday but forgetting which one it is.
Tact is the ability to do and say the right thing at the right time in the
right way. Tact is often the cause of success, and lack of it, a shortcut to
failure. (CYLVIA A. SORKIN)

A sultan called in one of his seers and asked how long he would live.
    "Sire, you will live to see all your sons dead."
    The sultan flew into a rage and handed the prophet over to the guards
for execution.
    He then asked a second seer, who said, "Sire, I see you blessed with a
long life, so long that you will outlive all your family."
    The sultan was delighted and rewarded the seer with gold and silver.

379

Both prophets knew the truth, but only one had tact.
(ANCIENT CHINESE STORY)

A young man proved himself wise when a young widow asked him how old he thought she was.

He answered, "I am just doubting about making you ten years younger on account of your looks, or to make you ten years older on account of your intelligence."

Silence is not always tact, and it is tact that is golden—not silence.
(SAMUEL BUTLER)

Tact is like a girdle. It enables you to organize the awkward truth more attractively.

TALENT

There is a good deal of wasted talent in the world, and some of the waste comes from sheer ignorance. People simply do not know how to apply their energies.
(GILBERT HIGHET)

Talents are not usually dished out in dozen lots. It is for each to take what skill he has and put it to work in the place where he is.

Talent is God-given; be thankful. Conceit is self-given; be careful.
(THOMAS LA MANCE)

Encourage individuals to use their talents in their own ways and they will often turn a squirrel cage of frustration into a ladder of success.
(CRAWFORD H. GREENEWALT)

It is an old but pertinent illustration that the fish in Mammoth Cave lose their eyes because they do not use them; that unused muscles atrophy; that talents which are not put into action soon fade away.
(WILLIAM L. STIDGER)

As tools become rusty, so does the mind. A garden uncared for soon becomes smothered in weeds; a talent neglected withers and dies.
(ETHEL PAGE)

No talent can survive the blight of neglect. (EDGAR A. WHITNEY)

Talent is what you have. Person is what you are. It is the person who uses the talents; and if the person is inadequate, the talent won't account for much. Most of us look at an unusually talented person and assume that all it takes to win is talent. Don't be fooled. Talent is only the beginning. . . . A great person takes a small talent and develops it as a tool for serving others. A small person with great talent soon fizzles, and wonders why. (LLOYD D. MATTSON)

TALKING (see CONVERSATION, MOUTH)

Talk is by far the most accessible of pleasures. It costs nothing in money, it is all profit, it completes our education, founds and fosters our friendships, and can be enjoyed at any age and in almost any state of health. (ROBERT L. STEVENSON)

The more you say, the less people remember. (ANATOLE FRANCE)

A gossip talks to you about others; a bore talks to you about himself; a brilliant conversationalist talks to you about yourself. (JIFFY WIT)

It's often better to slip with your foot than with your tongue. (BOYS' LIFE)

Talk is cheap because supply exceeds demand.

Many people who have the gift of gab don't know how to wrap it up. (LIONS MAGAZINE)

I got a high compliment the other day from an admirer. He said, "Every talk you make is better than the next one."

As you go through life you are going to have many opportunities to keep your mouth shut. Take advantage of all of them. (WEST VIRGINIA GAZETTE)

It's a toss-up as to which are finally the most exasperating—the dull people who never talk, or the bright people who never listen. (SYDNEY HARRIS)

The trouble with a fellow who talks too fast is that he is liable to say something he hasn't thought of yet. (DON RADDE)

If you don't say anything, you won't be called on to repeat it. (CALVIN COOLIDGE)

An overly talkative person is like a cat. He licks himself with his tongue.

The difference between a successful career and a mediocre one sometimes consists of leaving about four or five things a day unsaid.

Conversation is the art of telling people more than you know.

Two great talkers will not travel far together. (SPANISH PROVERB)

Waiting for some people to stop talking is like looking for the end of a roller towel. (NUGGETS)

Don't be afraid to talk to yourself. It's the only way you can be sure somebody's listening. (FRANKLIN P. JONES)

TASTE

If this is coffee, please bring me some tea; but if this is tea, please bring me some coffee. (ABRAHAM LINCOLN)

TAXES (see INCOME TAX)

In making out your income tax return, remember it's better to give than to deceive. (JOAN WELSH)

Psychiatrists say it's not good for a man to keep too much to himself. The Internal Revenue Service says the same thing. (HAROLD SMITH)

It has reached a point where taxes are a form of capital punishment.

Don't get excited about a tax cut. It's like a mugger giving you back carfare. (ARNOLD GLASOW)

The three basic needs of the average American are food, clothing, and tax shelter. (FRANK WALSH)

Death and taxes may be the only certainties in life, but nowhere is it written that we have to tax ourselves to death. (NATION'S BUSINESS)

There's only one kind of tax that would please everybody—one that nobody but the other guy has to pay. (EARL WILSON)

It seems a little ridiculous now, but this country was originally founded as a protest against taxation.

Patrick Henry should come back and see what taxation *with* representation is like. (AMERICAN FLINT)

If Washington is the seat of government, then the taxpayer is the pants pocket. (MICKEY PORTER)

A man pays a luxury tax on his billfold, an income tax on the stuff he puts in it, a sales tax on whatever he takes out, and an inheritance tax if there's anything left in it when he dies.

April is the month when the green returns to the lawn, the trees, and the Internal Revenue Service. (EVAN ESAR)

Internal Revenue Service auditor, to nervous citizen: Let's begin with where you claim depreciation on your wife.

Internal Revenue Service man, to Sherlock Holmes: You make a lot of amazing deductions.

Poverty is catching. You can get it from the Internal Revenue.

(ROBERT ORBEN)

My uncle is an optimist. He just asked the Internal Revenue to take him off their mailing list.

We would like to say that those guys in our legislature tax our patience, but we don't want to give them any ideas.   (HERM ALBRIGHT)

It looks as though the taxpayer will be the first of America's natural resources to be completely exhausted.

(NATIONAL RETIRED TEACHERS ASSOCIATION JOURNAL)

TEACHERS AND TEACHING
(see INSTRUCTION, PEDAGOGY)

The mediocre teacher tells. The good teacher explains. The superior teacher demonstrates. The great teacher inspires.   (WILLIAM A. WARD)

It is not what is poured into the student, but what is planted, that counts.   (EUGENE P. BERTIN)

Teacher's note on report card: Your son excels in initiative, group integration, responsiveness, and activity participation. Now if he'd only learn to read and write!

The best teachers in the world are not those who sledgehammer facts into people's heads. To know everything is not to be educated.

(GILBERT HARDING)

When asked the subjects she taught, she answered that she did not teach subjects—she taught *children!*   (GOOD READING)

A little girl ran into the classroom and told the teacher: "Two boys are fighting out on the playground, Teacher, and I think the one on the bottom would like to see you."

The teacher largely governs the moral and spiritual atmosphere of the classroom. After all, the self of the teacher is taught along with the regular materials of study. The right kind of person teaching history, literature, or chemistry will do far more good than will the wrong kind of person trying to teach a course in Bible. (RODNEY CLINE)

Teachers are great resource centers. They are constantly involved, or should be, in the learning process. Hence they are accumulating learning from two perspectives—from their own discoveries, and from the experiences of their pupils. (C. NEIL STRAIT)

A good teacher is one whose ears get as much exercise as his mouth. (NEA JOURNAL)

A lot of children almost never talk to the teacher. But they talk to each other, and I can listen. (STANLEY KIESEL)

The teacher is often the first to discover the talented and unusual scholar. How he handles and encourages, or discourages, such a child may make all the difference in the world to that child's future—and to the world. (LOREN EISELEY)

Though a teacher cannot teach what he does not know, he can sure enough inspire students to learn what he doesn't know. A great teacher has always been measured by the number of his students who have surpassed him. (DON ROBINSON)

A great teacher is not simply one who imparts knowledge to his students, but one who awakens their interest in it and makes them eager to pursue it for themselves. He is a spark plug, not a fuel pipe. (M.J. BERRILL)

I can teach it to you, but I can't learn it for you.

The object of teaching is to enable those taught to get along without a teacher. (BITS AND PIECES)

It is very difficult to teach anything without kindness. . . . Pupils should feel that the teacher wants to help them, wants them to improve, is interested in their growth, is sorry for their mistakes, is pleased by their successes, and sympathetic with their inadequacies. (GILBERT HIGHET)

The good teacher needs to be more than a well-educated specialist who can communicate with his students. He needs, also, to be a person of sound mental health. A neurotic does not teach; he infects. (CRAIG W. JAMES)

Successful teachers . . . share certain traits that have contributed greatly to their success. For one thing, they prize creativity. For another thing, they know how and when to maintain discipline. They can also judge and evaluate people accurately. They have a sense of humor. And they have open minds—they are alert to new ideas and new developments in teaching. (PATRICIA HOCKSTAD)

It is possible for a teacher to be quite a personage to his pupils and yet to be written off as a nonentity by parents, supervisors, or other adults. Conversely, a person who impresses adults may have little impact on the pupils. (J.M. STEPHENS)

Student: I don't think I deserve a zero on this paper, Teacher.
   Teacher: Neither do I, but it's the lowest grade I'm allowed to give.

Filling out a series of reports at the end of the school year, one tired teacher came upon this line: "List three reasons for entering the teaching profession."
   Without hesitation she filled in: "(1) June, (2) July, (3) August."
(SUNSHINE)

Only two personal characteristics appear to be conspicuous in teachers nominated for teacher-of-the-year awards: (1) a nebulous quality called dedication, and (2) the attribute of energy, which someone has called the "trademark of good teaching." (PHI DELTA KAPPAN)

A Colorado study asked 3,000 high school seniors about their best teachers and received this composite: He is (1) genuinely concerned and interested in students as individuals, (2) requires students to work, (3) is impartial in dealing with students, and (4) is obviously enthusiastic about teaching. (THE REPORT CARD)

The new role for teachers is to become talent-developers. Research has shown that students grow more in knowledge when teachers are not the center of focus but merely the means of developing talents.
(CALVIN TAYLOR)

There are three things to remember when teaching school: Know your stuff; know whom you are stuffing; and then stuff them elegantly.
(LOLA MAY)

A professor who had taught for many years was counseling a young teacher. "You will discover," he said, "that in nearly every class there will be a youngster eager to argue. Your first impulse will be to silence him, but I advise you to think carefully before doing so. He probably is the only one listening." (JIM KELLY)

TEAMS (see SPORTS)

A team is where a boy can prove his courage on his own. A gang is where a coward goes to hide.   (MICKEY MANTLE)

When a football coach wants to build a good team, he does not send it out on the field to play with soft pillows; he puts it to work against rough opponents, a bucking frame, a tackling dummy, and he puts it through exercises that are strenuous. God does the same thing with us, to give us the strengths of steadfastness and patience in our character: He marches us at times against tough opponents, against temptation, against public opinion, against discouragement.   (LOUIS H. EVANS)

TEARS

The soul would have no rainbow had the eyes no tears.(JOHN V. CHENEY)

Tears shed for self are tears of weakness, but tears shed for others are a sign of strength.   (BILLY GRAHAM)

More tears are shed in our theaters over fancied tragedies than in our churches over real ones.   (FRANK C. RIDEOUT)

TECHNOLOGY (see SCIENCE)

Radar spelled backward is radar; they've got you coming and going.
                                                              (BILL LEARY)

TEENS (see YOUNG TEENS, YOUTH)

Life goes on and there comes a time when you don't have to pay girls to spend the evening with your son.   (GENE YASENAK)

Mother Nature is providential. She gives us 12 years to develop a love for our children before turning them into teenagers.   (EUGENE P. BERTIN)

Kids aren't interested in putting their shoulders to the wheel these days—all they want to do is get their hands on it.

To get his teenage son to clean his room, one father just throws the keys to the family car in there once a week.   (LANE OLINGHOUSE)

I take a very practical view of raising children. I put a sign in each of their rooms: "Checkout Time is 18 years."   (ERMA BOMBECK)

When my teenager butters me up, I know that he's going to put the bite on me.   (CHARLESTON [W. VA.] GAZETTE)

Let's face it. Some kids are like ketchup bottles. You have to hit them to get them moving.

The best way to keep teens home is to make home pleasant—and let the air out of the tires. (EUGENE P. BERTIN)

A teenager is a person who gets up on a Saturday morning and has nothing to do, and by bedtime has it only half done. (ROUGH NOTES)

It's always hard to get teens to hang up things—coats, towels, jeans, shirts—and especially the telephone.

They really want and expect rules. Seventy-five percent of one group of teens stated that "obedience and respect for authority are the most important habits for children to learn." . . . More than 50 percent of them felt that their parents, schools, churches, and law-enforcement agencies coddled them too much. (HAZEN G. WERNER)

A survey revealing teenagers consider acne their most serious problem will surprise many parents who thought *they* were. (QUOTE)

The problem of communicating with the younger generation would be less complicated if parents knew a little more about what was going on under that male or female hair. One way to find out, I have discovered, is to act as chauffeur for a group of teenagers. Keep your mouth shut, and within minutes of starting out you will be forgotten and conversation will go on as though you were an automatic pilot. I don't know if this is considered an illegal form of bugging, but it is effective.(PAUL K. CUNEO)

I have never talked with a young person who has not wished to be accepted and loved by his or her parents. They all need love and acceptance at home as much as in the group. (THOMAS A. FRY, JR.)

Kids really aren't worse than in our day—it's just that they're less sneaky about it. (AL BERNSTEIN)

It is amazing how quickly the kids learn to drive a car, yet are unable to understand the lawnmower, snowblower, or vacuum cleaner. (BEN BERGOR)

There's nothing wrong with teenagers that reasoning won't aggravate. (H.E. MARTZ)

American teenagers tend to live as if adolescence were a last fling at life, rather than a preparation for it. (TIME)

Bert: My teenage son obeys me perfectly.
  Gert: Amazing. How do you do it?
  Bert: I tell him to do as he pleases. (JIM KELLY)

There's a new government program to eliminate teenage crime. It's called the War on Puberty. (ROBERT ORBEN)

Conversation with a teenager is almost impossible, I have discovered, unless by chance you are also a teenager. In that case it is ridiculously easy or, when overheard by an adult, easily ridiculous. (RICHARD ARMOUR)

The way kids dress today, it's kind of dangerous putting them out on the curb at 7:30 in the morning. One kid was picked up twice for garbage. (ROBERT ORBEN)

I've never met anyone who wanted to be a teenager again. (ENID A. HAUPT)

The best principal I ever worked for gave teachers this wonderful admonition regarding teenagers: "Treat them as adults, but don't expect them to act that way." (R. LOWELL DAVEE)

The teacher was admonishing the high school boy for coming in late to class: "Don't you ever listen to the voice of conscience?"
  After a moment's hesitation the boy replied, "I don't think so—what channel is it on?" (WALL STREET JOURNAL)

Ours seems to be the only nation on earth that asks its teenagers what to do . . . and tells its golden-agers to go out and play. (JULIAN GEROW)

TELEPHONES

My teenage daughter is at that awkward age. She knows how to make phone calls, but not how to end them. (MODERN MATURITY)

The bathtub was invented in 1850 and the telephone in 1875. Had you been living in 1850, you could have sat in the tub for 25 years without the phone ringing once. (ARNOLD GLASOW)

A Vermonter dropped in on his neighbor and found him busily filling out a lengthy mail-order catalog form. All the while his telephone rang persistently.
  "Bill," said the visitor, "ain't that your ring?"
  "Yep," answered the Vermonter.
  "Well, why don't you answer it?"
  "Tom," said Bill not looking up, "I'm busy, and I put that blame thing in for *my* convenience." (THOMAS LaMANCE)

TELEVISION

Television is the literature of the illiterate, the culture of the lowborn, the wealth of the poor, the privilege of the underprivileged, the exclusive club of the excluded masses. . . . Television is a golden goose that lays scrambled eggs. And it is futile and probably fatal to beat it for not laying caviar. Anyway, more people like scrambled eggs than caviar.

(LEE LOEVINGER)

Television will not go away; it is embedded in the culture now, like frozen lasagna, golf carts, and sociology departments. Those who would deny that it has been a boon to individuals in their private lives can be brushed aside; there is simply no question that television has answered the most desperate of human needs, the need for escape from boredom, escape from self. For those multitudes who cannot escape through their work or their reading or the experience of art, television has been about as close as they could hope to come to a heaven on earth.

(MARTIN MAYER)

Our broadcasts have not improved. If anything, their quality has declined. The tube has become a trip, a national opiate, a baby-sitter who charges nothing, something to iron by, and to shave to, and to doze over.

(ROGER MUDD)

An egghead finally succumbed and bought a TV set. He said he had to do it because everyone in his family is an opera lover: he, grand; his wife, soap; his kid, horse.

(TELEVISION AGE)

Public Television used to be known as Educational Television. The change in name was made because education has become synonymous with dullness.

(PHI DELTA KAPPAN)

I don't think that television has corrupted man. But I do think that man has invented it to flee from reality.

(MALCOLM MUGGERIDGE)

Television is called a medium because so little of it is rare or well done.

(FRED ALLEN)

The primary danger of the television screen lies not so much in the behavior it *produces* as the behavior it *prevents*—the talks, the games, the family activities, and the arguments through which much of the child's learning takes place and his character is formed.

(URIE BRONFENBRENNER)

Our children sit on their butts and are bored, displeased, or frightened, as the case may be, with the television stuff. So they reach out and switch to another offering of stuff. What a shock they will get some day to discover they will have to get off those butts and contend with real life because they can't turn to another channel.   (CARL RIBLET, JR.)

Television is simply automated daydreaming.   (LEE LOEVINGER)

Television requires nothing of us, but in requiring nothing, takes the most valuable possession we have: our time.   (NUGGETS)

Why people prefer TV to radio: They'd rather look at something bad than hear something good.   (FRED ALLEN)

One of the educational aspects of television: It puts the repairman's kids through college.   (JOAN WELSH)

A good picture is worth more than 1,000 words from a TV repairman.

Geneticists predict that because so many people stare at TV, future generations will have rectangular eyes.

Television has made a family semicircle out of the family circle.
     (PETER FRANKENFELD)

Television teaches children that grownups tell lies for money.
     (LEO GREENLAND)

Our summer TV cup rerunneth over.   (FRED PROPP, JR.)

There is little communication between members of the family. The communication is between each member and the television screen. It is an open admission that TV is more interesting than father, mother, or children.   (ART LINKLETTER)

In the old days (before television) the kids' domain was outdoors—summer or winter. Occasionally they had to be pried out, but once they were there it was tough getting them to come in. You would yell "Supper's ready!" and wind up organizing a search party that headed for the playground or alongside the creek. Children loved to take long walks with their friends, build orange-crate scooters, dip their hands into a bowl of papier-mâché. All this has changed. There is that electronic box forever calling to them to come inside, and the job of marching the kids outside again takes renewed effort. From the child's standpoint it is easier to plop down on the floor and be entertained, and it is easier for the parent to allow this to happen than it is to keep thinking up constructive things for them to do. In this never-ending tug-of-war other activities are curtailed in favor of TV viewing.   (NORMAN S. MORRIS)

A TV set is only a machine—glass, metal, wires, and little gadgets—until you place it in your home. . . . In some homes, TV becomes a baby-sitter, for babies of all ages. In other homes, TV is a narcotic, an escape from reality. Or it may be a thief, stealing time, thoughts, friendships, creativity, and opportunities for much-needed recreation and companionship. In too few homes, TV is a servant, providing information, insight, commentary on life, news, laughter, music, and worthwhile entertainment.

What TV becomes depends on you, the user. If you accept it as a tool, use it sparingly, wisely, and purposefully, it can become a servant. If you accept it as a friend, watch and listen continuously, it will become your master. (DAVID AUGSBURGER)

The easiest way to find more time to do all the things you want to do is to turn off the television. (O.A. BATTISTA)

Television has made us a sitting generation. We sit and see the problems portrayed on the screen, then make a sandwich and go to bed—heedless of the need. We have put on a veneer of indifference and very much resemble the people around the cross of Christ, of whom it is said: "Sitting down they watched Him there."

TEMPER (see ANGER)

Temper is a funny thing. It spoils children, ruins men, and strengthens steel. (L & N MAGAZINE)

Anybody who's always hitting the ceiling probably doesn't have his head all together. (FRANKLIN P. JONES)

Keep your temper. No one else wants it. (CRACKER JACK)

The most important time to hold your temper is when the other person has lost his. (HAROLD SMITH)

The man who is bigger than his job keeps cool. He does not lose his head, he refuses to become rattled, to fly off in a temper. The man who would control others must be able to control himself. There is something admirable, something inspiring, something soul-searching about a man who displays coolness and courage under extremely trying circumstances. A good temper is not only a business asset. It is the secret of health. The longer you live the more you will learn that a disoriented temper produces a disordered body. (B.C. FORBES)

We must interpret a bad temper as the sign of an inferiority complex. (ALFRED ADLER)

A tart temper never mellows with age, and a sharp tongue is the only edged tool that grows keener with constant use. (WASHINGTON IRVING)

The worst-tempered people I've ever met were people who knew they were wrong. (WILSON MIZNER)

When you are right you can afford to keep your temper; when you are wrong, you can't afford to lose it.

TEMPERAMENT (see PERSONALITY)

Temperament is not meant to be kept in its original form; nor is it to be obliterated. Instead, it should be disciplined, modified, sanctified.

Hear about the temperamental guy? Easy glum, easy glow.

TEMPTATION

You are not tempted because you are evil; you are tempted because you are human. (FULTON J. SHEEN)

Temptation is not sin but playing with temptation invites sin.
(J.C. MACAULAY)

The forces of temptation often attack a man's garrison of resolution by surprise, to win a quick victory and blow up the walls of fortification.
(DOUGLAS MEADOR)

Apart from God we're weak as water.

A little boy was punished by his mother for a misdeed. "You should turn a deaf ear to temptation," she scolded.
    In tears, the little boy protested, "But Mommy, I don't have a deaf ear."

We are never strong enough to risk walking into temptation.

The number of times the average man says no to temptation is once weakly. (PRINTS OF PARIS)

It's remarkable that cold feet are often the result of burned fingers.
(KIRK KIRKPATRICK)

Temptations, unlike opportunities, will always give you a second chance.
(O.A. BATTISTA)

There are several good protections against temptation, but the surest is cowardice. (MARK TWAIN)

What makes resisting temptation difficult for many people is they don't want to discourage it completely. (FRANKLIN P. JONES)

Most people who flee from temptation usually leave a forwarding address. (AUSTRALASIAN MANUFACTURER)

Nothing makes it easier to resist a temptation than a more attractive one. (QUOTE)

Many of the world's most attractive temptations are like some television commercials: frequently deceptive and frightfully costly. (WILLIAM A. WARD)

Temptation can cause us to succumb, sink, sin, or stand. (WILLIAM A. WARD)

Temptations discover what we are. (THOMAS À KEMPIS)

Youth is the age of temptation and the greatest temptation of all is to do what the rest of the gang are doing, right or wrong. Too often it is wrong, for wisdom comes only with maturity, and the road to the maturity of self-understanding and self-discipline is long and hard and there are those who never reach the end of that road. (PEARL S. BUCK)

Middle age is that perplexing time of life when we hear two voices calling us, one saying, "Why not?" and the other, "Why bother?" (SOMERSET [MASS.] SPECTATOR)

You're getting along in years when you don't dare to resist temptation for fear you won't get another chance. (QUOTE)

You needn't worry about avoiding temptation after you pass 60. That's when it starts avoiding you. (JOBBER TOPICS)

That person who is no longer tempted has long since been laid to rest! Temptation is part of the price of being human. (JERRY W. McCANT)

TENACITY (see PERSISTENCE)

A great oak is only a little nut that held his ground.

TENNIS (see EXERCISE)

The term "love" in tennis comes from the French word "oeuf" for egg. When a tennis player failed to make a point in France, the scorekeeper called out "L'oeuf," meaning the goose egg or zero. The pronunciation being close to the English "love," that word soon became standardized in tennis for nothing or no score. (QUOTE)

Fortune favors the brave. (JOHN NEWCOMBE)

People enjoy doubles more than singles because they have less work to do and a partner to blame. (BILL TILDEN)

Everything in this game is within. (ARTHUR ASHE)

When you get too keyed up about winning, you put added psychological pressure on yourself. That's why so many players never do their best in important matches. (JIMMY EVERT)

You've got to get to that stage in your life when going for it is more important than winning or losing. (ARTHUR ASHE)

Tennis is one of the very few sports that effectively reconciles the generation gap. I don't mean only father-and-son or mother-and-daughter doubles teams, but one-against-one competition. Many a 50-year-old tennis player can hold his own against someone in his twenties. In most other sports you'd be risking your life to try it. (BILL TALBERT)

The time your game is most vulnerable is when you're ahead. Never let up. (ROD LAVER)

Death is nature's way of giving somebody else your tennis court. (JOHNNY CARSON)

It is usually more blessed to serve than to receive. (LLOYD CORY)

The way some people play tennis, they ought to be fined for contempt of court. (JOAN WELSH)

Playing tennis is like raising children. You keep on thinking you're going to do better.

TENSION (see STRESS)

The short history of some men is that they live so tense that they soon become past tense. (JIM GOODWIN)

Learning to live with your tensions is a lot like learning to ride a bicycle. The sooner you get your mind off yourself, the sooner you are likely to go zooming along in balance. And you can't learn how to ride a bike by reading a book. It's all right to read how. But sooner or later you must mount the bike and start pedaling. (ARKANSAS BAPTIST)

Anyone, in any line of work, is likely to go into a slump. That condition in which you get off the beam can be caused by becoming tense. And a basic cause of tension is too much concern about how you are doing, or a hectic sense of competition with others. A calm effort just to do the best you can and to compete primarily with yourself is the corrective. As a well-known baseball player told me, "When I get tense and self-conscious and go into a slump, I forget I'm a big shot. I get my thinking straightened out. That is my cure for a slump." And it's a good cure for anyone. (NORMAN V. PEALE)

Tensions in human life are something like fleas on a dog. A reasonable number provides interest, excitement, a spur to achievement, and happiness. (O.A. BATTISTA)

We hear a lot about relaxing, but after all, if you're totally relaxed, you're dead. To win a baseball game, to run a mile, to beat last year's production record, to plan next year's production peak, you have to be full of tensions. (RICHARD J. CUSHING)

You will never be the person you can be if pressure, tension, and discipline are taken out of your life. (JAMES G. BILKEY)

TERROR AND FORCE

The one means that wins the easiest victory over reason: terror and force. (ADOLF HITLER)

TEXANS

A Texas newspaper recently conducted a contest, offering a valuable prize for the best essay on "Why I Am Glad to Be a Texan"—in 50,000 words or more.

A Texan was dictating his will: "To my son I leave $3 million—and he's lucky I didn't cut him off entirely." (LION)

One Texas oilman asked another what he was going to give his son for his birthday.
"Motors."
"Electric or gasoline?"
"General." (CAROLINA HIGHWAYS)

A Texan bought a 10-gallon hat, but he had an 11-gallon head.

THANKSGIVING (see GRATITUDE)

Thanksgiving is the attitude of the life that acknowledges the contribution from God, from others, from life. (C. NEIL STRAIT)

Thanksgiving was never meant to be shut up in a single day. (ROBERT C. LINTNER)

One Thanksgiving some understandably disgruntled American Indians gathered at Plymouth Rock to mourn the day the first whites set foot on those then Indian lands. Said Brave Bay, a Mohawk: "Plymouth Rock should have landed on the Pilgrims." (FORBES)

If you can't be satisfied with what you have received, be thankful for what you have escaped.

Be grateful for venetian blinds. If it weren't for them, it'd be curtains for all of us. (EARL WILSON)

No duty is more urgent than that of returning thanks. (ST. AMBROSE)

Surveys indicate the average American will gain two pounds between Thanksgiving and the new year. Now that's what I call expanding with the economy. (LOU ERICKSON)

Thanksgiving is when one species ceases to gobble and another begins. (R.E. MARINO)

A very interesting phenomenon in children is that gratitude or thankfulness comes relatively late in their young lives. They almost have to be taught it; if not, they are apt to grow up thinking that the world owes them a living. (FULTON J. SHEEN)

If a fellow isn't thankful for what he's got, he isn't likely to be thankful for what he's going to get. (FRANK A. CLARK)

Attitudes sour in the life that is closed to thankfulness. Soon selfish attitudes take over, closing life to better things. (C. NEIL STRAIT)

Thanksgiving puts power into living, because it opens the generators of the heart to respond gratefully, to receive joyfully, and to react creatively. (C. NEIL STRAIT)

The modern American seldom pauses to give thanks for the simple blessings of life. One reason is that we are used to having so much. We simply assume that we will have all the good things of life. Another reason is that it hurts our pride to be grateful. We do not want to admit that God is the Provider of all good things. We are simply His stewards. Being thankful requires humility and faith in God. When we have these, we can be grateful. (RICHARD B. DOUGLASS)

There's one thing for which you can be thankful—only you and God have all the facts about yourself. (DUB NANCE)

Thou who hast given so much to me, give one thing more—a grateful heart! (GEORGE HERBERT)

THEOLOGY (see BELIEFS)

Your theology is what you are when the talking stops and the action starts. (COLIN MORRIS)

Many are preaching as a substitute for Christ's work in man's behalf, man's work in his own behalf. This is as dangerous as telling an artist with cancer that he can cure himself with his great art and needs not a physician and surgeon. (PAUL RADER)

THEORY

A thirsty man may know that water exists, may know its chemical formula, but he will die of thirst unless he is willing to take a cup and drink. (RYLLIS G. LYNIP)

There's nothing like a little experience to upset a theory. (BITS AND PIECES)

Theory may raise a man's hopes, but practice raises his wages. (HIGHWAYS OF HAPPINESS)

THINKING (see BRAINSTORMING)

Thinking is like living and dying. Each of us has to do it for himself. (JOSIAH ROYCE)

The man who has no inner life is the slave of his surroundings. (HENRI AMIEL)

There is no expedient to which a man will not go to avoid the real labor of thinking. (THOMAS EDISON)

Thinking is a habit, much like piano playing, not a process like eating or sleeping. The amount of thinking you can do at any time will depend primarily on the amount of thinking you have already done. (CONSTRUCTION DIGEST)

"Thinking," said the little boy, "is when your mouth stays shut and your head keeps talking to itself." (ARKANSAS BAPTIST)

Ours is an age which is proud of machines that think, and suspicious of any man who tries it. (HOWARD M. JONES)

The thinking you do before you start a job will shorten the time you have to spend working on it. (ROY L. SMITH)

Don't let yourself say or even think, "I am busy," "I haven't time," "I am tired." This makes you feel busier, or more rushed, or more tired than you actually are. (WILLIAM B. GIVEN, JR.)

The smaller the mind, the more interested it is in the rare, the extraordinary, the sensational; the larger the mind, the more interested it is in studying the obvious, examining the ordinary, and investigating the commonplace. (SYDNEY J. HARRIS)

The creative process requires more than reason. Most original thinking isn't even verbal. It requires a groping experimentation with ideas, governed by intuitive hunches and inspired by the unconscious. The majority of well-educated men are incapable of original thinking because they are unable to escape from the tyranny of reason. Their imaginations are blocked. (DAVID OGILVY)

I think and think, for months, for years; 99 times the conclusion is false. The hundredth time I am right. (ALBERT EINSTEIN)

Guard well thy thoughts; our thoughts are heard in heaven. (OWEN D. YOUNG)

Thinking is the hardest work there is, which is probably why so few engage in it. (HENRY FORD)

A great many people think they are thinking when they are really rearranging their prejudices. (EDWARD R. MURROW)

The trouble with most people is that they think with their hopes or fears or wishes rather than with their minds. (WALTER DURANTY)

Thinking is one thing no one has ever been able to tax. (CHARLES F. KETTERING)

The probable reason some people get lost in thought is because it is unfamiliar territory to them.

Tie the arm to one's side and it withers; cease exercising the mind for a prolonged period and thinking can no more be recovered than spoiled fruit can regain its freshness. It is use, practice, exercise that gives muscle to the faculties, all faculties—intellectual and spiritual as well as physical. (LEONARD E. READ)

The human tongue is only inches from the brain, but when you listen to some folks they seem miles apart. (P-K SIDELINERS)

Thoughts should be tested before they are transmitted. If our thoughts taste unkind, critical, or unfair, we should refuse to release them into the dangerous world of words. (WILLIAM A. WARD)

With some people, thought is merely an impediment to conversation. (BETTER FARMING)

When you hear, "Now this is just off the top of my head," expect dandruff. (QUOTE)

Negative thoughts breed doubts and despair. Such thinking enslaves life and keeps it from reaching out for the best. Such thinking makes life a stranger to possibility. . . . Negative thoughts poison the mind. What a mind poisoned with negative thoughts contributes, then, to life is not progress, but problems. (C. NEIL STRAIT)

To overcome troubles you must use the good mind God gave you. Think through and understand them. And you cannot think clearheadedly while seething with a sense of outrage, hating other people or life or even God for some harsh experience that has befallen you. Neither can you weep and wail about it—and at the same time think. (NORMAN V. PEALE)

I believe that if you think about disaster, you will get it. Brood about death and you hasten your demise. Think positively and masterfully, with confidence and faith, and life becomes more secure, more fraught with action, richer in achievement and experience. (EDDIE RICKENBACKER)

Two thoughts cannot occupy the mind at the same time, so the choice is ours as to whether our thoughts will be constructive or destructive. (BETTY SACHELLI)

Our best friends and our worst enemies are our thoughts. A thought can do us more good than a doctor or a banker or a faithful friend. It can also do us more harm than a brick. (FRANK CRANE)

If you make people think they're thinking, they'll love you. If you really make them think, they'll hate you. (ELBERT HUBBARD)

Think like a man of action and act like a man of thought. (HENRI BERGSON)

Thinking is more precious than all five senses. (NACHMAN OF BRATSLAV)

Every man should have a room where he can be by himself to think and meditate. If not a full room, then a corner, or a place in the basement. (WILFRED A. PETERSON)

Where all think alike, no one thinks very much.   (WALTER LIPPMAN)

Nobody has ever thought out anything in a shower because it's too fast and too efficient.   (DON HEROLD)

To tell a man what to think is, in the long run, equivalent to telling him not to think at all.   (T.V. SMITH)

THOROUGHNESS

I have always made a fetish of thoroughness. A thing that separates the men from the boys, in my opinion, is the ability to follow through and make sure all the buttons are in place.   (LEO BURNETT)

THREATS

Threats are the arrows of a defeated foe.   (J.C. MACAULAY)

THRIFT (see MONEY)

Thrift: A moss-grown obsession of those primitive men whose accomplishment was to create the United States of America.   (FIFTH WHEEL)

People don't understand what a large income thrift can be.   (CICERO)

Thrift used to be a basic American virtue. Our folklore is full of it. Now the American virtue is to spend money.   (DAVID BRINKLEY)

A saver grows rich by seeming poor. A spender grows poor by seeming rich.   (BANKING)

TIES

I have a hankering to go back to the Orient and discard my necktie. Neckties strangle clear thinking.   (LIN YUTANG)

TIME

Lots of folks who wouldn't swipe paper clips from their bosses think nothing of stealing time for which they're being paid.(FRANK A. CLARK)

When a person gets into the habit of wasting time, he is sure to waste a great deal that does not belong to him.   (SUNSHINE)

The great dividing line between success and failure can be expressed in five words: I did not have time.   (FRANKLIN FIELD)

We master our minutes, or we become slaves to them; we use time, or time uses us.   (WILLIAM A. WARD)

Always give people time to become familiar with a concept before you ask them to vote on it. People will always vote no on anything that is strange or threatening to them. (ROBERT A. COOK)

It isn't what you know that counts; it's what you can think of in time. (BITS AND PIECES)

There is a time to let things happen and a time to make things happen. (HUGH PRATHER)

Time flies. It's up to you to be the navigator. (ROBERT ORBEN)

There is no way on earth to save time; all you can do is spend it. (MERRILL E. DOUGLASS)

Time is too slow for those who wait, too swift for those who fear, too long for those who grieve, too short for those who rejoice. But for those who love, time is not. (HENRY VAN DYKE)

Striker's picket sign: Time Heals All Wounds. Time and a Half Heals Them Faster! (EARL WILSON)

Time is a great healer, but a poor beautician. (LUCILLE S. HARPER)

Time wounds all heels.

Time, obviously, is relative. Two weeks on a vacation is not the same as two weeks on a diet.

Some people can stay longer in an hour than others can in a week. (WILLIAM D. HOWELLS)

The management of time should be the No. 1 priority for us. Without some organization of our day, it will waste away without purpose and drain away without accomplishment. (C. NEIL STRAIT)

Our days are identical suitcases—all the same size—but some people can pack more into them than others. (GRIT)

Most time is wasted, not in hours, but in minutes. A bucket with a small hole in the bottom gets just as empty as a bucket that is deliberately kicked over. (PAUL J. MEYER)

A minute is never long enough for those who ask you if you can spare one.

Dost thou love life? Then do not squander time, for that is the stuff life is made of. (BENJAMIN FRANKLIN)

The moment passed is no longer; the future may never be; the present is all of which man is the master. (JEAN-JACQUES ROUSSEAU)

There are three things a man can do without fretting about wasting his time—make love, make war, and make art. (PAUL PICKREL)

Time you enjoy wasting is not wasted time.

The wheel goes round and round and the fly on the top'll be the fly on the bottom after a while. (LAURA I. WILDER)

Most of modern man's troubles stem from too much time on his hands and not enough on his knees. (IVERN BOYETT)

Make time to think—it is the source of power.
Make time to play—it is the key to freedom and relaxation.
Make time to read—it is the gateway to knowledge.
Make time to worship—it washes the dust of earth from your eyes.
Make time to help and enjoy friends—no other happiness matches this.
Make time to love—if you don't it will fade away.
Make time to laugh and pray—these are two things that lighten life's load.
Make time to be alone with God—He is the Source of everything.
(GUARDIAN OF TRUTH)

No great thing is created suddenly, any more than a bunch of grapes or a fig. If you tell me that you desire a fig, I answer you that there must be time. Let it first blossom, then bear fruit, then reopen. (EPICETETUS)

Time is a dressmaker specializing in alterations. (FAITH BALDWIN)

There are four kinds of thieves—the love thief, the embezzler, the base runner safe at second, and the thief who steals your time. The latter is the worst thief because, while love can be replaced, stolen gains can be repaid, and the base runner put out at third, time can never be renewed.
(CARL RIBLET, JR.)

One of the best ways to save time is to think and plan ahead; five minutes of thinking can often save an hour of work. (CHARLES C. GIBBONS)

TIMES

Good times are when people who used to go barefoot complain about the price of shoes. (MAURICE SEITTER)

Whether these are the best of times or the worst of times, it's the only time we've got.   (ART BUCHWALD)

TITHING (see GIVING, STEWARDSHIP)

If every church member were suddenly placed on public relief and gave a tithe of his average welfare payment, the income of American churches would be 35 percent greater.   (R.K. HUDNUT)

At a social event one man told another: "I've met you before but I can't place you. And you look much like somebody I have seen a lot. This person you look like is somebody I don't like. I resent him very much, but I don't know why I resent him. Isn't that strange?"

The other man declared, "Nothing strange about it. You have seen me a lot and I know why you resent me. For two years I passed the collection plate in your church."   (QUOTE)

Pastor: You say you can't give to the church because you owe everyone. Don't you feel that you owe the Lord something?
Member: Yes, of course I do. But He isn't pushing me like the others.
                                          (CAROLINA COOPERATOR)

TODAY

Live one day at a time. You can plan for tomorrow and hope for the future, but don't live in it. Live this day well, and tomorrow's strength will come tomorrow.   (CHARLES W. SHEDD)

TOGETHERNESS

I finally got it all together, but I forgot where I put it.

Coming together is a beginning; keeping together is progress; working together is success.

In France . . . I was the weekend guest of a couple in their mid-60s who lived a solitary country life, depended mainly on each other for company, and still conversed together with the interest and animation of old friends catching up after a long absence. When I remarked on this, my host said, "To feel really close to another person one must keep a little distance." In other words, we must avoid the aggressive shaping of one person by the other. How seldom we are aware of the tremendous pressure we put on our families and friends to be as we want them to be, rather than the unique persons they are. The basic message of human communication is, "Here I am; there you are. We are not alone."
                                          (JOHN K. LAGEMANN)

TOLERANCE

Tolerance is the quality that keeps a new bride from reforming her husband right away. (MIKE CONNOLLY)

The trouble with being tolerant is that people think you don't understand the problem. (SOMERSET [MASS.] SPECTATOR)

Tolerance comes with age. I see no fault committed that I myself could not have committed at some time or other. (GOETHE)

TONGUES

A tongue three inches long can kill a man six feet tall.
(JAPANESE PROVERB)

When you've got a word on the tip of your tongue, it's sometimes as well to leave it there.

A tongue doesn't weigh much, but many people have trouble holding one. (GRIT)

A sharp tongue invites a split lip. (EVELYN ZEMKE)

Sometimes I doubt whether there is divine justice. All parts of the human body get tired eventually—except the tongue. And I feel this is unjust.
(KONRAD ADENAUER)

TOOLS

The man who has a full set of tools has no children. (ROY HATTEN)

TORMENT (see SUFFERING)

Lord, on You I call for help against my blind and senseless torment, since You alone can renew inwardly and outwardly my mind, my will, and my strength, which are weak. (MICHELANGELO)

TOUGHNESS

When the going gets tough, the tough get going.

TRADE (see WORK)

It is not enough to learn the tricks of the trade—you must learn the trade. (SAMSCRIPTS)

TRADITION

Does Protestantism have a heritage of worship? . . . Yes, although this does not imply doing things in church "just because the Reformers did." Calvin wore a hat in church . . . because the church had (a) drafts and (b) pigeons. (ROBERT M. BROWN)

TRAINING AND EXPERIENCE

Training means learning the rules. Experience means learning the exceptions. (INDIANAPOLIS TIMES)

TRAVEL

Travel broadens the mind, flattens the finances, and lengthens the conversation. (LOIS HAASE)

However far your travels take you, you will never find the girl who smiles out at you from the travel brochure.

A tip for those going abroad: In an underdeveloped country, don't drink the water; in a developed country, don't breathe the air.(CHANGING TIMES)

If it costs 1¢ to ride a thousand miles, a trip around the world would cost 25¢; to the moon $2.38; to the sun, only $930; but a trip to the nearest star would cost $260 million. (GOOD READING)

TRIAL AND ERROR

When you stumble today pick yourself up tomorrow. That's what tomorrows are for. (JANET COLLINS)

TRIBULATIONS (see TROUBLES)

It always looks darkest just before it gets totally black.(CHARLIE BROWN)

The Lord doesn't take us into deep water to drown us, but to develop us. (IRV HEDSTROM)

TROMBONES

There are so many things to be thankful for. For instance, let's be thankful the trombone has never become as popular as the guitar. (ROBERT ORBEN)

TROUBLES (see ADVERSITY, SORROW)

Trouble is what gives a fellow his chance to discover his strength—or lack of it. (FRANK A. CLARK)

It takes a world with trouble in it to train men for their high calling as sons of God, and to carve upon the soul the lineaments of the face of Christ. (J.S. STEWARD)

I believe in getting into hot water. I think it keeps you clean.
(G.K. CHESTERTON)

The gem cannot be polished without friction, nor men perfected without trials. (CHINESE PROVERB)

In the presence of trouble, some people grow wings; others buy crutches.

Trouble is a sieve for separating friends from acquaintances.
(J. GUSTAV WHITE)

A troublemaker is a guy who rocks the boat, then persuades everyone else there is a storm at sea.

Don't borrow trouble. Be patient and you'll have some of your own.
(GEORGE GOBEL)

When it comes to borrowing trouble, a man's credit is always good.
(O. SHUCKS)

The capacity for getting into trouble and the ability for getting out of it are seldom combined in the same person.

You don't know what trouble is until your kids reach the age of consent, dissent, and resent—all at the same time. (ROBERT ORBEN)

If you see 10 troubles coming down the road, you can be sure that 9 will run into the ditch before they reach you. (CALVIN COOLIDGE)

Troubles are often the tools by which God fashions us for better things.
(HENRY W. BEECHER)

Never attempt to bear more than one kind of trouble at once. Some people bear three kinds—all they have had, all they have now, and all they expect to have. (EDWARD E. HALE)

No one should surrender to trouble, letting it crush him. At the same time, no one should resent trouble as though it were an intruder. Trouble is a natural part of life. Consequently, it is wise to accept trouble and bear it without complaining. (ROBERT W. YOUNG)

There should be more pleasure getting into trouble; it is so hard to get out. (FARM JOURNAL)

Warning! Following are the names of the seven Mischievous Misses who are responsible for most of our troubles: Miss Information, Miss Quotation, Miss Representation, Miss Interpretation, Miss Construction, Miss Conception, Miss Understanding. Don't listen to them. (WILLIAM J.H. BOETCKER)

It's not the magnitude of the mess that matters; it's the measure of the man in the midst of the mess. (GARY GULBRANSON)

Sign on army chaplain's door: If you have troubles, come and tell us about them. If not, come in and tell us how you do it.

With me, a change of trouble is as good as a vacation.

As long as you laugh at your troubles, you may be sure that you will never run out of something to laugh at. (BENDIXLINE)

The easiest way to get into trouble is to be right at just the wrong time. (GRIT)

Jesus spoke more about trouble and crosses and persecution than He did about human happiness. (W.T. PURKISER)

Trouble has not diminished since man first turned from God. It does not wear out. Its energy surges unabated. No laboratory is dedicated to its demise. No medicine paralyzes its clutching hand. No light eclipses its glare. The so-called progress of mankind has not led him from its kingdom of sorrow. (V.H. LEWIS)

To be right with God has often meant to be in trouble with men. (A.W. TOZER)

No one is more exasperating than the guy who can always see the bright side of our misfortunes.

I am an old man and have known a great many troubles, but most of them never happened. (MARK TWAIN)

Most of us seem able to meet the big crises, even head-on. We get up, bruised and even bleeding, from the ground to which we've been flung, and go on somehow. But the little things throw us like restive horses which we haven't learned to ride. (FAITH BALDWIN)

A wise businessman we know has what he calls his "Trouble Tree." It is located about a block away from his house, where he has to pass it every evening on his way home.

"When I reach that tall poplar in the evening," he explains, "I leave all the troubles and worries of the day right there. 'Let them hang on the branches if they want to,' I say to myself. 'I'm through with them for the day.' And I throw back my shoulders and stir up a grin and get ready for a fine evening with my family. I used to take my troubles home to my wife, and often they would stay with me all night, and I'd get up the next morning with a grouch.

"But no more! I hang them on the Trouble Tree, and five nights out of six they have all blown away by morning." (QUOTE)

TRUST

There's only one thing finer than a friend you can trust, and that's one who trusts you. (ISIS)

If you can't trust people, who *can* you trust? (JOHN WIDDICOMBE)

The man who trusts men will make fewer mistakes than he who distrusts them. (CAMILLO DI CAVOUR)

If you think you have someone eating out of your hand, it's still a good idea to count your fingers regularly. (BALANCE SHEET)

Trust is a treasured item and relationship. Once it is tarnished, it is hard to restore it to its original glow. (WILLIAM A. WARD)

Better to trust the man who is frequently in error than the one who is never in doubt. (ERIC SEVAREID)

That the Almighty does make use of human agencies and directly intervenes in human affairs is one of the plainest statements in the Bible. I have had so many evidences of His direction, so many instances when I have been controlled by some other power than my own will, that I cannot doubt that this power comes from above. (ABRAHAM LINCOLN)

People whom we trust tend to become trustworthy.(SOLOMON FREEHOF)

There are many people who when trouble comes focus more on what they've lost than on what they've got left. They go through life counting their blessings on their fingertips and their burdens on their pocket calculators. (PAUL W. POWELL)

TRUTH

A truth that's told with bad intent
Beats all the lies you can invent. (WILLIAM BLAKE)

The truth is rarely pure, and never simple.   (OSCAR WILDE)

A man who is proud that he always tells the truth should first make sure that he tells necessary truths for honorable motives, and not unnecessary truths for hurtful motives.

An unblessed soul filled with the letter of truth may actually be worse off than a pagan kneeling before a fetish.   (A.W. TOZER)

Truth often suffers more by the heat of its defenders than from the arguments of its opposers.   (WILLIAM PENN)

Truth is incontrovertible. Panic may resent it; ignorance may deride it; malice may distort it; but there it is.   (WINSTON CHURCHILL)

When you stretch the truth, watch out for the snapback.(BILL COPELAND)

The trouble with stretching the truth is people are apt to see through it.
                                                        (QUOTE)

Always tell the truth. Then you don't have to worry about what you said last.   (ROBERT A. COOK)

Some people live their whole lives just around the corner from the world of truth.   (CARL F.H. HENRY)

Men occasionally stumble over the truth, but most of them pick themselves up and hurry off, as if nothing had happened.(WINSTON CHURCHILL)

The truth shall make you free, but first it shall make you miserable.
                                                        (BARRY STEVENS)

The more serious I am about reality, the more I have to remind myself that when I recognize some aspect of truth in the words of my bitterest opponents, I must concede that truth.   (VIRGINIA R. MOLLENKOTT)

Sometimes the kindest thing you can do for a person is to tell him a truth that will prove very painful. But in so doing, you may have saved him from serious harm or even greater pain.
    In a world such as ours, people must learn to "take it." A painless world is not necessarily a good world. (SYLVANUS AND EVELYN DUVALL)

Of course the truth hurts. You would too, if you got kicked around so much.   (FRANKLIN P. JONES)

Add one small bit to the truth and you inevitably subtract from it.
(DELL CROSSWORD PUZZLES)

In Washington there are three kinds of truth—truth that must be hidden because of fear, truth that must be saved for the right moment, and truth that is leaked. (CARL RIBLET, JR.)

Most truths are so naked that people feel sorry for them and cover them up, at least a little bit. (HELMUT WALTERS)

Four high school boys, afflicted with spring fever, skipped morning classes. After lunch they reported to their teacher that their car had a flat tire.

Much to their relief, she smiled and said, "Well, you missed a test this morning, so take seats apart from one another and get out your notebooks."

When they had settled down, she said, "First question: which tire was flat?" (FOSTER QUINN)

Truth has to change hands only a few times to become fiction.
(DAWSON COUNTY [GA.] ADVERTISER)

The truth is stranger than autobiography. (QUOTE)

Truth is always strong, no matter how weak it looks, and falsehood is always weak, no matter how strong it looks. (PHILLIPS BROOKS)

The great truths are too important to be new. (SOMERSET MAUGHAM)

It is much easier to recognize error than to find truth, for error lies on the surface and may be overcome; but truth lies in the depths, and to search for it is not given to everyone. (GOETHE)

TYPOGRAPHY

The type in some of the mammoth new paperbacks gets smaller and smaller and one anguished reader has struck back at his tormentors.

"I propose," he writes, "that these typographical monstrosities henceforth carry this legend on the last page:

" '*A Note on the Type in Which This Book Was Set*

" 'The type in which this book was set is known, quite unfavorably, as one half point Myopia, and was designed in 1622 by that noted sadist, Feodor Astigmatism. It bids fair to become one of the most heartily disliked faces this side of Fidel Castro. It is perfect for engraving the complete text of *The Brothers Karamazov* on the head of a pin.' "
(C. KENNEDY)

ULCERS

Ulcers are something you get from mountain-climbing over molehills.

(LOCAL GOVERNMENT NEWSLETTER)

It's not what you eat that gives you ulcers. It's what's eating you.

ULTIMATES

The rarest thing in the world is sincerity; the greatest, kindness; the most satisfactory, the untroubled mind; the most difficult to encounter, the swelled head; that which is most desired, a friend who understands; the hardest to endure, selfishness; the most aggravating, prejudice; that which we most admire, courage; the most valuable, character; that which we need most, faith.

(FRIENDLY CHAT)

UNBELIEF (see ATHEISM)

In 1938, a man with a home on the south shore of Long Island ordered himself a long-desired barometer from Abercrombie and Fitch, the famous New York City sporting goods store.

The barometer arrived on the morning of September 21st and the owner proudly hung it up on the back porch. Half an hour later he took a peek at his high-priced toy and was irritated to find the needle stuck at "Hurricane."

Quickly he sat down and wrote an angry letter to Abercrombie and Fitch, demanding a new barometer. When he returned home from the local post office after mailing the letter, both barometer and house were missing. September 21, 1938, it developed, was the day of the worst hurricane ever to hit Long Island. (BITS AND PIECES)

Thomas Paine on his deathbed expressed the wish that all copies of his most famous work, *Age of Reason*, had been thrown into the fire, for "if the devil has ever had any agency in any work, he has had it in writing that book." (QUOTE)

UNCERTAINTY

Nothing beats uncertainty to make tomorrow more interesting. (WHEELER MCMILLEN)

UNDERSTANDING

Confidence is the feeling you sometimes have before you fully understand the situation. (BANKING)

To know a little less and to understand a little more: that, it seems to me, is our greatest need. (JAMES R. ULLMAN)

It is nothing for you to worry about if you are misunderstood. But you had better get all steamed up if you don't understand. (CONSTRUCTION DIGEST)

Most of us really want to be half-understood. Not to be understood at all is frustrating; to be wholly understood is humiliating. (SYDNEY HARRIS)

General Grant is said to have retained an incompetent officer on his staff for a single purpose. "If he can understand my orders, anyone can," explained Grant. (AUREN URIS)

Understanding can wait. Obedience cannot. (GEOFFREY GROGAN)

To understand another does not mean that one has to agree with all that he says or does. Understanding, however, is the basis for getting along with people in our daily contacts. Friction, bickering, and confusion in our environment cannot exist where there is understanding. (REGINALD C. ARMOR)

The essential point of any human relationship is to try to understand what is on the other person's mind, what his objectives are. I think if one does that, it's much easier to be a useful member of whatever community you're living in, including your own family. (AVERELL HARRIMAN)

The next time you think a person is being unreasonable or dense, try this: Instead of arguing or explaining, restate his position in your words so that he agrees that you have got it straight. You will find it more difficult than you think, and you may have to try more than once to get it right. Once you've succeeded, however, you will have reached a deeper understanding of the other person and, surprisingly, you may find that he seems to understand you much better. This is a big step toward a meeting of minds. (HAROLD MAYFIELD)

UNDERTAKERS

Undertaker's problem: How to look sad at a $10,000 funeral.

And there's the sarcastic undertaker who's always running people into the ground. (SHELBY FRIEDMAN)

UNFORGIVENESS (see FORGIVENESS)

A chip on the shoulder usually comes from the block above it.
(E. ROGER JONES)

UNHAPPINESS (see HAPPINESS)

The most unhappy of all men is he who believes himself to be so.(HUME)

Unhappiness is in not knowing what we want and killing ourselves to get it. (DON HEROLD'S MAGAZINE)

Unhappiness is man's inheritance; all of us are bound to be sad and even grief-stricken at times. The capacity to feel sad is perhaps just the other side of the capacity to feel happy. So the most useful thing we can teach is that life is complex and difficult—and the more roses you seek, the more likely you are to fall upon thorns. (ELAINE CUMMING)

Life to the unhappy person is not unlike marriage to the platonic husband. Neither is getting all he could. The happy person gets more out of life. More people like him and want to help him. And he is usually more successful in accomplishing his own goals. (ROSE TECHNIC)

Nine-tenths of our unhappiness is selfishness, and is an insult thrown in the face of God. (G.H. MORRISON)

UNISEX

The battle of the sexes will have to be called off, if it gets any harder for one side to identify the other. (FRANKLIN P. JONES)

UNITED STATES

No matter what other nations may say about the United States, immigration is still the sincerest form of flattery. (PATHFINDER)

UNIVERSITIES (see SCHOOLS)

A university president says he is working hard to develop a school the football team can be proud of. (GEORGE CROSS)

UNIVERSE

It would seem incredible to me that of all the other planets in the universe, we should be the only one with life. I believe there is life on other planets with principalities and sovereignties, perhaps different from us, but all a part of God's universe. (BILLY GRAHAM)

UNSELFISHNESS

The secret of being loved is in being lovely; and the secret of being lovely is in being unselfish. (J.G. HOLLAND)

URGENCY

Your greatest danger is letting the urgent things crowd out the important. (CHARLES E. HUMMEL)

USEFULNESS

Visibility and usefulness are not the same. (DAVE McCASLAND)

Have nothing in your house that you do not know to be useful, or believe to be beautiful. (WILLIAM MORRIS)

USELESSNESS

Nothing is as useless as the right answer to the wrong question.

VACATIONS

This summer, one-third of the nation will be ill-housed, ill-nourished, and ill-clad. Only they call it vacation. (EUGENE P. BERTIN)

Rules for vacationing, for benefit to both mind and body: (1) Before you travel with anyone, be sure you know him, her, or them quite well. (2) Don't overwork before you start your holiday—it takes longer to unwind. (3) Don't expect too much from your vacation; for example, a trip probably won't save a marriage. (4) Allow a reentry day. Don't rush straight from your trip to your job. (5) Use your vacation to go some-where, do something different. (6) Learn to relax without feeling that you're just doing nothing. (7) Keep your vacation free of work; don't take along a briefcase or stay home to clean closets. (8) Finally, family visits usually don't count as vacation time. (FRANCIS L. CLARK)

Last year we discovered a vacation spot that's convenient to get to, comfortable, relaxing, where we don't have to get dressed up, and that's priced within our budget. It's called the living room. (ROBERT ORBEN)

I got a vacation postcard: "Having a wonderful time; wish I could afford it."

No family should attempt an auto trip if the kids outnumber the car windows. (TERESA BLOOMINGDALE)

A vacation is like a romance: anticipated with pleasure; experienced with discomfort, remembered with nostalgia. (Lou Erickson)

After all, the best part of a holiday is perhaps not so much to be resting yourself, as to see all the other fellows busy working. (Kenneth Grahame)

An efficiency expert went in to see his boss about his vacation. He came out with a depressed expression on his face. Asked what was wrong, he replied, "I only get one week. The boss says I'm so efficient I can have as much fun in one week as other people have in two." (Voice)

When packing vacation clothes, take the line of crease resistance.
(Millie Wertheim)

The ideal vacation cottage is one that visits 12 and sleeps 2.
(Don Epperson)

No one needs a vacation so much as the fellow who has just had one. (Bits and Pieces)

Doctor to patient: I want you to skip your vacation this year and get a good rest. (Lucille S. Harper)

I took a long vacation,
  Was gone for many days;
Canceled my newspaper,
  Had them shut off the gas.

But I found out that Nature,
  In her capricious ways,
Had completely forgotten
  To shut off the grass.

(Quote)

Many people feel no change after a vacation—not a nickel!
(Adrian Anderson)

An executive who works 12 months in the year does not work more than 6 months. It is the man who works 10 or 11 months and does something else for 1 or 2 months who works for 12 months. (B.C. Forbes)

Vacations are times to spend re-creating the energies of life—physical, mental, emotional, and spiritual. In a busy workaday world, too often the vital areas of life are neglected and spent. Vacation time should be an opportunity to check out the energy levels of life and to replenish the low ones.

Every person needs a period away from the toil and routine. He needs a time to replenish his mental energies, regroup his physical powers, reconsider his emotional needs, and review his spiritual progress.
(C. Neil Strait)

VALUES (see IDEALS)

People who have no values have no value. (Burton Hillis)

It is said that about 200 years ago, the tomb of the great conqueror, Charlemagne, was opened. The sight the workmen saw was startling. There was his body in a sitting position, clothed in the most elaborate of kingly garments, with a scepter in his bony hand. On his knee there lay a New Testament, with a cold lifeless finger pointing to Mark 8:36: "For what shall it profit a man, if he shall gain the whole world, and lose his own soul?" (ORIGIN UNKNOWN)

If we spend 16 hours a day dealing with tangible things and only five minutes a day dealing with God, is it any wonder that tangible things are 200 times more real to us than God? (WILLIAM R. INGE)

[A] writer . . . expresses the opinion that the greatest social problem in America is not racial integration or drink or divorce or juvenile delinquency, but the emphasis that we are putting on material values. Whether we agree with the appraisal or not, the statement cannot be lightly dismissed. . . . If our emphasis on earthly values is not our greatest problem, it is surely a habit that brings poverty to the soul.
(CHRISTIAN OBSERVER,

A speck cuts the value of a diamond in half. A race horse that can run a mile a few seconds faster than any other is worth twice as much. That little extra all through life proves to be the greatest value.
(JOHN D. HESS)

A greater poverty than that caused by lack of money is the poverty of awareness. Men and women go about the world unaware of the beauty, the goodness, in it. Their souls are poor. It is better to have a poor pocketbook than to suffer from a poor soul. (THOMAS DREIER)

Houses are visible, but homes are not. Churches can be seen, but the fellowship of believers that makes the church is an invisible spirit. Citizenship papers are seeable, touchable, and weighable, but patriotism is not. A marriage license is purchasable, but love is not. Birthday and anniversary gifts can be measured in terms of dollars and cents, but thoughtfulness and appreciation cannot. (HAROLD E. KOHN)

Many wise men have said in many different ways that there are at least four things by which men must live in the world. They were speaking, of course, of spiritual values, not of material necessities. Food, shelter, clothing, and the like man must also have. But if he has nothing more than these, life will be barren indeed. The other things that he must have are *love, work, play,* and *worship.* There can be no lasting happiness without *love;* there can be no satisfaction of achievement without *work;* there can be no release from tension without *play;* and there can be no experience of the joy and peace and power of life without *worship.*
(CHRISTIAN OBSERVER)

VANITY (see PRIDE)

A vain man can never be utterly ruthless; he wants to win applause and therefore he accommodates himself to others. (GOETHE)

VEGETARIANS

Could she be carrying her vegetarianism too far? She won't even eat animal crackers.

VEXATIONS (see DIFFICULTIES)

Some people can accept a staggering setback with much more resignation than they can put up with the little vexations and difficulties of daily living. However, it is the small things that most reveal one's spiritual stature. (WAR CRY)

VICTORY

Victory is gained only through conflict.

We can retreat from life or meet it head-on. God has a plan for each life, but we'll never find that plan or victory by a head-in-the-sand approach to life. When it comes to problems, the way out is the way through.

To the victor belong the responsibilities. ·(AL BERNSTEIN)

One of the greatest victories you can gain over a man is to beat him at politeness. (BITS AND PIECES)

He . . . got the better of himself, and that's the best kind of victory one can wish for. (MIGUEL DE CERVANTES)

Be careful that victories do not carry the seeds of future defeats.

I feel sorry for someone who has to win at everything. (SNOOPY)

VIEWPOINT (see OUTLOOK, PERSPECTIVE)

To get a person to understand our point of view, we must first get to understand his.

We see things not as they are, but as we are. (GOOD READING)

End of kids' argument, Janet to Steve: Dolls are not stupid—*guns* are!

Sometimes it is only a change of viewpoint that is needed to convert a seemingly tiresome duty into an interesting opportunity.
(ALBERTA FLANDERS)

We look at our neighbors' errors with a microscope, but at our own through the wrong end of a telescope. Every vice has two names; and we call it by the flattering and minimizing one when we commit it, and by the ugly one when our neighbor does. (F.B. MEYER)

When the other fellow takes a long time, he's slow. When I take a long time, I'm thorough. When the other fellow doesn't do it, he's lazy. But when I don't do it, I'm busy. When the other fellow does something without being told, he's overstepping his bounds. But when I do it that's initiative. When the other fellow overlooks a rule of etiquette, he's rude. But when I skip a few rules, I'm original. When the other fellow pleases the boss he's an apple-polisher. But when I please the boss, that's cooperation. When the other fellow gets ahead, he's getting the breaks. But when I manange to get ahead, that's just the reward for hard work. (AMERICAN SALESMAN)

An idealist believes the short run doesn't count. A cynic believes the long run doesn't matter. A realist believes that what is done or left undone in the short run determines the long run. (SYDNEY HARRIS)

The faults of others are like headlights of an approaching automobile— they only seem more glaring than your own. (CHEWELAH [WASH.] INDEPENDENT)

A big-league umpire once remarked that he could never understand how crowds in the grandstand, hundreds of feet from the plate, could see better and judge more accurately than he, when he was only seven feet away.
Another man commented that in life too, we call strikes on a chap when we are too far away to understand. Perhaps, if we had a closer view of the man and his problems, we would reverse our decisions. (INFORMATION)

VIOLENCE

In the era before television there were about a dozen manufacturers turning out toy guns and such . . . weapons for children. Now there are about 300. (THE COUNTRY INDEXER)

VIOLINS

Dad says I play the violin as if the strings were still in the cat. (NONEE COAN)

VIRTUOUS DEEDS

Distinction between virtuous and vicious actions has been engraven by the Lord in the heart of every man. (JOHN CALVIN)

VISION

It would be easier to develop great statesmen if vision were as available as television. (INDIANAPOLIS TIMES)

Vision is the world's most desperate need. There are no hopeless situations, only people who think hopelessly. (WINIFRED NEWMAN)

It is not the darkness that blocks your vision so much as what is between you and God. (GAIL B. TRAFFORD)

VITALITY

Vitality shows not only in the ability to persist but in the ability to start over. (F. SCOTT FITZGERALD)

The Bible says, "Where there is no vision, the people perish." Have you a vision? And are you undeviatingly pressing and pushing toward its accomplishment? Dreaming alone will not get you there. Mix your dreaming with determination and action. (B.C. FORBES)

It is the dream within the person that counts more than anything else. If a parent can give a child a vision, he has given him one of the best gifts. If a teacher can create an idea of what life might be, she has done her part. (GERALD KENNEDY)

A motorist was telling about the trouble he's had driving to and from work lately. It used to be easy, he said. No traffic problems, no mad rat race. But now—wow! Cars coming from all directions. "And it's been that way," he added, "ever since I got my new glasses."

(GENERAL FEATURES)

VOCABULARY (see SPELLING, WORDS)

Stressing the importance of a large vocabulary, the high school English teacher told his class, "Use a word ten times, and it will be yours for life."

In the back of the room a pert blonde senior closed her eyes and was heard chanting, under her breath, "Fred, Fred, Fred, Fred, Fred, Fred, Fred, Fred, Fred, Fred." (TRACKS)

WAITING (see HESITATION)

Most things come a lot faster to those who won't wait.

(AMERICAN SALESMAN)

The while we keep a man waiting, he reflects on our shortcomings.

(FRENCH PROVERB)

Never run after a bus, a woman, or an educational theory; there will be another one coming along very soon. (M. PEYRE)

Simply wait upon Him. So doing, we shall be directed, supplied, protected, corrected, and rewarded. (VANCE HAVNER)

WALKING

In this age of high-speed travel, the best way to enjoy America's sights, sounds, and smells is the slowest way—on foot. (CHANGING TIMES)

If a thousand people visit a park on Sunday, 900 of them won't move more than 100 feet from their cars. Of those who walk around, only a handful will penetrate the woods deeper than a couple hundred yards. If you can find a place more than a mile from a road, you may not see another human being for days. (RICHARD FRISBIE)

Unquestionably, our current preoccupation with physical fitness is due at least in part to the fact that walking has for many years been considered a sign of extreme poverty or outright eccentricity. (CHARLES F. JONES)

Walking, because it's so unstructured, impromptu, and natural, is the most modern family exercise, though as long ago as 1786 Jefferson pointed out, "Of all exercises, walking is the best." The Hindus say, "Walk much for long life." . . . One wise old American, asked his recipe for continuing health, answered, "I have two doctors, my left leg and my right." (REBECCA WARFIELD)

Walkers not only do a great service to their bodies by habitual long walks, but they enrich their minds as well. All nature gives to them its choicest smile, and every bird offers a serenade. (GEORGE M. ADAMS)

WANTS (see NEEDS)

The practical man is the man who knows how to get what he wants.
The philosopher is the man who knows what man ought to want.
The ideal man is the man who knows how to get what he ought to want. (EDGAR S. BRIGHTMAN)

WAR (see FIGHTING)

In memory's eye I could see those staggering columns of the first World War, bending under soggy packs on many a weary march, from dripping dusk to drizzling dawn, slogging ankle deep through mire of shell-pocked roads to form grimly for the attack, blue-lipped, covered with sludge and mud, chilled by the wind and rain, driving home to their objective, and for many, to the judgment seat of God. . . .
Twenty years after, on the other side of the globe, again the filth of murky foxholes, the stench of ghostly trenches, the slime of dripping dugouts . . . the horror of stricken areas of war.
(DOUGLAS MACARTHUR, NEAR THE END OF HIS LIFE)

In war there is no prize for the runner-up. (OMAR N. BRADLEY)

War is like a giant pack rat. It takes something from you, and it leaves something behind in its stead. It burned me out in some ways, so that now I feel like an old man, but still sometimes act like a dumb kid. It made me grow up too fast. (AUDIE MURPHY)

The world's biggest heavy industry is war. (DUBLIN OPINION)

I hate war as only a soldier who has lived it can, only as one who has seen its brutality, its *stupidity*. Yet there is one thing to say on the credit side—victory required a mighty manifestation of the most ennobling of the virtues of man—faith, courage, fortitude, sacrifice. If we can only hold that example before our eyes; moreover, if we can remember that the international cooperation then so generously displayed points the sure way to ... success ... then the war can never be regarded as a total deficit.   (DWIGHT D. EISENHOWER)

It is the people and the politicians who make war and the soldiers who make peace.   (HUGH L. SCOTT)

A father had just finished giving his son a long account of the part he had played in the war.

The little boy thought for a while, then said, "But Dad, why did they need all those other soldiers?"   (QUOTE)

In every war we give our best men and women, not our worst. Only those who can pass the physical and mental tests are crippled and slain.   (HAROLD E. KOHN)

It is only a generation after a war that the ordinary people begin to admit that it was a futile, foolish, and unnecessary one—which is something the prophets, poets, and philosophers were nearly stoned for saying as it began.   (SYDNEY HARRIS)

The following mobilization order, issued by Haile Selassie when the Italians invaded Ethiopia in 1935, is considered by Pentagon officials to be a model of simplicity.

"Everyone will now be mobilized and all boys old enough to carry a spear will be sent to Addis Ababa.

"Married men will take their wives to carry food and cook. Those without wives will take any woman without a husband. Women with small babies need not go.

"The blind, those who cannot walk, or for any reason cannot carry a spear, are exempted.

"Anyone found at home after the receipt of this order will be hanged."
                                            (THE HANGING DOG NEWS)

History teaches us that when a barbarian race confronts a sleeping culture, the barbarian always wins.   (ARNOLD TOYNBEE)

I can set your mind at ease; there will be no nuclear war. Why do the Soviets need war when they can break off nation after nation, piece by piece, from the West?   (ALEKSANDR SOLZHENITSYN)

We must have military power to keep madmen from taking over the world.   (BILLY GRAHAM)

I don't know what kind of weapons will be used in the third world war, assuming there will be a third world war. But I can tell you what the fourth world war will be fought with—stone clubs. (ALBERT EINSTEIN)

WARNING

Just because the river is quiet, don't think the crocodiles have left.
(MALAY PROVERB)

WASTE

The greatest waste in the world is the difference between what we are and what we could become. (BEN HERBSTER)

ATER

The water's so hard in my town, our Maytag got a hernia.
(SHELBY FRIEDMAN)

WEAKNESS

Discover your weak points and then build a fortification at each.
(DEFENDER)

Samson's weakness was his fondness for showing off his strength.

A weakness may be any disadvantage that makes your living more difficult. Let your weakness be what it will; one of the strangest paradoxes and at the same time one of the most encouraging facts in human life is that your weakness can be your greatest asset. Men, like kites and airplanes, rise against and not with the wind. You cannot be blamed for your weakness but you should blame yourself for not trying to turn it into your greatest asset. (CARRIE M. HAZARD)

Although men are accused of not knowing their own weakness, yet perhaps as few know their own strength. It is in men as in soils, where sometimes there is a vein of gold which the owner knows not of.
(JONATHAN SWIFT)

WEALTH (see MONEY, RICHES)

Discipline begets abundance. Abundance, unless we use the utmost care, destroys discipline. (MEDIEVAL MONK)

Wealth is the relentless enemy of understanding. (J.K. GALBRAITH)

The futility of riches is stated in two places: the Bible and the income tax form. (GILCRAFTER)

WEATHER (see NOAH)

Probably the last completely accurate weather forecast was when God told Noah there was a 100 percent chance of precipitation.

(ROBERT ORBEN)

Don't knock the weather; nine-tenths of the people couldn't start a conversation if it didn't change once in a while. (KIN HUBBARD)

WEDDINGS (see MARRIAGE)

Bride: I don't want to overlook the most insignificant detail of my wedding.
Mother: Don't worry. I'll see that the groom is there.

A kindly country parson who had just married a young couple had a parting word for the groom: "Son, God bless you. You're at the end of all your troubles."

A year later the groom returned to the scene of the crime and moaned, "What a year I've gone through! And you told me I was at the end of my troubles."

"So I did, son," smiled the parson. "I just didn't tell you which end." (BENNETT CERF)

WEIGHT (see OBESITY)

Putting on weight is the penalty for exceeding the feed limit.

(BLIGHTY, LONDON)

You are overweight if you are living beyond your seams.

Logic is when you come to the conclusion that either you're gaining weight or the holes in your belt are healing up.

Manufacturers are producing a new reducing belt—which you tie around the refrigerator.

Many of us don't know what poor losers we are until we try dieting.

(THOMAS LaMANCE)

I'm practicing the power of positive shrinking. (HOWARD HENDRICKS)

You can't reduce by talking about it. You have to keep your mouth shut. (GRIT)

When weighing it does very little good to hold your stomach in.

(NONEE COAN)

"He's not as big a fool as he used to be."
"Getting wiser?"
"No, thinner."

I seem to find the weight that other people lose.   (WAYNE BERGMAN)

Overweight is caused by leading the gut life.   (QUOTE)

Signs in reducing salons:
    Let us help you win the losing game.
    A word to the wide—Reduce!

Underexercising rather than overeating may well be the more important cause of overweight today.   (JEAN MAYER)

WEIRDOS (see UNDERSTANDING)

A young man who gets along famously with all kinds of people, of all ages, was asked how he did it. His reply: "When I first meet somebody, I always tell myself, 'He (or She) is a weirdo,' because everybody has idiosyncrasies and eccentricities. Then when that person does something weird I'm not surprised or disenchanted. I still *like* the guy or gal."

WHISTLING

Many a man will remember youthful moments when he whistled while afraid. Walking through a dark alley. Or along a trail in the woods. Or over the rocks in a fast creek. Must be a most natural reaction. Investigators of air disasters checked out the voice recorders recovered from 450 plane crashes. In 364 they heard whistling by crew members.(L.M. BOYD)

WICKEDNESS (see SIN)

No man ever becomes wicked all at once.   (BITS AND PIECES)

WIDOWS

"A widow," said Johnny, "is a woman that has lived with her husband so long that he died."   (C. KENNEDY)

Widows are divided into two classes—the bereaved and the relieved.   (MARILLA W. RICKER)

Widow Jones inherited a million dollars from her deceased husband, but she was terribly lonely. "I'd give ten thousand of it," she sighed, "if I could have him back."   (QUOTE)

WILL

Put your will in neutral so God can shift you.   (DECISION)

The will of God (biblical rule of thumb): God is more concerned about who you are than what you do, and He is more concerned about what you do than where you do it.   (GARY GULBRANSON)

Never be afraid to do what God tells you to do—it's *always* good.
(MALCOLM CRONK)

WINNERS AND LOSERS

It's harder to be a good winner than a good loser—one has less practice.

The winner glories in the good; the whiner majors in the mediocre.
Winners' thinking processes differ from other people's. As part of their
normal, moment-to-moment stream of consciousness, winners think constantly in terms of *I can* and *I will.* Losers concentrate their waking
thoughts on . . . what they should have done . . . would have done . . .
what they can't do. When the mind's self-talk is positive, performance is
more likely to be successful. The huge majority of our negative doubts
and fears are imaginary or beyond our control.   (DENIS WAITLEY)

The winner persistently programs his pluses; the loser mournfully magnifies his minuses.   (WILLIAM A. WARD)

Cripple him, and you have a Sir Walter Scott.
Lock him in a prison cell, and you have a John Bunyan.
Bury him in the snows of Valley Forge, and you have a George Washing-
ton.
Raise him in abject poverty, and you have an Abraham Lincoln.
Subject him to bitter religious prejudice, and you have a Disraeli.
Afflict him with asthma as a child, and you have a Theodore Roosevelt.
Stab him with rheumatic pains until he can't sleep without an opiate, and
you have a Steinmetz.
Put him in a grease pit of a locomotive roundhouse, and you have a
Walter P. Chrysler.
Make him play second fiddle in an obscure South American orchestra,
and you have a Toscanini.
At birth, deny her the ability to see, hear, and speak, and you have a
Helen Keller.   (ABIGAIL VAN BUREN)

Everybody likes a good loser—provided it is the other team.

It isn't whether you win or lose. It's how you place the blame.

Every race is a tiring race. But you're not very tired when you happen to
win.   (MARK DONOHUE)

If you cannot win, make the one ahead of you break the record.
(JAN MCKEITHEN)

WINTER

Be like the sun and the meadow, which are not in the least concerned about the coming winter. (BERNARD SHAW)

Winter is when your car won't start running and your nose won't stop.

WISDOM

Scholars are a dime a dozen, but a man of wisdom is a rare bird.
(FRANCIS B. THORNTON)

There are no locks on the doors of wisdom, knowledge, honest enterprise, and opportunity. (MEGIDDO MESSAGE)

The wise know too well their own weaknesses to assume infallibility; and he who knows most, knows how little he knows. (GRIT)

A man becomes wise by watching what happens to him when he isn't. (BITS AND PIECES)

Wisdom does not consist so much in knowing what to do, as in knowing what *not* to do when you are ignorant; the chief fault of the unwise is driving toward conclusions from insufficient premises. (SYDNEY HARRIS)

Wise men talk because they have something to say; fools, because they have to say something. (PLATO)

By reading a lot one grows wise; by seeing a lot one grows tolerant.

From the errors of others a wise man corrects his own.(CRYPTOQUOTE)

Committing a great truth to memory is admirable; committing it to life is wisdom. (WILLIAM A. WARD)

A wise man listening to a fool will learn more than a fool listening to a wise man. (NUGGETS)

The wise man reads both books and life itself. (LIN YUTANG)

A word to the wise is superfluous, and a hundred words to the unwise are futile. (SYDNEY HARRIS)

If you realize that you aren't as wise today as you thought you were yesterday, you're wiser today.
(BULLETIN, JEFFERSON AVE. PRESBYTERIAN CHURCH, DETROIT)

A man should never be ashamed to own that he has been in the wrong;

that is but another way of saying he is wiser today than he was yesterday. (MEGIDDO MESSAGE)

Wise are they who have learned these truths: Trouble is temporary. Time is a tonic. Tribulation is a test tube.

WISHING (see DREAMS)

A man will sometimes devote all his life to the development of one part of his body—the wishbone. (ROBERT FROST)

If a man could have half his wishes, he would double his troubles. (BEN FRANKLIN)

It is not good for all your wishes to be fulfilled. Through sickness you recognize the value of health, through evil the value of good, through hunger satisfaction, through exertion the value of rest. (HERACLITUS)

Most folks don't know what they want, but it's something different than what they have. (ARNOLD GLASOW)

WIT

To make witty remarks, think of something stupid and say the opposite. (DUBLIN OPINION)

Wit has truth in it; wisecracking is simply calisthenics with words. (DOROTHY PARKER)

WITNESSING (see SOUL-WINNING)

When it comes to talking about Christ, are you a conversation dropout?

The world is far more ready to receive the Gospel than Christians are to hand it out. (GEORGE W. PETERS)

What do we mean by "witnessing"? Spouting a lot of Bible verses to a non-Christian? Not quite. Witnessing involves all that we are and therefore do; it goes far beyond what we say at certain inspired moments. So the question is not *will* we witness (speak), but *how* will we witness? When we're trusting Jesus Christ as Lord as well as Saviour, He enables us to live and speak as faithful witnesses. (PAUL E. LITTLE)

No man can give at one and the same time the impression that he himself is clever and that Jesus Christ is mighty to save.(JAMES DENNEY)

Are your conversations and your facial expressions good advertisements for your faith?

WIVES

In Nahuatl, the ancient Aztec language, the word for "wife" was a set of syllables that translate "one who is the owner of a man." (L.M. BOYD)

Trying to outfox my wife is like trying to sneak a sunrise past a rooster. (LESTER CASE)

A word to the wives is insufficient. (JACK KRAUS)

The parishioners were asked to bring something to a church auction that they didn't have any use for. Several women brought their husbands. (SHELBY FRIEDMAN)

Some men seem to have been inspired by their wives to do great things. Others may do great things as a way of getting away from their wives. (SYLVANUS AND EVELYN DUVALL)

She not only reads her husband like a book; she gives the neighbors reviews. (BOB GODDARD)

A happy wife sometimes has the best husband, but more often makes the best of the husband she has. (MARK BELTAIRE)

I figure my wife is going to live forever. She has nothing but dresses she wouldn't be caught dead in. (BOB GODDARD)

WOMEN

In Sunday School one little girl was asked if she knew the story of Adam and Eve.

She replied, "First God made Adam and then looked at him and said, 'I think I can do better,' so He created women." (HILIGHTS)

Being a woman is a terribly difficult task since it consists principally in dealing with men. (JOSEPH CONRAD)

Did you ever wonder how many fig leaves Eve tried on before she said, "I'll take this one"? (OKLAHOMA JOURNAL)

Some gals don't want to be marry go-getters. They're looking for already-gotters. (POWERGRAMS)

Arguing with a woman is like getting caught in a rainstorm. The best thing to do is to take shelter somewhere until the storm passes. (O.A. BATTISTA)

No matter how happily married a woman is, it always pleases her to discover that there is a nice man who wishes she were not.

Women were made with a sense of humor so they could love men instead of laughing at them.   (WILL ROGERS)

I think that I shall never see a tree as lovely as a knee.(EARL WILSON)

Women's fashions keep changing, but their designs are always the same.

Hair, to women, must have some deeply symbolic or sexual meaning far beyond the mere physical appearance, for nothing else explains the vast amount of time, money, and energy devoted to care of the hair; nor is this merely a modern obsession—in biblical times, the Book of Timothy warns women against excess in attention to the dressing of the hair.
                                                        (SYDNEY HARRIS)

In a survey . . . it was found that 15 percent of the ladies tinted their hair, 38 percent wore wigs, 80 percent wore rouge, 98 percent wore eye shadow, 22 percent wore false eyelashes, 93 percent wore nail polish. And 100 percent of the ladies voted in favor of a resolution condemning any kind of false packaging.   (CAROLINA COOPERATOR)

A smart guy once said a woman was created beautiful and foolish. Beautiful, that man might love her, and foolish, that she might love him.

Tell a woman, "You have a face that would stop a clock" and you have made an enemy.
    But tell her, "When I look upon your face, time stands still" and you have made a friend for life.   (ROBERT P. JOYCE)

Intuition is what enables a woman to put two and two together and get your number.   (SUPERVISION)

A woman can talk with less effort than a man because her vocal cords are shorter than those of the male. Not only does this cause her voice to be higher pitched; it also requires less air to agitate the cords, making it possible for her to talk more, yet expend less energy. (GOOD READING)

Some women, when they quarrel, become hysterical, while others become historical—they dig up the past.   (MUTUAL MOMENT)

A foremost anthropologist supported the idea of coed conscription, but draws the line at letting the ladies be battle-axes: "I do not believe in using women in combat, because females are too fierce."
                                                        (MARGARET MEAD)

When a woman is speaking to you, listen to what she says with her eyes. (VICTOR HUGO)

The fear of women is the basis of good health. (SPANISH PROVERB)

The Chickenization of Women: Women are frequently referred to as poultry. We cluck at hen parties. When we aren't henpecking men, we are egging them on. In youth we are chicks. Mothers watch over their broods. Later we are old biddies with an empty-nest syndrome. Is it just a coincidence that so many women's wages are chicken feed? (ASSOCIATION OF OPERATING NURSES JOURNAL)

I've known a certain lady for years. Our friendship goes back a long way—when we were both the same age. (QUOTE)

A Berkshire (England) schoolteacher, who was explaining to her class that women live longer on the average than men, asked if anyone could tell her the reason.
"Yes," said an 11-year-old boy, "they don't have wives." (PETERBOROUGH DAILY TELEGRAPH)

One of the most important things for a woman, I think, is to respect herself. 'Cause a woman usually gets from men the same amount of respect she has for herself, almost to the ounce. Men have a second sense about women and when they sense that a woman has no respect for herself, they're very quick to follow in her footsteps. (MICHAEL CANE)

While many would not hesitate to say that great beauty is the characteristic that makes most women outstanding, several experts on the subject tend to disagree. They say that responsiveness is a woman's most outstanding attribute. If she is responsive to the moods and emotions of others, if she can share joy, humor, and even problems, she will have no difficulty in attracting friends. (EDWARD R. AND CATHEY PINCKNEY)

There are a few things that never go out of style, and a feminine woman is one of them. (JOBYNA RALSTON)

There are two kinds of women in the world: those who take a man's strength and those who give a man strength. (IHRE FREUNDIN)

The questionnaire an applicant for a job was asked to fill out included the query, "Age?"
She answered, "Nuclear." (BENNETT CERF)

It was to a virgin woman that the birth of the Son of God was announced. It was to a fallen woman that His resurrection was announced. (FULTON J. SHEEN)

Policeman, to woman driving a station wagon full of children, after she had run a red light: Lady, don't you know when to stop?
Lady: I'll have you know that all of them are not mine—it's my day in the car pool. (ROCK HILL HERALD)

While equality of the sexes is a fine ideal, it's unlikely that women would ever allow it. (FRANKLIN P. JONES)

The easiest way to change a woman's mind is by agreeing, disagreeing, or saying nothing. (QUOTE)

Woman showing well-dented car to garageman: The fender's been acting up again. (QUOTE)

There isn't enough to do in a modern home to keep any really intelligent woman busy. (MRS. THEODORE WEDEL)

A Parisian psychoanalyst has said: "My women patients can be divided into two categories: the ones who work and the ones who stay at home. The former suffer from a guilt complex, the latter from frustration." (REGINE GABBEY)

The trouble with women in business, according to one Detroit businessman, is that if you treat 'em like men they cry; and if you treat 'em like women, darned if they don't get the best of you. (BARB WILLIAMS)

Women, it is said, do not concentrate. They can attend to the subject in hand, but their attention has not the wholeheartedness of a man's. If so, it is just possible that since women have been cooking the supper, mending clothes, listening to half a dozen children talking at once, and keeping them good-tempered and amused since before the dawn of history, they have learned to be able to attend to several things at a time. A man, on the other hand, focuses his mind. (DAVID GARNETT)

It is true that all sensible women think all studious men are mad. (G.K. CHESTERTON)

WOMEN'S LIBERATION

I'm more confirmed than ever in my Christian feminist beliefs because I care about human justice and full personhood for all persons—males and females alike. I'm convinced that men as much as women will benefit by rethinking gender roles. (LETHA SCANZONI)

Women who insist upon having the same options as men would do well to consider the option of being the strong, silent type. (FRAN LEBOWITZ)

A minister was discussing Women's Lib with one of the ladies of his church, and the woman argued that the church was pro male. To make her point she said, "Why do they say Amen instead of Awoman?"

The minister calmly replied, "Because we sing hymns, and not hers."

(ROUGH NOTES)

Yesterday I was at a wedding where the minister looked at the couple and solemnly pronounced them person and person.　(ROBERT ORBEN)

If the Women's Lib people were really serious about the movement, they would do something about their poor sisters who are forced to live on large alimony handouts from men they simply can't stand.

My wife decided to join Women's Lib—and I'm glad. Now she complains about *all* men—not just me!　(CURRENT COMEDY)

Recently, on the subway, I got up and gave my seat to a lady who was holding onto a strap. She was rather surprised and said, "Why did you do that?"

Seeing that she was incapable of understanding a spiritual reason, I said to her, "Madam, I tell you, ever since I was a little boy, I have had an infinite respect for a woman with a strap in her hand."

(FULTON J. SHEEN)

Women get more unhappy the more they try to liberate themselves. A woman is a tender and sweet person. She will lose that if she tries to be like a man.　(BRIGITTE BARDOT)

Supreme authority in both church and home has been divinely vested in the male as the representative of Christ, who is the Head of the church. It is in willing submission rather than grudging capitulation that the woman in the church (whether married or single) and the wife in the home find their fulfillment.　(ELISABETH ELLIOT)

WOODPECKERS

Woodpeckers must be very superstitious. They're always knocking on wood.　(SHELBY FRIEDMAN)

WORDS (see SPELLING, VOCABULARY)

It's a strange world of language in which skating on thin ice can get you into hot water.　(FRANKLIN P. JONES)

Much wisdom can be crowded into but four words:

This too shall pass.
Still waters run deep.
Love laughs at locksmiths.
Charity begins at home.
Nothing ventured, nothing gained.
Let sleeping dogs lie.

Live and let live.
Bad news travels fast.
Nothing succeeds like success.
Politics makes strange bedfellows.
Man proposes, God disposes.
In God we trust.

(BITS AND PIECES)

Words are the lubrication of the mind because it cannot run any more smoothly within itself than its command of words allows. A man's thinking is exact only to the degree that he has words to make it so. We can think in nothing but words. When our words run out, we come to the end of our thinking; all we can do is to repeat ourselves.

(ELMER G. LETERMAN)

Have you a googler in your office? (Cy Frailey says a googler is one who never uses a short word if he can think of a long one with the same meaning.) (ADVERTISING AGE)

Little keys can open big locks. Simple words can express great thoughts.

(WILLIAM A. WARD)

There is a relationship—an almost uncanny relationship—which exists between a man's income and his ability to use his language. Words are tools . . . and the more tools we have, the more jobs we can handle.

(EARL NIGHTINGALE)

Cold words freeze people, and hot words scorch them, and bitter words make them bitter, and wrathful words make them wrathful. Kind words also produce their image on men's souls; and a beautiful image it is. They smooth, and quiet, and comfort the hearer.   (BLAISE PASCAL)

The five most expressive words are: alone, death, faith, love, no.

(WILFRED FUNK)

The 10 most persuasive words in the English language are: you, easy, money, save, love, new, discovery, results, proven, guarantee.

(HENRY J. TAYLOR)

Four-letter words that changed the world: love, hope, care, heal, work, feel, duty, home, good, kind, pity, rest, seek, pray, live.

Kind words can never die, but without kind deeds they can sound mighty sick.

WORK (see EMPLOYER/EMPLOYEE, PROFESSIONALS, TRADE)

Not everyone who seeks a job is looking for work; not everyone who wants a promotion is looking for more responsibility. (QUOTE)

People who don't come in to work on Monday are not necessarily sick—but they may be in a weekend condition.

Working people are brighter than we think. Their jobs may be drab, but they transcend them. (STUDS TERKEL)

How do I work? I grope. (ALBERT EINSTEIN)

The recent graduate, a thoroughly modern youth, was asked if he was looking for work.
    He thought a moment, then replied, "Not necessarily, but I would like a job." (TEXAS OUTLOOK)

The number of people who are unemployed isn't as great as the number who aren't working. (FRANK A. CLARK)

Rest and play are the desserts of life. Work is the *meal.* It is only a child who dreams of a diet of dessert alone. (HAROLD MAYFIELD)

The world is full of willing people; some willing to work, the rest willing to let them. (ROBERT FROST)

"Been to the zoo recently?" asked the manager.
    "No, sir," answered the new delivery boy.
    "Well, you should," said the manager. "You'd enjoy it and get a big kick out of watching the turtles zip by." (QUOTE)

The instructor at a company-sponsored first-aid course asked one of the workers: "What's the first thing you'd do if you found you had rabies?"
    Answered the worker without pause, "Bite my supervisor." (EXECUTIVES' DIGEST)

Those persons who want by the yard and try by the inch need to be kicked by the foot. (W. WILLARD WIRTZ)

We were not put here on earth to play around. "Life is real; life is earnest," Longfellow wrote. We are not here to "have fun," which seems to be the chief ambition of so many. There is work to be done. There are responsibilities to be met. Humanity needs the abilities of every man and woman. (ALDEN PALMER)

I've been working all my life, but somehow it seems longer.
(ROBERT ORBEN)

Nothing's harder work than not having a job.　　(FRANKLIN P. JONES)

No man will work for your interests unless they are his.(DAVID SEABURY)

Find a job that's suited to your talents and then do a lot more work than
you're paid for. In time you'll be paid much more for what you do.
Workers who get what they can, as fast as they can, as easily as they
can, are bound to be disillusioned. Such people fail to make progress
simply because they aren't profitable to the people who hire them.
(WALTER HOVING)

Samuel Gompers spent his life trying to keep Labor from working too
hard, and he certainly succeeded beyond his own dreams.(WILL ROGERS)

Two people working with you are worth 12 people working for you.

I have never known any man or woman to succeed in any business or
any profession who was jealous of the hours he gave to his job.
(ALDEN PALMER)

Just because you have a job, don't feel you must stop looking for
work.　　　　　　　　　　　　　　　　　(H.J. KORDSMEIER)

To get the true measure of a man's capacity, note how much more he
does than is required of him.　　　　　　　　　(GRIT)

Sign on office bulletin board: Would you like to find out what it's like to
be a member of a minority group? Try putting in an honest day's work
occasionally.　　　　　　　　　　　　　　(KELLY FORDYCE)

"The best way to prevent a nervous breakdown is to work hard," says a
psychiatrist. What's the next best way?　　　　　(GRIT)

There is a low correlation between brilliance and performance. There
are people who have nothing but potential.　　　(JOHN FLAHERTY)

Out of ten people who are promoted with every hope of success, about
two live up to their own and their employer's expectations.
(PETER DRUCKER)

Do not pray for easy lives. Pray to be stronger men. Do not pray for
tasks equal to your powers. Pray for powers equal to your tasks.
(PHILLIPS BROOKS)

When zest departs, labor becomes drudgery. (OWEN D. YOUNG)

Some are bent with toil, and some get crooked trying to avoid it. (HERBERT PROCHNOW)

We've come from the Puritan work ethic to the new work ethic, from living to work to working to live. The current work attitude among younger people: you have a job you want done. I have a life I want to live. Let's make a deal. (ROGER BLACKWELL)

For a real quick energy boost, nothing beats having the boss walk in. (ROBERT ORBEN)

The biggest goof-offs in industry are the people whose jobs have an air of mystery about them. Find out what everybody is doing.(HERB TRUE)

"Some folks remind me of blisters," says the contemporary sage. "They don't show up until the work is done." (ATLAS NEWS)

Nobody can think straight who does not work. Idleness warps the mind. Thinking without constructive action becomes a disease. (HENRY FORD)

Nothing breeds crime like unoccupied time. (ARNOLD GLASOW)

I know hardly anyone who works too hard. I believe in hard work and long hours of work. Men do not break down from overwork, but from worry and from plunging into dissipation and efforts not aligned with their work. (CHARLES E. HUGHES)

Few men drop dead from overwork, but many quietly curl up and die because of undersatisfaction. (SYDNEY HARRIS)

Times are always hard for those who seek soft jobs. (THE DEFENDER)

The average human being in any line of work could double his productive capacity overnight if he began right now to do all the things he knows he should do, and to stop doing all the things he knows he should not do. (ELMER G. LETERMAN)

The only man who ever got all of his work done by Friday was Robinson Crusoe. (MRS. M.M. REEVE)

What is happening to our drive, to our spirit, to our initiative? This morning I saw two robins standing in line for worm stamps. (ROBERT ORBEN)

I've met a few people in my time who were enthusiastic about hard work. It was just my luck that all of them happened to be men I was working for at that time. (BILL GOLD)

People who think they are too big to do little things are perhaps too little to be asked to do big things.

When a man tells you that he got rich through hard work, ask him: "Whose?" (DON MARQUIS)

It is questionable if all the mechanical inventions yet made have lightened the day's toil of any human being. (JOHN STUART MILL)

The old Dale Carnegie students' "class yell": I know men in the ranks who are going to *stay* in the ranks. Why? *I'll* tell you why: simply because *they haven't the ability to get things done!*

The hardest thing about making a living is that you have to do it again the next day. (QUOTE)

No man goes before his time—unless the boss leaves early.
(GROUCHO MARX)

Kids today aren't afraid of hard work for the same reason I'm not afraid of an African lion. They never get too close to it. (CURRENT COMEDY)

The best security a parent can give his children is an insatiable thirst for hard work. (O.A. BATTISTA)

Hard work beats all the tonics and vitamins in the world.
(COL. HARLAND SANDERS)

Hard work is an accumulation of easy things you didn't do when you should have. (CUBA CITY [WIS.] NEWS-HERALD)

Truth as old as the hills is bound up in the Latin proverb, "Necessity is the mother of invention." It is surprising what a man can do when he has to, and how little most men do when they don't have to. (WALTER LINN)

We are judged by what we finish, not by what we start.

Don't do nothing halfway, else you find yourself dropping more than can be picked up. (LOUIS ARMSTRONG)

It's what a worker does, not what he is capable of doing, that shows in the record of achievement. (TIT-BITS, LONDON)

A man grows most tired while standing still.　　　　(CHINESE PROVERB)

I never remember feeling tired by work, though idleness exhausts me completely.　　　　(SHERLOCK HOLMES)

Unless a man has to do more than he can do, he will not do all that he can do.　　　　(GORDON COOPER)

If there is one thing that's unhealthy in America, it's that it is a whole civilization trying to get out of work—the young, especially, get caught in that. There is a triple alienation when you try to avoid work: first, you're trying to get outside energy sources/resources to do it for you; second, you no longer know what your own body can do, where your food or water come from; third, you lose the capacity to discover the unity of mind and body via your work.　　　　(GARY SNYDER)

In order to do an urgent and important work, two things are necessary: a definite plan and not quite enough time.　　　　(GRIT)

Nothing of a worthwhile, durable nature in the world has ever been produced without sweat.　　　　(HERBERT LOCKYER)

I am wondering what would have happened to me if . . . some fluent talker had converted me to the theory of the eight-hour day, and convinced me that it was not fair to my fellow workers to put forth my best efforts in my work. I am glad that the eight-hour day had not been invented when I was a young man. If my life had been made up of eight-hour days I do not believe I could have accomplished a great deal. This country would not amount to as much as it does . . . if the young men had been afraid that they might earn more than they were paid.　　　　(THOMAS A. EDISON)

My grandfather once told me that there are two kinds of people: those who do the work and those who take the credit. He told me to try to be in the first group; there was much less competition there.(INDIRA GANDHI)

Iron rusts from disuse, stagnant water loses its purity and in cold weather becomes frozen; even so does inaction sap the vigors of the mind.　　　　(LEONARDO DA VINCI)

Anyone can do any amount of work, provided it isn't the work he is supposed to be doing at the moment.　　　　(ROBERT BENCHLEY)

Too many people are ready to carry the stool when there is a piano to be moved.　　　　(INDIANAPOLIS STAR)

It is good for the hearts of men, as of women, to do their own chores, to cut the grass, to shovel the snow, to dig and weed the garden, to chop the firewood, to put on and take off the storm windows, and even to take out the ashes. It gets us down to earth, keeps us humble, is good for our health, and, incidentally, saves us money. (PAUL D. WHITE)

The greatest producer of real work is necessity.

Don't tell me how hard you work. Tell me how much you get done. (JAMES LING)

Work is the greatest thing in the world, so we should always save some of it for tomorrow. (DON HEROLD)

When you do not know what you are doing, do it neatly. (GROUND RULE FOR LABORATORY WORKERS)

Everybody is proficient at sounding the fire alarm, but few people are willing to help put out the fire. (MARY E. LEBAR)

There are far too many people in the world who live without working, and far too many who work without living. (DIOGENES)

Thank God every morning that you have something to do, whether you like it or not. Being forced to work and forced to do your best, will breed in you temperance and self-control, diligence and strength of will, cheerfulness, contentment, and a hundred other virtues the idle never know. (CHARLES KINGSLEY)

Without work, all life goes rotten. But when work is soulless, life stifles and dies. (ALBERT CAMUS)

If it were desired to reduce a man to nothing, it would be necessary only to give his work a character of uselessness. (FEODOR M. DOSTOEVSKI)

The humanizing of work is making work more appropriate and fitting for an adult to perform. By this criterion, humanized work: (1) should not damage, degrade, humiliate, exhaust, or persistently bore the worker; (2) should be interesting and satisfying; (3) should utilize many of the valued skills the worker already has, and provide opportunity to acquire others; (4) should enhance, or at least leave unimpaired, the worker's ability to perform other life roles—as spouse, parent, citizen, and friend; and (5) should pay a wage sufficient to enable the worker to live a comfortable life. (ROBERT L. KAHN)

It's not so much how busy you are—but *why* you are busy. The bee is praised. The mosquito is swatted. (MARIE O'CONNOR)

A man who is too big to study his job is as big as he will ever be. (WILLIAM E. NORTH)

Man's work is an extension of himself, a revelation of his inner life, both to others and to himself. (RICHARD LYNCH)

No man needs sympathy because he has to work, because he has a burden to carry. Far and away the best prize that life offers is the chance to work hard at work worth doing. (THEODORE ROOSEVELT)

"Gung Ho" came to us from American Marines in the South Pacific during World War II. "Gung" is the Chinese word for work, and "Ho" is the word for harmony. (QUOTE)

Great works are performed not by strength but by perseverance. (SAMUEL JOHNSON)

Blessed is he who has found his work; let him ask no other blessedness. (THOMAS CARLYLE)

No one has a right to sit down and feel hopeless. There's too much work to do. (DOROTHY DAY)

Many fellows have gained reputations as good workmen by simply developing the uncommon habit of putting everything they've got into everything they do. (PHOENIX FLAME)

He who begins too much accomplishes little. (GERMAN PROVERB)

There is no such thing as a big job. Any job, regardless of size, can be broken down into small jobs which, when done, complete the larger job. (WALTER P. CHRYSLER)

For doing important things, set aside large blocks of time. (JOHN FLAHERTY)

You don't have to do great things, but the little things you are doing in your sphere of influence can be done with great conviction, great beauty, and great love. (RUTH K. JACOBS)

When love and skill work together, expect a masterpiece.(JOHN RUSKIN)

Roll your work onto the Lord and your plans will be achieved. (PROVERBS 16:3, MLB)

To some men who follow *Him*, God gives not only a vision of unlimited horizons, but a strong back and a determined mind to push on toward those horizons. As always, the horizons are ever moving ahead of them— ever out of reach—yet *God's men stride on!*   (VICTOR E. CORY)

Next time you're faced with the need for an extra burst of energy, or you need a little extra creativity, or there's some extra brain work to be done, give it a try. Find a cool place to work—60 to 65 degrees Fahrenheit is not terribly uncomfortable. And a shiver now and then will do you good. It's a sign that body metabolism is increasing in order to maintain a normal temperature. You may amaze yourself at how efficient you can be.   (PREVENTION)

People may forget how fast you did a job, but they will remember how well you did it.   (BITS AND PIECES)

The Japanese have learned it matters not whether you win the war; it's how you play the game afterward.   (KIRK KIRKPATRICK)

Talkers are not good doers.   (WILLIAM SHAKESPEARE)

Work brings profit; talk brings poverty.   (PROVERBS 14:23, TLB)

If I could do it all again, I would do less, and allow God to do more through me.   (VANCE HAVNER)

Work is fine, but when it's mixed with fun it's a lot better. Don't be a fun pauper. Get into the delights a good God has put into the world.
               (NORMAN V. PEALE)

I never did a day's work in my life—it was all fun.   (THOMAS EDISON)

Ask God's blessing on your work, but do not also ask Him to do it.   (WAGGERL)

Church bulletin board: Work for the Lord. The pay isn't much, but the retirement plan is out of this world.   (QUOTE)

If God simply handed us everything we want, He'd be taking from us our greatest prize—joy of accomplishment.   (FRANK A. CLARK)

Work can be our friend or our foe, our joy or our woe.(WILLIAM A. WARD)

I don't like work—no man does, but I like what is in work: the chance to find yourself, your own reality—for yourself, not for others—what no other man can ever know.   (JOSEPH CONRAD)

For all of man's ages-old preoccupation with work, no one has yet been able to come up with a very satisfactory definition of it. For work is a paradox, simultaneously a curse and a blessing. A man works when he is hungry; and it is equally obvious that he continues to work when he is well-fed, well-clothed, and well-housed. A man devotes nearly half of his waking hours to work. Some men make work out of play, and some make play out of work. But man cannot free himself from work nor, according to repeated studies, would he do so if he could.

(HARRY LEVINSON)

As you comtemplate it, work seems awfully repulsive, even nauseating. But as you embrace it, you find it is not bad at all; in fact, it is far more comforting than mere scheming and dreaming. The more closely you become acquainted with it, the more friendly and familiar it seems.

(JAMES MANGAN)

Hard work is a thrill and a joy when you are in the will of God.

(ROBERT A. COOK)

Most men are proud to be called hard workers. They like to brag about the tension, strain, and work of their duties. Working hard is a religion with them. Modern psychology, however, points out that it is more important to be an easy worker than to be a hard worker. Instead of working at high tension, the easy worker relaxes. He knows how to let go and rest mind and body. He keeps fresh and vigorous, and gets more done than the hard worker! Learning to be an easy worker is not easy. But mastery of this art is the salvation of the American businessman.

(HIGHWAYS OF HAPPINESS)

Every now and then go away, have a little relaxation. For when you come back to your work, your judgment will be surer, since to remain constantly at work, you lose power of judgment. Go some distance away because then the work appears smaller, and more of it can be taken in at a glance, and a lack of harmony or proportion is more readily seen.

(LEONARDO DA VINCI)

How to get a job done: (1) Coordinate all persons and processes necessary and set each in motion at the right time. (2) Follow through so that no step or link in reaching that final result has been omitted or forgotten. (3) Maintain the required level of quality. (4) Set time limits and see that each phase is done on time. (5) Demand cooperation from all people involved. (6) Do a "plus" job—just a little more than the minimum called for.

(DANIEL STARCH)

WORKAHOLICS

The workaholic, like the alcoholic, is a sick person. His enjoyment is employment.

(LOU ERICKSON)

You can become a workaholic, as addicted to slave-driving yourself as a tippler is to his booze or his bender. . . . Doctors, counselors, psychiatrists, pastors are all discovering that some of the men we most admire, tireless demons for work, are as sick as the men we most disadmire, drug addicts and alcoholics. (DAVID AUGSBURGER)

I'd rather be that [a workaholic] than what most people are—lazaholics. (REGINA ZYLBERBERG)

WORKTEAMS (see COMMITTEES, PARTICIPATION)

A group becomes a team when each member is sure enough of himself and his contribution to praise the skills of the others. (NORMAN SHIDLE)

We can use associates like drunks use lamp posts, for support instead of light.

The larger the number of people involved in any given decision, the greater the pressure for conformity. (PSYCHOLOGY TODAY)

The question should never be who is right, but what is right. (GLENN GARDINER)

It is always easier to command than it is to convince.

WORLDLINESS

The essence of worldliness is exclusion of God. (HENRY JACOBSEN)

WORMS

Pound for pound, a worm is 1,000 times stronger than a man. (QUOTE)

WORRY (see ANXIETY)

At first glance there seems to be little connection between the physical act of "strangling" and the mental process of "worrying." However, the word "worry" is derived from the old German word wurgen meaning "to choke." Somehow, by extension, the term came to be used to denote "mental strangulation" . . . and then, to describe the condition of being harrassed with anxiety or care. (AMERICAN DRUGGIST)

Worry is a thin stream of fear trickling tnrough the mind. If encouraged, it cuts a channel into which all other thoughts are drained. (A.S. ROCHE)

Worry is faith in the negative, trust in the unpleasant, assurance of disaster, and belief in defeat. . . . Worry is a magnet that attracts negative conditions; faith is a more powerful force that creates positive circumstances. . . . Worry is wasting today's time to clutter up tomorrow's opportunities with yesterday's troubles.   (WILLIAM A. WARD)

Worry is the traitor in our camp that dampens our powder and weakens our aim.   (WILLIAM JORDON)

Blessed is the person who is too busy to worry in the daytime, and too sleepy to worry at night.   (LEO AIKMAN)

If you want to test your memory, try to remember what you were worrying about a year ago.   (LEONARD THOMAS)

Most worries are reruns.   (CLAUDE McDONALD)

You can't change the past, but you can ruin a perfectly good present by worrying about the future.   (DECISION)

Worry is a cycle of inefficient thoughts whirling around a center of fear.   (CORRIE TEN BOOM)

Worry grows lushly in the soil of indecision.   (NORMAN SHIDLE)

Worry is to life and progress what sand is to the bearings of perfect engines.   (ROGER BABSON)

Worry is interest paid on trouble before it falls due.   (WILLIAM INGE)

Worrying is the only game in which, when you guess right, you don't feel any better.   (SUNSHINE)

The Bureau of Standards in Washington . . . tells us that a dense fog covering seven city blocks, 100 feet deep, is composed of something less than one glass of water. That amount of water is divided into some 60 thousand million tiny drops. Not much there! Yet when those minute particles settle down over the city or countryside they can blot out practically all vision. A cupful of worry does just about the same thing. We forget to trust God. The tiny drops of fretfulness close around our thoughts and we are submerged without vision.   (A. PURNELL BAILEY)

People who like to worry have a greater and more varied number of things to choose from than ever before.   (GRIT)

A Harris survey asked a cross section of Americans to tell what worries them most. More than 70 percent said they worried about wasting too much time, especially watching television. About the same number stated they worried about not reading enough, not attending church regularly, and not being active in community affairs. About 60 percent said they often felt guilty about eating too much and being out of shape physically. One-third of those surveyed felt guilt pangs over spending more than they could afford. Twenty percent worried about personal debt and the same number about drinking too much.

Worrying does not help anything and hurts everything.(GEORGE PATTON)

Worry won't kill you if you face problems squarely and solve them. But sidetrack those problems and internal tensions increase. Repression of our natural safety valves causes these tensions to find outlets in the stomach, heart, blood vessels, etc. And this will eventually kill you, says one of the outstanding psychiatrists. (SUPERVISION)

Worry doesn't empty tomorrow of its sorrow; it empties today of its strength. (CORRIE TEN BOOM)

Don't tell *me* that worry doesn't do any good. I know better! The things I worry about don't happen. (BOB FOSTER)

Worry affects the circulation, the heart, the glands, the whole nervous system. I have never known a man who died from overwork, but many who died of doubt. (CHARLES H. MAYO)

Some people don't want advice—they just use you as a wastebasket for their worries. (BITS AND PIECES)

There is no use worrying over things over which you have no control. If you *have* control, you can do something about them instead of worrying. (GRIT)

Don't be worried over the fact that you have worries. Everyone has them. Don't play the hero by sticking it out and suffering with your anxieties. Take a trip or engage in some activity that enlists your interest and energy. Get yourself out of the rut and clear your mind so you may cope with pressure lying ahead. In this way, you can control anxiety. (ALFRED K. ALLAN)

A big worry drives out a small one and, since there's always a still bigger worry coming along, you have nothing to worry about.(DUBLIN OPINION)

WORSHIP

To worship means to recognize supreme worth. (HAROLD C. BONELL)

One of the acid tests of a Christian is his attitude toward his possessions. Someone has figured out that one out of every four verses in the

Gospels is related to this attitude. I think the emphasis can be condensed into a single phrase: *What we worship determines what we become.* If we worship material possessions, we tend to grow more materialistic. If we worship self, we become more selfish still. That is why Christ continually endeavored to direct men's worship.   (HARVEY F. AMMERMAN)

Worship is, in part, listening to what God might say to us, through music, through words, through fellowship. It is also our response to what He speaks. Worship has occurred when life responds with an openness to how God could change our lives.   (C. NEIL STRAIT)

Those who are wise consider how God responds to their worship.
          (DAVID MAINS)

Worship is not a text but a context; it is not an isolated experience in life, but a series of life experiences.   (GARY GULBRANSON)

WRITERS AND WRITING

Jorge Luis Borges, 82, author, on why he writes: "So that I wouldn't have to spend my life correcting manuscripts [editing]."

Thinking is the activity I love best, and writing is simply thinking through my fingers.   (ISAAC ASIMOV)

I don't enjoy writing, and I certainly would not do it for a living. Some people do, but some people enjoy flagellation.   (PRINCE PHILIP)

Have something to say, and say it as clearly as you can. That is the only secret of style.   (MATTHEW ARNOLD)

Every author should remember that you've got to read before you can write.   (O.A. BATTISTA)

The most important attributes a writer must have are faith, hope, and clarity.   (WILL CONWAY)

One difference between a writer and a talent is the number of wastebaskets the writer has filled.   (JOHN CIARDI)

The only important thing a writer needs is a subject. What the reader hungers after is not accomplished craftsmanship nor even correct grammar but a frank report of the things a writer has done, seen, and thought. None of these can be learned in the library or classroom. They have to be learned in the unsheltered world of living where men get slivers of the truth beaten into their heads.   (BROOKS ATKINSON)

No writing comes alive unless the writer sees across his desk a reader, and searches constantly for the word or phrase which will carry the image he wants the reader to see, and arouse the emotion he wants him to feel. Without consciousness of a live reader, what a man writes will die on his page. (BARBARA W. TUCHMAN)

A reporter, trying to track down the wellspring of the creative process, asked Edna Ferber why she writes.

Her reply was at once startling and satisfying: "Because it is less agonizing to write than not to write." (EVELYN W. WENDT)

Writing is a chore, an onerous one. A writer will do almost anything to get out of it. It takes as much out of you as a bad spell of sickness. (JOHN FAULKNER)

All authors are blind to their own defects. (JOHN DRYDEN)

The third-grade teacher was giving writing hints. "Don't copy what other people write," she said. "Be original. Write what's in you."

Little Tommy followed her advice. He wrote, "In me, there is a stomach, a heart, two apples, one piece of pie, and a lemon drop." (CATHOLIC DIGEST)

You are subjecting yourself to tough things as a writer. It erodes a person. That's why the casualty rate is so high. You fear the exhaustion of your reserve, the collapse of your ambition, involuntary retirement by your readers. The psychic drain is enormous. (LEON URIS)

Talking or writing that is too long is generally the result of thinking that wasn't long enough. (BITS AND PIECES)

What is written without effort is in general read without pleasure. (SAMUEL JOHNSON)

Writing books for children is hard work, a lot harder than most people realize. And it never gets easier. The most important thing about me is that I work slavishly—write, rewrite, reject, and polish incessantly. I know my stuff all looks like it was rattled off in 23 seconds, but every word and every sentence is a struggle. (THEODOR SEUSS GEISEL)

Good writers are not those with the largest vocabulary of difficult words, but those who have mastered the simple words. (GUSTAV HASFORD)

No author dislikes to be edited as much as he dislikes not to be published. (RUSSELL LYNES)

Brief review of new book: The covers are too far apart. (HOUGHTON LINE)

Ambiguous reply to a bad author, who had sent an advance copy of his book: Many thanks. I shall lose no time in reading your book.

(BENJAMIN DISRAELI)

A budding author sent a poem to an editor and wrote: "Please let me know at once if you will use it, for I have other irons in the fire."

The editor wrote back: "Remove irons and insert poem." (LION)

French publisher Gaston Gallimard was asked by an author if he had read his latest work.

"I have indeed," Gallimard replied. "It reminded me of Charlemagne's sword."

Intrigued, the writer looked up the reference. The sword is described as "long, flat, and deadly." (TIME & TIDE)

Most of the great classic tales that have survived were written for bread. (PAUL GALLICO)

The average barber now makes more money per word than the average writer. (LANE OLINGHOUSE)

Writing is a lonely profession. It always has been; it always must be. The author may be a philosopher, poet, historian, biographer, essayist, or novelist, but his ideas, his vision, have to be communicated in loneliness. Only by a dredging of his own consciousness can he get at the kind of power with which to remake an experience or to reformulate a concept and shed light that has not been shed before on conditions, ideas, and situations. (E.W. MARTIN)

A publisher friend of mine says that most writers are not real writers; they are just people who "want to have written." Real writers are those who want to write, need to write, have to write. (ROBERT P. WARREN)

Any writer knows that it's hard to write on an empty stomach. That's why most of 'em use paper. (JACK HERBERT)

Being a writer is a solitary vocation. Occasionally, letters or phone calls provide evidence that someone out there is reacting—usually in vehement disagreement. But it is exceeding difficult for a writer who does not also teach to experience a continuum of face-to-face challenge and response to his ideas. You shoot an arrow and most of the time you have no way of knowing what impact it had, if any. (Which may be why even the most depressed writer can be instantly buoyed by seeing someone on the subway reading one of his books or articles.) (NAT HENTOFF)

Put it before them briefly so they will read it, clearly so they will appreciate it, picturesquely so they will remember it, and above all, accurately so they will be guided by its light. (JOSEPH PULITZER)

I write every paragraph four times—once to get my meaning down, once to put in anything I have left out, once to take out anything that seems unnecessary, and once to make the whole thing sound as if I have only just thought of it. (MARGERY ALLINGHAM)

Writing a book is an adventure. To begin with it is a toy and an amusement. Then it becomes a mistress, then it becomes a master, then it becomes a tyrant. The last phase is that just as you are about to be reconciled to your servitude, you kill the monster, and fling him about to the public. (WINSTON CHURCHILL)

I have no advice for beginning novelists except a series of "nevers." Never give up, never lose faith, never ignore constructive criticism, and never, never stop writing. (SUSAN HOWATCH)

To write what you want to say in a way that it can be understood is not easy. It takes real effort. . . . Do your writing in four bite-size portions. Doing one of these at a time makes your writing easier and your results more effective. Here are these four steps: (1) Define your purpose and learn your subject. (2) Organize your material in the light of your readers' abilities and interests. (3) Write to best express yourself (and your ideas). (4) Edit and polish your writing so that it is easy to read, is easy to understand, and is good English. (FRANK E. McELROY)

The love of language must be in the heart of every really superior writer. This is the thing that distinguishes a real craftsman from a hack. For the craftsman the English language is an instrument of beauty and precision, and he works and works and reworks his manuscript until it has smoothness, cohesiveness, easy readability, and above all a choice of words that convey the exact meaning he wants. (BEN HIBBS)

There is really no such thing as a "writer," generically speaking. Instead, there are men and women who write fiction, poetry, articles, and so forth. Very few of them are adept at more than one form. . . . The term "writer" is as misleading as the term "athlete"—for who would send a baseball pitcher to run in the high hurdles? (SYDNEY HARRIS)

Creative people have few of the endearing qualities that attract many friends. We have the bad habit of being too candid. We're too inaccessible. . . . We don't have time for the fabric of friendship. So where do characters like us find our best friends? Only within ourselves. The writer—like the artist—must be his own best friend. Because he already is, it goes without saying, his own worst enemy. (MARION ODMARK)

Writers are most fortunate of all in not having to retire when they grow older. Like actors, they may have a big public, but the public does not care how writers look. The thoughts of 60 or 70 are not absurd or pitiable as faces of the same age may be when revealed to a great public. If you embrace the writing profession it is as a close and long embrace. It lasts for life and may be as vital at the end of life as it was in the first young approach. (MARGARET C. BANNING)

WRONGNESS AND RIGHTNESS (see SIN)

Lord . . . where we are wrong, make us willing to change, and where we are right, make us easy to live with. (PETER MARSHALL)

People would rather be wrong than be different. (HENRY JACOBSEN)

YAWN

A yawn is a silent shout. (G.K. Chesterton)

YESTERDAY (see PAST)

Four-year-old, explaining the difference between the past, present, and future to her two-year-old sister: Yesterday we called today tomorrow.
(Janet Cory)

One thing I do . . . is to forget what is behind me and do my best to reach what is ahead. (Philippians. 3:13, GNB)

Yesterday ended last night. (Cyrus H.K. Curtis)

YOUNG TEENS (see TEENS, YOUTH)

Between the ages of 10 and 13 or 14, typically, the child goes through almost as great a transformation as that seen when a tadpole changes into a frog. (Lois B. Murphy)

YOURSELF (see SELF)

You give but little when you give of your possessions. It is when you give of yourself that you truly give. (Kahlil Gibran)

YOUTH (see TEENS, YOUNG TEENS)

We are only young once. That is all society can stand. (Bob Bowen)

Young people find it nearly impossible to conceive of their parents as ever having been young; but this is because they find it just as hard to conceive of themselves as ever being old. (SYDNEY HARRIS)

The young man who has not wept is a savage; the old man who will not laugh is a fool. (GEORGE SANTAYANA)

You are only young once, but you can stay immature indefinitely. (WISCONSIN GENERAL NEWS)

Youth is not properly definable by age. It is a spirit of daring, creating, asserting life, and openly relating to the world. (MALCOLM BOYD)

I remember my youth and the feeling that will never come back any more—the feeling that I could last forever, outlast the sea, the earth, and all men. (JOSEPH CONRAD)

One of the virtues of being very young is that you don't let the facts get in the way of your imagination. (SAM LEVENSON)

Sometimes a young person is bad because he hates to waste a reputation. (JOHN K. YOUNG)

Modern youth has been tried and found wanting—everything under the sun. (BALANCE SHEET)

When we're young, we take so casually every sacrifice offered by the old. (WALLACE STEGNER)

Most teenagers think that their family circle is composed of squares. (DAN BENNETT)

I was born in the wrong generation. When I was a young man, no one had any respect for youth. Now I am an old man and no one has any respect for age. (BERTRAND RUSSELL)

We are living in a day when young people are encouraged to believe that they are infinitely wiser than their elders. Of course growing boys and girls have always had a bit of this, but it is rather more so today. It should be remembered that young people have not yet been old, but older people have been young. So older people understand younger people better than younger people understand older people. (J.C. MACAULAY)

Young people simply have responded to propaganda—and part of the propaganda, including that of the advertisements, is that youth is a better thing than age. So they conclude that 17-year-olds naturally are wiser than their fathers and mothers. They really believe this . . . [but] they'll get over it. The wonderful thing about cockiness is that it can be overcome by a little maturity. (D. ELTON TRUEBLOOD)

Parents of teens soon discover that youth is stranger than fiction.

Young people should be helped, sheltered, ignored, and clubbed if necessary. (AL CAPP)

A society that hates its youth has no future. (E. PINTO)

Absorbed in his own minor tribulations of coin and conquest, the adult too often forgets that youth is a jarring time, full of excruciating first experiences and full-blown tragedies. It is a pimple on the cheek which everyone will see with distaste; it is the clothes which never seem to fit a gangly body; it is the ultimate disappointment, a broken promise by a parent. It is a training ground for adulthood, a place and time to try for independence, a place and time to try and fail and succeed. (LION)

Formerly, the personality of young people often developed by identification with their father and mother. It develops today by identification with friends and comrades of the same age-group and with teenage ideals, since their former source of security has vanished with the repeated abdication of their parents. (MARCEL HICTER)

The thing our teenagers need . . . right now is part-time jobs on weekends and especially in the summer. Not, in most cases, because they need so badly to learn the joys of working and getting paid for working. Old Satan is still going around finding mischief for idle hands to do, and the sooner we fill those hands . . . the better for our young people and the better for our country. (MAX RAFFERTY)

Don't fight the establishment—try to work within it, we keep telling the kids. If organized crime can do it, so can they. (CHANGING TIMES)

In youth we learn; in age we understand. (MARIE EBNER-ESCHENBACH)

Today's accent may be on youth, but the stress is still on the parents. (EARL WILSON)

As I approve of a youth that has something of the old man in him, so am I no less pleased with an old man that has something of the youth. (CICERO)

The error of youth is to believe that intelligence is a substitute for experience—while the error of age is to believe that experience is a substitute for intelligence. (WAYNE MACKEY)

ZEAL

I don't know about having too much zeal; but I think it is better the pot should boil over than not boil at all.　　　　　　(AN AMERICAN INDIAN)

ZOO, Russian style

An American visiting the Moscow zoo was amazed to see a lion and a lamb in the same cage. "Do they get along well?" he asked the Russian guide.

"They get along fine," the Russian replied, adding, "Of course, we have to put in a new lamb every day."　　　　　　(LEO AIKMAN)